Advance praise for

GIMME A CRISIS

"Howard Green's *Gimme a Crisis* is not simply a thorough and entertaining biography of Rick Waugh, a central player in Canada's financial history and a stellar crisis manager; it is a meticulously researched and detailed chronicle of the biggest financial events of our time, delivering concrete guidance for today's policymakers."

—Stephen Poloz, former governor of the Bank of Canada and author of *The Next Age of Uncertainty*, winner of the 2023 National Business Book Award

"Howard Green has done it: Written a riveting adventure story about what really happens—and happened—behind the scenes in Canadian banking, and also laid out leadership lessons from a very human banking CEO."

—Geoff Smith, executive chair of EllisDon

"This isn't just a biography of one of Canada's most influential bankers through trying times. It is a close examination of the architecture of Canada's banking legacy on a global stage. Howard provides rare access to the inner workings of Canada's untold financial history and by extension, a window into Canadian history itself. We often tout our banks as among the safest in the world. But rarely do we stop and ask, why? Howard does. He provides us with a desperately needed accounting of our own story. What should be a dense and complex exploration of Canada's banking sector, is made refreshingly accessible by Howard's elegantly simple and highly entertaining storytelling. You'll read a book about a man, but come away knowing so much more about our system and our country."

—Amber Kanwar, former BNN Bloomberg anchor
and host of *In the Money with Amber Kanwar*

GIMME A CRISIS

ALSO BY HOWARD GREEN

Railroader: The Unfiltered Genius and
Controversy of Four-Time CEO Hunter Harrison

Distilled: A Memoir of Family, Seagram,
Baseball, and Philanthropy (with Charles Bronfman)

Banking On America: How TD Bank Rose to the Top
and Took on the U.S.A.

GIMME A CRISIS

IN THE ROOM *with*
GLOBAL BANKER RICK WAUGH

HOWARD GREEN

VIKING

VIKING

an imprint of Penguin Canada, a division of Penguin Random House Canada Limited

Canada • USA • UK • Ireland • Australia • New Zealand • India • South Africa • China

First published 2025

Viking, an imprint of Penguin Canada
A division of Penguin Random House Canada
320 Front Street West, Suite 1400
Toronto, Ontario, M5V 3B6, Canada
penguinrandomhouse.ca

The authorized representative in the EU for product safety and compliance is Penguin Random House Ireland, Morrison Chambers, 32 Nassau Street, Dublin D02 YH68, Ireland, https://eu-contact.penguin.ie

LIBRARY AND ARCHIVES CANADA CATALOGUING IN PUBLICATION

Title: Gimme a crisis : in the room with global banker Rick Waugh / Howard Green.
Names: Green, Howard, 1959- author
Identifiers: Canadiana (print) 20250144034 | Canadiana (ebook) 20250144050 |
ISBN 9781037801440 (hardcover) | ISBN 9781037801457 (EPUB)
Subjects: LCSH: Waugh, Rick. | LCSH: Chief executive officers—Canada—Biography.
| LCSH: Bankers—Canada—Biography. | LCGFT: Biographies.
Classification: LCC HC112.5.W39 G74 2025 | DDC 338.092—dc23

Cover and book design by Matthew Flute
Typeset by Terra Page
Cover images: (building) © Bloomberg / Contributor / Getty;
(sky) © Petros / Adobe Stock

Printed in Canada

10 9 8 7 6 5 4 3 2 1

Penguin
Random House
VIKING CANADA

For Susan

*

A smooth sea never makes a good sailor.
—attributed to Franklin Delano Roosevelt

CONTENTS

Introduction   1

Chapter One: *Great Timing*   11

Chapter Two: *As Canadian as Hockey and Tim Hortons*   25

Chapter Three: *From Halifax to the World*   38

Chapter Four: *No, Mr. Trump: Lending to Americans*   45

Chapter Five: *How to Snag a Raptor*   72

Chapter Six: *Good Wine, Rotten Barrels*   97

Chapter Seven: *Every Country Needs a Good Bank*   140

Chapter Eight: *Friday Afternoons Were the Worst*   162

Chapter Nine: *In the Room*   215

Chapter Ten: *Close Calls for a Deal Junkie*   254

Chapter Eleven: *Does She Mind Going Down One Floor?*   274

Epilogue   301

Acknowledgements   313

Bibliography   319

Notes   340

Index   351

INTRODUCTION

In the innocent days before 9/11, passengers on airliners were often invited up to the cockpit for a view from the front seats. Since that horrific day, however, flight decks the world over have been sealed off for security reasons. But I can't think of a time when the cockpit of a major Canadian bank—and in this case, a global bank—was open for viewing. This book, though, will take you there, through the eyes of a CEO who piloted one through remarkably turbulent times.

The bank is Scotiabank, or The Bank of Nova Scotia. Hailing from an out-of-the-way peninsula in Canada's Atlantic region, over its almost 200-year history, Scotia grew into one of the world's most international banks. Its chief executive officer for ten years was Rick Waugh, a lifer at the bank, where he spent more than four decades. Aside from having been a leading banker on the world stage, Waugh also believes in the recording and telling of business history. He and I share that passion, and this book is the result of a multi-decade relationship. Waugh made himself available for extended questioning, opened doors to other key figures, and provided certain personal documents so important stories, events, and situations could be captured and understood more fully. Early in the project, I casually described this exploration as a rare glimpse inside the executive realm, and eventually CEO suite, of a huge bank. I'll amend that. It may be unprecedented.

That's of course what grabbed me. But my interest in writing about business history runs deeper. I'd started my journalism career in daily news, at regional newsrooms covering whatever was assigned—strikes, forest fires, provincial premiers, helicopter crashes, a day in the life of a maximum-security prison guard, or the downright frivolous—eventually moving into longer-form magazine and documentary programming and business coverage.

But a seed may have been planted in the fall of 1980 when a documentary miniseries, *The Canadian Establishment,* aired on CBC Television. I watched. I was in my last year of Carleton University's journalism program, and I still remember a telephoto shot of a line of black Cadillac limousines making their way to a cemetery to bury a titan of business. The scene seized me. The series was based on a 1975 book of the same name by author Peter C. Newman, written to crack the shell of an otherwise impenetrable group—those who own and/or control the country's biggest companies and economy.

In 1988, I began covering business, perhaps because of that series about business big shots. I had wondered: Who are these people? What are they like? What do they do? And most important, what is their impact? The answers, for me, would form a view of how the world worked. While others covered Parliament, I would cover business, a seemingly closed club with no daily question period on television.

My initiation was chronicling entrepreneurs. But I soon started nosing into big business and, by the late 1990s, banks. Banking is central to everything, the circulatory system of the economy. Without credit, people can't buy cars or houses. Businesses can't get started and can't grow. And because we want money from them, bankers can also poke their way into every cranny of our affairs—they see everything. In Canada, there is also something of an aura around our big banks. They are pillars of our society, our economy. They're also in our faces. The main drag in just about every small town has had at least one branch. In Toronto, aside from the CN Tower, it is their skyscrapers that dominate the view.

There's also an aura around those who lead the banks. Notwithstanding the rise of the tech oligarchs, bank CEOs are at the top of the executive food chain, particularly in Canada, where they loom large. With luxurious offices on hushed executive floors, augmented with the finest art, they're ushered to important, private gatherings. They weigh in on public policy and pull levers that make the country work.

Bankers, while necessary, can also bugger things up. Undue risk-taking, slippage of risk practices, misaligned incentives, as well as poor and fragmented oversight can wreck companies and put economies, the entire financial system, and people's livelihoods in peril, not to mention stressing taxpayers. Bankers not only have immense responsibility to their companies and their shareholders, but also, arguably, to society at large. Some haven't always lived up to it, while others have risen to meet the moment.

In 1999, as part of the team that launched what's now BNN Bloomberg, an all-business television network, I began interviewing bankers regularly. I covered them for the next fifteen years. That included chief executive officers (CEOs), chief financial officers (CFOs), chief risk officers (CROs), and assorted other chiefs. I would devour quarterly reports, analyst reports, and what others in the financial community had to say. Over time, I would meet and speak with approximately twenty Canadian bank CEOs—a few generations at each of the major banks—as well as international bankers and those who ran smaller banks. In 2013, I published my first book—about what else, banking.

One leading banker from that period was different than the others. Although part of a rarified, sometimes standoffish club, Rick Waugh was approachable. Loud, given to laughter and a slap on the back, he was fun to be around. I interviewed him for the first time in 2004, early in his CEO tenure. Subsequently, we spoke numerous times, both at the BNN studio, where I hosted the flagship interview program, as well as at the bank, via a remote link, and on stage at conferences. Aside from what was going on at the bank, in the financial system, and with the economy, a frequent line of questioning during our interviews was about CEO compensation, something I raised with all the bank CEOs, as well as those who led other big companies. It was not only a business issue but also more broadly a social concern, given discussion of income and wealth inequality. I tried not to make it personal, although I may have failed at times because it can be hard to separate. But Waugh, a gregarious, seemingly game-for-anything person, would field any question.

During one of our conversations, this time recorded on the executive floor of Scotiabank, I said something to the effect that the big Canadian banks, which go back to the 1800s and operate within a protected oligopoly, basically ran themselves and the main job was to not screw things up. I was being provocative. Their CEOs certainly had to be deeply skilled, strategic leaders of huge organizations. But the people running them weren't typically entrepreneurs; they were custodians—so why did their CEOs need to be paid so much? That lit Waugh's fuse. At the end of the segment, he leaned over and slapped me firmly on the knee. "Ya got me," he said, irritated with himself for taking the bait—and miffed with me, I think. From then on, anytime I saw Waugh, he joked about compensation. It became a running routine between us.

In late July 2023, almost twenty years on, I drove to his summer home north of Toronto to speak to him about writing this book. Driving along his private road into his expansive property, which sits high above the water, I clocked the new tennis court, the swimming pool, the great room overlooking the pool with a bay vista—the accoutrements of a highly successful forty-three-year banking career that saw the Winnipeg boy rise from teller to CEO. His wife, Lynne, was in the city, so he was alone. He greeted me cheerfully, clad in a well-worn, untucked shirt, grey jeans, and slightly tattered moccasin loafers. He was still tall, although not quite as tall as I remembered him from when he ran the bank. He was now seventy-five, the skin on his face crinkled. Inside the newly built house sat one of his jukeboxes, ready to play one of his fifteen hundred 45s. Born near the end of 1947, Waugh is a first-wave baby boomer, with a record collection reflective of first-wave rock.

He fetched me a bottle of water while he grabbed a Gatorade ("for electrolytes") as we discussed the risks of dehydration. Measuring risk is Waugh's obsession. It's the occupational hazard—or strength—of being a banker, and the kind of banker he was. We quickly settled into two black leather chairs in his study, which was immaculate. In fact, the whole house seemed incredibly orderly, somewhat at odds with Waugh's flailing arms and disarming, at times, shambolic way. Even as a CEO wearing a suit and tie, there was never a buttoned-down sense about Waugh, more everyman than establishment man.

It may seem a peculiar comparison, but when you listen to the Rolling Stones, sometimes it seems like the band is barely holding it together. But they do and somehow that's the magic, rather than overproduced perfection. Underneath the prancing, twanging, and growling is a meticulous sense of knowing what works. Although Waugh's a long way from Mick and Keef, like them, he somehow holds it together. He switches instantly from messy to pinpoint, shooting a series of penetrating questions, with a knack for finding the weakness in a loan application or sniffing out a path to a deal—painstaking when trolling for risk. Bankers, after all, lend money and fear getting hosed.

Once settled in, Waugh got talking, which he loves to do, often to the consternation of those who've had to listen for hours. For an author, however, it was gold. He was keen to share stories for the spine of this book—not as the main subject of an autobiography or biography, but as the principal character in a narrative history exploring the issues and situations he bore witness to and participated in along with a large supporting cast. Here was a key business person who'd been in the room when momentous events—frequently crisis after crisis—occurred in the modern era of banking and finance. Indeed, from when he started in 1970 until 2009, there had been fifteen banking-related crises somewhere on the planet, significant enough to attract the attention of global policy-makers.[1]

The story swirling around Waugh is one of a moment in time in global banking. His career began in the age of typewriters and adding machines. By the 1980s, when Waugh was a young executive, the world was transitioning to computerization and globalization. And by the time he retired as CEO in late 2013, he'd survived an earth-shaking financial crisis and acquired an online-only bank now called Tangerine. A few years after, digitization and social media would, astonishingly, create a bank run in seconds.

Alongside vast technological change, there was also vast social change. When Waugh started in banking, there was scarcely talk of climate change, or diversity, equity, or inclusion. Indeed, there were no women executives or board members, and Waugh capped his tenure with a concerted push to include them. When he started, the industry was adjusting to a profound regulatory shift that opened banking to wider opportunities. By mid-career, there would be a significant unshackling of regulation in Canadian and global banking that permitted comingling with other financial businesses like securities dealers. In the twilight of his career, regulatory tightening was afoot, a response to that vicious financial crisis.

This is to say nothing about the rise of corporate governance. When Waugh began, and for much of his career, the CEO was also the chairman of the bank's board, with supreme command. That changed. Bank CEOs became accountable to independent board chairs. Boards also shrunk, changed composition, and were pushed to sharpen up, rather than just be a vehicle for members to down a good Scotch at cozy gatherings. When Waugh started, bank employees had to get permission to get married and few bankers had university educations. Leading bankers were canny, steely, streetwise characters who learned on the job. Among other things, credit was often granted based on a reading of character, not a verdict of software. Issy Sharp, founder of Four Seasons Hotels and Resorts, banked with Scotia from the outset. The numbers may not have pointed to acceptable risk, but the bank believed in him.

Waugh's career was notably defined by crises. While still a relative youngster at Scotia, an energy crisis and high inflation almost sunk Western economies, while loans to developing countries almost sunk banks. The violent default of Argentina in 2001–2 put Waugh at the epicentre of an international crisis and a crisis for Scotiabank. People were dying in the streets near Scotia's subsidiary bank in Buenos Aires. Soon after, a Caribbean nation would fall into economic chaos, with Waugh and Scotiabank instrumental in the bailout. And, of course, there was the global financial crisis from late 2007 into 2009, the worst banking-system breakdown since the Great Depression. This found Waugh at the height of his leadership, not only at his bank and in Canada but also in global banking circles as the sector raced to reform before regulators did it for them. He thrived on crisis. It motivated him.

That July afternoon, and in many more lengthy sessions over almost two years, stories came tumbling out in his garbled syntax, the dialect of Waugh, or, in the fond parlance of colleagues, "Rick-isms," some of which were deemed so funny that a list of greatest hits was compiled. Suggesting his speech was impacted by a neurological condition, Waugh seemed to enjoy the ribbing he got; it was just part of his rumpled calling card. "But everyone knows what I mean," he told me firmly.

What came out that summer day was a blur of words, tangents, and anecdotes. At one point Waugh, who can be charmingly self-aware, laughed at himself and said, "*Focus, Rick.*" Indeed, as a listener, you must constantly decode what he's saying, connecting the strands of a brain that's racing while the mouth tries to catch up. But you do get it. By then, I had known him for two decades, so I had a running start.

As the afternoon wore on, Waugh reclined in his chair to chaise longue level, his head way back, feet up, making me secretly feel as though I was the therapist. Over three hours, he was part global banker, part razor-eyed analyst, part rambling raconteur, part jokester, and part pissed-off retiree, recalling and processing stories and situations. When talk turned serious, his face tightened and darkened. His speech crystallized.

Waugh was visibly tired by the time we were done, while I had to drive back to Toronto in rush hour. He was concerned I get home before a forecasted tornado and heavy rains hit. Again, it was his risk radar humming away. He reminded me of it in virtually every conversation for this book. Calculating and pricing risk was his life's work. It bled into everything. He couldn't not talk about it. This inescapable theme underpins this book's narrative.

Over the previous year, he'd had his own personal risk and threat to his life—a ruptured appendix requiring emergency surgery. Unfortunately, a day or two after the operation, he described being in excruciating pain again, as he'd experienced prior to surgery. Despite having an appendectomy, the poisons from his burst appendix were still coursing through his body. He was septic again, at risk of dying twice that week. It took a year to regain his strength. Now he wanted to speak for the historical record, implying the risk of not being around forever to do so.

His years running Scotiabank were good years for the bank, including, it turns out, during the financial crisis. When the risks were most dire, Waugh had skippered the organization through safely. Not only did the bank survive, it prospered. By all accounts, he was reluctant to leave the post, a job he loved, but he knew an orderly succession was required. Lynne Waugh told me retiring from the bank was difficult for her husband, and by extension for her. He missed it. It electrified him. And he missed the people.

Waugh was also known to be the life of the party, electrifying others with that booming laugh and loud voice. As a top executive at one of the other big Canadian banks told me, when Waugh walked into the room, everyone gravitated to him, including other CEOs who are used to getting attention. Waugh simply never wanted the party, or the challenge, to end. Not only did he love the bank, but he also loved the problems. In fact, the bigger the better, and he was blessed with the temperament to address them. Furthermore, banking had been his ticket to the world—the very top of the financial world. *He was in the room.*

It's also undeniable that his is a remarkable story from working-class Winnipeg, of one who'd risen from the bottom of the bank to the pinnacle, becoming a noteworthy CEO. He was proud of his accomplishments and didn't think he should have to apologize for his compensation. Clearly, even though it's public information, it's a touchy subject, as it would be for most. He likes to relate to people as a regular guy, and his wealth is anything but regular. He told me that, at one point, he was the largest individual shareholder of the bank. Not only did he amass stock options and shares as a large part of his compensation, but he also purchased more stock during the financial crisis. He once told me he sold in the ninety-dollar range, an all-time high in early 2022. But in the spring of 2024, he was buying Scotiabank shares again—the then-lagging price was not far off where it had been when he left the bank ten years prior. Although I don't know his net worth, it would not be outlandish to suggest it's well into nine figures. To his and Lynne's credit, they have made philanthropy a serious vocation.

Although this book unavoidably has a strong strain of biographical elements that bring the story to life, it is intended to be a historical account. Waugh's career is the useful lens that helps capture and frame that history. Due to Scotiabank's then-operations in fifty-plus countries, which allowed Waugh entry into the decision-making salons of the world, his experiences and the recollections of colleagues and others illuminate part of our times. Whether it's trying to temper the chaos of yet another default in Argentina, the hairy challenges of operating in the Caribbean, or the behind-the-scenes of 2008, when the entire financial system stared into the abyss, Waugh was in the middle of it. From lending to the biggest companies in America, to advising heads of government, to dealing with leaders of central banks, he was there, reading the room and the people in it.

While the book has a main character, it also has a formidable cast of ensemble players. Indeed, if good governance is a sub-theme, one of its hallmarks is that it takes a team. The truth is that individuals, including bank CEOs, while forces in their own rights, do not exist in a vacuum. Waugh recognizes and embraces this. They are also part of a continuum— of family history, of national history, of banking history, of corporate history, and of political and social history. To his credit, Waugh knew he needed a team. So, in addition to hearing from the captain of the team, as well as material drawn from published and private documents, you will hear from many of Waugh's teammates and others who've graciously shared recollections to help fill in the blanks of a gripping period of global financial history—participants who occupied front-row seats. The fact that the bank—a character itself in the story—was founded in my home-town of Halifax and grew into a far-reaching international company also provides a connection for me personally. Obviously, I'm biased. But there's a movie in here somewhere.

CHAPTER ONE

Great Timing

His timing was perfect. When Richard Earl Waugh was born at Misericordia Hospital in Winnipeg on December 23, 1947, not only was he part of a demographic shift that would remake Canada, but also the banking world he would enter a couple of decades hence would shift with it, creating enormous opportunity. Rick Waugh would be part of the second year of the baby boom generation, and Canada would feel that boom greater than any other Western nation. Between 1945 and 1954, Canada had the highest birth rate in the Western world.[1] Immigration was also increasing rapidly. The country was growing. People wanted houses. They wanted cars. They wanted consumer loans. They needed a banking system to meet those needs. Rick Waugh would grow up in tandem with that economic and social change and eventually become a financial leader not only in Canada but also globally.

Waugh was raised in a family that was eons away from a bank tower and a CEO suite. Originally, Waugh's father, Earl, hoped to be a police officer. But the idea of tagging his friends with speeding or parking tickets was distasteful. Instead, he fought fires, surviving being thrown off moving fire engines and falling through burning roofs. Ultimately, smoke inhalation damaged his heart, and he died at just fifty-four. Waugh was already a young banker living in Toronto and had rushed home after being told to come quickly. "As I drove up the front, he was having his last heart attack," Waugh said. Years later, the memory still brings tears to his eyes. Unfortunately, he didn't make it in time to speak with his father.

Until Waugh was in his early teens, the family home was at 379 Victor Street in Winnipeg's west end, what he would refer to as a hyphenated district—full of immigrants or "hyphenated" Canadians. The house was his grandparents', purchased with money saved by his grandfather, who had a barber shop at the city's best-known corner, Portage and Main. Waugh, though, didn't get his hair cut in a barbershop until he was twelve. He got his locks trimmed at home, on Saturdays around the kitchen table.

The home was small but housed seven people: Rick's grandparents, his parents, Waugh and his brother Ron, as well as their aunt. The two boys shared a bedroom, while his grandmother lived in an insulated shed and his grandfather slept in the dining room. Supper was frequently Kraft Dinner, while dessert was homegrown rhubarb with brown sugar. To this day, Waugh can't stand KD or rhubarb.

Waugh's mother, Frances Mary Richardson, was of Irish heritage, and looked after her diabetic mother-in-law. Her mother, after all, had looked after her, bringing her to Canada to get away from her alcoholic father. Earl Francis Waugh had Scottish roots, traced to Edinburgh. Stationed in England during the Second World War, he served for the Allied forces in Egypt. He was a bombardier when dropping a bomb from an aircraft was a manual procedure. In one instance, when Earl tried to let one drop, it detonated and burned him badly from the waist down. The plane landed, but Earl spent months in a Cairo hospital with severe burns. Eventually he made it back to Winnipeg where he met Frances, who worked in a beauty parlour.

Dad "was like me," Waugh says. "He made no enemies or tried to make no enemies." On the other hand, Waugh's mother "had an opinion on everything." He laughs. "She called it like she saw it. Dad was always the one who smoothed things over. My father always wanted to work things out." While Waugh describes having his dad's trait, when you're a banker there are limits to niceness. "You haven't seen me angry," he says. "She [his mother] brought a toughness into me to get things done in the right ways. My dad taught me the social skills to convince people to do it in the right way." Both skillsets were vital for running a global bank.

Waugh made friends easily and kept them. Unfortunately, though, when he was in public school, he contracted tuberculosis, a highly contagious pulmonary illness that can kill. He reckoned he caught TB from his grandfather, with whom he'd often play cards. Waugh was taken daily by ambulance for treatment, getting needles every day in his rear end. For a period, he was also in isolation in hospital, and was out of school for a year. To help him keep up, his mother arranged for a tutor who came to the house every day. Kids in his class also brought him schoolwork. In defiance of the doctors, his mother wouldn't allow her son to be admitted to a sanitarium where Waugh's grandfather had been admitted and subsequently died. While he had a jolly exterior, Waugh developed a steely core not unlike many who survived severe childhood illnesses.

Certainly, in a hostile climate like Winnipeg's, you were motivated to get along. Harsh winters fostered neighbourliness and pride of place. You never knew when your car would need a boost from the person next door. Waugh has maintained many of his Winnipeg connections. One of his best friends to this day is Bonnie Lovelace. She and Waugh started together at the University of Manitoba in 1966, and her husband, Dave Hudson, played football with Waugh in high school. She describes Winnipeg as an "isolated city" where the culture runs deep. As kids, it was skating, hockey, and marbles. There were kitchen parties, and grandmothers poured whisky into their teacups. The bonds stick for lifetimes.

"We'd call it the Manitoba mafia," Waugh says. That someone like Rick Waugh, *a bank CEO*, could for decades remain close to Gary Doer, *an NDP premier* (and later Canadian ambassador to the United States), speaks volumes about Manitobans' ability to get along. The two played football against each other in high school. While Doer says they were both competitive, when Waugh's team lost, "Rick didn't talk to me for two weeks." Despite competing and occupying different political wavelengths, they're still buddies from Winnipeg who hung out in community clubs listening to Neil Young, Burton Cummings, and Randy Bachman before they were stars.

"We were all hustlers a little bit," Doer says, laughing. They'd sell popcorn at football games and get to see the Blue Bombers play. Working as ushers, Doer said they scored front-row seats for a Rolling Stones concert. Doer says he and Waugh "came from the culture of *Let's Make a Deal*," the popular American game show hosted by Winnipeg's Monty Hall.

Meantime, Waugh loved school. He studied commerce and finance and lived at home, unable to afford digs elsewhere. School was social and action-packed, like he was. He tried every activity and was never in a rush to leave at the end of the day. In his final year, Waugh was known as "Senior Stick," a nickname for class president, or in more colloquial terms, "big man on campus." At Grant Park High School, he'd also been student council president.

Being Senior Stick was another clue about Waugh's popularity and ambition. In that role, he introduced federal finance minister Edgar Benson in front of a thousand people.[2] Bonnie, the "Lady Stick," was one of about a dozen women in the class who were vastly outnumbered by about 180 men. She says whenever Waugh was around, there was a "mighty racket." If he was in the room, you knew he was there. Her first recollection was hearing him bellow, "We have a freshie float to build! Who's coming to build it?" A float needed to be constructed for the freshman parade down Portage Avenue. So, who stepped up as general contractor, telling everyone what to do? It was simply a natural desire to lead, fuelled by a bursting tank of energy.

A parade float was one matter. Civil disobedience was another, and Waugh's leadership would soon be tested. While he pursued commerce in class, other students were busy rebelling. The giant company Dow Chemical was coming to campus to recruit and "all our guys had interviews," Waugh says. But Dow was controversial among students then—the Vietnam War era—because it made napalm and Agent Orange, high-profile chemical weapons that came to be symbols of America's war against communism. By the late 1960s, the war had lost popular support in the United States, particularly on university campuses, and it was no more popular in Canada. To protest the company's presence, students put chains on the "manpower centre," as it was known then.

Waugh flipped into problem-solving mode. He used the personal touch, like his father would. And for support, he brought along a few members of the football team to help open the shackled gates. By lucky coincidence, Waugh happened to be dating the sister of one of the protesters. "You can protest, but you're going to open the gates," he warned the guy, while threatening to have the sister intervene. He was making a demand but wrapping it in humour. He'd pulled out the old Waugh charm to smooth things over while firmly solving a problem without people getting hurt. He would have to do this in spades as a banker, not only in Canada but also in the United States, Caribbean, South America, and Asia.

For an elective in his final year, Waugh studied sociology. He doesn't mind saying, "I was really good at it," adding that he's "big on human behaviour." Meantime, Angus "Gus" Reid, later the well-known Canadian pollster, was in graduate school and supervised the lanky, enthusiastic student. Waugh, as is his wont, made it personal, writing a term paper about his own experience—with neighbourhoods.

After his grandfather died his parents sold the house on Victor Street and used the proceeds to purchase a home at 862 Borebank Street. It was in a decidedly more prosperous neighbourhood. His essay described how his family's move from the "hyphenated," less affluent west end—populated by Ukrainian-Canadians, Scottish-Canadians, whomever—to the upper-middle-class, urban-professional River Heights enclave in the south end, changed his life. His theme: where you live and who your neighbours are can be differentiating factors in how you fare in life. Suddenly, he was interacting with another socio-economic strata and learning from that exposure.

If you had to 3D-print a personality suited for banking, you might squirt out someone like Waugh. He was an instant pal who could authentically put his arm around you and close a lending deal. At the same time, he had the requisite ice coursing through his veins—the guy who'd have no problem knocking on your door to demand the bank's money be paid back.

In banking, he started as a teller on September 1, 1970, at the Windsor Park branch of Scotiabank in a Winnipeg strip mall for $7,400 per year. He had turned down $9,000-a-year jobs in the oil patch because he figured that in Calgary, as an accountant, he wouldn't have the same status as the petroleum engineers. He also chose Scotia because it held his job while he hitchhiked around Europe that summer. A local newspaper article appeared highlighting the new teller. Waugh says Gary Doer helped orchestrate it. Doer says Waugh wanted the article to impress his mother and "his mother's bridge club." If it was in the Winnipeg paper, Waugh's mother believed it.

Within weeks of hiring on, though, Waugh was shipped to Toronto
to work in the investment department as an analyst and/or portfolio
manager. *What do those people do?* he asked the HR person. "I don't
know," was the response. Before accepting, he sought advice from a fellow Winnipegger, Arni Thorsteinson, who he also knew from student
days. Thorsteinson has had a long, successful career in real estate and
was on the board of private equity firm Onex for forty-two years. He
had been Senior Stick the year before Waugh and had worked for two
summers as a securities analyst. "I loved the business, and I explained all
of this to Rick," Thorsteinson says. "He should jump at the opportunity," he told him. He knew his friend could do better than being a
teller. Waugh said he was one of the first university graduates hired by
the bank just out of school and one of three Manitobans hired by head
office in Toronto that year.

The flight to Toronto was Waugh's first trip on a plane. He was put
to work on the eleventh floor of 44 King Street West alongside the chief
economist, and Jane Nokes, the bank's archivist. Waugh soon fell in love
with investing (he said he "was a natural") and within a few years was
head of equity research. At twenty-four or twenty-five, he was writing
reports recommending how the bank should invest managed accounts
or its pension fund. Just a few years into a career, he was overseeing hundreds of millions of dollars of investments, with access to some of the
best minds on Bay Street—Eric Sprott, Tony Arrell, and Ira Gluskin. All
would become prominent in the investment community. "We'd meet on
Friday afternoons at Hy's for drinks."

Waugh oozed industriousness. He'd delivered newspapers, worked at
the public library, in retail, at a glass factory, during summers in the
Alberta oil industry, and done security at football games. He was driven.
In those early years in Toronto, taking advantage of the bank's education
benefit, he studied for his MBA at York University at night (the University

of Toronto wouldn't give him any credits from the University of Manitoba). So, after work, he drove his Triumph GT6 from downtown up to York. He'd taken out a car loan from Scotia, bought the little sportscar in Winnipeg, and shipped it. Through his studies he added to his investment knowledge, which he says is firstly "determining what the risk is." That dovetailed well when he moved into lending. "The principles are largely the same." To save time, he would submit research reports he'd written at the bank for his MBA assignments. "That's a trick I taught him," Thorsteinson said.

In short order, Waugh was in contact with top executives of the bank, including Robert MacIntosh, one of the first PhDs in Canadian banking. He advised Waugh to move into the credit department. MacIntosh supervised the data centres at the bank, and according to Thorsteinson, he not only had a huge presence on Bay Street but also "knew more about the Canadian banking system than any bank president." Credit, MacIntosh told Waugh, was the bloodstream of banking. That meant that credit was a non-negotiable necessity for career success. "I will never become CEO of Scotiabank, and I think you have a possibility. I won't because they never regarded me as a real banker because I never had credit experience." Waugh never forgot the lesson.

Understanding credit was key to the culture at Scotiabank. Waugh, who has a knack for distilling seemingly complex matters down to the essentials, says that banking is two things: earning the trust of customers who hand over their deposits to you for safekeeping, and then, lending money. Lending is credit—knowing how to lend, who to lend to, how much to charge, and how to get your money back. At the most basic level, it's how banks make money and don't lose it. The idea is to pay for deposits and then get paid more for loans, which are funded by the deposit base. Furniture companies make sofas. Banks make loans. There are many complexities and offshoots beyond that—other businesses banks have expanded into—but credit is fundamental. If Waugh eventually wanted the brass ring at the Bank of Nova Scotia (BNS), he'd have to learn how to be a good lender.* Thorsteinson, meanwhile, heard MacIntosh talking up Waugh. "We hired a fireman's son from Winnipeg, and someday he's going to be a leader, maybe even the president of the bank."

From the investment department, in May 1979 Waugh moved to branch banking, and not to just any branch, but the main branch in Toronto, "the flagship." At thirty-one, he was managing almost five hundred employees at the corner of King and Bay, including fifteen to twenty assistant managers older than him. Not long after getting the job, his university pal Bonnie came to visit at his grand office. "You have to see my personal bathroom," he told her. "It's bigger than my room at home used to be." There was also a shower, but it had been years since it was used. One evening, getting gussied up to attend a fancy event, the future CEO of the bank jumped in, shocked to discover only cold water was available.

Cold showers aside, the job had been a powerful stepping stone for executives of the bank—including past CEOs Bill Nicks and Cedric Ritchie. Of course, there was still lots Waugh didn't know. Customers would arrive wanting to deposit big cheques and wanting to speak with the manager—*him*. Laughing, Waugh says he always brought his deputy manager to these meetings "'cause I didn't know how to open up an account." Nonetheless, he had novel ideas. Cultivating relationships on Bay Street, he'd keep the branch vault open after hours to handle large, late-in-the-day deposits from investment dealers—good for customers, good for the bank.

It wasn't long before the chairman and CEO, Cedric Ritchie, who would run Scotia for two decades, installed Waugh on the boards of a few companies in which the bank had investments. The young banker

---

* While it's The Bank of Nova Scotia, in 1975 the company began operating as Scotiabank. Throughout the book, the names will be used interchangeably. The bank may also be referred to as BNS, its stock exchange ticker symbol, or simply as Scotia.

understood a fundamental metric when it came to credit—EBITDA, earnings before interest, taxes, depreciation, and amortization. It's crucial because it's not a figure you can fiddle with via non-cash items like depreciation, which is formulaically applied for accounting purposes. EBITDA, a gauge of cash flow, tells you whether the customer can handle the loan. And Waugh has a rule: follow the money. So, when lending, follow the EBITDA. He said that one day, Ritchie, who was then chief general manager of the bank, called Waugh to his office to explain what EBITDA was. "He literally didn't know," Waugh says. Warren Buffett's late partner Charlie Munger was known for calling EBITDA "bullshit earnings." Waugh, in the metric's defence, said, "I never called it earnings. It's free cash flow. You gotta have the cash." And a lender wants to know if you've got the cash to pay them back.

As a relatively neophyte banker, Waugh says he stood his ground, even if it meant going above people senior to him at the bank, including the head of credit, George Hitchman. If necessary, Waugh would go to the ultimate boss, Ritchie, to make his case. Possessing his father's collegiality attracted business for the bank. At the same time, possessing his mother's toughness protected the bank from lending to deadbeats. It was a potent combination for someone who wanted to go far in the organization. He could play the happy major chords that made everyone smile and gravitate towards him. But when needed, he could hit a chilling minor chord with a darker message. One minute he was Dick Van Dyke in *Mary Poppins* dancing on the rooftop; the next minute he was Scrooge, clinging to the loot. And even though he went over Hitchman's head to Ritchie, the chief of credit liked Waugh.

"I'm reading this credit presentation, Mr. Waugh, *and it reminds me of how I would write a credit presentation,*" Hitchman pronounced in puffed-up tones. No doubt, a certain characteristic of bosses can be vanity. They like to see themselves in their protégés. Mr. Hitchman, who would become deputy chairman, liked what he saw in Mr. Waugh (everyone was Mr. then).

Waugh's wife, Lynne, comes from Camden Town in North London in England. Also from modest means, she was born in 1948, the third of four children in a blue-collar family. Her mother, who was half Irish, was a cleaner. Her father, who was Italian, was a carpenter. Her grandfather delivered coal in Camden Town. On Saturdays, when she was just ten or eleven, Lynne worked in the coal yard with a cousin. The two of them bundled wood.

Like Waugh, she too was an early baby boomer, fortunate to miss the war years and the bombing of London endured by her mother and two older sisters. Lynne, an A student in multiple languages, wanted to be a teacher and came to Toronto to continue her studies, but ended up working for Simpsons, the now-defunct department store. She met Waugh at a pub, the Butcher's Arms, in downtown Toronto.

Prior to getting married, Waugh had to get permission from the bank's human resources division, then known as the personnel department. Having to seek permission from your employer to get married is now unfathomable given today's social norms and pushback against patriarchal attitudes. Back then, it was custom and procedure, and not just at Scotia.

Their wedding reception was held in a hotel at the corner of Mount Pleasant and Soudan with sixty or seventy guests. The newlyweds had to pay for everything themselves. Waugh's signature humour couldn't be contained. Because Lynne worked at Simpsons, any suits he bought were eligible for 25 percent off. "I married her for the discount," he joked in his speech, ever the banker. Not letting him get away with anything, Lynne says, "I married him for my Canadian citizenship."

The first night of their honeymoon was spent at the Four Seasons, where the couple used a half-price voucher. Discount suit, discount room. By the second night, they were in Freeport in the Bahamas staying at the Holiday Inn. As was often the case in Caribbean resort-land, hustlers were looking to sell time-shares to the besotted just-married crowd—and maybe even the second-marriage crowd—all anxious to secure a slice of paradise. So, what the hell, they signed up for the information session. "We'd do anything for a free meal," Lynne laughs. "Then they threw Rick out because he asked too many financial questions." It was the future banker's first foray into what would eventually be deep involvement in Caribbean banking. But this time, he got a door slammed in his face.

While he was still learning the basics of banking, Lynne was already a successful buyer for Simpsons, later bought by the Hudson's Bay Co. Her pay was seventy-two dollars a week. Accepted into a management training program, she worked at Simpsons for ten years, flying overseas or to New York. According to Waugh—with a tone of amazement and disbelief—Lynne was flying first class to Hong Kong while he hadn't even flown in a plane until he was twenty-two.

Nonetheless, by the late 1970s, he was well on his way in banking. In late 1976 and 1977, when Waugh was supervisor of investments for the bank, he published a series of three articles about markets in the *Canadian Banker & ICB Review*. One was about the Canadian money market, another about the bond market, and the third about equity investing and the stock market. Equity investing means taking an ownership position. While it can be done privately, typically it means buying a company's publicly traded stock or shares. Stock (or equity) is issued by a company to help finance itself, usually as a complement to debt. In the latter article, Waugh explained stocks, how to value them—among other things, assessing their price versus earnings—and what they mean to an economy. "Without equity investment, the private sector could not exist," Waugh wrote. A strong, active stock market "is the necessary basis for a strong, growing economy."

In his article about the money market—a short-term market of 1 to 364 days where cash can earn a yield—he wrote about liquidity. Liquidity, or the ability to get quick access to cash, would be crucial to him and the bank over the course of his career, particularly during the global financial crisis of 2007–9. Waugh wrote: "Most important is the need for a cushion of liquidity on the part of corporations, individuals, governments and financial institutions to allow them to carry out their normal operations and meet unexpected demands. This is a primary function of the money market: to provide a highly liquid haven for those needing liquidity and safety while at the same time earning income." Moreover, "there is always risk arising out of the need for refinancing when the short-term debt matures. The money market is a vitally important market to the banks," he argued. "Without such a market, any given bank would have to keep large amounts of cash on hand to meet its statutory requirements and to meet unexpected demands for funds by its customers." Gauging the risk of insufficient liquidity was central to Waugh's modus operandi.

On bonds, Waugh wrote about the banks' role in that market—as "purchasers, issuers as well as distributors." When he published this in 1977, he said, "Chartered banks hold about 35 per cent of the outstanding debt of the federal government, excluding Canada Savings Bonds," with a similar amount held by the Bank of Canada and the rest by the public and financial institutions. He also addressed the risks (credit risk and interest rate risk) and rewards of bonds. A bad credit means you may not get paid back, while moves in interest rates impact bond prices.

The net effect of reading the articles is the realization that, at a young age, Waugh was not only telegraphing ambition, but he already had a deep appreciation and understanding of markets. He was cultivating an expertise in risk, the seeds of which seemed sprinkled in his DNA, a fit with the bank's culture. Also, between understanding markets, credit, and people—and possessing the internal circuitry capable of withstanding crises like tuberculosis—whether he knew it or not, Waugh was assembling a leadership hand. As a result, he was getting noticed by top executives like MacIntosh, Hitchman, and Ritchie. At the same time, the Canadian banking industry not only was evolving with Waugh's era but also had been historically set up to succeed.

CHAPTER TWO

As Canadian as Hockey and Tim Hortons

In addition to their skill and leadership, Rick Waugh and his peers in Canadian banking owe much to the stable financial system the country built over time. While much has been written about America's founding fathers, less is touted about those who conceived the framework of Canada and the founding document of the country. Of all things, those responsible included banking in the British North America Act of 1867, which served as the country's constitution until repatriation in 1982. It mentions banking explicitly as a federal responsibility.[1]

From the outset, Canadian political leaders appreciated the role of finance. The key proponents of Confederation—Sir John A. Macdonald and George-Étienne Cartier—were both lawyers who served on boards of banks, among other companies.[2] Macdonald was also the first president of Manufacturers Life, now Manulife. Aside from Macdonald and Cartier, finance ministers in Canada's early days, including the first,

Alexander Tilloch Galt, had a strong awareness of banking.[3] An entrepreneur, Galt was a business leader in real estate and railroads.

The banking sector wasn't without its conflicts. Banks were created by the merchant class to facilitate credit, allowing businesses to function and get paid. They were necessary. But because communities were so small, perhaps more so than today, leading business people were intimately and unavoidably tied to government and vice versa. As a result, Galt, like others at the top of the power structure, was by modern standards of governance conflicted. In 1867, as finance minister, he was a significant shareholder in a failing Ontario bank.[4] William McMaster, who started the Canadian Bank of Commerce (predecessor to Canadian Imperial Bank of Commerce, CIBC) in 1867 and served as its president until 1886, was in 1870 appointed chairman of the Senate Banking Committee— *while he ran a bank*.[5] In the 1890s, when Canada's population was under five million, Sir John Abbott was prime minister and on the board of Bank of Montreal.[6]

Banking and strategies about it predate the country itself. While modern Canada was not officially created until 1867, in 1858, during the run up to Confederation, Galt proposed a federal government that would oversee "trade, currency and banking." The thrust was to head off the kinds of financial crises that frequently occurred in the United States. But it was Canada's third finance minister, Sir Francis Hincks, who is credited with being the "'father of Canadian banking.'" Hincks headed inspection of banks, had been a premier, and got the first Bank Act passed in 1871.[7] It was 6 pages long. By 1980, it had grown to 245 pages, not including 262 pages of regulations.[8]

As Christopher Kobrak and Joe Martin argue in their comprehensive historical comparison of Canadian and American banks and financial systems, Canada drew from an American model that was rejected by the United States. President George Washington's secretary of the treasury, Alexander Hamilton, favoured a broadly dispersed national branch banking network. Thomas Jefferson disagreed. As author of America's Declaration of Independence and later third president of the United States, Jefferson disputed Hamilton's view. Jefferson, who was also a farmer, architect, vintner, and slave owner, believed in decentralization of power. That applied to banking as well. Jefferson and his supporters won out, and the United States developed a banking system that was for much of its history dominated by the individual states, to the point where interstate banking was prohibited.[9]

Canada, meanwhile, determined that Hamilton's idea suited the Canadian political landscape and its geography.[10] A branch banking system—also a Scottish influence—would be most appropriate. As Malcolm Knight, the former number two at the Bank of Canada and later CEO of the Bank for International Settlements wrote, the United States experienced a tsunami of immigration in the 1800s, leading to thousands of banks in new communities. In Canada, though, there was a small population, and the nation's focus was resources and transport sectors. It needed big banks to bring in foreign capital. A highly concentrated banking sector also turned out to be the most stable.[11] Rather than the crazy quilt of state regulators and thousands of small banks that constituted the American system, Canada had federal oversight (the Bank Act came up for review every ten years), and it had a relatively small number of large banks with dependable, national deposit bases. It would be a protected oligopoly, "tightly regulated in a grand bargain whereby chartered banks would provide financial stability in exchange for the Canadian government limiting entry into the industry."[12] Canada's small number of large banks still exists, and they continue to prosper and make billions of dollars for shareholders. The big six employ more than four hundred thousand people.* Five of their head offices are

---

* The big five are Royal Bank of Canada, Toronto-Dominion Bank, The Bank of Nova Scotia, Bank of Montreal, and Canadian Imperial Bank of Commerce. The big six includes National Bank of Canada.

within a stone's throw of each other. Like a watchtower, there's even an office nearby for the federal Ministry of Finance and the Bank of Canada. Banking is bred in the Canadian bone.

Bank of Montreal, founded in 1817, fifty years before Confederation, was the first of the major banks. For the next century, it was the country's dominant bank, and one of the most important in North America. The Bank of Nova Scotia was established fifteen years later in 1832 and installed an agent in New York in the same year.[13] Rick Waugh would successfully run that agency in the 1980s and early 1990s, lending to the biggest companies in America. In 1866, the Canadian Bank of Commerce was launched after a Bank of Montreal director resigned, believing the bank restricted credit to Ontario. That director was William McMaster, the new bank's first president. McMaster University is named for him.[14]

Despite embracing the Hamiltonian model, Canada's banking system hasn't been perfect. There were failures in the 1800s and the early 1900s, and 1923 saw the devastating collapse of the Home Bank of Canada, which wiped out tens of thousands of depositors, including prairie farmers. Bank inspection began in Canada soon after, in 1925, although in later years, it was exposed as weak. In the mid-1980s, two Alberta-based banks went bust in the years following the reviled National Energy Program and the associated recession—the Canadian Commercial Bank (CCB) and Northland Bank. Fortunately, they weren't large in the overall scheme of Canadian banking, but they were a blight on what had arguably become a complacent system and revealed inadequate supervision. Loans had been highly concentrated in Alberta real estate and oil and gas, cyclical sectors. As well, many of the loans were bad, made by banks that wanted to aggressively expand lending.

A federal inquiry into the two failures was scathing. Supreme

Court Justice Willard Estey called out management, directors, audi-tors, and regulators for failure to address overstated income and loan values. Specifically, Northland had a CEO with no banking experi-ence and board members borrowed from the bank, via an approval process that "bordered on the cavalier," although that was not a primary factor in the bank's demise, Estey wrote. But he cut to the quick: "The financial statements became gold fillings covering cavi-ties in the assets and in the earnings of the bank." Estey's report laid much of the blame for the failures on the Office of the Inspector General of Banks, referring to bank regulation as "wink and nod."[15] Meantime, depositors were compensated—taxpayers and the major banks ponied up—while investors were wiped out.[16] Coincidentally, an investigator brought in to scrutinize CCB's books was none other than Waugh mentor and no-nonsense credit overseer George Hitchman, who found more than 40 percent of the Alberta bank's loan portfolio to be worthless.[17]

Another low point occurred in the 1980s when troubled loans by Canadian banks to least developed countries (LDCs) amounted to $24 billion out of $285 billion lent by banks globally, seriously pinching the big five. In 2024, that would be equivalent to $59 billion, which would largely wipe out the annual combined profits of Canada's major banks. In 1987, as a response to the LDC situation and failures in Alberta, the Office of the Superintendent of Financial Institutions (OSFI) was created. But no major Canadian bank failed because of the LDC crisis, nor did any fail during the global financial crisis of 2007–9 and they have continued to pay dividends and grow them. While Scotiabank reduced its dividend during the Great Depression, it has never stopped paying one since its founding.

The United States has seen a different story play out. During the Great Depression thousands of American banks failed, leading President

Franklin Roosevelt to close banks in 1933 to prevent further runs.[†] That same year, the Macmillan Commission, headed by Lord Hugh Macmillan from Britain, argued in favour of the establishment of a Canadian central bank. When it was finally decided by the five members of the Royal Commission, it was a squeaker, passing 3–2 in favour.[18]

The banks fought the proposal, proving that even bankers' emphatic certainty can still sometimes be completely wrong. Waugh mentor Bob MacIntosh, in his history of Canadian banking, *Different Drummers*, tells us "there was one thing on which all the banks were agreed, and this was that they would suffer a severe loss of earnings if a central bank were created. The chartered bank note issues would disappear, to be replaced by paper currency issued by the central bank." Through their circulation and the financing of assets, their own bank notes generated a yield for banks. They feared they'd lose that income stream. But they were short-sighted. A central bank would create a stabilizer for the system. An impetus for the formation of the Bank of Canada was the Depression, MacIntosh wrote, citing former deputy minister of finance Robert Bryce. Despite pushback, the Bank of Canada opened for business in 1935. Initially, believe it or not, people could buy shares in the central bank. However, in 1936 the government took 51 percent control and fully nationalized it in 1938.[19]

The banking environment changed rapidly after the Second World War, along with Canadian society. During these years—the years that

---

† According to the National Bureau of Economic Research (NBER), banking in the United States was fragmented, with "institutions that were small and fragile." In parts of the country, "all of the loans made by a local bank would depend ultimately on the value of a single crop." Aside from during the Great Depression, the NBER reported that between 1837 and 1890, there were eight years in which there were bank panics in the United States. With a weak banking system, the NBER said the United States developed robust capital markets instead, yielding "shadow banks" that were lightly regulated. (Michael D. Bordo, Angela Reddish, and Hugh Rockoff, "Why Didn't Canada Have a Banking Crisis in 2008 (Or in 1930, Or 1907, Or . . .)?" National Bureau of Economic Research, Working Paper 17312, August 2011).

followed the birth of Rick Waugh—a high birthrate and high immigration levels would dramatically change the country and its banking system.[20] While the residential mortgage business is now foundational to
the strength of Canada's big banks—Waugh once told me mortgages
pay the overhead—it would surprise many to learn that banks weren't
permitted to offer mortgages until 1954. Until then, life insurance companies and trust companies provided them, or even individuals through
lawyers. But burgeoning families full of baby boomers required housing, and there simply wasn't enough financing available due to the legal
constraint on banks, which held the savings of most people. In 1954,
an amendment to the Bank Act, spearheaded by Canadian Bank of
Commerce general manager Neil McKinnon, changed that.[21] The mortgage market opened further in 1967 with changes to the Bank Act.[22]

It was then the media's turn to look ridiculous. An editorial in a
Bowmanville, Ontario, newspaper bellowed: "What evil genius has per-
suaded the government to force the banks into the mortgage business?
Has the government forgotten that the first duty of the banks is to their
depositors?" Not to be outdone, the Moose Jaw *Times-Herald* wrote,
"The proposal strikes at the very heart of the Canadian banking system.
It will not strengthen it; rather it will weaken it."[23]

The banks soon got permission to make consumer loans, which
included lending for auto purchases. Prior to that, finance companies
had charged interest rates of 16 to 24 percent on loans for cars or appli-
ances. Of course, banks needed to fund those consumer loans. If
deposits weren't sufficient, their investment portfolios could earn
money or be liquidated to make loans. But more importantly, banks
were also becoming more reliant on short-term loans in the money
market—via commercial paper with maturities in months.[24] The world
of banking was opening wide for a young banker like Waugh who was
fascinated by the intersection of credit, markets, and investing—and
the underlying theme, risk.

Banking was breaking out from what could be described as a contained, static state. For more than a century there was a cap on how much interest the banks could charge—6 percent.[25] The latter rule was lifted after the Bank Act revisions in 1967, just three years before Waugh started as a teller. The revision of the act was the culmination of a process that had begun seven years earlier with the establishment of the Porter Commission. As long-time central banker Malcolm Knight wrote, the 1964 report was "a classic" and Canada's financial system "evolved consistently with the recommendations of the Porter Report." He added that subsequent revisions through the late 1980s created a path of "phased deregulation," allowing banks to acquire securities dealers and trust companies, trade in government and corporate securities, and broaden into investment counselling and wealth management.[26] Dealers could issue and trade securities such as stocks. Trust companies oversaw estates and trusts. Wealth managers looked after people's investments. The revised Bank Act also put a 10 percent ownership limit on Canadian banks (later increased to 20 percent), which effectively became a shield against takeovers by foreign financial institutions. Kobrak and Martin wrote that this limit came into force not long after Citibank (First National City in the United States) bought control of Canada's Mercantile Bank from a Dutch bank in 1963—in defiance of the finance minister and governor of the Bank of Canada.[27] Despite being given an exemption to hold 25 percent—enough for Citi to control Mercantile—it influenced Ottawa to bring in the ownership limit in September 1964.[28]

While the Mercantile affair was part of it, Dick Thomson, who ran TD Bank for some two decades, added a colourful story when I interviewed him for *Banking on America,* my book about Toronto-Dominion's US expansion.[‡] In 1963, as assistant to then TD chairman and president Allen Lambert, Thomson encountered David Rockefeller of Chase

---

‡ In 1985, after CCB and Northland failed, Mercantile had liquidity issues and was forced to merge with the National Bank of Canada.

Manhattan Bank, who Waugh would cross paths with years later. Rockefeller was business and American royalty, grandson of John D. Rockefeller, a business titan, the force behind what became Exxon. The Rockefeller family's wealth was staggering, not to mention its political heft. At the time, TD was interested in retail banking in the United States, and Lambert instructed Thomson to go to New York and watch how Chase, today part of JPMorgan Chase and Co., operated. In return, someone from Chase would visit Toronto to see how TD did things. Thomson soon figured out Rockefeller wanted to buy TD Bank. The American banker was, it turns out, on good terms with Prime Minister Lester Pearson.

Meanwhile, Allen Lambert phoned Pearson's finance minister, Walter Gordon, to let him know what was cooking. Rockefeller meantime had a cordial meeting with Pearson, who wrapped up by saying, "I'd like you to meet Walter Gordon, and I'll take you to his office." Gordon was a staunch Canadian nationalist and told the richest person in the world, "I want to tell you that I'm introducing a bill in Parliament that restricts your ownership to 10 percent." That put an ownership limit on Canadian banks, to restrain the Yanks.[29] Waugh would feel the effects of this legislation many years later.

Explaining what led to the rule, Bob MacIntosh cited Pearson's memoir. The prime minister wrote of a dinner he had with Rockefeller when he told him in no uncertain terms Chase couldn't buy TD.[30] While TD wanted to block Chase, Scotiabank was opposed to the ownership limit, given its burgeoning international operations.[31] Arguably, the ownership limit has benefited Canadian banks.[§] They've been protected and have avoided the frequent mishaps associated with American banking. They have also been good investments for decades. Not only did they grow as the country grew but also in the late 1980s there was a regulatory change that allowed them to buy investment banks and trust companies.

---

§ In February 2025, in the midst of a trade war, US president Donald Trump said he wanted American banks to have more access to operate in Canada.

Investment banks, also referred to as dealers, help companies raise capital via securities issuance, advise on major transactions, and act as brokers or intermediaries. Trusts, in addition to administering estates, trusts, and pension plans, also provided bank-like services such as deposit-taking and mortgages. Prior to regulatory reform, banks, insurance companies, trusts, and investment banks were kept separate. They had been known as the four pillars of the financial system. But regulatory reform nick-named "the big bang" in Britain in 1986 was also felt in Canada, where it was referred to as "the little bang."[32] Deregulation in Britain led to similar deregulation in Canada, setting off a series of deals. Canadian banks bought investment banks and trust companies and began offer-ing insurance.

By the late 1990s, Canada's banks were plenty big, but that did not squelch their aspirations (and later, Waugh's) to be bigger. Early on the morning of January 23, 1998, Royal Bank of Canada (RBC) and Bank of Montreal (BMO) announced they wanted to combine and create a mega-bank. But they made a grave strategic error. Neither the prime minister nor the finance minister heard the news from the banks them-selves. A reporter, the late Kevin Doyle of Bloomberg News, received a tip from "very senior financial industry people" and called the late Jim Peterson, who was secretary of state for financial institutions. Peterson got on the phone to finance minister (and later prime minister) Paul Martin, who was furious. "It was clear that this was an attempt to pres-sure me. I wasn't going to be pressured. It backfired," Martin says in an interview for *Banking on America*. The prime minister, Jean Chrétien, was equally incensed. "Can you believe it? They didn't even call us first," he told a retired banker that morning.[33]

A few months later, TD and CIBC joined the sweepstakes, announc-ing their intention to combine, leaving Scotia and National Bank with-out deals. Some believed the TD-CIBC arrangement was, at a minimum, designed to block RBC-BMO. Either way, the banks had been tone-deaf, thinking Ottawa would approve their proposals. How could shrinking the big five to the big three, with BNS being a distant third and National even smaller, be a sounder system? Certainly, there had been periods of Canadian bank consolidation in the past—in the 1910s and 1920s.[34] Also, in 1955 a merger of the Bank of Toronto and the Dominion Bank created Toronto-Dominion, and in 1961 the Canadian Bank of Commerce and the Imperial Bank merged to create CIBC. In the latter case, there had been fear of a foreign takeover. Barclays Bank of Canada had acquired 20 percent of the Imperial Bank of Canada, which motivated Imperial Bank to merge with the Commerce.[35]

But Paul Martin says he clearly recalled the 1994 bankruptcy of insurance company Confederation Life, the 1985 bank failures in Alberta, as well as the collapse of Royal Trust in 1993, which served as cautionary tales. Canadian banks were already too big to fail. So, the prospect of the failure of an even bigger, merged bank could be catastrophic for the system. There was also the likely issue of branch closures and layoffs, which would be a political nightmare.

Aside from the insult of Royal Bank and BMO side-swiping Ottawa, they had done so prior to the release of a major task force report on the future of financial services.[36] The government was unlikely to approve the mega mergers, but it would make the banks twist in the wind for a year as it conducted an official review. Chrétien had even been on the board of directors of TD Bank during his political wilderness years after John Turner took over the leadership of the federal Liberal Party. But in 1998 he was prime minister, with a finance minister who wanted to be (and would become) the next prime minister. There was no political upside to approving bank mergers.

Theoretically, it was also conceivable that if approved, one of the newly combined mega-banks would have swaggered off south of the border and paid too much for an American bank that would have greatly exposed the Canadian financial system to the 2008 subprime mortgage crisis, a harrowing period when Waugh would be CEO. From the point of view of nurturing a stable financial system, in retrospect, the federal government's rejection of the merger proposals looks like sound public policy. Further proof of that is that the big banks have remained strong without in-country consolidation, and all survived 2008.

"It raised the 'too big to fail' issue that we talk about today. If there had been mergers there would have been serious problems in Canada during the [2008] meltdown," says Scott Clark, who was deputy minister of finance at the time. "We saved their bacon."[37] On December 14, 1998, the government rejected both merger proposals as "not in the best interests of Canadians," saying the mergers would lead to "unacceptable concentration of economic power" resulting in a "significant reduction in competition." Still, given the limited size of the Canadian market, there's only so much business each bank can snare from competitors in Canada. Strong capital generation, competitiveness, and ambition have made them all expand abroad, mostly to the United States, while Scotia has ventured further afield, before and during Waugh's tenure.

But the Canadian system, from its earliest days, has both nurtured banks and shielded them. Aside from being funded by stable national deposit bases and having legal protection from foreign takeovers, they have had to hold more and better-quality capital than banks elsewhere and been subject to rigorous supervision. They've also typically held loans to maturity on their balance sheets, which has motivated them to lend prudently.[38] Canada's branch banking system, while concentrated among half a dozen major banks, created diversification. Deposits were dispersed, sitting in accounts across the country. Such diversification is glue. It holds things together. In more recent years, new business lines such as wealth management, investment banking, and international expansion would add further diversification. A history of banking as

a national, federally regulated priority has endowed Canada with a rug-
ged, resilient system that has provided credit to the country and allowed
banks to make handsome profits. While Waugh would push back at
regulators at times, he believed the country had been well served by the
system and understood the need for prudent regulation.

The history of Scotiabank is a separate story, and one that would
expose Waugh to the wider world and turn him into a global banker.

CHAPTER THREE

From Halifax to the World

In the early 1800s, Halifax, Nova Scotia, had fifteen thousand civilians and a couple thousand soldiers. They were fortified by 180 taverns. It was a thriving seaport and garrison. Shipments of brandy, silk, spices, and gold gave way to fish, lumber, rum, sugar, tobacco, and other trade. Beyond routes to Boston, New York, London, and the Caribbean, by the late 1820s, ships were arriving from India. Trade was getting more complex. The most widely accepted currency was "specie," gold and silver coins, valued by their weight and issued by many countries. There were also "bills of exchange" for payments, but they relied on how creditworthy their issuers were. It was all terribly complicated, and reliable credit and flow of funds was needed if commerce in Nova Scotia was to flourish.[1]

On the last day of 1831, a meeting was held at the Merchants Exchange Coffee House to discuss the establishment of a public bank.*

---

* There was a private bank in Halifax, but merchants found it inaccessible.

On January 31, 1832, 184 citizens signed a petition sent to the House of Assembly. Two months later, a law was passed, and Bank of Nova Scotia came into existence.[†] Shares had been sold, raising £50,000 in initial capital. There was a president, a board of thirteen, and a cashier, who ran the operation. There were also two tellers and a messenger—the bank had more board members than staff.[2] It had a vault, took deposits, issued banknotes, weighed specie, and in its first year grew assets, presumably by making loans. The first dividend was paid in July 1833.

Long before it expanded internationally, the bank expanded outside of Nova Scotia. In 1882 it took over the Union Bank of Prince Edward Island. This was despite the maritime provinces falling on hard times at the end of the age of sail—and the rise of steam and rail. This meant not only shipbuilding suffered but lumber and other industries as well.[3]

Also in 1882, the bank reached beyond the Maritimes. It opened a branch in Winnipeg, Waugh's hometown, amid a boom in the west that coincided with the building of the transcontinental railroad. Amidst heavy losses due to bad loans when a speculative real estate bubble popped, it closed in 1885, and the bank didn't reopen in Winnipeg again until 1899. Nonetheless, expansion continued. Next stop, south of the border, the year the bank closed shop in Winnipeg. Wheat and flour drove the Minnesota economy, and the bank thought it could mill money via lending and foreign exchange. In October, the Bank of Nova Scotia hung its shingle in Minneapolis.[4]

While money was lost in Winnipeg, profits were made in Minnesota. But in 1892, the bank shuttered Minneapolis and moved to Chicago, a city on a parabolic growth trajectory.[5] Scotia's American roots were taking hold. Almost a century later, Waugh would lead US lending to new heights, putting him on the CEO track.

---

† In 1871, the name was changed to The Bank of Nova Scotia.

Within Canada, the bank fanned out again from the Maritimes. Montreal was the bull's eye, and in 1888 a branch was opened there. This move was spurred by the Merchants Bank of Halifax, which was doing the same. "Merchants" would later be called the Royal Bank of Canada, and would move its head office to Montreal in 1907.

And then came the Caribbean. In 1889, a branch opened in Kingston, Jamaica. Opening in the West Indies was a first for a Canadian bank, as was expanding outside of the United States or Britain. Amazingly, Scotia had not yet opened in Toronto. That happened eight years later, in 1897. More significantly, in 1900 the bank's general manager and staff moved from Halifax to Toronto.[6]

In the first twenty years of the twentieth century, bank mergers were not unusual in Canada. It was easier to buy than to build, and that's how Bank of Nova Scotia grew. Between 1913 and 1919, it bought the Bank of New Brunswick, the Metropolitan Bank, which was concentrated in Toronto, and the Bank of Ottawa, giving it branches in Ontario, Quebec and the Prairies, and British Columbia. It now had more than three hundred branches across Canada, not including its operations in the Caribbean and the United States, as well as an office in London.[7]

The bank entered the darkness of the 1930s in solid shape, conservatively positioned. In 1929, it had the highest earnings in its history— $2.8 million, in part due to a national construction boom. Following years of bumper crops in the 1920s, there was more construction, which meant more loan business. That flow of credit fuelled building and meant activity for businesses associated with construction. Credit was economic nourishment and good for the bank too.[8] A signal of its stability during the Depression, in 1931 it opened a new head office building in Halifax, a stunning example of Beaux-Arts architecture that still stands.[‡] While the bank continued paying a slightly diminished

---

‡ It is no longer head office but is the main branch in the area.

dividend due to an eventual rise in non-performing loans, dividends became a public policy lightning rod, particularly in western Canada, where the Depression was felt acutely. The general manager (and later president) of the bank, J.A. McLeod, wrote to one of his directors in 1933 that the dividend was "somewhat embarrassing." If banks paid out less in dividends, so went the argument, they could lend more cheaply to those who needed it, including governments and municipalities and others.[9]

While the American banking system struggled in comparison, the United States was ahead of Canada in a fundamental way. It had a central bank. The Federal Reserve had been established in 1913 in the years following the 1907 financial panic, which saw John Pierpont Morgan—J.P. Morgan himself—play the role of central banker. In 1933, Canada's Royal Commission on Banking and Currency recommended the formation of a central bank.[10] The Canadian Bankers Association had publicly fought the idea the year before. The bankers lost the battle. The Bank of Canada was formed in 1935, and in the long run, the banks benefited from the establishment of a central bank, not only as an inflation fighter but also as a backstop during future crises. Among other things, it could coordinate actions with global central banks as the world's financial system became more interconnected. Rick Waugh, like all bank CEOs, would rely on the strength and guarantee of central banks—in Canada and in the many countries in which Scotiabank eventually operated.

In the 1950s, the bank grew alongside Canada, one of the world's most prosperous economies. A new twenty-five-storey building was opened in 1951 at the corner of King and Bay. It became the main branch, where Waugh would become manager. It still stands, and its opening was mentioned by the *New Yorker*, which praised how succinct the nine speakers had to be at the event—under forty-eight seconds each.[11] Three-quarters of the bank's branches were now outside of the Maritimes.[12]

In the 1950s, Scotia also appointed its first general manager who wasn't a Maritimer—Bill Nicks, a Winnipeg native like Waugh. Described as a "restless" character, he started working for the bank when he was sixteen. Nicks would rise to the position of president and chairman, running the bank for a decade and a half, transforming it into a global player.

While working in Halifax, Nicks made connections with Greek shipping owners that led to significant business for the bank. In 1959, he formed the bank's investment department, where Waugh would land after his short stint as a teller. By the mid-1960s, the bank was looking for new recruits who had more education than previous hires—young people who'd attended university.[13] Waugh was one of those, among just a handful of university graduates hired by the bank in 1970.

The last few years of the Nicks era were calamitous. In the late 1960s, a gas explosion racked his Rosedale home, injuring his chauffeur.[14] In 1972, he died of a heart attack at home. But Nicks had laid the groundwork for Scotia to become an international bank.[15] Waugh would be only two years into his banking career when Nicks passed away. But the platform Nicks left behind would be what his successors over the next forty-plus years—Cedric Ritchie, Peter Godsoe, and Rick Waugh—would continue to build on. While there was a caretaker CEO after Nicks died, his effective successor was the autocratic and demanding Ritchie.[16] There was an interlude after Nicks's death when Thomas Boyles was chairman and CEO, but by the end of the year, Ritchie became president and chief executive officer. Boyles remained chairman for two years.

Ritchie was born in 1927 in a small New Brunswick town along the Saint John River. His father died young, and his mother supported the family as the postmistress. With no funds for university, "the lone bank in town was Bank of Nova Scotia," where he started as a teller in Bath, New Brunswick. He rose to chief accountant at age thirty-three and then to various top management roles before becoming CEO in 1972, adding the chairman title in 1974 and keeping it until his retirement in 1995. Described as a "workaholic," Ritchie was hard-driving, "fueling himself with chocolate bars." Brisk and sharp-edged, he told one of his executives that his job was to make decisions, not phone for help—and that the banker's lending limit was only limited by his judgment.[17] This would be the Scotiabank that Rick Waugh would absorb.

Arguably, Scotia turned outward long before Nicks and Ritchie. As historian James D. Frost described, a brutal commercial depression hit the Maritimes in the 1880s. "The crisis had a profound material and psychological effect on the Bank of Nova Scotia," Frost concluded, writing that it "shattered the bank's faith in the region." It was during this period, under Cashier (General Manager) Thomas Fyshe, that the bank expanded into more populated parts of Canada (Montreal), the United States (Minneapolis), and Jamaica, where a railway was being built. By 1888, lending was growing more in Minneapolis than in the Maritimes (based on Frost's detailed research of deposits and credit flows). Four years later, Minneapolis would give way to Chicago, where the bank would finance the likes of the International Harvester Company and a predecessor of Pillsbury Company. Fyshe drove the bank's national and international expansion based on disaffection for opportunity in the Maritimes. By 1910, lending in the Maritimes constituted just under 20 percent of the bank's loans.[18]

The bank's cultural obsession with credit also may have its roots with Fyshe, who'd begun his training in his native Scotland. When appointed general manager in 1877, Fyshe observed that the bank did not have a "systematic lending policy." Frost wrote that Fyshe changed that. The banker was quoted in a circular as saying, "the main consideration of success in banking is not large profits but small losses." Waugh, who repeatedly talks about first understanding the downside of any loan, transaction, or investment, would no doubt agree with Fyshe. In other words, lend well, and not for long periods.

In another circular, Fyshe said, "There are really very few men anywhere who can be trusted to handle prudently and safely unstinted loans
of money."[19] Much may have changed since those early days, but credit
judgment and risk management would become a point of pride at Scotia.
They would become preoccupations of Waugh's mentors, and he would
absorb their lessons in full. He would see bad credit decisions play out in
the least-developed-country debt crisis of the 1980s, as well as in financial
calamities he had to manage—the default of Argentina and the global
financial crisis half a decade later. It's no surprise Rick Waugh believes
history repeats.

CHAPTER FOUR

No, Mr. Trump
Lending to Americans

Not yet forty, in the mid-1980s, Rick Waugh left Toronto. Having established himself at the main branch, he relocated to New York. If successful there, he would still have a couple more rungs to climb, but he would be one step closer to consideration for the top job at the bank. His predecessor as CEO, Peter Godsoe, said if you wanted to get anywhere in your career, at some point, you'd have to work in New York. "Because *he* did," Waugh laughs, adding that Godsoe was right. According to Rod McQueen's *The Money Spinners*, Godsoe went there to learn from American bankers.[1] While Waugh was inwardly resistant to going, he says he wasn't given a choice; "people who I respected such as Peter Godsoe and others, I took their advice seriously."

In the mid-1980s to early 1990s New York was certainly the place to be for a Canadian banker. The financial sector had the rocket boosters associated with the Reagan epoch of laissez-faire capitalism. Business was brisk. In keeping with the zeitgeist, there's a photo of a young Rick Waugh in New York, decked out in red suspenders, emblematic of the go-go era.

More important, US banks had not yet merged to create the goliaths of today. The landscape was dominated by thousands of smaller, stand-alone state banks. Until the 1990s, American banks couldn't even do business across state lines. As a result, when Waugh landed in New York in 1985, Canadian banks were bigger than the biggest American banks. Crucially, US banks had *lower* lending limits than Canada's, so the latter lent to major American companies. "It was a great place to make money," Waugh says. Scotia already had decades of expertise lending internationally, including in the United States. Now it was applying more than 150 years of experience to substantially grow commercial credit in the country.

Among those who called Waugh scrounging for money was none other than Donald Trump, then just a publicity-seeking braggart taking up the oxygen in Manhattan's real estate sector. Waugh says anyone like Trump who needed money "would eventually find us." In Trump's case, it was Trump's brother (Robert) who found Scotia.

"Would I mind coming up to Trump Tower?" came the request. So, Waugh went. He recalled waiting in the reception area, staring at a ten-year-old magazine sporting Trump's picture on the cover. Once Waugh was in his office, Trump pointed out his window at the Plaza Hotel, boasting, "I own that." Waugh says the brash New Yorker then outlined a scheme involving his company, Resorts International, whereby Trump would borrow against the cash flow from his Nassau hotel and casino to get a loan from Scotiabank to build out casinos in Atlantic City. Waugh says he told Trump, "Very unlikely and we wouldn't do it." Explaining why, he told Trump the Bahamian government wouldn't allow him to build a casino in Atlantic City to compete with the casinos he had in the Bahamas.

"Rick, with due respect, you're not the CEO of the bank," Trump said.

"No, I'm not," Waugh conceded.

And then, out came a full load of Trump's trademark chutzpah. "Well, I'd like to meet the CEO." That, at the time, was Cedric Ritchie, who frequently visited the New York area. According to Waugh, Ritchie "loved to call on customers," so he and Waugh had that in common. "I was always looking for people to take him around [to]," Waugh recalls, adding, "I had a lot of quality time with Ritchie." When the CEO was freed from the tight schedule of head office, Waugh knew he could be at Ritchie's side without others clawing for his time. While it was good for the bank, helping develop business in New York, it was also good for Waugh.

Back at Trump Tower, this time with Ritchie in tow, the same old magazine with Trump's mug on the cover was in the reception area. Waugh describes Ritchie decked out in a three-piece suit, looking every bit the bank boss from central casting. "I can tell who the CEO is," Trump said upon seeing the suit. As always, Trump was focused on appearances, and in this instance, in full suck-up mode. Ignoring Waugh and zoning in on the CEO, Trump proceeded to roll out his stock lines for Ritchie. *See that hotel? That's the Plaza. I own it.*

Trump then outlined his plan for Paradise Island in the Bahamas, which Ritchie knew intimately, courtesy of Scotia's significant Caribbean presence. After the meeting, Waugh and Ritchie were descending in the elevator and Waugh said, "Well, Mr. Ritchie. You've met the Donald. What do you think?"

"That guy knows what he's talking about," Ritchie told his young colleague. Waugh recounts Ritchie's response with a bemused smile and raised eyebrows—as if to say, *Can you believe this?* Could this hard-boiled CEO, a no-nonsense, successful, lifelong banker, have been hoodwinked by Trump?

Waugh says he then interjected, "But we're not going to lend him the money, right?" Ritchie agreed with him. Waugh believed the Bahamas would immediately shut down Trump's casino there (he said Scotia's country manager in Nassau happened to be related to the prime minister). Trump did eventually build a casino empire in Atlantic City, but after piling up debts, the odyssey ended in tatters, with multiple visits to bankruptcy court over several years. A lengthy 2016 report by the *New York Times* ("How Donald Trump Bankrupted His Atlantic City Casinos, but Still Earned Millions"*)* citing "a close examination of regulatory reviews, court records and security filings," said there was "little doubt that Mr. Trump's casino business was a protracted failure." It added that "the burden of his failures fell on investors and others who had bet on his business acumen." By the early 1990s, one of his Atlantic City casinos was in bankruptcy court. A year after, so was the Plaza Hotel.[2]

Trump aside, by Waugh's telling, lending in the United States was open season for Scotiabank. Not only had Godsoe tilled the soil there, but Godsoe's number two, Bruce Birmingham, had as well. With ten American offices—including New York, Chicago, Atlanta, and Houston—Waugh says, "I just took it to a higher level," adding that he used credit to a greater degree than the other two, "the ability to lend large amounts of money" quickly. Or, as Birmingham reportedly said, "big bucks, fast and cheap." To get attention and scoop business in the United States, for a time Scotia charged less than American banks. But clearly the judgment was that no amount was worth the risk of lending to someone like Trump.*

"Peter [Godsoe] was very important to my career," Waugh reflects. "Bruce Birmingham was equally important," he adds, calling them both

---

* During Trump's first term as president of the United States, I asked Waugh's successor Brian Porter at a Scotiabank/United Jewish Appeal event on February 8, 2018, whether the bank would ever lend to Trump. The answer was unequivocal—no.

mentors. Waugh described Birmingham as very hands on, a credit guy and a "great guy," who would go to bat for him.[†] As Waugh had absorbed years earlier from Robert MacIntosh and George Hitchman, credit was the beating heart of banking. And you were unlikely to get anywhere at Scotiabank without knowing how to lend, how to make money from it, and how to get paid back.

The New York assignment was high times for Waugh. As a Canadian bank, "I could work with Chase Manhattan one day and Chemical Bank the next day and I wasn't considered a competitor. I would come in as an equal partner with them. The challenge was [the] Americans had hundreds of very capable bankers and we had maybe fifty. They had ten teams to our one team," Waugh says, sitting at the kitchen table of his luxurious Toronto condo. He describes how in New York cold calling became a calling card. "I would just go out and call on senior people in these American banks." Waugh would tell them that if they had a big loan, why not give half of it to Scotia to spread the risk? "We would be probably the first or second call," he says, "if an American bank was looking for someone to be partner in a big financing." The approach worked quickly, he says, and led to direct customer relationships.

"It wasn't just lending. We had to go out there and market." All bank officers under Waugh in the United States had to do a minimum number of cold calls—twenty to thirty a month. "You never get business on the first call, and if you do, watch out." But he and his team sold the ability to make quick decisions on large loans. "We Canadians, we can act like Americans if we have to. Except we're kinder, gentler, and always say we're sorry." This, of course, belies an inner toughness, and perhaps a passive aggressiveness that may not be apparent to Americans at first.

One of Waugh's cold callers had in fact been hired at Scotia because he'd cold called the bank itself for a job. Jim Tryforos grew up in Queens,

---

† Birmingham died in 2010. A hotel in Stratford, Ontario, is named for him—the Bruce Hotel—and run by his daughter.

New York, an engineering student who played varsity football for Columbia. His gridiron skills got him into MBA school at McGill in Montreal, where he described tuition then as dirt cheap. As he approached graduation in 1979, he sent out 180 letters, the equivalent of cold calls. Five of them went to the heads of the big Canadian banks. He told them he was an American graduating from McGill and wanted to work in New York. At the time, it was hard for Canadian banks to get Canadian MBAs into the United States, so Tryforos used the competitive advantage of an American passport to get in the door. From all the letters he sent, he received one response—on Cedric Ritchie's letterhead. He was amazed. But he later discovered Ritchie had a *room full of people* answering his correspondence. Nevertheless, he got a job at Scotiabank working at 67 Wall Street, and was henceforth known as "the guy who wrote a letter to Ced Ritchie." As it turned out, being a fearless cold caller was a valuable skill. He and others on the Waugh squad would call on Fortune 500 companies to see what financing they needed. In Canada, there was a history of local branch managers doing this. Waugh had done it as manager of the main branch. But in the United States, there weren't branches of Scotiabank, so corporate bankers like Tryforos had to do it.

Another member of Waugh's cold calling crew was Stephen Lockhart. Lockhart grew up in the village of Bath, New Brunswick, population 476, just a ten-minute drive from where Ced Ritchie was born and raised. It "sort of gave me a special relationship with Ritchie," he says, given that the CEO knew Lockhart's father, the local physician. Lockhart joined Scotiabank in Toronto and spent three years in the branch system before resigning and enrolling at Western for his MBA. He rejoined the bank in 1977 in—what else?—the credit department in Toronto. A couple of years later, he was transferred to Chicago. That's where he met Waugh, who burst into the room late and onto a call already in progress, overwhelming the person on the other end of the line with his thunderous entrance. The guy on the line, experiencing full-on Waugh for the first time, "didn't know whether to have a poop or wind his watch," Lockhart cracks.

No matter. Scotia, Lockhart recalls, had a leg up. The creditworthiness of the borrower wasn't the only factor because *banks were also given credit ratings*. And if you were a borrower, the credit rating agencies wanted to know the ratings of the banks with whom you were dealing. A lot of American banks, Lockhart says, were only single-A rated, whereas the Bank of Nova Scotia was rated more highly, a material advantage. Scotia was better run, so it had a better credit rating, making it more attractive to the rating agencies assessing borrowers. If you had Scotia lending to you, that gave comfort to them, as though the borrower had the *Good Housekeeping* seal of approval. A higher-rated bank would be more likely to have stable funding, an obvious plus for a rating agency. "It wasn't as hard as you might think to make a cold call on a large corporate [company] in the US to get your foot in the door."

But was Waugh limited by how much he and his team could lend? "I had no limit," he says. "I had to go to Toronto for everything and that was a good thing. But I got twenty-four-hour turnaround." Although sometimes, he allowed, it was forty-eight hours. To ensure speedy service, Waugh had access to the key credit decision makers at head office. Of course, Ritchie, Godsoe, and Birmingham were the top deciders, but supporting them were Terry Fryett, who became chief credit officer, and Sylvia Chrominska, who was senior VP of corporate credit, the bank's first female executive vice-president (EVP) and ultimately the bank's head of human resources.

Unquestionably, the ability to give a rapid-fire answer to borrowers "was a competitive advantage," Waugh says. "We could commit large dollars very quickly." By way of hypothetical example, American bank Manufacturers Hanover might be able to lend $100 million but needed $200 million. In that case, it would come to Scotia, a non-US bank "but a good look-alike," Waugh likes to say with a laugh. Often, it came down to a nighttime phone call. "You could definitely phone somebody at eight o'clock at night." The final decisions were all made in Toronto by the bank's risk committee first thing in the morning. "That's when Ritchie was CEO, when Peter was CEO, when Rick was CEO," Waugh says. "If I can think of other things that made us successful in New York, that was it. The turnaround time for any amount."

As with all junctures in his career, several other Scotia bankers figured prominently during Waugh's New York days. One was Stephen Hart, who met Waugh in 1976 when he was an intern in Scotia's investment department. Hart said the future CEO was already a "hotshot VP" and larger-than-life character, although Waugh interacted with juniors like him, which "wasn't done at this time." Hart was assigned to do financial analysis, even though he said he'd only taken one accounting course. Clearly, he was well cast. Hart would also eventually be the bank's chief credit officer and its chief risk officer (CRO).

Godsoe sent Hart to Chicago from 1981 to 1986, overlapping with the beginning of Waugh's years in the United States. Hart began interacting more with Waugh when he was moved back to Toronto as supervisor of corporate credit for the east from 1986 to 1991—which included Waugh's region in New York. Hart's boss in credit was Sylvia Chrominska, who would become one of Waugh's top executives when he was CEO. In those days, Hart says, there was no chief risk officer, now an independent voice reporting to the bank's CEO. Back then, each group had its own credit group, and they reported to Godsoe, who oversaw corporate banking—which Hart calls very bad governance. Nonetheless, at the time, two decades before the financial crisis of 2008, it somehow worked.

As for the theme of Waugh's time in New York, Hart described Scotia as "aggressive." He jokingly echoed Birmingham's famous line. "Does the phrase 'big bucks, fast and cheap' mean anything to you?" It was a strategy and marketing line wrapped into one. Scotiabank typically took a piece of a "syndicated" loan, banks joining forces to lend together. That allowed Scotia to move more quickly, given that another bank led the deal and had done much of the grunt work. It was also the era of the fax machine, and there were a lot of faxes, Hart says. Typically, a fax consisted of a "ten-thirty-five," the code for a corporate credit application. The loans were usually between $25 million and $100 million.

Even though Waugh said he didn't have limits, Hart says there were single-name limits. Hart said the data out of the United States—such as information on competition—was better than in Canada, so that was a plus when analyzing a credit. "The disadvantage is you're not the lead bank," he says, adding that "you pick up the pennies." But there were a lot of pennies. "We moved fast," Hart continued. "If it was a rush deal, we'd rush it." Eventually, the bank concluded it could lead deals. Business was good, and closing dinners were all the rage, with "very expensive steak and wine."

In 1977, Terry Fryett was a McMaster MBA interviewing for a job with Scotia at the old headquarters at 44 King Street West. Coincidentally, one of the people interviewing him was Rick Waugh, barely thirty years old. Waugh was working in the treasury department, which interested Fryett as well. He later moved to corporate banking and there was Waugh again; he soon became manager of the main branch in Toronto. "That was a really big deal," Fryett says of Waugh's ascension to running the main branch, a signal about his future. The two reunited in New York, with Fryett spending a dozen years there.

While Waugh boasted he could get twenty-four-hour (or forty-eight) turnaround on loan approvals, Fryett suggested a certain hyperbole. "Twenty-four hours might be really fast," he says, and Waugh later amended it to a few days, rather than the weeks it took American banks. However, Fryett allowed that the team was "extremely responsive." Fryett says it was not unusual to stay up all night to finish a job. He indicated it was always helpful to have Rick on the phone, talking to the two or three people in Toronto who would have the final say—Chrominska,

Birmingham, and, if necessary, Godsoe. "He [Waugh] would do a lot of the legwork, a lot of the explaining." During that period, Fryett said there was a lot of merger and acquisition activity (M&A), and the bank plugged into it. Big companies were buying other companies, or combining. And buyers borrow to do so. Scotia lent to a lot of these deals because it could lend a lot, quickly.

When one of Waugh's New York deals floated up to Chrominska's committee, there would be questions to ensure the structure, risk, and price were appropriate and that the terms and conditions would protect the bank. While the proposed transaction would go to the senior credit committee for approval or to "loan policy" for ultimate approval (i.e., the top bosses), obtaining quick turnaround on American loans had an incentive attached. Chrominska said if the bank committed within forty-eight hours, it got a bonus fee up front.

But taking pieces of big loans did not mean swallowing the due diligence of the lead banks holus-bolus. Chrominska said Scotia did its own detective work. How much debt was there? How much equity? What was management like? While others suggested there were limits, Chrominska said there was no limit on the size of transactions. If the bank was leading a syndicated deal, the issue was "how quickly we could sell down," meaning how quickly could you off-load pieces of a big loan to other banks. "It absolutely had to be syndicate-able." Sometimes it wasn't and was painful, she said.

While Chrominska respected how hard Waugh's team worked to get a deal and encouraged her team to find ways to endorse a loan application, they did sometimes say no, avoiding what they saw as a potential loss. Nonetheless, Waugh was aggressive, and he and his group pushed hard. "He [Waugh] was perceived as a bit of a deal junkie. He usually got very, very excited about transactions. Very excited," she said. "If we didn't endorse the deal, he would get pretty agitated, clearly."

Meantime, Fryett observed that there was traditionally a philosophy at Scotia: one that encouraged the bank to be aggressive in the United States but discouraged it from being the lead on a deal. "'We shouldn't do that,'" Fryett said, mimicking the thinking. "We should always have a US bank that would be leading." He isn't certain how this conservative policy developed, but hypothesizes that if a loan got into trouble and ended up in American courts, the belief was that it was better to have a US bank out front than a Canadian one ("I don't believe that," Waugh said, when presented with the viewpoint). But Fryett maintains the attitude in Toronto was "Get a friend, get a friend"—meaning an American bank as a cushion against trouble. Perhaps, he allowed, it was because Scotia was in so many countries and so often the foreign bank, and "because we had our head handed to us as a foreigner sometimes."

However, on the question of how aggressive Scotia should be in New York, Waugh's take was that historically, head office in Canada "didn't believe we had the skill level. But over [a] time of several years, their confidence increased," he says, adding that he and his team had to prove themselves. Previously, the bank had been content "as long as we got invited to the closing dinner; we didn't care if we led or not." But as the management team in New York got more successful and confident with leading, they did, "but it was never a strategy." Until, he said, an American bank asked Scotia to lead a credit because the US bank couldn't take it on due to a conflict of interest. (If it was an acquisition loan, for example, perhaps the US bank had another customer in the bidding and couldn't represent more than one side.) However, another issue was capacity. While Waugh had no doubt Scotia had the skill to lead deals, he ran a relatively small team in New York compared to American banks. "We didn't have the capacity to do more than one or two [lead] deals at a time."

But Fryett indicated Waugh wanted to push the envelope. "Rick convinced people in Toronto that we could lead, and we did," he said, adding

that "there were two or three years where we were number five in the
league tables" (a performance ranking based on financial measures
such as the value of deals or revenue). It included US and global banks.
"[Waugh] took it from zero to number five in the league tables. He
really elevated the game plan for the bank, big time." A good ranking
helped Scotia promote itself as a player. It was third-party verification
of the bank's skill.

What's more, Waugh would include everyone in the conversation, even junior people. "He would challenge you on the credit,"
Fryett says, and surviving the Waugh meat grinder was painful. The
questions were relentless. Who's the management team? For how
long? Who's the board? How well is the company governed? What
were the numbers? Were the assumptions too rosy? What could go
wrong that would prove the assumptions were unrealistic? What was
the collateral? What were the protections in the covenants? Why are
they coming to us for a loan when they've been dealing with this
other bank for years? Why is this point important for the borrower?
What am I missing here? What's driving this loan application? Why
is this leverage important? Was the borrower under pressure? Waugh
was the credit prosecutor, poking and probing everything. Stephen
Hart says there were other questions, too: What makes the business
special? What's the competitive advantage? Does it have access to
cheap raw materials? Patent protection? A long list of clients? What's
going to keep it alive when others fail? What keeps you up at night?
"I've never seen a borrower's projection," Hart said wryly, "that says we
won't pay you back in five years."

"This is how well you need to know your deal," Fryett says, "before
you recommend these big numbers to the bank. You need to understand these credits inside out." Fryett confesses to initially not knowing
his material as well as he should have and getting scorched by Waugh.
Once you passed muster, though, Waugh would pick up the phone and

call his counterpart in risk, saying "this deal is coming up on Monday and I like it." "When it had his support, it carried a lot of weight." Years later, when Fryett became the bank's chief credit officer, he "found it so easy." Waugh had taught him how to do it.

Macro events inevitably impacted Scotia's approach in the United States. Because of the burgeoning Eurodollar market—which had nothing to do with euros, but rather US dollars that were deposited outside of the United States—foreign banks started making short-term loans to big top-rated companies like Texaco or Pfizer, with small margins over LIBOR, the London Interbank Offered Rate. Although since phased out, LIBOR was considered the benchmark for how much banks would charge each other for loans. Most of what Scotia was doing, Tryforos said, fell into that category: lending to very large borrowers at cheaper rates than US banks could. It would participate in large revolving credit lines for highly rated companies. Nonetheless, even as perhaps the tenth-largest lender in such deals, it was lucrative business, and the cultural barriers were low. "Canadians weren't Americans, but they were close," he said.

But establishing a reputation as a quick-footed lender was core to what Scotia did in the United States. In 1981, a few years before Waugh arrived in New York, Texaco had been on Tryforos's target list. One otherwise dull Friday morning in early July, he got a call from the assistant treasurer at what was then one of the giants of the oil industry. Texaco was putting together a multi-billion-dollar financing for an acquisition. It wanted Scotia to lend it $300 million, and it wanted the answer by 3 p.m. that day. Normally, Tryforos said, such a loan application would involve a detailed credit analysis four or five pages long and would take a week or so. But Texaco was Texaco—huge—and in 2001, it became part of Chevron. It was hardly an unknown. So Tryforos wrote a two-pager and sent it by telex to the bank's credit jury. As requested, the loan was approved by 3 p.m.

Eventually, cable television came into view. The industry could be confusing, and was losing money because of huge up-front capital investment. If you were an uninitiated lender, you'd say, "I'm not going near that," Tryforos said. But Scotia and Waugh, like TD, which also went big into cable lending, understood that cable, via monthly subscriber fees, generated enormous cash flows to pay back loans. As Robin Korthals, the late president of TD Bank said, "You'll give up your refrigerator before your cable television."[3]

In 1985, Scotiabank gave the cable and media file to Tryforos, who worked with another banker, John Eby. By 1990, under five years of Waugh in New York, the bank had billions in loans to US cable companies. The bank took certain comfort in knowing that TD was also financing cable firms, Tryforos said, because Scotia "didn't want to have something blow up" and be "the only dumb Canadians" lending to key industry players. While bankers coolly analyze numbers, they're also flesh-and-blood humans trying to avoid the embarrassment of losses or being beat by competitors. During the late eighties and early nineties, Stephen Hart says the key financial ratios on which the bank would anchor credit judgments when lending to cable companies would shift for convenience. "We went nuts in cable," he said. (He described oil and gas as another phase of frenzied lending.)

Hart rhymed off examples of ratios used to rationalize a cable loan. There was debt-to-population. There was debt-to-subscribers. "You found a way to get a ratio that made everyone comfortable, to justify the loan." Was it bad governance? "Oh, terrible. It was the 'everyone's doing it' syndrome." It wasn't as if the bank went rogue, Hart explains. Rather, the approach was simply in vogue. "The bank was good," he said, adding, "We knew credit. Ritchie was a credit guy. [Gordon] Bell [Ritchie's number two] was a credit guy. Godsoe was a credit guy. Rick was a credit guy." They all spoke the same language and wore the designation like a badge. But there were limits on how many deals a foreign bank like Scotia could lead. Clients wanted their lead bank to do their cash management or payroll, which Scotia couldn't do—the capacity issue Waugh cited. In the late 1990s, the bank appointed its first chief risk officer, and there were industry limits and country limits. "We wanted diversification," Hart says. "That's the first road for risk management."

Aside from understanding the fundamentals of the company and the transaction, Waugh was interested in "idiosyncratic risk," the fly in the ointment or the out-of-the-ordinary scenario. His early training and experience at the bank was in investing, and he says he treated lending like investing, specifically value investing in the spirit of Benjamin Graham and Warren Buffett.

"I always viewed lending, like investing, as an art, not a science." He adds that there's no algorithm that can teach you how to lend. And with big loans or credits, there's the problem of concentration rather than diversification. A corporate loan portfolio is different than a portfolio of hundreds of thousands of mortgages, which theoretically spreads risk widely.

Of course, the cable business brought Waugh into contact with a whole other realm of American society, and those who knew how to play the schmooze game at an entirely different level, with a spritz of glitz. Exhibit A: media mogul Ted Turner, he of the America's Cup sailing extravaganza, the Atlanta Braves of Major League Baseball, and best known for founding CNN. Launched in 1980, the twenty-four-hour Cable News Network revolutionized television news, and perhaps geopolitics along with it. The 1991 bombing of Baghdad or the 2001 destruction of the World Trade Center could be watched in real time. The model later spawned Fox News and MSNBC.

Alongside this broadcasting convulsion, the Bank of Nova Scotia, like TD, was a pre-eminent lender to the North American cable and media sector. "It's an industry I knew well," Waugh says, while not divulging whether Turner was a client. But he does allow that an

invitation from Turner led to one of the best breakfasts of his career—
held at Trump's pile, the Plaza Hotel. Perhaps not surprisingly, a TD
banker was also present. In those days, Waugh says, Toronto-Dominion
was the bank Scotia always "benchmarked against." It was "the bank
most like us at the time," similar in culture, nimble, and entrepreneur-
ial, and there was a mutual respect.

But back to the breakfast. Aside from his broadcasting and sporting
ventures, Turner was known for squiring starlets, at the time the
Hollywood actress and workout queen Jane Fonda. On this particular
day, the sly Turner figured he knew who he was dealing with, a couple
of easy-to-impress Canadian hayseeds who made loans.

"And who walks in but Jane Fonda," Waugh said. "And we just melted."

"Why don't you come in and say hello?" Turner asked her.

"It worked," says Waugh. Fonda spent time charming the eager
bankers, telling them how much she loved Toronto and jogging in its
ravines. "She did most of the talking," Waugh recalls.

This era coincided with the trend towards leveraged buyouts, or LBOs,
whereby the acquiring firm takes on a high level of debt to make the
purchase using the target's assets as collateral. The bank lent to such
deals. "Rick would have been one of the driving forces," Jim Tryforos
says. For example, he cites Scotia's involvement, in 1987, as an equity
investor in a fund run by famed buyout firm Kohlberg Kravis Roberts
and Co., or KKR, perhaps best known for purchasing snack food and
tobacco giant RJR Nabisco for a staggering $25 billion in 1988. The
deal was immortalized in a book, *Barbarians at the Gate*, and later in a
movie starring James Garner as president and CEO F. Ross Johnson.
Coincidentally, Johnson was, like Waugh, from Winnipeg. LBO culture was sharp, opportunistic, aggressive, and secretive. If the deal was
right, huge sums were made. It was a long way from Thomas Fyshe's
day. But if you wanted to be a lead bank and participate in deals with

the famous private equity firm, investing alongside KKR in its fund
was a "ticket to entry." The LBOs of the second half of the 1980s,
Tryforos said, "changed the entire banking business."

This phenomenon introduces another key cog in Waugh's New York
machine, Seth Mersky. Born in Delaware, Mersky went to the University
of Delaware and wore a blue Delaware T-shirt with gold letters when
he spoke to me via Zoom from the Bahamas. He looked every bit the
retired boomer chilling in a beach house. A stuffed blue, turquoise, and
yellow mahi-mahi—caught in 1967—was mounted on the wood panel-
ling. After university, Mersky went to Houston and worked for about
a year in Exxon's tax department. Socially, he met some Scotia bankers
posted there and was soon working for the bank. Mersky first spoke
with Waugh around 1986 or 1987. It was the early days of LBOs, and
Mersky was intrigued by that business. He was also interested in loan
syndication—distributing pieces of large loans to a group of participating banks. Waugh moved Mersky, who was twenty-eight at the time, to
New York. Mersky believed in being the distributor of the loan—in
other words, the lead bank. "I wanted to lead more deals and be in that
position," he said, whereas older forces in the bank didn't. Waugh, he
recalled, was in the middle.

Overwhelmingly, though, Mersky said the biggest part of Scotia's business then was getting "the first call" from the major banks of the day—
Manufacturers Hanover, Chemical Bank, Citi, or Bank of America—to
participate in their loans.[‡] Mersky believed Waugh wanted to be more
aggressive too but didn't want to upset the bigger piece of the business—
taking large chunks of loans from other banks. Being one of ten banks
that would take $100 million was often a slam dunk versus being lead or
co-lead, which carried more risk but potentially higher returns.

Mersky said a senior banker sitting in Canada was much more able

‡ In the 1990s, Chemical acquired Manufacturers Hanover and Chase Manhattan, form-
ing the nucleus of what is now JPMorgan Chase.

to gather risk-related intelligence for major Canadian lending. "Peter Godsoe used to say it was a thirty-phone-call country," he said. He meant there were thirty people in Canada who, between them, could fill you in on just about anything. In the mid-1980s or early 1990s in the United States, Mersky suggested Scotiabank was not in that privileged position, so it was harder for the bank to assess risk there if it wanted to lead. After all, the United States was ten times larger, population and GDP-wise, and there were better-connected people there than those who worked at Scotiabank, no matter how good Scotia's people were.

Waugh, however, pushes back on Mersky's assertion, defending his New York team's ability to do the kind of due diligence and risk assessment Godsoe could get done with his thirty phone calls in Canada. "Those [American] deals made a lot of money for the bank with a lot of constrained risk," he says. In certain deals, US banks would give Scotia the safest part of the loan—the working capital—which was short-term, thereby mitigating term risk. "And we never got greedy," Waugh emphasizes. In those days, the bank made literally hundreds of corporate loans in the United States. In June 2024, the CEO of Scotiabank, Scott Thomson, told a Canadian Club audience in Toronto that while the bank still did not have a retail (branch) presence in the United States, it had three thousand corporate clients there.

Meantime, Mersky couldn't argue with the fast-turnaround lending Waugh revelled in describing. "He [Waugh] could get a loan turned around in a day or so for hundreds of millions of dollars." Waugh, he says, could speed things up, calling Birmingham, Godsoe, or even Ritchie. It was Scotia's credit chromosome at work. Mersky believes Waugh and those leaders "just had a sixth sense for finding the weakness in a proposal and focusing attention on it till he was satisfied that it was addressed." Every business, every proposal, every loan application has a flaw, and it was that ability to detect a flaw that set them apart, Mersky says. In lending, there are the three C's, or rules of thumb: capacity (can they pay), collateral (what's backing the loan), and character (can you trust the borrower). But it's not that simple. Some people, Mersky says, had great character but "wanted to do stupid things." Others were lacking in character but had a brilliant idea. There was a thicket of information to absorb, analyze, and judge.

"I certainly believe I had it [judgment]," Waugh says. "Peter, Bruce, and I thought very much alike," he adds, "on most things." He also says that "the CEO or the president is always the chief risk officer," whether there was officially a CRO or not. During Waugh's New York days, if he really wanted to do a deal and the policy committee or credit committee said "you're crazy," he wouldn't do the deal. He says that didn't happen very often, though, because he presented them with deals that made sense to them.

"He [Waugh] was very adept at distilling a loan or a business enterprise," Mersky said, "into its most important essence." He had an ability to acquire a quick understanding of a situation, and act as a good salesperson for or communicator about it. "Rick didn't start many sentences with 'it's complicated,'" he said. In fact, Mersky said that if someone starts a presentation by saying how complicated a situation is, it's a red flag to him. He also doesn't think that great bankers, lenders, or investors are formulaic; therefore, one financial ratio isn't sufficient to give comfort. If lending or investing was formulistic, he says, everyone could do it. He pointed to the cable industry, which in its earliest days had no earnings or cash flow. All the money that came in went into building the network, an arms race of sorts. A ratio, he says, couldn't capture it. You had to believe in the future of the business. Scotia and TD did.

Among the memorable deals for Mersky was a loan to Newmont Mining Corp. (now Newmont Corporation), which he said was the biggest loan of physical gold to a company (a million ounces) ever. In 1987–88, Newmont needed money to fight off the late corporate raider T. Boone Pickens, who led a hostile bid for the company. To make Pickens go away, the gold company basically paid him off. In addition to cash, Newmont borrowed gold and then sold it to pay a special dividend— basically a corporate ransom payment to make Pickens retreat. At the time, it was cheaper to borrow gold than to borrow cash. And if you owned a gold mine, Mersky said, you were naturally "long" gold—you were producing it. Every month, every quarter, and every year, you were producing the precious metal with which you could pay back the loan at a bargain-basement borrowing rate. So, Scotia led a syndicated loan with what Mersky recalled as a group of approximately ten banks. The lenders would get paid back in gold plus the fee. "It was a big success."

The gold deal also showed that the customers Waugh and Scotia loaned to were not all New York based. Besides Newmont, the bank lent to many private hospital companies headquartered in the southern United States. "Our loan book in Nashville equalled probably to New York," Waugh says, chuckling about it. Who in Tennessee had ever heard of the Bank of Nova Scotia? "Where's Nova Scotia? We were quite an oddball business in Nashville," covering the south via the bank's office in Atlanta. Given his prominence as a lender in the area, there is a ship on the Mississippi named for him: the *Richard E. Waugh*.

In Las Vegas, Scotiabank lent to casinos, hotels, and resorts. In New York, Greek shipowners would drop into the bank's offices to say hello, tied to the Bill Nicks era, when the bank began financing the Greek shipping industry through its relationships in Halifax. That dated back to the post–Second World War years, when Canada sold off navy ships, which were purchased by Greek shipowners.

Not all the lending went swimmingly. Mersky recalled deals with two high rollers from Australia. One was a loan to the late property developer George Herscu, who wanted to build malls and own the anchor tenants. It was a great idea until the economy intervened and retail suffered. Mersky calls it "an embarrassment." Real estate developers were a frequent cause of banking trouble, given the cyclical nature of the business—so much so that according to Stephen Lockhart, Mersky cracked, the bank would be better off just *giving* them each a million dollars and telling them to go away.

The other sour Aussie loan was to the late Alan Bond, also a prominent businessman. Both Bond and Herscu did time in jail—in Bond's case, twice. While Herscu fancied real estate, Bond wanted to corner and consolidate the second-tier beer business in the United States. Unfortunately, events intervened. Mersky says there was a price war on salted snacks that infiltrated the beer industry. The prices of premium brand beers dropped in tandem, so why buy a second-rung brew when you could now get top of the line cheap?

Several times during our discussions, Waugh said "beware the credit officer who says they never made a bad loan." Even so, he tightens up when talking about swinging and missing. Such discussion treaded on dangerous territory for him, professionally. "Then who was the guy who defaulted? That's customer confidentiality." More broadly, he said there were various reasons why loans went bad. They could be macroeconomic or idiosyncratic, or maybe "we relied on a borrower who had been successful" who then disappointed, failed to execute. "We put too much confidence in management, and I think that's probably the number one" reason loans went bad. Of course, no loan portfolio is bulletproof. That's why it's a portfolio.

That said, Scotia took its bodychecks along with the goals it scored. Some deals were just higher risk. The bank was co-lead with Security Pacific, involving a storied company more than a century old. BNS helped finance a corporate raider's bid for the company and earned significant fees. The company ended up in bankruptcy and was turned over to the workout group, which sold the loans for one hundred cents on the dollar or face value.§ It was an all-round success—loans, banking fees,

---

§ A workout group typically tries to renegotiate with a borrower the terms of a loan that's in default to increase the chance of recovering the loan.

syndication. The idea was to get into a large loan that most people didn't want any part of and potentially make a lot of money, but definitely not lose money. "We went right to the brink a couple of times. It was too close to hell for a lot of people's liking," Lockhart said. "It worked out well, but it was a close call."

Going to the brink meant coming "very close" to a loss, having to nurse a troubled borrower through a problem, with a high risk of not being paid back. But a bank or banking group charges more for such nursing. Therefore, a loan in which a bank goes to the brink with no losses can be among its most lucrative. Waugh says you never intend to make a bad loan, but bad loans are a cost of doing business, and "you feel like hell" when they happen. However, he maintains if you structure loans correctly, you can mitigate or avoid losses. In one instance, he says, the bank lent to a best-in-the-business company that unfortunately went bankrupt. Scotia took ownership, brought in a new CEO, restructured the business, sold it, and got its money back. But being at the brink requires nerve. While many have described Waugh's sense of calm and empathetic approach, Mersky did recall seeing him lose his temper a couple of times, though not in a table-pounding manner. "He did not like to be intentionally deceived or misled," Mersky said, noting that his anger was never rooted in a loan going bad but due to market conditions.

Sometimes, though, what with going to the wall and working all night, mistakes were inevitable. Although Waugh doesn't remember this, Terry Fryett recalls forgetting to add the bank's fee into a deal for a mining company's financing. Fryett says they appealed to company officials, who wouldn't budge, saying "too bad, a deal's a deal." But what goes around comes around, and on another occasion, it was the mining company wanting something from the bank. Not forgetting the company's hard-assed response to the fee error, Fryett and Mersky folded their arms and said no to the company's request, which resulted in the bank's fee finally being paid. They excitedly called Waugh to tell him, expecting he'd be instantly pleased, but ever the sang-froid banker, Waugh was initially unimpressed. "What did you have to give up to get it?" he asked. He was constantly on guard—in this case, wanting to understand the motivation for a concession. As always, he wanted to know the downside.

"He's very, very demanding. You need to be on your game," said Fryett. "But he wanted people to have fun. And he wanted to have fun." The fun was also part of team building, which was good for business.

Since Waugh's retirement, Fryett allowed, the scope of risk has changed. While the basics such as credit risk, liquidity risk, and market risk are still crucial, there's now cyber risk, ESG (environmental, social, and governance) risk, pandemic risk, war, DEI (diversity, equity, and inclusion) risk, reputational risk associated with social media, and technological risk, not to mention the rise of artificial intelligence (AI). He cited the speed at which deposits were withdrawn online from Silicon Valley Bank in March 2023 as an example of the changing environment. When presented with the view that it's a different world now, Waugh was unperturbed, insisting he'd be a better CEO the second time around. Certainly, the business world is always searching for the magic elixir of emotional intelligence, analytical skill, judgment, decisiveness, and strategic thinking—all proven traits, and traits he's exhibited. But it's also true anyone can become out of step with the times. At any rate, the point is moot—we'll never know.

Like Waugh, Mersky eventually moved to Toronto. But he left Scotiabank in 1998 for the private equity firm Onex, where he stayed for more than twenty years. Onex's founder and CEO, Gerald Schwartz, hired him away from the bank. Mersky's departure upset Waugh. "I told Gerry Schwartz at the time that [it] pissed me off," Waugh says, but clearly Schwartz could pay more than the bank. Mersky said he still feels bad about leaving a leader who had been so good to him. "To this day, I still have some misgivings about that." (When I relayed this to Waugh,

Waugh said Mersky should have misgivings.) Mersky says Waugh was the leader he "always wanted to please." He made people want to achieve for him, turning them into loyalists. "Rick never said to me, 'You stay here till you get that done.' You wanted to go to the wall for him" because of his leadership and inspiration. "He compelled, impelled people to want to achieve for him."

While they all worked hard, Mersky describes working for Waugh as "a very familial environment," with "Rick being kind of [a] patriarchal figure," and, in Mersky's case, a mentor. They all laughed—including Waugh—at his penchant for butchering speech, his so-called Rick-isms, which were chronicled by Lockhart into a top-ten list. In one legendary instance, Waugh was visiting a silver refiner. He apparently spotted a coin on the client's desk and said, "Oh, look at that." He continued to explain that just by "happenchance" (meaning happenstance) he had a similar coin, although his had no "pneumatic" (meaning numismatic) value. That, Waugh explained, was because someone's initials were "embezzled" (meaning emblazoned) on it. Around the office, this one was fondly known as the "triple play." Colleagues would tease Waugh about such instances. "What did I say? What did I say?" he'd ask.

Nonetheless, Mersky asserts, "Rick was one of the most deceptively intelligent people I've ever known in my career." While he was as smart as anyone in the room, Waugh had a disarming way of carrying himself that did not require showcasing it. Nor did Mersky ever believe it was an act, a nervous reaction, or a reaction to stress. Besides, being a smooth talker might be overrated. It doesn't equate to good judgment or wisdom. Mersky certainly remembered his time in New York nostalgically. While those glitzy closing dinners were nice, they are not what pops most readily to mind for him. When the team would work late into the evening, it was not uncommon for Waugh to come in and say "Hey, let's order some pizza and some beers—and I'll treat." Waugh also had access to a limousine, chauffeured by his trusty driver, Charlie Prentiss. It was a stretch limo, but not an ostentatious one, more presidential than prom night. The car was maybe a foot or two longer than normal, but with enough room for a jump seat so a group could get in the back.

There was, of course, a story behind the limo. Both Cedric Ritchie and Peter Godsoe would visit New York often, and Waugh decided the car and dedicated driver were required for security. Prior to that decision, Ritchie had flown into the city and needed to make a phone call. He was being driven by a random driver who pulled up to a phone booth in the South Bronx so Ritchie could make his call. When Waugh heard about it, he said, "It's time we had a limo and our own driver." He recalls it was a six-to-eight-seater and, in addition to pizza and beer, the team would talk about deals, socialize, and get a ride home to Bergen County, New Jersey, where they lived.

"These were like management meetings." Waugh couldn't recall whether the limo was a Cadillac or Lincoln, but being Scotia, "we would go for the cheapest." He was also pleased to say that one specific transaction paid for the car multiple times over. Scotia was in a co-agency deal with an American bank, and the team climbed into the limo to drive uptown to a meeting with the client and the other bank. The American bank had indicated the fee the client would pay to put the deal together, a fee Waugh thought was low. The car had a telephone, and on the ride uptown, the Scotia team managed to track down another fee the client had previously paid, which was more. That fee was accepted, and "it paid for the car ten times over."

The limo was particularly valuable to Stephen Lockhart. When he was transferred to New York, he bought a house in the town contiguous to where Waugh lived. As a result, Lockhart lived closer to Waugh than any of his colleagues and would ride with him in the limo to and from work. Waugh had to have two passengers in the car to use the HOV (high-occupancy vehicle) lane, "So, I was the logical balance," Lockhart recalls. He reckons that over the next five or six years, he rode with Waugh two to three times a week. "He was my direct boss, so I could get things done in the car," Lockhart said. "I had the access in the morning or the evening to run things by him." He is the only member of Waugh's New York crew, including Waugh, who remembered what kind of car the limo was (a Cadillac), although he said Waugh would also tool around in a Chevette, a sub-compact Chevrolet of the era. "He called it his Vette."

Aside from being the boss, Waugh could also be one of the boys, throwing big Christmas parties at his house. "He would spend as much time with the guys from the mail room" at the parties as he did with his team, Tryforos recalled. While Waugh "had no airs," Tryforos observed that there were limits to his being one of the gang, noting that Waugh "did keep his own counsel." No one really knew what he was thinking or planning. "He never discussed his career aspirations with anyone in New York." However, "when he came to New York he had to know he was one of the chosen ones." After Godsoe and Birmingham, "Rick no doubt saw himself in that chain of guys."

Although he hadn't wanted to move to New York, global banking was now in his blood, and he'd become a force at Scotiabank, expanding its US business. One day in the early nineties, the inevitable call came from head office: Godsoe wanted him back in Canada. Waugh conceded that the next thing he did was cowardly—he phoned Lynne. "He didn't even have the nerve to tell me in person," she said. "*He called me. I was sobbing.*" Now it was Lynne Waugh who didn't want to move. She liked where they lived, but they both soon came around to the wisdom of going back to Toronto. Their boys were growing up, the United States would become embroiled in foreign wars, and Waugh was ready for the next rung at the bank.

He had also learned other things—geopolitical lessons. In the United States, he had been involved in the Americas Society. There were at least two days a year that included a State Department gathering plus a dinner. David Rockefeller usually chaired the meeting during the day. At one of the dinners, a leading business person from Venezuela spoke about Hugo Chávez, who would become the country's firebrand leader for more than a dozen years. The speech was not complimentary. Shortly thereafter, American government assistance to Venezuela was restricted. "It showed me the power of the US. And their ability to act very quickly," Waugh recalled. This would be an invaluable education for Waugh, who would have to deal more intimately with Latin America in later years— not to mention the United States, particularly during the financial crisis.

While Waugh has said publicly that he never had a grand plan to become CEO, he was clearly a high-octane go-getter. You don't spend time at the State Department absorbing foreign affairs instead of being home for dinner if you don't have grander ambitions in mind. Waugh's years in New York had made him confident moving among the titans of Wall Street. Aiming to be a titan of Bay Street was only logical.

CHAPTER FIVE

How to Snag a Raptor

L ending is one thing. Making major transactions click is another. Rick Waugh's time running Scotia's main Toronto branch and its New York agency proved he knew credit and how to lend large amounts. By the time he left the United States and returned to Canada in 1993 he was also a senior executive vice-president who knew a lot of people, including those who ran major enterprises and did deals. Given the sheer volume of customers and clients he'd dealt with, Waugh had come to appreciate that dealmaking is about more than understanding financial minutiae; he knew that it was also about the so-called social issues—understanding personalities and what they want from a business arrangement. With big mergers, it can be the question of which CEO will run the combined company, or whose name and colour scheme will prevail.

While these weren't the obstacles when luring the Raptors to town, other matters came to the fore as Toronto sought and secured a National

Basketball Association franchise—and Waugh and Scotiabank were at centre court. Who knew that at its highest levels, professional basketball can be as much about governance and social issues as it is about rebounding, passing, and jump shots? Egos, styles, personal motivations, and opportunities for redemption all come into play. Such concerns surfaced again a couple of years later as the team's initial bidding group evolved and ultimately exited the basketball business, selling to someone Waugh knew well.

Initially, there were a handful of significant parties involved in the bidding process for an NBA team, and Waugh had relationships with all but one. There was broadcasting billionaire Allan Slaight; the hard-driving entrepreneur and self-described basketball junkie John Bitove Jr.; and the former premier of Ontario David Peterson. There was also the construction magnate and later professional sports owner Larry Tanenbaum, whose father Waugh had known from managing the main branch. The key player Waugh didn't know was the NBA, the sports league then run like a kingdom by its late commissioner, David Stern, who made the game into a global entertainment product. Waugh would have only limited contact with Stern, but observing him closely would influence the outcome of the bidding.

It was a striking irony that while basketball was invented by a Canadian, Canada did not have a team in the NBA even a hundred years after the first basketball game was played. Canadians did have Major League Baseball—beginning with the Montreal Expos in 1969 and adding the Toronto Blue Jays in 1977. The Blue Jays even won two World Series in the 1990s.* Given the increased integration of Canadian and American economies under the North American Free Trade Agreement (NAFTA), the lack of an NBA team in Canada was a gaping hole. That changed in 1995.

---

* The Expos departed Montreal in 2004, becoming the Washington Nationals.

By the 1990s, Toronto had come into its own. An annual film festival brought Hollywood stars to town. The city became a tapestry of cultures, with few metro areas like it anywhere on the planet. Not only were the Blue Jays winning but there was also a burgeoning restaurant and café scene kick-started by an influx of Italian immigrants after the Second World War. Toronto was a city on the move. It was growing and admired, and there was a sense of possibility (rather than current frustration over gridlock, a lack of housing, and aging infrastructure). It was a magnet.

Rising along with the city was an ambitious young executive, Rick Waugh, now in his mid-forties and transitioning back to Toronto after a successful run in New York. Waugh was also interested in sports. While in New York, he played basketball in a city league. In addition, during his stint in Manhattan, he'd become familiar with the Dolan family. Not only were the Dolans major players in cable television, but they also controlled Madison Square Garden and owned the NBA's New York Knicks and the NHL's New York Rangers.

But pro sports were quirky. They were show business, city pride, and the childhood dreams of owners all wrapped into one. Choosing the right executive to handle a basketball franchise file wasn't something you could pinpoint on an organizational chart, like lending to a widget factory. Nor, according to Waugh, was his boss Peter Godsoe an org chart guy. If you were the person who could do the job, you'd get the call. "He'd get the right horse for the course," Waugh says, implying Godsoe had calculated that the Waugh horse could help snag a raptor. Besides, Godsoe wasn't a basketball guy. Waugh was. While not in the headlines, he would be a critical hinge.

Of course, it started with a client, and Waugh was a client guy. In this case, the client was one of Scotia's most treasured, and one Waugh knew well, and he became central to the pursuit of a franchise, drawing the bank and Waugh into the process. That client was the late Allan Slaight, whose radio career began on air in Moose Jaw, Saskatchewan.

Eventually, Slaight became a Canadian radio mogul, widely estimated to be a billionaire. Under the banner of Standard Broadcasting, which he'd purchased from Conrad Black, Slaight amassed a radio empire of fifty-one stations, the flagship being Toronto's CFRB. It was a lucrative business that Slaight eventually sold to Astral Media in 2007.[†]

Slaight's former chief financial officer David Coriat, who started working for him in 1986 and looks after his estate, said Slaight had a banking relationship with Scotia going back at least to the mid-1980s. "Scotia was really our banker," Coriat said. That included what Coriat described as a very close relationship between Allan Slaight and Peter Godsoe. But Slaight and Coriat also knew Waugh, citing a relationship almost as long.

"Rick has always been a great friend for the Slaights," Coriat said. "And he's always been there for us." According to Coriat, the Slaights' relationship with Waugh went back thirty-five years. Just as he went back decades with the Tanenbaum family to his days managing the main branch, Waugh had been the Slaights' account manager. It's hard to imagine how AI could replicate such relationships.

Coriat described Slaight as a "brilliant entrepreneur" with a knack for making decisions. Meetings were short and to the point. Issues were dealt with in seconds, rather than hours or days. Memos to him couldn't be longer than a page. Scotia lent to the Slaights based on the family's broadcasting cash flow. "We ended up borrowing a fair bit of money," said Coriat, adding that this was where Waugh was "instrumental" in helping the family avoid pitfalls, such as meeting certain difficult loan covenants. He described the connection between Waugh and the family as an open relationship. "We always told him what was going on and he was always there for us." Waugh, he said, "was very gracious about us and gave us the relief we needed." Relief meant "warehousing"—or the

---

[†] Astral was later purchased by BCE.

setting aside of $50 million in debt so payment could be delayed—"so covenants would not be breached. This was necessary due to cash flow challenges. The debt was eventually repaid in full."[1]

There are various recollections of how the Raptors initial ownership group came together. Cobbling the parties together was David Peterson, premier of Ontario from 1985 to 1990. In the early 1990s, post-politics, Peterson's phone rang at his office at Cassels Brock, the law firm that, coincidentally, had its offices in Scotia Plaza, the skyscraper housing the bank's headquarters. The call was from John Bitove Sr., an entrepreneur who'd been financially successful in the catering and restaurant business. Would Peterson see his son? The answer was yes. John Jr. soon told Peterson, "I'm going after an NBA franchise in Toronto." Peterson asked him who was on his team. "And Bitove said, 'Well, if you are, it's you and me.'"

Bitove was a sports fanatic. His father had told Peterson that as a boy "John would be designing sports stadiums in his room." He was especially keen on basketball. Peterson said he followed up with some basic questions about Bitove's idea, and then went home that night and told his kids what had happened at work that day.

"Dad, Dad! This is better than politics! You've got to do this." So Peterson, after admitting he'd done zero risk analysis, told Bitove he was in. "What the hell, why not try?" he said, adding that "my job was to put the ownership group together." But the field was already crowded. Peterson said it was the first time in the history of the NBA that three groups were chasing the same franchise; typically, the bidding was between cities. In this case, it was between high-profile groups *within* a city.

The most prominent was headed by Larry Tanenbaum, who had partnered with CIBC. Tanenbaum was highly respected in the sports world and had previously tried to lure a team to Toronto.[2] In the late 1970s and early 1980s, Tanenbaum's father, Max, would pop into Scotia's main branch on Friday afternoons after having lunch at the Royal York hotel. He'd sit and chat with Bev, Rick Waugh's secretary at the time. And then he'd visit with Waugh, the young branch manager, telling him the bank charged him too much. "So, we got on good," Waugh recalls fondly. As with Slaight, it was old-time relationship banking. The third bidder for the franchise included the head of EMI as well as concert promoter Michael Cohl, known for staging shows featuring the Rolling Stones. They had their own hoop star, Magic Johnson, as part of the bidding lineup.

While the Bitove family had a lot of money, "we decided we needed a bank," Peterson said, to offset Tanenbaum's partnership with CIBC. Scotia's involvement, Peterson recalled, became fundamental and can be traced to a dinner party at venture capitalist Ben Webster's house. Also in attendance was Peter Godsoe. "Peter," the former premier remembered saying, "would you look at this [the franchise idea] and come in and take a piece of it?"

Peterson allowed that while this may have caught Godsoe's ear, the CEO of Scotiabank was influenced far more heavily by Slaight, a major customer and a friend of Godsoe. Waugh confirmed this. "It was through Allan Slaight," Waugh said. "It was client driven." A good Scotia customer was interested in basketball, so the bank was too.

While Bitove and Slaight would have the largest interests at 44 percent each, the bid had Godsoe's backing, and he handed the file to Waugh. "We were lucky to have him," Peterson said. "He liked sports," and Scotia came in for a 10 percent interest. "We wanted their name on the bid," the former premier said, "[which was] more important than the money really." Scotia and Waugh would be like the cartilage between two big bones, helping them work together. Peterson and packaging entrepreneur Phil Granovsky would round out the bidding group with 1 percent each. While the latter two would have relatively small equity stakes, each would be persuasive.

David Coriat said Slaight's involvement was a business venture, "complementary to the broadcasting business," rather than an infatuation with basketball. John Bitove Jr. was clearly the infatuated one, and, as Peterson described, "the brains of the whole operation." While Bitove Jr. was the chief legal presence at his family's substantial food and catering business, he was, as his father had indicated, deeply drawn to sports. He grew up playing basketball. There were other factors that positioned him well. Bitove Jr. had been involved in the bid for the 1996 Olympics, which Toronto lost to Atlanta, and he already had an international basketball feather in his cap. According to James Christie, who covered the birth of the Raptors for the *Globe and Mail*, Bitove "made big points with the NBA by salvaging the 1994 World Basketball Championships from war-torn Yugoslavia and bringing them to Toronto."

While Larry Tanenbaum had been persistently trying to land a Toronto team for years and was widely considered the front-runner, Bitove was also a true believer. With confidence to spare, he spoke with conviction. For someone so young, Bitove also had presence. It wasn't just salesmanship, which he had in spades. There was passion, not to mention business sense. "I always felt it was mine to lose, because I had the working relationship with the league," Bitove said.

In many ways, the key business players in Canada were a relatively small group (and still are). They often live in the same neighbourhoods and summer and winter in the same enclaves, and it seemed as if Waugh knew all of them. Not only did he know Slaight and Tanenbaum, but Waugh also lived across the street from Bitove Jr.'s sister, and Waugh's three sons knew her three boys. He and Bitove Jr. knew each other socially. Cue the relationships. While Waugh can exhibit the hard shell of a banker, he's also a social animal, still Senior Stick from university, getting people to help build the parade float. He also liked a party and a belly laugh, while never losing sight of the plot line. Peterson said that when Waugh became head of the bank, financier and by-then board member Gerry Schwartz threw a party for him. Peterson described Waugh unabashedly singing "Red Red Wine" with his kids (Terry Fryett called Waugh "the worst singer in the world"). Schwartz says he "did like to sing."

For his part, Bitove Jr. said, "I might not have had the Raptors" without Waugh. Prior to getting involved in the NBA bid, Bitove's main bank had been CIBC, but it was already lined up with Tanenbaum's group. While Bitove did meet first with Peterson (like Waugh, Peterson also knew everyone), in a subsequent conversation with Slaight, Bitove said he asked who Slaight banked with and Slaight told him Scotiabank. Slaight then set up a three-way meeting with him and Scotia. A lot of things were happening quickly between the parties. Bitove reckons that all these conversations occurred in the span of a week. "It happened really, really fast."

Coriat confirmed Bitove's characterization of the timeline. Godsoe talked to Waugh. Waugh had a meeting with Bitove and Slaight. Any phone calls Bitove had with Godsoe yielded the comment, "Deal with Rick." While Waugh happily took the file, he also delegated. He put another banker, Borden Osmak, on the case, reporting up to him. Osmak, Peterson said, was as straitlaced as Waugh was not. According to Peterson, Waugh seemed "like a big goofy dog sometimes." Meanwhile, Waugh jokingly nicknamed Osmak the bank's "vice-president of basketball." When you give someone a nickname, it's playful, but it's also a subtle form of control, managing.

As a senior executive of Scotiabank, Bob Brooks attended a lot of board meetings, even though he was not on the bank's board. Brooks recalled Osmak "coming into the board meeting bouncing a basketball" to announce that the bank had entered a partnership with Allan Slaight to bring an NBA team to Toronto. One of the bank's board members was David Morton, the late CEO of Alcan, a Brit with a dour, droll manner. Morton, Brooks recounted, began listing three reasons big organizations like Scotiabank got into trouble.‡ The first was trophy real estate (as they all sat there in Scotia Plaza, a recently constructed sixty-eight-floor building). Number two was acquiring a corporate jet (Scotia had recently bought its first). "And the third is to own a sports team." Basketball would complete a trifecta, and not in a good way.

Osmak had worked for the bank in New York for almost eight years prior to Waugh's arrival. There he worked with future president and Waugh mentor Bruce Birmingham. The job meant knocking on doors. Despite being described as straitlaced, at least compared to Waugh, Osmak has a salesman's charm (he kept calling me "young man," like a friendly uncle). Back in Toronto, the bank was expanding its corporate lending business, and Osmak got to know Bitove Jr. When it came time for the bid, Osmak said Slaight asked Godsoe to not only take an interest but also to watch over the process. "He said to Rick, have you got somebody? [And] Rick looked at me [and said], 'Well, he knows Bitove.'" Of course, Waugh also knew Bitove. Osmak said Waugh was deft at handling the various relationships and "was a good guy to work for and work with," citing Waugh's ever-present sense of humour. While sitting next to him at dinner, Waugh told Osmak about becoming a father.

"Well, I have a son," Waugh said.

"What's his name?"

"Otto." OttoWaugh: a groaner for sure, but fun to be around.§

Osmak said Scotia in fact did have familiarity with pro sports. At one point, the bank held a minority interest in the NHL's Montreal Canadiens. Meantime, he described David Peterson as a very good politician (Coriat would call him "the glue" of the group). And as a former politician, he was perfectly cast. Peterson, Osmak said, knew that from a political perspective, the ownership group had to be diverse. On that front, Granovsky,

---

‡ Brooks died in November 2024.
§ Waugh has three sons: David, Stephen, and Christopher.

who like Peterson had a one percent interest, was an immigrant, Jewish, and a self-made entrepreneur with a compelling personal story that would later resonate with the owners of other NBA teams, the voters on granting a new franchise.

While Osmak would handle day-to-day business on Waugh's behalf, Waugh would emerge at crucial times. Fast-forward to a dinner in New York that included Waugh, NBA commissioner David Stern and his deputy, Russ Granik, along with Bitove, Slaight, and Peterson, who chaired the ownership group and, according to Waugh, also provided a community presence and view. This dinner meeting was key. It was a "get to know you" with Stern at 21 Club, a Waugh favourite from his New York days. Waugh says he knew the owner of the famous restaurant and got a private room for the group. At the meeting, Waugh watched Stern closely and listened carefully.

While broadcasting revenue was an important consideration at the meeting, the focus of the trip, Waugh says, was Stern. Along with his deputy, Granik, Stern had crafted a new form of sports entertainment. "He turned basketball into the hottest game in the world," Peterson said, and was considered the best commissioner in modern sports. As Stern, who ran the league from 1984 to 2014, said, "We think we have a great American product, and we would like to market it on a global basis with as much class and success as we can."[3] An NBA game had been turned into more than just basketball. It was now a show. Although the league was looking to expand and Toronto had much to offer, Stern would be picky about who would get to hang the NBA shingle in the city.

While Waugh's group was certainly after votes from owners, he believed there was a vital lesson to be learned: "Listen to the commissioner." The commissioner, Waugh says, was the CEO of the league, and if you didn't have your CEO on side, you were in trouble. Nine times out of ten, he reckons, the board will support the CEO. The owners, Waugh argued, would back the recommendation of the commissioner.

"Rick went down and saw the whites of David Stern's eyes," Bitove said. He was putting himself in the boss's shoes, shoes he would soon wear. For all intents and purposes, Waugh was back in sociology class at university, reading people. With Stern, he wouldn't be wrong.

But it wasn't just shrewd strategy on Waugh's part that helped seal the deal. Others stumbled. Bitove suggested that one of the other two bidding groups got offside with Stern by going to the All-Star Game in Salt Lake City to put on a show for the other owners. In no uncertain terms, Bitove said, Stern had issued a warning to his group. "I'm telling you not to do that. And if you do that, I'm not going to like it," he recalls. The commissioner saw such behaviour as an end run. He, Stern, ran the process. "Don't outwardly campaign," was the message. Waugh, Bitove, and Slaight all heard Stern loud and clear, so they worked quietly. "We did no press releases. We did no press conferences," Bitove said.

Whatever their approach, they were still clearly the underdogs. The overdog was Larry Tanenbaum. This made things slightly awkward between Waugh and Tanenbaum, who knew and liked each other. Tanenbaum's late father, Max, had been very close to the senior team at Scotiabank, including head of credit George Hitchman and Gordon Bell, Cedric Ritchie's co-pilot. But Larry said his father did his banking with a young fellow named Rick Waugh, manager of the main branch. "And my dad absolutely fell in love with the guy." Tanenbaum says that one day, his father told Hitchman that Waugh would eventually be president of the bank. "My dad picked him out." Max Tanenbaum died in 1983, so he didn't live to see his prediction come true. But Larry Tanenbaum knew full well the Bank of Nova Scotia became involved in basketball because of Allan Slaight. "The Slaight family was very close to Scotiabank," as was Tanenbaum's family. Thus, the awkwardness. Nonetheless, business was business, so they each did what they had to do.

Because he'd been trying for some time, Tanenbaum's group was the odds-on favourite to win. He was determined, despite previous unsuccessful attempts. In the early 1990s, he'd been approached to bring the Denver Nuggets to Toronto. Tanenbaum's principal business was heavy construction, and the team needed an arena. And "Maple Leaf Gardens," he says, "would never be approved as an NBA arena." What followed was what Tanenbaum described as "a dance." He would build the arena, but he wanted ownership of the team: "I didn't want to be a landlord." It was during this time frame when he met David Stern. Moving the Nuggets, however, "became problematic," Tanenbaum says. It needed the approval of the Maple Leafs and the city. A possible injunction loomed about moving the team. So on to another idea.

Next came the San Antonio Spurs. A broker for the franchise wanted $5 million, and Tanenbaum would have to pay $75 million for the team. He says he brought it to Stern and Stern said no—saying Tanenbaum couldn't possibly move the team because it was the only professional sports franchise in the city. "Why don't you try the New Jersey Nets?" he was told. There were eight owners of the Nets, and Tanenbaum spoke with them. Four agreed, he says, while four didn't.

So now it was three strikes with the NBA. But Tanenbaum was not out. He says he made an argument to Stern that the NBA, with twenty-seven teams, should consider a twenty-eighth—and it should expand to Toronto. Then the league could have an equal number of teams in two divisions, east and west. Stern, he says, told him that if Tanenbaum could convince twenty-seven owners to support the idea, then it might be possible. It sounded as if Tanenbaum *needed to campaign*—to win votes—as much as listen to the commissioner, the latter of which was Waugh's strategy.

"I went around to twenty-seven owners. I visited twenty-seven arenas," Tanenbaum recalls, adding that he even got to know the owners' families. The timing would have been ideal, he indicated, because the Blue Jays were winning, which had put Toronto on the map as a major league sports town. For Tanenbaum, there was a narrative that could work.

In 1993, the board of governors of the NBA agreed to an expansion. But afterwards, Tanenbaum says, Stern took him into his office. "Look, I want to make sure you're the best guy to own a team here." It was yet another blow, and Tanenbaum said he wasn't happy, "but what am I going to do about it?" Tanenbaum had competed for business all his life, and he would do it again, so long as the ground rules were the same for everybody. Clearly, given his history of trying to secure a team for Toronto, Tanenbaum and his bidding group—which included CIBC and Labatt Brewing Company—were looking like a good bet.

Unsurprisingly, given his background, David Peterson has his own view of the process. "It was a political campaign," he says. Therefore, who are the voters? How do you appeal to them and show you'll be the best custodians of the franchise? It wasn't as though there was disagreement among the bidding group about the approach, but there were certainly two schools of thought, schools that perhaps operated concurrently.

Keeping to the dictum of not campaigning openly, Peterson, Bitove, and Osmak, Waugh's deputy, went on a discreet road trip to a handful of NBA cities to see teams, arenas, and owners. Osmak said they visited about half a dozen key teams across the league to rustle up votes—"the people we thought would influence the rest of the board." They went to Charlotte, Seattle, Phoenix, Milwaukee, and Chicago.

Osmak agreed with Peterson's assessment that it was a political campaign. "Oh, yeah. Absolutely." Clearly, this was not Waugh's view. "I'm not saying Rick's wrong," Osmak said, but "visiting the teams was important for us," and he believed Peterson had put together the right group of partners, people who would resonate with the owners.

Of course, the bank was a key component in getting the contours of the bidding group just right. CIBC had a minority stake in the back-to-back-championship Jays, and Bitove said "it was a proven, successful model" to have one of the big banks onside. "We were just going to copy that model," he said, adding that Waugh "was there whenever we needed him on any important decisions." It was also good to have a third party as an offset to the two main owners, Bitove and Slaight. According to Russ Granik, the number two at the NBA, "The inclusion of a major bank in the bid was an important element in terms of confirming the financial strength of the group."[4] Scotia's presence meant money wouldn't be a problem.

Eventually, each of the three bidders would present to Stern and the team owners at a New York hotel, a glitzy affair. Peterson's recollection: "For me it was just the star power. Television cameras everywhere. It was just reeking of American hustle." Osmak describes the presentation as a "deal-breaker." The group, he said, would have about half an hour in front of the commissioner and owners. Everyone in the group said something, and when Osmak spoke, he mentioned the bank's association with the Montreal Canadiens. Most important, there were rules to follow. For instance, the league didn't want to hear any mention of a name for the proposed team. "We were playing by their rules," Osmak says. Aside from Waugh's focus on social issues, he also stressed governance—in this case, the league's way of doing things. The NBA was also very concerned about the location of the arena. The group's proposed location at Bay and Dundas, near the Eaton Centre, was just so-so. There would be a better one.

Unlike other bidders, however, Peterson says their group didn't have a slick video—or, for that matter, any sort of video. Instead, their ad person, Himal Mathew of the firm Cossette, arranged a novel approach. He had the room go dark. "Nobody knew what was going to happen." Then the voice of a well-known basketball play-by-play announcer was heard (Peterson said it was the voice of the New York Knicks). It set up an imaginary scene of the first night of the NBA in Toronto. "It was an absolute winner," Peterson says. When it came to speaking, though, one member of their bidding group stood out. Phil Granovsky made an appeal to the owners. Peterson described Granovsky as "not a big bombastic sports guy." His was an emotional pitch, with the ultimate message to the owners being, "we're your kind of people."[5]

"He was batting cleanup," Bitove says, "not knowing he'd knock it out of the park." The major owners were one thing, but Granovsky and the bank provided a compelling storyline. "Not only are we creative, but money's not a problem—that was the message from Scotia," Bitove says.

When he heard the bid had prevailed, Bitove was at his cottage in Collingwood. Then came the price. Slaight had said to Bitove, "If it's over 110 [US$110 million], I don't want to do it." But now they'd won the bidding, and the price was higher—US$125 million. Bitove, who was just in his early thirties, told his father the news and his dad gave him a hug. "You didn't ask me the price," Jr. said.

"Does it matter?"

"It's 125."

"So what?" his father said.

While the bid had been put forward by a group of hard-nosed business people, a well-known politician, and a major bank, Peterson said they hadn't known how much they'd have to pay for the franchise. "We had no idea."

At a meeting the following Monday, Bitove said, Slaight shrugged his shoulders at the price and "just kind of smiled," in his way. Did it really matter whether it was 105, 110, or 125? Today, Bitove says the franchise is worth $2.5 billion. "That's just the power of the NBA." Peterson says the price didn't matter: "We'll pay whatever it is." After all, this wasn't selling radio ads, slinging sandwiches and coffee at the airport, or lending money. This was big-time sports. This was a rush. This was fun. And they were buying something scarce. It was worth the price of admission.

As for Slaight and Coriat, when the group's bid prevailed, Coriat says they were surprised, "'cause all of a sudden our world changed." Now they had to run a team, and John Bitove Jr., the keeper of the basketball flame, would be the operator. The deal he had with Slaight, Coriat says, was that if John and Coriat agreed, it carried. If there was a disagreement, Coriat and Bitove went to Slaight to resolve it. This mattered. A couple of years later, the group would split. But first, they celebrated. Osmak described a big reception at Wayne Gretzky's restaurant and sports bar.

The *Toronto Star* was gaga over the prospect of a team. There was a full-page spread with three stories, including a headline shouting "Basketball Fans Jump for Joy."

The person not celebrating was Larry Tanenbaum. From the outset, Tanenbaum says, the arena where a new team would play was an issue. He knew the only way a team could work economically was if hockey and basketball were under the same roof. Osmak says Bitove, Slaight, and the bank "weren't even thinking about hockey." Although he didn't own the Leafs at the time (he acquired an interest in 1996), Tanenbaum was friends with Steve Stavro, the team's owner, and was able to bring the hockey team into the picture. But he'd lost, and he was despondent.

"I thought for sure we would get this franchise," Tanenbaum said on the phone from Florida. But he was acutely aware of John Bitove Jr. "He's got sharp elbows. He's going to do what he has to do." But, Tanenbaum added, Bitove was making difficult-to-deliver promises, such as an arena at the corner of Dundas and Bay Streets. Even though it was close to the subway, Tanenbaum said it was too small for both the NBA requirements and for parking. Osmak added that not only did the plan have a smaller footprint than where the Raptors ended up but also the construction costs would be high and the property didn't have adjacent land development opportunities.

But the Bitove-Slaight-Scotiabank group had prevailed, "in part because they didn't have hockey and the NBA didn't want hockey," Tanenbaum said. Bitove, he knew, was a basketball-only guy. Tanenbaum maintained that the Bitove group was "on the wrong piece of property" in Toronto and that the building "wasn't going to be a high-class city arena." But "they [the NBA] didn't want to hear it." As well, Tanenbaum said, Bitove was willing to pay whatever was necessary, even if it was just a million more than "the Tanenbaum group will pay." While there were twenty-seven owners in the league, Tanenbaum recognized Stern as "the king" who awarded the franchise to Bitove, Slaight, and Scotiabank.

"I was incredibly disappointed, to say the least," Tanenbaum said, adding that he even had a name for the team ready to go, as well as swag. He had a vision to spread the team's story across the country. He was so down about the decision that he "didn't watch basketball for two years, three years, four years."

As for the two schools of thought about which had been the most influential approach—securing the owners' votes or focusing on commissioner Stern—Coriat agrees with Waugh's interpretation. "We knew what Stern wanted, that was primary." Stern, he says, "had a very rigid control over the NBA." He was "the quarterback that directed the traffic and he was the key figure." Bitove believed both approaches were important. However, he added, "I think Rick at that dinner [at 21 Club] saw that David Stern had our confidence."

Even though Waugh knew Tanenbaum was a savvy business person and "good guy," he believes Tanenbaum did not win the bid because he had, in Waugh's view, irritated the commissioner by campaigning openly among the owners. But what was Tanenbaum supposed to do? By his telling, after his third attempt had foundered, Stern had, in effect, encouraged him to get to know the owners. In the long run, though, it wouldn't matter. Patiently waiting in the weeds, Tanenbaum would eventually get what he sought. He even became chair of the board at the

NBA. For Waugh, getting the franchise meant more than just sealing another financial deal. His sons got to be ball boys at exhibition games. Given that Waugh worked long hours and didn't see his kids much, this was a family bonus, a social issue for him.

Winning a franchise and operating one, however, are two different matters. After a year spent on the bidding process, the group operated the team for two years. A new arena was part of the deal, and the group now wanted to construct a joint building with the Maple Leafs. It was logical. As Tanenbaum had argued, two sports under one roof would be better business, even though the NBA had not been keen on the idea during the bidding. However, the Leafs would not agree to any deal that meant an equal partnership. Jerry Reinsdorf, the owner of the NBA's Chicago Bulls, had told Bitove to make sure he was top dog. "Don't you dare do this if you're not in control," Bitove recalls Reinsdorf saying. But Leafs owner Steve Stavro (Bitove's uncle) had different thoughts. "It's hockey, it's Canada," he said. We must own it, he added, and you [the NBA team] can be the tenant.

And so the tension began. According to Bitove, Slaight thought there were issues between Bitove and his uncle. Stavro wanted control, and Coriat said the Slaight side tried to see whether the Raptors and Leafs could live under one roof. But that only made sense if there was one owner for both teams. There was also a new collective agreement in the NBA, so the economics of building an arena had changed. Both parties started getting nervous. Bitove was concerned about the impact of the new union agreement; he saw all teams losing money. The Raptors alone were projected to lose $30 million in the next year. As well, Bitove says, Slaight "was nervous about doing the arena alone."

While Bitove operated the team with the brio and know-how he'd brought to the bid (the bank thought he had the right ideas), it would only be a couple of years before the ownership group would fray and change, including Scotiabank's stake, which would put Waugh at the negotiating table. For starters, the team wasn't doing well, and player salaries were going up. There was also the question of where the team would play long term.

The arena issue had been there from day one, a concern of the league. Osmak recalled that Deputy Commissioner Granik warned them not to put the arena "out there wherever it's called," meaning Mississauga, the suburb that the American couldn't pronounce. Initially, the Raptors played in the SkyDome, now the Rogers Centre. Then, the old Canada Post building just south of Bay and Front Streets became available, conveniently located next to Union Station, where you could grab the subway or GO Train. Waugh was quoted in the *Globe and Mail* in 1994 regarding the still un-financed new arena: "BNS senior executive vice-president Richard Waugh affirmed 'as a ten percent owner, I can say we've got every confidence that this will be financed on a sound and sensible basis.'"

But the ground began to shift. On the Bitove side, Coriat said, there was a disagreement within the family about whether to build the Air Canada Centre, and there was a provision in the franchise agreement that if an arena wasn't built by a certain date, there would be a signifi-cant financial penalty ($50 million, he said). This concerned Slaight, although Coriat said the Bitove family didn't believe the NBA would enforce the penalty, that it could be negotiated. While Slaight had a good relationship with Bitove ("I think John viewed Allan as a mentor," Coriat said), the two sides were moving apart. Aside from the arena penalty issue, each had a different style. Was Bitove too aggressive for Slaight? "For sure," Coriat says. "It's just a different operating philoso-phy. That's all it is."

Osmak confirms this. "As much as I like John [Bitove Jr.], sometimes he pushed a little too far." At a certain point, it became uncomfortable for Slaight, who Coriat describes as getting "a little nervous." Osmak added that tension like this is inevitable when there are two large, equal partners. Each had a different approach and comfort level, but only one could be the lead. "And the bank had to be loyal with Allan," Osmak said. "He was our customer. He was our client. He was the reason we came in."

By 1998, Slaight wanted out. "Peter [Godsoe] said, if he's [Slaight] selling, we're selling. We're not going to hold him up."

Ultimately, Slaight triggered the "buy-sell agreement," otherwise known as the shotgun clause, in the agreement with Bitove. Coriat says either party could have triggered it, setting off a predetermined chain of events. The party that pulls the trigger must state a number—a price at which the other party could buy it out. Coriat says Slaight put forward a number, at which point Bitove had thirty days to buy. If he chose not to, Slaight had the right to buy him out at that number, and that's what happened.

This was a surprise. Tanenbaum says everyone thought Bitove would buy out Slaight, given that he had been the front man and driving force behind the bid. But Slaight was confident. Tanenbaum had remained good friends with Slaight, who told him, "Larry, there's no way he's going to take this. This is mine." The night of the shotgun, Slaight and his wife invited Tanenbaum and his wife to dinner at North 44, a fancy uptown restaurant. Then they went to the Slaights' house to celebrate at midnight. Slaight would now own most of the team, while Scotiabank still owned 10 percent.

When Slaight activated the shotgun agreement, Bitove decided to sell, take the money, and do other things. Of the Bitoves' decision, David Peterson says "They could have bought it. But . . . the family came to a decision not to extend the financial risk, and let Allan take it." While Bitove had been the fire in the belly of the original bid, in the end it was business. "We got along great," Bitove says of his partnership with Slaight. "We just had a different view on the next step." He thought Slaight's strategy was to take him out and then convince the Maple Leafs to do the arena jointly, with Slaight as the sole owner. But Bitove says he was convinced the Maple Leafs would have eventually seen the benefit of being in a new arena with basketball and sharing the building. "Allan saw that as too risky." According to Coriat, the Slaight side certainly believed that it had to move on with construction, and the only way to do that was with one proprietor. That was the road to Slaight becoming the principal owner of the team. At least for a while.

A couple of years later, lawyer Dale Lastman called Coriat one Friday afternoon. Lastman represented the Maple Leafs and Larry Tanenbaum. Tanenbaum may not have watched basketball for a couple of years after his lost bid for the Raptors, but he'd been hibernating, just waiting for the right time to re-emerge. Finally, that time had arrived.

Lastman wanted to know whether Slaight was interested in selling the Raptors. By then, things in the basketball world had changed. For one, player salaries were pushing higher. "[It] got to be very onerous at the time to own the franchise," Coriat says. After Lastman's call, Coriat phoned Slaight, who gave him the go-ahead to discuss a sale.

"I met with Tanenbaum and Dale that Sunday afternoon at Larry's house," Coriat recalls, where they began the negotiation to sell the Raptors, which he says took a couple of months. That would once again draw in Waugh, representing Scotiabank's 10 percent holding.

It had only taken a few years for conditions to shift. At the start, Bitove and Slaight were all-in. But construction, strategic, and control issues arose, and family business cultures bumped up against each other, a not-disinterested uncle hovered, and new financial risks emerged. Then Bitove was out. Then Slaight wanted out. Then Tanenbaum, who was out, wanted in. Sports franchises are tangled webs of dreams and commerce. Top business people talk about the need and ability to extract emotion from financial equations. But when the asset is a sports franchise, it can be a challenge. However, for Slaight, basketball was never a passion. And for Waugh and the bank, it had all been about support-ing Slaight.

Meantime, Peter Godsoe called Tanenbaum and Slaight to a meeting at the bank. "I'm going to put the two of you in a room," Tanenbaum recalls Godsoe saying as he ushered them into the CEO's boardroom. "You guys make a deal." Tanenbaum was finally getting his chance to own an NBA team. Slaight, Tanenbaum says, wasn't interested anymore and was ready to sell. This was 1997, two years after the team launched. In 1996, Tanenbaum had bought his initial stake in the Toronto Maple Leafs as a minority shareholder, partnering with the Ontario Teachers' Pension Plan (OTPP). He brought their CEO, Claude Lamoureux, onside for this deal, and the group bought 90 percent of the Raptors from Slaight for $125 million. A few years earlier, that had been the price of the entire stake.

But the dealing wasn't done. Re-enter Rick Waugh. Now Tanenbaum and OTPP wanted Scotia's piece, too; Tanenbaum believed they needed it to integrate fully with the holding in the Leafs. The then-existing shareholders of Maple Leaf Gardens Limited, which owned the Leafs and the Gardens, "saw no way to have BNS be able to hold a separate 10 percent interest in the Raptors," Tanenbaum explained in an email. "The key guy was Rick." The intermarriage of hockey and basketball was about to occur, as Tanenbaum had originally envisioned, but he needed Waugh and the bank to play ball—and initially, Tanenbaum recalls, Waugh was resistant. For his part, Waugh says Tanenbaum had begun talking to the remaining shareholders. Each shareholder (Slaight and Scotia) had the right to sell or not sell, and Waugh said Tanenbaum came to his office at ten at night to talk. (Tanenbaum recalled that they both worked "twenty-four hours a day, so meeting at 10 p.m. would not be unusual for either one of us.") Waugh told him Slaight's price was fine for Scotia, but the bank needed other things. While continuing to own part of the team was not "on-strategy," Scotia wanted an ongoing relationship with the team, principally for day-to-day banking, including payroll, ATM machines in the stadium, and the opportunity to become sponsors and private bankers to the athletes.

"As good friends as I am with Rick, he was as tough as could be," Tanenbaum says. "He was a great fan. He loved basketball." And he was also an investor who wanted the best deal. "He actually said no." While Waugh says that there was one evening meeting at which the deal was done, Tanenbaum recalls half a dozen before Waugh finally relented and approved the sale. "It wasn't just at that meeting that we shook hands, I can tell ya," Tanenbaum says.

Tanenbaum would agree to what Scotia needed from the deal aside from price, Waugh says, but there was one more thing that needed sorting out. Tanenbaum's banker was TD, and he needed to make sure they were onside with the concessions. Tanenbaum told Waugh to check with TD, and if it was fine with them, it was fine with him. Waugh says he got that okay from Steve McDonald, a TD executive Waugh knew from New York who later worked for him at Scotia. TD was in it for the financing, not the day-to-day banking.

Whatever the contours of the negotiations between Waugh and Tanenbaum, the result was a new brand: Maple Leaf Sports & Entertainment. In addition to the purchase price for the team, Tanenbaum says it cost his group—OTPP and TD—another $60 million to make the arena suitable for both hockey and basketball. That was on top of $200 million for the arena itself. "It would have been a huge mistake if it was basketball only," he says. "I always thank Rick for accommodating us, even though he didn't really want to do it."

"I'm sure if Rick didn't trust me," Tanenbaum reflected, "a lot of things might not have happened." Patience, persistence, empathy, and transparency were the governance takeaways. "I knew Rick was comfortable with me, and it dates back to him dealing with my father."

While that's all very nice, Waugh's first obligation was to the bank. Slaight had been a client, the catalyst to getting involved. Now Slaight was out, so Scotia would be too, but in a way that would be a financial win. Waugh not only extracted a price for the bank's 10 percent stake that mirrored what Slaight got from Tanenbaum but also secured future benefits from an ongoing association with the team and arena. Just like he'd done countless times in New York, he'd cut a deal—good business for the bank.

But for Waugh, the essential point was that the handling of the social issues had won the day. They were as important as the financial issues. Handling the personalities in the correct manner, he believes, created the deal. And in Waugh's experience, compromise is by far the number one strategy. Tanenbaum went on to lead Maple Leaf Sports & Entertainment, in partnership with Rogers and Bell,[¶] putting both the Leafs and the Raptors in what's now the Scotiabank Arena (the bank got the right to rename what had been the Air Canada Centre). Being affiliated with the team and the arena had been a hit, he says, with the bank's sports-minded clients, not to mention the marketing and sponsorship manna.

Waugh still has a memento, a deal "tombstone" showing Scotia as co-lead on a $170 million senior secured credit facility with NationsBank, which he says was known as a sports financing bank. They'd led the financing of the building along with Scotia. "And they [Scotia] should have kept what they had then because they wouldn't be paying $40 million a year for the naming rights," Bitove jokes.

While at one point during our conversation Bitove said he had no regrets about selling and moving on, he allowed it was still emotional for him to let go of the Raptors. A top lawyer in Toronto told him, "Johnny, you're not going to believe this. But it's going to take you a while to become a fan again after what you've gone through." "And he was

---

¶ Bell sold its interest in 2024.

absolutely right," he says. Larry Tanenbaum hadn't been able to watch basketball for a few years after initially losing his bid, and now it was equally hard for Bitove. At games, he felt like "an unwelcome guest" at a party. But he's convinced the group's success at bringing the Raptors to Toronto forever changed the country. "From that first meeting of Rick, Allan, and I [*sic*]."

In 2019, almost twenty-five years after the team launched, the Toronto Raptors won their first NBA championship title. Canadians were behind the team all the way, chanting "We the North." A million people filled the streets of Toronto for the victory parade. While Bitove, Slaight, and Tanenbaum had been up front in bringing the Raptors to Canada, Waugh had been an integral pivot, proving once again he could stand out in another league. What would come later would be considerably rougher than the NBA.

CHAPTER SIX

Good Wine, Rotten Barrels

Lending to huge American companies and partnering in a pro basketball team had their challenges and risks. But it was kids' stuff compared to trying to save a bank and its staff in a violent, volatile country. At the dawn of the millennium, Scotiabank and Waugh would be severely tested in South America. In fact, the crisis would expose an unusual misapprehension of risk by BNS, which had been seduced into buying a bank in Argentina, a nation of serial economic failures. In 2001–2, Waugh would witness first-hand the economic collapse of a country, political turmoil, violence, employees in dire distress, and a bank failure. Terrified of losing their savings, people began pulling cash out of the bank there—like other banks—making it like a wounded patient losing blood. Waugh would also be part of a spy novel–like escape from hostile territory.

In addition to making a bad purchase, what happened in Argentina was the net result of misguided economic policy, extreme politics and corruption, and, finally, financial system and bank dysfunction. And it all occurred while Waugh was leading the international division of Scotiabank, one step closer to the CEO position. As with all of Waugh's defining moments, there would be a supporting cast.

The history of Scotia's entry into the region was paved with gold, and its foothold traceable to entering the gold business. In 1958, after a regulatory change, chairman and president Bill Nicks put the bank in the gold trade—storing it, shipping it, trading it for investors and governments, and supplying jewellers in far-flung locales like South America. His Rosedale home was even known as "Fort Nicks."[1] Under his guidance, the bank became such a prominent player in the gold business that Nicks was featured on the June 6, 1964, cover of *Business Week*. Silver-haired, cigarette in hand, and wearing a double-breasted blue suit, he's standing in a vault in front of a pile of gold bars.

Retired Scotia executive Roy Scott built a lengthy career working for the bank in South America. For decades, Scott helped lubricate the bank's relationships throughout that continent, and remembers much about his experiences—many relating to gold—during this time. Born in Argentina, he began working for Scotiabank in 1966, five years after Scotia opened a small representative office in Buenos Aires.

Just two and a half hours by ferry from Buenos Aires is Montevideo, Uruguay. In the mid-1960s, the country experienced a financial crisis. At the time, Uruguay had no central bank, and didn't get one until 1967. Meantime, it needed cash. Scotiabank lent the country US$60 million but wanted its gold as collateral. Countries, however, were not permitted to pledge their gold reserves, so Scott detailed a creative workaround to make it all kosher. Scotia bought the gold and sold it back to Uruguay on a 180-day delivery contract. It would be stored in Scotia's vaults in Toronto. The bank became known in Uruguay for its can-do approach.[2]

In 1973, the military took over in Uruguay and the country wanted its gold back—so it could be paraded through Montevideo in a national celebration. In a series of events like something out of *Keystone Cops*, the gold missed its flight in Toronto and didn't arrive in time for the parade. So, the Uruguayan military faked it, driving armoured trucks through the streets, the public none the wiser.[3] Banking in South America was certainly different than in staid, genteel Canada.

Despite these cultural differences, Scotia honed and grew its expertise in gold. Every Thursday, Scott's office in Buenos Aires arranged for a shipment of gold bars from Toronto to be delivered to a Royal Bank of Canada branch there for use by jewellers. In 1970, the Central Bank of Ecuador asked whether Scotia could sell gold bars in the city of Cuenca, where there was an evolving jewellery business. Gold then opened the door to other business. As word spread about this Canadian bank, South American central banks and commercial banks deposited their inter-national reserves with Scotia. In 1965, the Bank of Nova Scotia took its first deposit from Peru's central bank—US$100,000. That led to its first corporate loan in the hemisphere a year later—US$3 million to Peru's national steel company.[4] Scott recalled that by 1968, 70 percent of Chile's international reserves were parked at the Bank of Nova Scotia. Typically, countries (central banks) would make these deposits at Scotia's New York Agency, which Waugh would later run for several years. In South America, Scotia was establishing itself as a wholesale bank, dealing with govern-ments and companies rather than retail customers at branches, a business that would come to the region later.

Latin American business also spread to Canada. A branch in Halifax, Nova Scotia, became deposit central for South American money. When unrest in Uruguay hit, an exchange house based in Montevideo began ushering its clients to Scotiabank, which in turn sent their deposits to out-of-the-way Halifax. At the time, Scott said, Nova Scotia offered such deposits preferential tax treatment compared to other Canadian prov-inces.[5] From his office in Buenos Aires, what began as a trickle of Uruguayan money flowing into that one Halifax branch was by 1985 a billion dollars ($2.624 billion in 2025 dollars).

The business climate in South America changed abruptly in 1982 when the then military dictatorship in Argentina invaded the wind-swept Falkland Islands, off the country's coast. The Falklands were still part of the British Empire, and there was a swift and ferocious reaction from Britain, under the leadership of the "Iron Lady," Prime Minister Margaret Thatcher. Even though the Falklands were a world away from the British and their daily lives, to Thatcher the invasion was a gross affront. It was war. Ships were sunk and many lives lost, and much of Latin America sided with Argentina, scaring off foreign investors and foreign bankers.

Meantime, many of these countries had been piling up huge debts after being on the receiving end of a years-long lending spree by foreign banks. When OPEC, the Organization of the Petroleum Exporting Countries, rose to prominence in the early 1970s, so-called petrostates were flush with cash due to the high prices they charged for oil. The money, which gushed into their bank accounts, didn't just sit there. This cash was put to work as banks lent to what the United Nations had designated as LDCs—least developed countries—which included Latin American nations.

Of course, when money is on offer, governments take it and spend. That led to huge expenditures, which triggered inflation—and debts mounted until countries could no longer afford to pay the interest. Then they defaulted on their obligations. Mexico was the first domino to fall; others followed. Not only did Mexico default but it also nation-alized its banking system. It was a bleak period in Latin America, and bleak for the foreign banks that had pushed credit their way, including Scotiabank. It had to set aside, or provision for, US$2.7 billion to cover its exposure in the region. Today, that would be about a quarter of the bank's annual earnings—a major hit, but not disastrous. In the 1980s, this was an enormous sum relative to the size and earning power of the bank.[6]

But if there's one constant in economics, it's that cycles end and new ones begin. Eventually, debtors crawl out from under the rubble and start afresh, as do banks, if they survive. In 1990, a new phase in Scotia's Latin American journey began. It now owned 25 percent of Banco Sud Americano in Chile, reflective of an evolving strategy of forging strategic alliances or buying minority interests in local banks, a way to expand, but cautiously.[7] By 1992, Mexico was offering opportunities as well. It was ready to return banks to the private sector, allowing for foreign investors to own small percentages. Buying into a bank there at a bargain-basement price, Scotiabank would soon, under Waugh's predecessor Peter Godsoe, be a major player in Mexican banking.* The Latin American landscape was looking up again for Scotia. However, all of this was just a backdrop for a disaster-in-waiting: Argentina's 2001–2 financial and banking crisis that would be a crucible for Rick Waugh.

The economic story of Argentina is shocking. Since becoming independent from Spain in 1816, Argentina has defaulted on its debt *nine times.* For a sovereign default to occur just once is a debilitating trauma for a country and its people; nine times makes it akin to a chronic disease. A recurring theme in Argentina has been hyperinflation, destabilizing in any society. When the value of your money erodes at a frightening clip, there's alarm, and often panic. When it happened in 2001–2, it took down Scotiabank's subsidiary in Argentina, Scotiabank Quilmes (SBQ), the seventh-largest bank in the country. It would be the most searing instance in Waugh's career to that point.

A series of events culminated in the crisis. In 1991, Argentina hitched the peso to the US dollar, so-called convertibility. One peso was deemed to be worth a dollar. Initially, the move seemed to dampen inflation. Over the next three years, inflation fell, the economy grew, and Argentina

---

* At the bank's April 2024 annual meeting, CEO Scott Thomson would declare Scotia a top five bank in Mexico.

embarked on reforms that were the flavour of the day for globalizers—deregulation, privatization, and reducing obstacles to trade. Argentina's growth continued until 1998. Foreign money poured in. But its national debt grew, and the International Monetary Fund (IMF) warned of "a meltdown," pledging loans if necessary. In 1999, Argentina's key trading partner, Brazil, had its own economic problems and devalued its currency. As a result, Argentinian exports dropped. The price of wheat, an export central to Argentina, fell. The country's budget deficit worsened. Interest rates rose. The country was in a dive. In 2000, Argentina tried tackling its deficit, only to make a bad situation worse.[8]

International investors saw heightened country risk, meaning Argentina had to pay higher interest to lure funds into the country. The IMF agreed to lend Argentina $14 billion. By mid-year 2000, with the country in the throes of a depression, bondholders swapped old Argentinian bonds for new ones, giving the country more time to pay. In the summer, government salaries and pensions were cut, and there was another $8 billion from the IMF. On December 1, 2001, in a measure it called the *corralito*, the government restricted bank withdrawals and transfers of money out of the country. Depositors could only withdraw $250, or 250 Argentinian pesos, a week. More so, it was a default on foreign debt.[9] Panic ensued, and the IMF cut off Argentina.[10]

Peso convertibility ended on January 6, 2002. GDP fell 11 percent, and the unemployment rate hit 25 percent. People were destitute.[11] As author Paul Blustein argued in his chronicle of the crisis, after the world's financial system had puffed up Argentina as the next wunderkind of globalization, it ultimately let the country down. This was the financial, political, and social cesspool Rick Waugh had to navigate.

Of course, Argentina couldn't escape its own troubled financial history and desire to be a player once again on the world's economic map. It had, after all, been a top-ten economy between 1860 and 1930, but then a coup set off nearly a century of political and economic instability—with the country swinging back and forth between military and populist governments.[12] Many blame the policies that began with the election of Juan Perón in 1946 and the ever-present inflation and corruption, as though they are coded into the political-economic genome of the country.

Despite the mayhem, Argentina is like a siren call—one that Scotia fell for. The country, Waugh remarks, looks marvellous on the outside. But beneath the surface, there's trouble, the result of nearly a century of violent upheaval. He also points largely to the Peronists, named for Perón—whose wife, Eva, was the subject of the hit musical *Evita*. Waugh likened dealing with the Peronists to dealing with the old Communist Party in China or Russia. "It's [corruption] ingrained in the Peronist system," he says. "The government of Argentina was corrupt." Waugh says he recognized this from his own experience in Russia. Scotia opened an office in Moscow during the glasnost and perestroika years, during the post–Soviet Union glow when it was hoped Russia would westernize, democratize, and capitalize. But he says the bank couldn't do any business, even with an office there. "I opened it and closed it."

While Argentina was hard to resist, Scotia went in with its eyes wide open. Not only did the bank have a history in the region, but it now had three decades of experience in Latin America and the cultures in the Southern Hemisphere. By the early 1990s, Argentina had recovered from yet another one of its serial financial crises and was one of the most richly endowed, sophisticated countries on the continent. "It all made sense," Waugh says. "These are smart, articulate people, educated, worldly in many respects." Waugh says he loved it. "It's a great country to visit. Good food. Good wine . . . very hospitable people."

But in the decades leading up to Scotia's Argentina fiasco, a stage had been set in many developing countries. The debt crisis that hit Latin America in the 1980s was concurrent with the rise of economic globalization and the spreading of free market ideology—the Thatcher and

Reagan years—beyond Western industrialized countries, leading to deeper integration of global economies. Swept up in this were South American countries like Argentina, which soon once again became a destination for foreign investment. Within a relatively short period of time, Argentina had gone from the reckless invader of the Falklands to a poster child for globalization. Capital was inbound. Foreign investors were buying Argentina's bonds to fund its development.

This coincided with a change at the top at Scotiabank. Peter Godsoe succeeded Cedric Ritchie as CEO in 1992, just as globalization was hitting a fever pitch. In January 1994, Godsoe went to the World Economic Forum's annual gathering in Davos, a hamlet in the Swiss Alps. Each January, the world's most powerful and wealthiest people assemble in this snowy village for the better part of a week. CEOs mingle with each other, along with world leaders, thinkers of the moment, billionaires, actors, musicians, and those on the international influencer circuit. Business leaders come away with either new notions, expert sales pitches, or hangovers. While it is most certainly a venue for speed-dating among decision makers and a place to hear the ideas du jour, Davos is also derided as a concentrated pit stop for the world's elites, a source of problems rather than solutions. If any event symbolizes globalization, it's Davos. It's a gathering of the *in crowd*. As a journalist, once you've cleared the ironclad security perimeter, you walk unencumbered amongst them, free to buttonhole anyone who walks by, from the CEO of JPMorgan to Al Gore to Emma Thompson to Bono.

It was amidst this frothy environment that Peter Godsoe met Domingo Cavallo, Argentina's economic minister. "In their brief conversation Cavallo invited Scotiabank to consider investing in Argentina, going at the time through one of its few better times" Roy Scott wrote in a privately published memoir, adding that he expressed strong reservations about the proposal, concerned that Argentina's ways were not Scotiabank's ways.[13]

Argentina is like the archetype of the promising child. As literary critic Cyril Connolly wrote, *Whom the gods wish to destroy, they first call promising.* That is Argentina. Buenos Aires is the Paris of South America, with broad boulevards, lip-smacking wines, and juicy steaks. Resource-rich, the country could be a world-leading economy, but it's repeatedly been a financial misfit. Nonetheless, Scotia was determined. Scott says his reservations were "strongly overruled," and Godsoe asked him to suggest names for a possible strategic alliance. "I selected three." One of them was Banco Quilmes, not unlike the Chilean bank in which Scotia had taken a minority interest. As in Chile, Quilmes was controlled by a "small family group" and had a "small but reasonable market share, clean name, needed professional assistance which they admitted, and [was] willing to entertain a strategic alliance."[14]

Godsoe visited the three banks and landed on Quilmes, "as they needed BNS' expertise and we could have a larger say in management, whereas the other two were well run and did not need us much." Ten months after the meeting with Cavallo in Davos, Scotia purchased 25 percent of Quilmes. As Gordon Bell, Ced Ritchie's number two, once prophetically told Scott, "Roy, a 25 percent ownership is 25 percent of the profits, if any, but 125 percent of the problems."[15] It turns out Scotia grossly underestimated the risks in Argentina, particularly macroeconomics and the corrosive effects of corruption.

By 2001–2, Quilmes was supposed to be on track to earn $20 million. But that trajectory slammed into reverse as the economy crashed and people began to frantically withdraw deposits from their banks—a bank run. Withdrawals from bank accounts were soon restricted by the *corralito*, intensifying the panic. Argentina, desperate to keep money in the country, put a halt to interest payments on foreign debt. It was a sovereign default. This would in turn make life impossible for Scotia-bank Quilmes. Like other banks in the normal course of their affairs, SBQ had issued bonds to raise funds and had an interest payment coming due—to investors outside the country. But it would now be against the law to pay the interest. Not making the interest payment would make the bank look like it was insolvent (it wasn't) and worsen the crisis of confidence among depositors. Although Quilmes was operating as an Argentinian bank, it would be painted as a foreign villain because it was owned by Scotiabank.

Ironically, according to Bob Brooks, Scotiabank's former treasurer in Toronto, Quilmes had already put the money in New York to pay the note or bond off at maturity. But with the Argentinian government's capital controls, Godsoe decided that it couldn't be paid off with money in New York. It would be a breach of Argentinian law, even though the money wasn't in Argentina. That led to Quilmes defaulting, which, in Brooks's words, "put it front and centre in Argentina as a pariah bank."

But there had been other issues. Waugh maintains "there were lots of warnings" that Argentina was a sketchy place to operate. Quilmes, founded in 1907, got its name from the beer called Quilmes, not unlike Molson in Canada, where there was a Molson Bank from 1850 to 1925. Inside the Quilmes building was a room surrounded by lead, "so people couldn't eavesdrop," says Waugh, with a tone of incredulity. It made one pause and think, "This is sort of different down here." It also raised the question of whether all the stones had been turned over when Quilmes was purchased by Scotiabank. Scotiabank initially paid US$57 million for a stake in a bank Godsoe described as "extremely conservative." The deal closed in January 1995.[16] Within a couple of years, though, Quilmes "ran into problems with its loan portfolio" and what Godsoe characterized as "a lack of focus in its franchise." It lost money for the first time in twenty-five years.

There was another key character involved in the Argentina saga.

Anatol von Hahn was born in Chile and raised in Montreal, where his parents insisted he speak Spanish one day a week. It was fortunate advice. Like Waugh, von Hahn is tall, has a magnetic personality, and is gifted with people. Also like Waugh, he didn't like accounting but liked banking. After two years at Continental Bank in Ottawa in the early eighties, von Hahn decided he wanted to be an international banker. So, he took an offer from Scotiabank, starting at Toronto's Eglinton and Bathurst branch. Eventually, he became one of the bank's top executives, running the Canadian banking network. But Argentina, he told me, is where he learned the most in the shortest time.

He'd already had an introductory crisis class. When von Hahn was in his late twenties, his career collided with another period of international banking turmoil, and one in which Scotiabank also took body blows—the least-developed-country crisis. "[CEO Cedric] Ritchie handled that file himself," von Hahn said. As Bill Nicks did from the late 1950s to the early 1970s, and Thomas Fyshe did in the late 1800s, Ritchie pushed the geographic boundaries of the bank.

In 1986, at just twenty-seven, von Hahn was drawn into the LDC vortex with Ritchie—attending debt restructuring meetings in New York with the CEO. In large part, he said, he was there because he spoke some Spanish. Then, von Hahn shipped out to Singapore for two years, at which point the bank decided it wanted him in Latin America. But he didn't want to go, preferring Asia, where he saw growth. He thought Latin America was a basket-case region—*and he was from the region.*

But Ritchie spoke to him. "I don't know you from a hole in the ground," the CEO said, and then told von Hahn he should go to Chile. "Look, you know Chile. You were born there." What's more, you speak Spanish, Ritchie said. Von Hahn protested, saying he spoke Spanish like an eight-year-old. "That's more than any of us do," Ritchie shot back. So, von Hahn went. After that, he bonded with Ritchie. When von Hahn's first child was born, Ritchie's wife, a nurse, helped von Hahn's wife with their baby in Chile. This thickened the lore that Scotia had a family-like culture.

In 1990, Scotiabank's purchase of a minority interest in a Chilean bank was timed well; it coincided with a boom phase. A democratic transition was occurring after the brutal Pinochet dictatorship with the installation of a freely elected president. Scotia's purchase was worth five times more in two and a half years.

In 1995, at just thirty-six, von Hahn would find himself in Argentina managing Quilmes, which was still controlled by two families. It was not unusual for Scotia to purchase stakes in Latin American banks from families. Scotia's due diligence had turned up what von Hahn described as "a weak bank." But Scotia had decided Argentina had a future. Within months of purchasing a stake in Quilmes, von Hahn said, Scotia discovered "this is a worse bank than what we thought it was. We did bad due diligence. We were too trusting." He conceded he was part of that process. So, the view became, let's work with the families.

The next generation of those families was now running the show, holding the top executive positions. One day, they came to talk to the Scotiabank people, who were now minority owners, and said there were "a couple of ghosts in the closet"—two large, problematic loans that had not shown up in the due diligence or, perhaps worse, had been obscured. It was an "oh my God" moment for Scotia in Argentina, von Hahn says. One Argentinian executive for the bank put it this way: Scotia "discovered after one year that the bank was not what they assumed when they bought the bank."

Roy Scott, of course, knew the scene on the ground and says it was very difficult to do proper due diligence in Argentina. "I don't think it's a Scotiabank failure. It's so easy to fool a foreigner when they come in to audit an operation. It's an unfair fight." After hearing about the ugly reality at Quilmes, von Hahn and Scott sat in Scott's car mulling it over.

"We have no choice," von Hahn said. "We got to go to Toronto. We got to tell them what's happening." It was a risk to speak up, given that Godsoe had been the spear carrier on the purchase of Quilmes. By now, it was 1997.

"Godsoe says, yeah, let's stick with it," von Hahn said. But the CEO insisted Scotia go to Argentina's central bank. Von Hahn described the governor at the time as a very ethical central banker, who told the Scotia bankers, "I want those guys out of the bank" and I want you guys in. "And if you don't get it fixed, I'll intervene." So, Scotiabank bought the rest of Quilmes and ran it.

"I think Scotia [then] takes a piece of shit and makes it into a small, clean, relatively well-run institution." Von Hahn said Argentinian employees started seeing "the values of a meritocracy," noteworthy in a country riven with corruption. Specifically, von Hahn said, leases had been signed for branches and suppliers, which then generated kickbacks. Loans had been made to friends. "It's endemic." Nonetheless, Quilmes was making money, but another Argentinian crisis was building. By the late 1990s, the economy was sputtering, and the country endured four years of excruciating contraction.

In 2000, Alan Macdonald arrived to run the bank, while von Hahn moved on to Scotia in Mexico. On one occasion, Godsoe visited Mexico City, and von Hahn travelled with him in a chauffeur-driven car. "What do you think about what's going on in Argentina," Godsoe asked, suggesting they have a drink. So, they repaired to Godsoe's hotel room and poured a couple. Von Hahn began telling Godsoe what the bank needed to do in Argentina, about a dozen things. "I'm writing it on a piece of paper. He's keeping it," von Hahn said. Two days later, Rick Waugh, who now had head office responsibility for Argentina, phoned von Hahn. "I've got a frigging piece of paper . . ."

———

Despite Waugh's description of the lead-lined room and the creepy signal it sent, Argentina aspired to be an international player. Not unlike
other countries, and with certain justification, Argentina exhibits strong
national pride and sense of self. "Argentinians have always considered
themselves European rather than Latin American, which has given them
a reputation for arrogance in Latin American circles," observed Tom
MacDonald, Canada's former ambassador there. When the banking crisis hit in 2001–2 and Scotiabank was severely impacted, Waugh said
Argentina was scared the Canadian government would use its influence
to have the country booted out of the G20 and be replaced by Chile, a
humiliation. There wasn't only mayhem and unspeakable poverty due
to the crisis. Pride was at stake.

On the ground in Argentina, running the bank became tense.
Donna Groskorth, who grew up in the Parry Sound region of Ontario,
had worked in credit, the magic department at Scotiabank. When the
bank was expanding in Latin America, she studied Spanish on her own
time in the event an opportunity arose. After spending six months in
Argentina, Chile, and Mexico in 2000, she was asked to move permanently to Argentina. She did, even though Argentina was embroiled in
what would be a multi-year recession.

When the *corralito* came into effect, it led to violent protests. Dozens
of people died. The Argentine president's offices in the Casa Rosada
(the Pink House) faced the Plaza de Mayo, a short walk from Scotiabank
Quilmes. "We were in the office ten minutes away from where the
majority of people were killed," Groskorth said, a sense of alarm in her
voice more than twenty years later. As the head of risk for Scotiabank
Quilmes in Argentina, she had a security guard. Groskorth said it was
decided that she required a female guard. "She wore spike heels." The
guard also carried a gun in her purse. "I don't know if she could outrun
anybody, but she could certainly do damage with those heels."

Groskorth recalled that the streets were increasingly dangerous. "People who said they needed food would just overwhelm a supermarket and just steal things." Amidst this, she had a traumatic personal experience. On a Saturday morning, she went to the supermarket and described wearing a "watch of economic value." Coming out of the store, in one arm she held a bag of groceries, in the other a bottle of Malbec. "A man came up behind me and grabbed me by the throat and ripped the watch off my arm." Previously, she said, Waugh had spoken with her about being more careful, and she subsequently received a checkup call from the bank's head of human resources, Sylvia Chrominska. As a result of the communication from Waugh and Chrominska, Groskorth said, employees at Quilmes felt heard by head office and were comfortable expressing their views on the situation.

As the protests intensified, events sped up. Cavallo, the economic minister who'd convinced Scotiabank to invest in Argentina, resigned, as did the country's president, Fernando de la Rúa. On December 21, 2001, he escaped via helicopter from the roof of the Casa Rosada. There was a revolving door of presidents—five in thirteen days. One lasted two days, while one lasted only a day. "What could be more graphic than that? It was chaos," Roy Scott said. Several provinces, he recounted, each issued their own currencies. Another bank staffer said that on the advice of a security firm, certain senior employees of Quilmes carried pistols (Waugh said he was unaware of this).

"The bank runs started at a slow pace in March of 2001," Groskorth said, adding that initially the loss of deposits looked manageable. "It wasn't a pronounced run, but deposits were starting to go down in the system and Scotiabank Quilmes as well." Meantime, Waugh was in Santiago, Chile, and asked the team in Buenos Aires to travel there to update him. "It was a pessimistic outlook," Groskorth said, "and Rick told us at that time to take specific measures and it just progressively got worse."

More deposits left the bank, the economy sagged, and there were more protests. The government was leaning more and more on the banks, she said. And there was more government exposure on the asset side—with banks having been pressured to hold government bonds, which were of questionable value—while on the liability side of balance sheets there was US dollar exposure. Deposits were vulnerable. By September, everything was more pronounced. And then 9/11 happened. Security on the American home front had been shattered. Any hope the United States would assist Argentina financially was now out of the question. Americans were focused on their own security.

Former Scotiabank vice-chairman Bob Chisholm described the Argentina debacle as "harrowing" for the bank's people there. Indeed. More than two decades later, a handful of them—including Groskorth and Anatol von Hahn, who would return for a dramatic finale—contributed to a paper about the experience entitled "Lessons Learned." Sections read like dispatches from a war zone. With protesters gathered in front of the bank's main building, metal bars were installed on windows. Threatening leaflets with images of Peter Godsoe and Alan Macdonald were distributed; the two were alleged to be responsible for the chaos. Bank employees were advised to dress casually—not like bankers—to avoid attracting the attention of thieves. Expats were provided with security guards when travelling to and from work. In one instance, a security guard, who was dressed in business attire, was "surrounded" by several teenage boys, would-be robbers. He pulled a gun, and they fled. One expat who worked for the bank was robbed in a taxi. Employees were also "requested to keep US$2000 in their residence" to pay "for transportation to leave Argentina if requested to do so by BNS." Canadian employees of Quilmes would depart work alongside Argentine employees as cover. One Quilmes employee left work by jumping from the roof of the bank to another roof, getting down via a fire escape. According to the bankers' paper, some employees in Argentina were naturally wired to cope with the turmoil while others were not. Some were "paralyzed." Others were "overwhelmed, demoralized." There was "no rule book, policies or procedures to follow to help guide them in day-to-day operations, decision making and strategy."[17] Some worried about losing their savings and/or their jobs.

In the early days of the crisis, SBQ had already begun preparing for trouble. While some there wanted to grow the residential mortgage portfolio, Claudio Hernandez, Quilmes's head of treasury—the person most familiar with the bank's liquidity—advised the opposite. Hernandez had been at the bank since 1984, a decade before Scotia bought its initial stake. He'd been through other Argentinian crises, specifically the hyper-inflation of the second half of the 1980s when the bank had to pay annual interest of *7,000 percent* to maintain deposits (he said the bank's computers weren't set up to handle four digits). Hernandez recalled the closure of the entire Argentine financial system for three weeks in the spring of 1989 because the central bank could not print enough bills to meet the inflation rate and satisfy the needs of the market. Bank branches, he said, became branches of the government, with deposits moved to the central bank. Credit to the private sector did not exist, Hernandez said. He had never seen long-term mortgages in Argentina.

A dozen years later, the nightmare was back. According to Hernandez, the bank simply didn't have the liquidity to fund more mortgages—assets. The ability to roll over (renew) debt to match the bank's mortgage portfolio had disappeared, and working to match assets and liabilities was crucial. Aside from deposits, investors must buy your bonds or short-term instruments—securities with maturities ranging from, say, thirty days to multi-year terms—to provide the liquidity to fund mortgages. Rick Waugh was informed of this and "ordered a stop to asset (loan) growth."[18] Waugh and Hernandez were on the same page.

"It was a constant progressive depletion of liquidity," Donna Groskorth said, as people took their money out of the bank. As the situation worsened, by day's end, Scotiabank Quilmes was "having to ask [Argentina's] central bank for funding." The SBQ bankers, she said, had "just no idea whether they would provide funding or not or to which banks they'd provide funding." There was the sense that the central bank was prioritizing local banks to force international banks like Scotia to inject new funds into their Argentinian subsidiaries. At the close of business, Groskorth said "every few minutes one of the treasury employees [of Quilmes] would refresh the computer screen to hopefully see that there was communication with the central bank that they'd provided us with funding." The peso, meanwhile, was convertible to the US dollar one-for-one, an unsustainable setup. "The central bank can't manufacture US dollars, so it was a great unknown," Groskorth said.

She remembered that at one point, the central bank announced it would match any dollar invested in an Argentinian subsidiary for liquidity. While "there wasn't a lot of trust in that," Scotiabank decided to test it and put in $5 million. The central bank did match it, but Groskorth said all the money quickly evaporated, "withdrawn by depositors" in less than twenty-four hours. "People were concerned that the banking system would fail them, and they would lose their money." That included employees of Quilmes. When they got paid, they'd withdraw the money, Groskorth said, sending it to Uruguay to deposit it there or stashing it in safe deposit boxes, even though there were worries the government would raid those. She also recalled uniformed police officers arriving at the bank, sitting down, and demanding bank files, a threatening scenario. According to the Scotia bankers' paper, police "claimed authority to enter the bank's vault to verify the amount of cash" if Quilmes said it didn't have the necessary amount. "The work around was to have very little cash in the vault at any time and to have the armoured vehicle delivering cash circle the branch until requested to deliver a limited amount of cash."[19]

Waugh estimated he travelled to Buenos Aires at least a dozen times during the crisis, working through weekends. He said he has no memory of where he stayed or what he ate because he was so focused on the task at hand and the people from the bank he met. Groskorth said Waugh would visit "and get us on track again." He told her that typically if a bank failed, it was due to liquidity. Waugh, along with Groskorth and Alan Macdonald, were trying to convince large foreign banks to make deposits with Scotia to bolster liquidity.

Aside from the eminently sensible Groskorth (Waugh would call her a hero),[20] there were many superb Argentinian employees of the bank. Miguel Jarsun, who ran the branches at Quilmes, spoke despondently of the *corralito*, the restriction on withdrawals. "You can't imagine that," he said, describing how everyone went to the bank and opened ten to fifteen separate accounts so they could transfer money from their main accounts. All these years later, he recalled, with anguish, his brother asking him whether it was safe to put money in the bank. If he said yes, he would be putting his brother's money at risk. If he said no, it was an indictment of the banking system and his own bank, which could make the deposit run worse. Jarsun spoke just as empathically about customers he'd known for twenty years, people who were like friends. He felt trapped, unable to tell them to take their money out before it was gone. To make matters worse, approximately 300 of Quilmes's employees out of 1,700 were on strike. The pressure was off the charts.

In all his banking days, Waugh had never experienced a bank run like Argentina's. Yes, there had been runs in small Caribbean countries, but they were at local banks. They were funded locally with currency that could be printed by the local central bank. But in Argentina, the peso had been pegged to the American dollar, an artificial construct that was destined to crack. The value of a currency reflects the perception of the local national economy, relative to other national currencies and economies. While pegging a currency to another may work for a while (in the early

1960s, the Canadian dollar was pegged at 92.5 cents to the US dollar), the practice has an inherent structural flaw. Put simply, convertibility, or dollarization, is phony. The peso was not the American dollar—and when that flaw surfaced, the peg broke, and chaos ensued.[†]

Newly appointed Canadian ambassador Tom MacDonald arrived in Argentina in 2001, presenting his credentials just one day after 9/11. Argentina was by then already in a bad slide. "It really went off a cliff in late November, early December," he says, after the peg broke. Money was rushing out of the country, and even if you had pesos, they were no longer worth a dollar.

MacDonald recalls his son visiting for Christmas. He nervously carried US$5,000 for his parents because they couldn't get access to their bank accounts. As for embassy staff, MacDonald reckons that 20 percent of his Canadian employees had been robbed, some at gunpoint. The percentage of his Argentinian staff who'd experienced similar crimes was much higher. "Kidnapping became incredibly common," he says, estimating some twenty a day in Buenos Aires. The citizenry was destitute, with slum ghettos not far from the embassy, no-go zones given the violence. People pushed wheelbarrows piled high with cardboard to sell for just a few pesos. In an email, MacDonald described Scotiabank-related demonstrations that took place in front of the embassy:[21]

> *There were normally up to a hundred or so demonstrators, including employees and depositors . . . We never had any violent incidents. But that was because the Argentine authorities placed a phalanx of about 12–15 police in front . . . They were equipped with helmets, Kevlar vests, hard plastic shields and billy-sticks (some no doubt also had handguns). They also had a few vicious-looking German shepherds. . . .*

---

† A similar situation unfolded during the Greek debt crisis, from 2009 to 2017; Greece was using the euro but didn't have the fiscal discipline to justify using it.

... I agreed to meet with a small representation from the group ...
I tried to explain the private sector nature of Scotiabank, that the
Canadian government had no direct role in its operations, and that the
problems at Quilmes were a function of Argentine policies, including
discriminatory treatment of the Canadian-owned bank as compared
with others. They listened but did not really hear ... Clearly the
Embassy and Scotiabank could not have been more closely aligned ...

Despite the chaos, Argentina had leverage, not so Canada. Scotiabank Quilmes was not viewed as a local bank. It was owned by a foreign bank and when trouble erupted, the local government worried about what it considered to be local banks first. "Local banks get treated differently than international banks," Waugh says, the latter occupying "a twilight zone." Even though Quilmes was in fact local and made money, it wasn't considered local.

Meantime, Argentinian politics tainted any attempt to run an advanced economy. The lead-lined room at Quilmes notwithstanding, Waugh said he negotiated with the governor of the country's central bank, whom he described as an internationally trained individual trying to act in a responsible way. "He and I were trying to see if we could find a way to save the bank," Waugh said. "He was trying to act like an independent governor of the [central] bank, in a good way." Waugh went on to describe an international meeting held in Washington at one of the major federal departments of the American government. He said Argentina's central banker was giving a speech about his independence. Waugh then described the governor's aide-de-camp coming down the aisle waving his hand as the governor spoke. The aide went up onto the stage and said the governor had a call from the president of Argentina— and had to excuse himself.

"What a loss of face," Waugh says in disbelief. "This was a message to everyone in the room that he's not an independent governor." This public humiliation, "this was the buildup to Quilmes." In countries where it operated, "we [Scotia] would take the guarantee of the central bank," Waugh says, not the guarantee of the country. "Argentina is a good example of when it didn't make any difference."

Despite the governor's public humiliation, it was a moot point. Waugh said a possible solution he discussed with the head of Argentina's central bank was of no interest to his bosses in Toronto. The fact remained he was not yet CEO and reported to Godsoe, who ran the entire bank. The Argentinians wanted to extract funds from Scotiabank, the parent company. They wanted foreign banks to inject money and buy Argentinian bonds to prop up the financial system. It was a game of who'd blink first. Argentina needed capital inflows and wanted money to come into the country, while Scotiabank wanted the reverse—for Argentina to lend to Quilmes. The tentative solution Waugh discussed was that BNS would put a token amount of money into the country. It could then exit gracefully, or perhaps stay. But Godsoe and his number two, Bruce Birmingham, believed that if the bank put more money into Argentina, the market wouldn't like it and it would affect the stock. "I totally understood the rationale," he says, conceding that stock price was important to the bank, "but [I] didn't like [it] as the local executive responsible." Still, he says, "probably for an all-bank solution it was the right move not to put money in."

There was also unlucky timing. Once the crisis hit, Quilmes was the first bank to reach a maturity date for an interest payment. As a result, Scotia was first up to bat, but because of the law forbidding payments to be sent out of the country, it decided it couldn't even swing. Waugh was quick to point out that it was "Scotia Quilmes's debt that came due, not Scotiabank." A lot of debt was held by offshore investors in US dollars. If it had been held in Argentina, Waugh said, it wouldn't have been the same issue. "Most of it was sold offshore, so the Argentines didn't care." They thought they wouldn't have to pay it.

"What do we do?" Waugh asked rhetorically when describing what happened. "We are Canadian. We obey the law." So, abiding by local law, the bank did not make the interest payment, and therefore Quilmes was in technical default, which would ultimately lead to the loss of the bank. But, this being Argentina, officialdom *hadn't expected Quilmes to follow the law*. Somehow, the situation had to be corrected. But the ending couldn't be prevented, even though it would take several months to play out. And then legal matters would linger for years.

"On January 2, 2002, SBQ defaulted on a US$55 million payment on a Floating Rate Note because of strict foreign exchange controls Argentina put into effect on December 1, 2001," the Scotia bankers wrote in their reflective paper. "There was no opportunity to learn from another bank's experience in the same situation." Depositors ignored the fact that the bank could have made the payment and focused on the fact that it had not paid. The run on the bank accelerated. It's estimated that over the course of the crisis more than 80 percent of Argentina's deposits left the country.[22] After being a darling in the 1990s, another internal meltdown had made Argentina radioactive once again.

By the time the crisis hit, Scotiabank was fully committed to Argentina. Internal troubles with Quilmes had led to Scotia buying the rest of the bank in July 1997 for $250 million. Not only was Quilmes the seventh-largest bank in the country, it was Scotia's second-biggest foreign investment. The bank had continued to be bullish on Argentina, given its then-robust GDP growth (5 percent) and the fact that only about a third of Argentines were customers of a bank.[23] But by 1999, investors and the media were questioning Scotia's Latin American strategy. An article by Susanne Craig in the *Globe and Mail* ("Scotiabank's Latin Obsession") described the perils of owning just a minority interest, not to mention the need for exhaustive due diligence. Rick Waugh was featured in the piece.[24]

When the crisis hit in late 2001 and early 2002, Waugh would report to the board back home each week. If Scotia were to stay, it would need

Argentina and its government to be part of the solution, which wasn't going to happen. Making SBQ squirm was a strong message to other foreign banks. From the government's point of view, Quilmes was "big enough to be noticed, but not too big to fail," said Tom MacDonald. "We were not so big in order to damage the industry," Claudio Hernandez, Quilmes's treasurer added, but big enough to make a point and put pressure on other foreign banks to help solve Argentina's financial problems. However, it wasn't worth the risk. "Peter [Godsoe] made the call, no more money for Scotia Quilmes," Waugh said. Ultimately, Waugh agreed. "Peter said no, and Peter was right." It would be like paying for hostages, he adds. You'd have to do it again and again. When would you stop? Aside from the safety of employees and looking after them following the default, a disturbing aspect of the failure was "they tried to make us the scapegoat," blaming Scotiabank. "They can afford it. Let's get them to pay," he says. It didn't happen. But both customers and employees of Quilmes were furious at what looked like an abandonment of the country by the parent in dire times.

Scotiabank Quilmes's operations were suspended by Argentina after the close of business on April 18, 2002. SBQ was informed of this decision in a meeting at the central bank. According to "Lessons Learned," when told of this, Waugh, who was in Toronto, "spoke by telephone individually with each person present to ask how each person was doing and to provide encouragement." Donna Groskorth described how Waugh spoke with key team members, including her, "asking how I was doing, how I was feeling" and talking about the road ahead. Godsoe sent an email to the expats to thank them for staying "in the midst of what was one of the most difficult situations we've ever faced as a bank. You made us proud."[25]

The subsequent suspension of Quilmes was ultimately a relief for the parent company. Scotiabank released a statement saying it would "not be putting new money into Argentina unless there are clear rules in place that give us confidence that the systemic crisis can be turned around."[26] In its 2002 annual report, Scotia described exiting the country as an "extremely difficult decision," but the day after Argentina's central bank suspended Quilmes, Scotiabank's stock rose 3.24 percent. Between the bank's announcement in early March of a $540 million (after tax) charge against Quilmes-related losses and the suspension of operations in the second half of April, the stock gained more than 10 percent. Scotiabank called the Argentina situation "unique in our 170-year history." A reportedly furious Godsoe thought Argentina (its central bank) should have lent Quilmes money under the lender-of-last-resort facility, given that the problem was liquidity, not solvency, believing Argentina could have lent against Quilmes's balance sheet. In a statement, Scotiabank said Quilmes had "substantial eligible assets to pledge."[27] But it was not to be. The bank was saying goodbye to Argentina.

Roy Scott knew he'd irritated Godsoe when the bank obeyed local law and did not pay interest on the foreign debt maturity. Scott argues that in Argentina, "you do not ask for permission, you ask for forgiveness" and that the bank should have paid it. Godsoe didn't appreciate the counsel. "Roy, for goodness [sake]. You and your advice," he said. "For goodness's sake, shut up." But Scott says he knew "Peter lashed out because he was under huge tension."

It was one thing to say no more money for Quilmes. It was another to get people out who were at risk. A judge had ordered an injunction preventing executives from leaving the country. Former ambassador Tom MacDonald said he was in frequent communication with Scotia's top person in Argentina, Alan Macdonald (no relation), who had previously been the bank's CEO in Venezuela, where he'd been "very successful," a "good, solid commercial and retail banker," according to Waugh. Scott described Macdonald as a "magician with computers." Now, he was akin to a hostage. "It was frightening for him. He didn't speak Spanish hardly at all." Tom MacDonald said the Scotia banker "was afraid that he could get shot by one of his depositors or one of his employees. Because they were all mad as hornets."

While the economic crisis had impoverished Argentinians, it was also a personal trauma for Macdonald. He had been prosecuted by a local judge without representation—denied a lawyer, denied an interpreter. Macdonald was wrongly accused of defrauding depositors during a run on the Argentinian banks, through no fault of his own. The Maritimer was being prosecuted for the failure of the bank. His life was at risk, and others were also ordered not to leave, including Roy Scott and Bill Sutton, a senior executive of the bank.[28] On one occasion, Waugh asked what he could bring Macdonald from Canada. "Scotch and Tylenol" was the answer. "I could get on a plane and go home, but Alan couldn't." Waugh recalled that Macdonald was ordered to show up at a hotel room every morning, where he had to stay. He said the Canadian ambassador would sit outside the door to send a message to Argentina that Canada was watching. Tom MacDonald remembered sending a message through other actions.

The embassy was prepared to give the banker refuge in the ambassador's residence, but it never came to that. The former ambassador also said he requested to be present at one of the court hearings, but the request was rejected. However, he believed the request sent a signal to Argentinian authorities that "the Canadian embassy was closely watching and there would be Canadian government intervention if it became necessary." When Alan Macdonald finally got out of the country, it was "partly using the rationale of health."

Eduardo Oteiza was drawn to academia and wanted to teach law. But he had a big family, so he started working for banks, first Deutsche Bank and then Scotiabank, when he was hired by Anatol von Hahn in 1997. Von Hahn, who was running Quilmes at the time, impressed Oteiza. Rather than discussing regulation, Oteiza said they talked about the bank's local culture and how to change it from the family-owned firm it had been. "He spent time with the people," Oteiza said, speaking via Zoom with his scholarly, laddered library in the background. In that sense, von Hahn was like Waugh. He would return to Argentina with Waugh and figure prominently in the bank's finale there.

When things spun out of control, Oteiza was intimately involved in Alan Macdonald's court case. He described the judge as biased. "We were afraid what could happen to Alan Macdonald during those days." He faced the risk of imprisonment "because of his honest work," Oteiza said. "He did not commit a crime, of course." Oteiza suggested a trial would be something of a kangaroo court on behalf of the government. Rather than testifying, where Macdonald would be subjected to the judge's questioning, Oteiza told him: "You can go to the [Canadian] embassy and in the embassy, you'll be protected." Macdonald, however, wanted to know who would go to court in his stead? Oteiza said it would likely have been Roy Scott, who headed the board of SBQ. "He [Alan] said no. That's my responsibility. I will wait for what will happen," Oteiza recalled. "A very brave man, I must say."

The *Globe and Mail's* Heather Scoffield covered the crisis extensively. In March 2002, she wrote about Macdonald being questioned in court for five hours without a lawyer or a representative from the Canadian embassy present. The allegations were that the bank had defrauded customers by obstructing access to deposits. They stemmed from the complaints of one customer—a woman who had not being able to withdraw funds. The judge was described as a low-level criminal court judge. Oteiza said Argentinian newspapers reported prominently on bank-related court cases and recalled "a total lack of impartiality from the judge." The trial, he said, was not open to the public. Meantime, some sixty thousand Argentines had gone to court, seeking their deposits. Raids were ordered on banks. The *Globe* wrote, "A dense row of police officers wearing bullet-proof vests stands outside each bank entrance."

Macdonald told Scoffield he had learned from reading in the newspaper that he had been restricted from leaving the country. If found guilty, he faced the threat of nine years in prison. Still, he said, "I'm needed here," and went on to declare, "It's our intention to stay here. We are long term players."[29]

Meantime, the situation was being closely monitored by the Canadian government, with finance minister Paul Martin saying the Argentine government had been asked to treat foreign banks the same as domestic banks.[30] President Eduardo Duhalde of Argentina told Canadian prime minister Jean Chrétien that the judge had been removed from the case.[31] As for Waugh, Oteiza said, "what I remember was the total support from him."

The truth is, while Scotiabank's ordeal with Quilmes was dangerous, chaotic, and an embarrassing loss, it was just one quarter's worth of earnings for a Canadian bank that would move on. Bankers, Waugh says, see the ups and downs of every cycle. "That's part of being a banker." But Quilmes may not have failed in isolation. Aside from the chaos in Argentina, Waugh hinted that there were circumstances at head office in Canada. 2002 was not only the year of Quilmes's demise; it was also the time frame in which Scotiabank had initiated talks with Bank of Montreal about a merger. "I wasn't at the table. I was not party to those discussions," Waugh says, although with a laugh he concedes this was happening "pretty well around that time" (meaning the time of the Argentina debacle).

In 1998, Scotia had been the lone bank out of the big five to sit out the merger deals that had ultimately been rejected by the federal government. But now, four years later, the situation had changed, and the merger issue was resurrected. In 2002, Scotiabank and BMO tried to merge, and the timing was not far removed from the troubles in Argentina. If consummated, combining the two banks would have been transformational. A quarter's worth of earnings lost because of Argentina's collapse certainly wasn't nice for Scotia, but the bank may have had a more important issue bubbling in the background. Who needs an irritant in another hemisphere when you're trying to remake the whole organization? Bob Chisholm was CFO of Scotiabank for ten years, then the head of the Canadian retail, commercial, and wealth division, and finally vice-chairman. He said he was involved in the talks with BMO. "We made it to the back door of the church. [But] we never made it to the altar." The two banks were within a couple hours of publicly announcing the deal when Godsoe got a call saying the deal was off.

Also intimately involved was Sarabjit (Sabi) Marwah, the CFO after Chisholm and later chief operating officer (COO), Waugh's number two. "I was dead centre in that," said Marwah, now a retired senator. Marwah says there were three people in the know at BMO and three people in the know at Scotia—plus maybe one other on each side. Marwah's counterpart was Karen Maidment, then CFO at BMO. He says they, along with two people from finance on each side, ran all the modelling and numbers. They would meet in a room at the Sheraton Centre in downtown Toronto. On one occasion, Marwah said he and Maidment arrived at the same time in the elevator. "Karen," he said, "this doesn't look good." They laughed. If successful, Scotia would have had a majority stake in the combined bank. The deal, Marwah says, came within a "millimetre. It was done. It was done." Marwah says while they had no explicit approval, the government hadn't said no. But "Chrétien heard about it and says over my dead body and that's it."

That fateful morning, Marwah says, he and an investment banking advisor to Scotia were ready to give the final pitch to the board when Godsoe came in and said it was off. Marwah says Godsoe got the news in a call from BMO because of the latter's discussions with Ottawa.‡ BNS

---

‡ A source on the BMO side said it was an internal "fuck-up" in the federal government, adding that once Chrétien advisor Eddie Goldenberg learned of the deal, "Eddie nixed it" on behalf of his boss.

had been ready to announce it, "that day, after the board meeting." Once the board had approved it, he explained, it would be a material event, so it had to be announced. If the merger had gone ahead, Godsoe would have been CEO for a short time, and then BMO's Tony Comper would have assumed the role for a few years. After that, Marwah says, it would have been wide open. Aside from Waugh, waiting in the wings at Scotia, there were contenders at BMO as well.

In Waugh's telling, it was a Scotia-driven deal, because Godsoe was initially going to be the guy. Then who takes over? "The board would decide who the successor was," Waugh says. "Peter knew me well . . . and knew I wouldn't take it well . . . so they kept it from me." As for how it all played out in Ottawa, "ultimately it would have needed the prime minister's okay . . . Obviously, it was presented to him very late in the game." Whatever happened behind the scenes in Ottawa or at the banks, a merger could have had a major impact on Waugh's career. He might not have become CEO or perhaps would have been forced to wait longer to get the job, resulting in a shorter tenure.

Comparing time frames, the Argentina crisis was at its most grave for Scotia from December 2001 through to April 2002, with the suspension of Quilmes. The next few months, through the sale of Quilmes in September, was a harrowing time. As for the merger talks, the *Globe and Mail* reported that discussions between BNS and BMO got serious in August 2002 (the merger was nixed in the fall), but that "for three years, Scotiabank had conducted an on-again off-again courtship to woo BMO."[32] Marwah disputes this, saying it was a much shorter time frame, a matter of months. As well, an insider from the BMO camp says it was a case of two interested parties. Nonetheless, Chisholm doesn't think a possible merger had anything to do with exiting Argentina. "My recollection is that they were quite divorced timewise," he says, adding, "there was no connection to my mind with it." Marwah wholeheartedly agrees with Chisholm that the two had nothing to do with each other, "zero," because what occurred in Argentina was "unplanned," therefore linking the two is not correct.

That may very well have been the case. But Godsoe was paid to think about the big picture and was considered a brilliant banker. Marwah says Godsoe had mergers on his mind well before the talks with BMO got serious in the summer of 2002—"the day the [1998] mergers fell apart" and the bank did lots of deal modelling during subsequent years. A big, historic merger would have, Argentina aside, capped his stellar career, a sweet denouement given Scotia was on the merger sidelines in 1998. If so, it's also conceivable Godsoe wanted Argentina in the rear-view mirror as quickly as possible. It's virtually impossible to know for certain. Godsoe died in December 2023.

When told that Marwah and Chisholm did not think merger plans played a role in turning off the tap to Argentina, Waugh had another view. He understood mergers and acquisitions, and if you're effectively doing a merger of equals, the share values must be aligned. Scotia's stock had been under pressure because of Argentina, so he says it could have been a problem for the deal, although he says he chose never to raise the issue with Godsoe or Birmingham. When the bank announced it was washing its hands of Argentina, its stock went up.

The market seemed to be saying that Argentina simply wasn't worth the trouble anymore. Chisholm calls it "one of our bad experiences" in the bank's portfolio of dozens of international exposures. But overall, he says, it was "small potatoes" for the bank, and the effect of the loss "wasn't something that lingered very long." The fact is, Scotia was "making lots of money" from its core Canadian business, as is the case with all the country's major banks. Canada is the cash cow, a banking oligopoly with retail branch networks that date back to the 1800s. International is "a higher risk strategy, ergo the return should be higher," Chisholm argues. In contrast to Argentina, Scotia's experience in the Caribbean was generally good. "The biggest asset loans," he says, "were in the real estate resort business."

The risk in the Caribbean was hurricane risk, given that one would hit an island every seven or eight years, but then the business would come back.

In hindsight, Waugh says, going to 100 percent ownership in Argentina "was probably a mistake." Perhaps if Scotia had still had local partners, it would have been better off. Roy Scott's words of warning hung in the air: the bank would have been better off just staying away. "You make the mistake when you go in," Waugh says. But with an operating portfolio in more than fifty countries, a handful were inevitably problematic, but never to the point of "jeopardizing Bank of Nova Scotia's capital."

When the situation was finally unravelling, Anatol von Hahn, the previous head of Scotia's bank in Argentina, came back into the picture. Among von Hahn's recommendations on that "frigging piece of paper" was that the bank should send Bruce Birmingham, Godsoe's number two. "We're not going to send Bruce Birmingham," Waugh firmly told him. "*You're going.*"

Within a few days, von Hahn flew to Toronto to meet Waugh. That coincided with a garden party Waugh threw in his backyard for the country heads who reported to him. Von Hahn said Waugh had a history of throwing great parties: you always went, whether you had to or not. This one, however, was poignant. The Argentinian court order preventing Macdonald from leaving the country had been reversed, and he was permitted to return to Canada for the bank's "country manager meeting." The local judge okayed it provided another bank executive was installed as a substitute. That was Jim Shields, already the head of retail and small business banking in Argentina who had previously served as a Scotia executive elsewhere in Latin America. Macdonald and his wife attended Waugh's party while Shields took his place in Argentina.§

---

§ According to von Hahn, Shields never formally took over Macdonald's job as CEO of Scotiabank Quilmes, but rather as the "face" and most senior Canadian on the ground.

"I was there when his [Alan Macdonald's] wife showed up," von Hahn recalled. She was visibly distraught. She had been asked how her husband was doing. It was all too much. "She was the detonator," von Hahn said. The situation in Argentina had become overwhelming. Waugh said he spoke with Macdonald and realized how stressful the situation was. Around 11 p.m., Waugh said, it was determined that the bank could not in good conscience send Macdonald back to Argentina, "for his own well-being and that of his family." Recalling the scene, Waugh got teary.

Instead of Macdonald going back, Waugh would take von Hahn to Buenos Aires. Initially, von Hahn resisted. His sister was getting married in Miami, so Waugh promised to drop him off in Florida on the way home. Waugh was hard to refuse, so von Hahn relented. On one day's notice, he and Waugh flew on the bank's jet to Montevideo, Uruguay. The assessment was that had they landed in Argentina, the plane would have been confiscated. After all, a private jet could be sold for US dollars, which Argentina sorely needed. Flying there was one thing, but getting home would be another. Von Hahn had two passports, Canadian and Chilean, so he was confident he could get out. The trick would be getting Waugh and Shields out. After landing in Uruguay, though, Waugh and von Hahn would fly commercial to Buenos Aires from Montevideo—a quick hop—do what needed to be done in Argentina, and then fly back to Uruguay to take the company plane home.

But there were complex, agonizing tasks to complete in Argentina before leaving. Among them was the fact that they couldn't take Shields out unless they named another country head. So, the plan was to appoint an Argentinian. Of course, the bank had first-class local people on staff—among them, the treasurer, Claudio Hernandez; the head of branch banking, Miguel Jarsun; and, in legal, Eduardo Oteiza. As the situation came to a head, Waugh and von Hahn met the three men at the Hilton. They were told von Hahn would be in the country "in the background" at the bank—he had been popular there during his previous posting. Waugh and von Hahn said they wanted Jarsun to become the in-country CEO. "Rick," Jarsun said, "you want me to be the fucking CEO? No fucking way." They told him they needed him to do this. "You're fucking crazy, but I'm going to do it," von Hahn recalled him saying.

Jarsun didn't quibble with von Hahn's version of what he said. Additionally, the bank would protect him and afterwards give him a job anywhere in the network. Jarsun told them he had to speak with his wife, but ultimately agreed to take the assignment for the good of the bank and its rank-and-file employees, who were concerned about their jobs, severances, and their own deposits. Von Hahn said Jarsun took this on at great personal risk—of being sued, jailed, and shut out of working ever again in Argentina; he called Jarsun a very honourable man.

Waugh, according to von Hahn, told the Argentinians they'd be running the bank, and that it wasn't about making money for Toronto. It was about the employees keeping their jobs while Scotia worked to find a buyer, in conjunction with the central bank. But they needed the employees, who were striking, back on the job.

Then there was the staff meeting in Quilmes's main banking hall. "To this day, it was scary as shit," von Hahn recalls. It wasn't just the employees, "it was their wives and their kids." It was hundreds of people. "The only one talking is me because they wanted to know what Toronto thought." He told the assembled group that the only chance the bank had was if the central bank permitted a sale of Quilmes. "They bought in." They knew von Hahn and trusted him. The strikes stopped.

Quilmes's leadership went to the central bank, saying they wanted to sell. A boutique investment banker, Alejandro Reynal, ran the process. Waugh said he didn't charge Scotiabank. A buyer was found, one that would agree to keep the employees and honour the deposits. However, the central bank then declared it didn't want this purchaser, and permitted it to buy only half of Quilmes. The rest would go to another bank. In the end, Quilmes was split between two acquiring banks, Banco Comafi SA and Banco Bansud SA.

As for Waugh, "I imagine he knew he'd be CEO," von Hahn said, but "he had the guts to go in when no one else would." Godsoe was being painted as the villain by protesters, so it was simply too dangerous for him to go. As head of international, it was Waugh's job, and he was respected in Argentina. He'd visited frequently and spoken to people. Von Hahn said "he [Waugh] understood what they'd been through. When he showed up, it showed them we were serious. They were really happy they had a face they knew [Anatol] and that they had a friend in Toronto [Rick]."

But Waugh sent von Hahn in to tell the employees the bad news that Scotia was pulling out. "He was having to explain to all the people why Scotiabank was leaving. I was sitting out in the car," Waugh said. "He was the CEO [previously], he had the credibility." Employees were shocked, felt abandoned, but would be provided severance [which was doubled]. And when Quilmes was sold, some twelve hundred out of seventeen hundred would get jobs with the acquiring banks. The parent company also offered many of them jobs elsewhere in the Scotiabank network. Von Hahn said seventy Argentinian employees got positions in other countries. But it would be a big move for most people. "Argentines love their country, and they never want to leave. Asking an Argentine to leave the country is a big ask," Waugh observed.

However, some did indeed move and were success stories elsewhere in the bank. Jarsun, for instance, went to the Dominican Republic, while Hernandez shared his expertise in Chile, Peru, and Venezuela until his retirement in 2014. Others worked for the bank in Toronto. Donna Groskorth became chief risk officer for the bank in Mexico, then worked for BNS in Chile and Puerto Rico. Could Scotiabank ever return to

Argentina and operate a bank? Waugh shook his head. "Once you leave a country where you're a local banker, once you leave you can't go back. You never say never, but it would be highly unlikely."

When he'd joined the Bank of Nova Scotia as a teller in Winnipeg, Rick Waugh could not have imagined the *Mission Impossible*-like scene that was now about to unfold. Some thirty years later, he stood in the customs line at the airport in Buenos Aires, trying to keep cool. A clandestine operation was underway. Secretly, Waugh and von Hahn had plotted— likely with advice from bank security—to get Jim Shields, Alan Macdonald's stand-in, out of Argentina and into neighbouring Uruguay, where Scotia's jet waited to fly the three of them home.

The Canadian government had been informed about the escape plan. Canada's embassy in Uruguay, under Ambassador Susan Harper, let the bank use its diplomatic pouch so documents could avoid border inspection. In case flying to Uruguay became problematic, there were two backup plans. If needed, a speedboat would be standing by to whisk Waugh, von Hahn, and Shields across the water—129 nautical miles— to Montevideo. There was also a ground route. A Scotia executive had a home in Bariloche in Patagonia, two days by car from Buenos Aires. Once there, you could hike to Chile.

But first they would try to fly. While von Hahn was inside the bank telling employees that Macdonald wasn't coming back and Shields was leaving, Waugh and Shields had been on the move. They had retrieved Macdonald's belongings as well as the $25,000 in cash he had on hand. Waugh also had a bodyguard. Von Hahn left the employee meeting and met them, appearing somewhat shaken by the experience.

Their vehicle headed off. Meantime, it was anarchy on the streets. If you stopped at a traffic light, you risked being robbed. They needed to get to an airport and there were two, the international one and the regional airfield. Waugh and von Hahn thought they'd be less likely to be stopped at the regional airport. But Waugh said passengers flying from Buenos Aires to Uruguay pre-cleared customs at the airport. This was where it could all go wrong.

The bankers schemed how they would get through. The three of them would check in separately. Memories, however, conflict. Von Hahn says he went last, figuring with his two passports he'd be okay. Waugh went first, followed by Shields. "I knew I had to be last in case one of them got caught," von Hahn says. Waugh, however, remembered it differently. He recalled von Hahn went second, because he'd lived in Argentina previously and now lived in Canada. Shields, Waugh says, went last because he was living there and was the biggest risk. If Shields got pulled aside, at least the other two would be through. "Big, brave me, I went first," Waugh joked. When presented with the discrepancy in the stories, Waugh deferred to von Hahn's version. Either way, it was risk management in practice, limiting the downside, one of Waugh's mantras. After clearing customs, the three would board a forty-eight-minute commercial flight to Montevideo, where the company plane was parked. On that short flight to Uruguay no one said a word, von Hahn says. "It was all in the eyes. Holy shit, we're out of here."

At the airport in Montevideo, Scotia's Challenger jet was waiting (in Waugh's latter years as CEO, the bank purchased a Dassault Falcon 7X, which he says could fly non-stop from Toronto to Peru, eliminating the need to refuel in Central America). Upon boarding the Scotia jet there also wasn't a word said, according to von Hahn. Waugh, he recalls, sat at the front on the right. Shields sat at the back. Waugh said Shields grabbed a bottle of Black Label and filled his glass to the top. "We all did and gulped it all the way down."

"It was stressful," Waugh admitted, saying he didn't feel endangered personally. "That just went with the territory," he said, joking that that's why he earned what he did. "That's how I justified it . . . solved the problem that I was hired to do." Meantime, stress be damned. Waugh was still

Waugh, and he couldn't resist one last act, totally in character. "I arranged to have a couple cases of Argentinian wine [Malbec] put on the plane."

The sale of SBQ closed on September 3, 2002. Certain employees left Argentina that day for Santiago, Chile, working out of Scotiabank's Chilean bank, Sudamericano, for ten days. That way they would avoid a possible ban on leaving Argentina and be close by so they could return quickly to Buenos Aires if necessary. Earlier that year, though, there had been a restriction on the use of credit cards, creating a problem for refuelling Scotiabank's aircraft in Argentina. There was, however, a plan B. Employees of the bank in Chile would fly from Santiago to Buenos Aires, "each with just under US$2000 in cash," the legal maximum a person could then carry into Argentina. If necessary, that cash would be used to refuel the plane. However, plan B was never required. The credit card restriction was lifted, but soon enough it was simply too risky for the plane to land in Argentina.[33]

Despite the drama and danger, Donna Groskorth has an amusing memory in connection with the aircraft. At the end of one of Waugh's many visits to Argentina, he asked "some of us" to join him on a call with Godsoe. Towards the end of the discussion, Waugh "sort of looked around the table" with a smile, saying, "Peter, just one more thing. There might be a bit of a problem with the bank plane." Clearly, Groskorth said, Waugh was having fun at Godsoe's expense, and it was the only time she'd ever heard Godsoe swear. She recalled that Godsoe repeated Waugh's name. "Rick, Rick. I don't care about you, Rick. But get that goddam plane out of there." It was the last time the Scotiabank jet landed in Buenos Aires.

It was an embarrassment. Big banks in Canada aren't supposed to lose money, so it's news when one does. More than an embarrassment, it was a deeply felt setback for the head of international—Rick Waugh, who had been on a meteoric career path. "We lost the bank," he told me on September 21, 2011, during a fireside chat in front of a financial services audience at the Metro Toronto Convention Centre. Sagging in his chair as he said it, Waugh clearly still felt the anguish of a debacle that went back a dozen years. The loss also called into question the strategy of Canada's most international bank, with exposure to dozens of countries, many of which, at a passing glance, would not appear to be the kinds of places you'd want to do business. Godsoe, who had picked Argentina, "was making me take the heat," Waugh said in an interview for this book, but added he appreciated why. He understood their relationship and his own position in the bank's pecking order. The two executives were close and had worked together for three decades. But a country in *Waugh's* division was in dire circumstances. He was responsible for the bank there, and he wasn't the CEO yet. In later years at global gatherings, Waugh said, then Bank of Canada governor David Dodge (later a Scotia board member) and Prime Minister Stephen Harper would poke Argentina's leaders about what happened to Scotiabank there. Waugh's work under fire and his "undercover ops" ironically helped position him to be CEO. He'd handled a major international crisis. However, Four Seasons Hotels and Resorts founder Isadore Sharp, who was a board member when Waugh was selected as Godsoe's successor, said it wasn't just one factor that made him a unanimous choice, but everything he'd done up to that point.

While Argentina was certainly a financial loss, the outcome was arguably the best of a bad lot of possibilities. Most important, the bank's people had escaped physical harm and those most at risk got out. Von Hahn said there was one more dose of "the Rick magic." Quilmes had agreed to give the bank away, losing the right to sue the government. "Do not give it to them," Waugh said. "Don't withdraw our ability—Scotia's— in the international courts." International courts were crucial. A foreign bank, they reckoned, couldn't possibly win in an Argentinian court. By 2005, Scotiabank was demanding Argentina pay it back, charging that its actions in connection with Quilmes were "expropriatory and discriminatory." The case went to arbitration.[34] It took years to resolve. Dieter Jentsch, a top executive when Waugh was CEO and afterwards, said that on a visit to New York as head of international from 2012 to 2016 under Waugh's successor Brian Porter, he collected the last $100,000 owed to Scotiabank in the settlement.

It was a major decision to pursue a sovereign state when the bank operated in more than fifty others. But it did so on behalf of shareholders. As Waugh puts it, there was a settlement so Argentina could say it was never sued by a foreign bank, and Scotia could say it never sued a sovereign nation. And the bank's reputation remained intact in Latin America. It had, in fact, wanted to remain in Argentina. "Did I regret it?" Waugh asked rhetorically. "Sure."

Waugh gets revved up and slightly defensive when pushed about the risk Scotia took in certain international investments. In response, he would turn the tables and criticize his competitors in Canada. "The history of Canadian banks in the United States has been terrible," he says, leaning over the conference table in his foundation office, his voice rising. "You name me one Canadian bank—the TD was the one outlier—that did well in the US."[¶] Meanwhile, "'stupid Scotiabank' with fifty-one countries," he said, aping critics of BNS's strategy over the years. So, what if you had a few Argentinas in the dumpster? "You had forty other countries giving you sustainable revenue."

"This is not just Rick Waugh," he continued. "This is Peter Godsoe and Ced Ritchie and before him it was Bill Nicks." Meantime, Waugh's

---

¶ TD had been an outlier until 2024, when the US Justice Department announced TD Bank pled guilty to multiple felonies, including conspiring to violate the Bank Secrecy Act and commit money laundering. Attorney General Merrick Garland said TD Bank became the largest bank in US history to plead guilty to Bank Secrecy Act program failures and the first US bank in history to plead guilty to conspiracy to commit money laundering. It was fined US$3 billion and was subject to an asset cap at its American operation.

successor, Brian Porter, consolidated the number of international markets in which Scotia would focus during his tenure—Mexico, Colombia, Chile, and Peru—and Porter's successor, Scott Thomson, announced a new strategic plan in December 2023. The bank would increasingly direct capital to Canada, the United States, and Mexico, given bullish expectations about North American trade. Different eras, different approaches.

A postscript to the SBQ story: In a country with a history of corruption, one Argentinian who worked for the bank talked about things he heard during Quilmes's last days. "Your bosses in Canada are stupid," he was told. Don't they know it's possible to fix the problem with some money? The former banker said he was proud to tell the official to forget it. Von Hahn had a similar story. At one point back in Buenos Aires, von Hahn was in a meeting with a senior official from the Ministry of Labour and the head of the union for bank employees. At the ministry, the official suggested they go for a walk. So, they went outside and started walking. "You know, your problem can go away," the official said. "It's going to take some money. We think it could be a million dollars to each [of us], and your problem goes away." There it was—a brazen attempt at corruption in broad daylight.

Von Hahn says the proposed corrupt payment was in connection with Quilmes's difficulties with employees, not the central issues the bank faced. Either way, von Hahn says he was clear, telling the Argentinians that this wasn't how things were done at a bank that had been around since 1832. "We're exiting the country." Aside from it simply being wrong, the bank didn't want to be known as a company that pays when in a pinch. "We'd rather have a write-off of $700 million than pay somebody."

Former ambassador Tom MacDonald, who is also a student of Latin American history, has strong thoughts on governance. "Argentina," he emailed, "is an object lesson in the importance of good governance, and the consequences when it is lacking." Citing a century's worth of governance disasters, he said "it is not surprising that Argentines are highly cynical about politicians of any stripe and mistrustful of government institutions. They are notorious tax evaders, rationalizing it on the basis that any tax which they do pay will only go to line the pockets of corrupt politicians. . . . All of this feeds a vicious circle of low tax revenues and low internal investment, endemic government budget deficits and debt burdens, recurring devaluations and defaults, and further deterioration of confidence in domestic political and economic institutions. One of the more pernicious aspects of this is that it always hits hardest on the Argentine middle class." Meantime, politics still poisons Argentina's economy. As Waugh was told by Sergio Marchi, a Canadian cabinet minister with Argentinian heritage: "Don't go anywhere near them. They may make good wine, but their barrels are all rotten."

Waugh liked to say "Gimme a crisis." Somehow, he seemed wired to handle stress. When I suggested that perhaps he inherited that trait from his father, the firefighter, he dismissed the notion, saying it was a stretch. Separately, though, he did seem to possess an iron constitution. Peter Cardinal, who was at one point executive vice-president for Latin America, was once out for a meal with Waugh in Mexico, where he said the CEO blithely ate a dish featuring worms, with no apparent effect. Once a sickly, bedridden boy with tuberculosis, a potentially deadly disease that kept him from school for a year, Waugh had developed an inner toughness with energy and enthusiasm to spare. Also, early on, he knew he wouldn't be a good accountant, saying his strength was never numbers. Rather, what he could do and liked to do, he said, was read people and understand risk. He was good with others and understood markets from his time in investments and credit at the bank. Argentina, while undoubtedly stressful, motivated Waugh.

"There's good stress and bad stress," he explained, noting that what stresses him are things like remembering names or working the remote on his TV. "If there's a big problem to solve, I'm very good as a problem solver and knowing what I'm good at. Adding up numbers, I'm not good at." While the latter is a somewhat peculiar admission for a banker, Waugh seemed slightly irritated when pressed on the point, assuring me he "can add efficiently" and knows numbers well enough (others say he's a whiz with figures). His point was that solving big problems excited him—big issues and executing on those issues. "If I can impact something, it really interests me to do it."

Miguel Jarsun added another layer to the description of Waugh's demeanour. The first time he met him, he said Waugh also met with Jarsun's colleagues Claudio Hernandez and Eduardo Oteiza. "He was very polite and kind" as everything in Argentina was falling apart around them. "In that situation, not many people are able to be polite and kind." Jarsun said he knew many leaders in lesser crises who would have blown up. "In the case of Rick, everything was very calm." Tom MacDonald said Waugh "prioritized the human element of it." Perhaps the year-long affliction with tuberculosis had also fostered an empathetic side.

Colleagues said Waugh didn't have Godsoe's intellect and wasn't viewed as a visionary like Ritchie. But he could run things. Without the need to show how smart he was, he could figure out complex situations (like Argentina) on the ground and get people to follow him. He could go into a place he didn't know and quickly process what was going on, weigh risks, and make decisions. "I'd go out with the local country manager and have dinner and go over what's happening," Waugh says. "I didn't want a presentation from an economist." He was a banker for the times in which he operated.

Over a period of several years, some of what Scotia lost in Argentina was recovered. Most important, while some no doubt suffered psychological wounds, Quilmes and Scotiabank employees had been kept physically safe. Waugh's job was done in Argentina. Soon he would be running the whole bank. The Argentina crisis, it turned out, would be just a warm-up.

CHAPTER SEVEN

Every Country Needs a Good Bank

On January 15, 2003, approximately a year after the Argentina drama, Rick Waugh became president of Scotiabank, one rung from becoming chief executive officer. Peter Godsoe was still chairman and CEO and would be for the rest of the year. But Waugh had checked all the board's succession boxes. As Isadore Sharp said: "He was clearly the 100 percent vote on succeeding Peter." He'd lent to the biggest companies, he'd run the US division, he'd run wealth management, and he'd run international. However, boards don't want to blow it. To complete the transition, Waugh would be president for a year, the understudy, overseeing day-to-day operations as second-in-command (Bruce Birmingham had retired).

Despite everything else he'd done, though, Argentina was invaluable training because 2003 would bring another banking and economic trauma. Yet another country in Scotia's portfolio would be brought to its knees. But this time, it would result in a win for Scotiabank, for the country, and for Waugh. The imperilled nation was the Dominican Republic (DR), which is both Caribbean and Latin American, principal areas of Scotia's international division.

Not unlike Latin America, the Caribbean is also another galaxy when compared to banking in Canada. Starting with Jamaica in 1889, Scotia's earliest days involved financing the shipment of lumber and wheat in exchange for rum. During Waugh's tenure, the bank was in more than twenty countries in the West Indies with some 370 branches across the region.* The Caribbean, Waugh says, might not have been the bank's best source of revenue, but it was consistent and diversified risk. While dozens of small countries were time-consuming to manage, Godsoe, Waugh recalled, referred to the islands as "a chain of pearls." Out of twenty or so pearls, even if one or two went through periods of difficulty, there were eighteen others making money. "It was a portfolio of countries," Waugh says. "Each one on its own would not make any sense," but as a region "it produced predictable, sustainable profits that were significant to the bank. It could be several hundred million a year." Aside from financing hotels and resorts in the region,[1] Caribbean cruise lines would become part of the bank's business there.

Haiti may have been a rough pearl, but it was nonetheless part of the chain and occupied the western side of Hispaniola, the island it shares with the Dominican Republic. Waugh explains that developing countries, even those like Haiti, offered inexpensive entry and fat spreads (what a bank earns on loans versus what it must pay for deposits). "It can work," Waugh says. "We were the big bank in Haiti. *Who banks in Haiti?*" But he says BNS made money there. "And we were loved in Haiti," he says, adding that the employees were good people. That said, "I always assigned a country risk to all countries, including Canada and the US, [each has] a country risk."

---

* As of 2024, the bank's website said it had 294 branches in the Caribbean and Central America, employing ten thousand people, with 99 percent hired locally.

But in Haiti, country risk also meant knowing how to navigate in a dangerous nation. Waugh would get driven around with high security. The guard in his vehicle toted a machine gun and wore a three-piece suit. "At any time, I could take over the country," the character told Waugh. "*But I make too much money not taking over the country.*" Waugh refers to the guard as "the gangster." When socializing, ex-pats went only to each other's homes, because there was security. But Waugh says Scotia lent to legitimate customers in Haiti and was considered a safe bank.

When he was head of international, Waugh says, he'd promised Haiti's country manager he'd visit after being told that nobody from head office ever went. "It was a tough place to visit," he says. As a result, the country managers from Haiti would typically come to Toronto for meetings. But Waugh decided to go and flew in on the BNS jet (he said Godsoe was generous with the plane). He was picked up at the airport by the country manager. They drove in a Jeep with the guard—the gangster—and Waugh spent about four hours on the ground. The first order of business was meeting staff. En route to the meeting, however, the country manager informed him that in honour of Waugh's visit, he'd promised the staff something. "You need to pay them a whole month's bonus," he announced as a *fait accompli*.

"How much was that?" Waugh wanted to know. The answer was about $40,000 to cover the bonus for about thirty people. While Haiti's labour pool wasn't costly, Waugh maintained the bank paid well on the island. "Okay, we'll do it," he told the country manager. "We go in, and he makes the announcement. They literally cried," Waugh says. "I was a hero. So, I was happy."†

Cuba was another rich story in Scotia's Caribbean (and Latin American) history. The bank had been in Havana since 1906, just a few years after the Spanish-American War. The economy was modernizing,

---

† In 2017, under Waugh's successor Brian Porter, Scotiabank sold its operations in Haiti to Unibank.

there was American investment, and production of sugar and tobacco was growing. The manager in Cuba, F.W. Ross, recalled the loneliness, not knowing the language, "and where the fear of fever hovered over everything."[2] In 1959, however, communists under Fidel Castro seized power from the corrupt, mobster-riven regime of Fulgencio Batista. The closure of Scotia's operations on the island took time, however. The bank stopped lending money after the revolution but couldn't collect what it was owed. Scotiabank's official history says by December 1960 the bank's office in Havana was closed, and the Castro regime nationalized the banks at the start of 1961. Victor Cox, who then ran the bank there, was put in jail. After an appeal by the Canadian government, he was released and permitted to leave the country.[3]

Cuba's minister of finance and central bank governor was Ernesto "Che" Guevara. Born in Argentina, the cigar-smoking, beret-clad revolutionary became immortalized on T-shirts the world over. On September 17, 1960, Che told all foreign banks—including the Bank of Nova Scotia, Royal Bank of Canada, Chase Manhattan, Chemical Bank, and National Westminster Bank—they'd be confiscated and should leave immediately. Scotia's representative was G.A. Griffiths, nicknamed Bonzo. Retired Scotia executive Roy Scott wrote that Bonzo was the last foreign banker about to leave the room after Che issued his orders. Che didn't know it, but Bonzo held powerful cards. The Bank of Nova Scotia stored Cuba's gold—in Canada. As a result, Griffiths got in a jab, saying "over his shoulder that in view of this confiscation, Scotia would keep Cuba's gold." Guevara, Scott said, heard Griffiths's remark and called him back. They negotiated an orderly departure after the bank got full payment of the book value of all its assets on the island[4] (the bank's official history says "approximately" book value).

Shortly afterwards, Scott said, the bank transferred Cuba's gold to the London branch of Moscow Narodny Bank. Meantime, Cuba's central bank kept a US dollar account at Scotia in Toronto,[5] with the bank's history saying the Cuban government's deposits were "sizeable." Scotia fared better than most foreign banks, despite the disappearance of revenue and the loss of eight branches and two hundred jobs.[6] According to Scott, two Scotia bankers later assisted the country in setting up the foreign department of Banco Nacional de Cuba, which for several years occupied Scotia's old main branch building in Havana (now Banco Metropolitano). It still had the Bank of Nova Scotia name and crest on the floor.[7]

Revolutions and weak economies were not the only risks in the Caribbean. Storms also devastated islands. Solutions were often improvised and situations downright bizarre. In 2004, a Category 5 hurricane—Hurricane Ivan—decimated Grenada, destroying homes and crops. It also destroyed a prison, allowing convicts to escape. "There was chaos in the country," Waugh says, and the bank wanted to provide humanitarian aid, but the Red Cross was not operational. He said Scotia's country manager found a priest who could decide who most needed the money, and the nearby nation of Trinidad also sent assistance. Incredibly, he added, the bank had the only working car on the island. So "they [the Trinidadians] could have the bank car if they'd just watch over the house where the country manager was living and the branch. And it all worked out." Weather-related chaos was not unusual. Wendy Hannam, who was executive vice-president of international retail banking at the time, recalled a severe storm while visiting St. Maarten for the bank. Roads were washed out, and she described three inches of water on the floor of her hotel room. This was part of doing business in the West Indies.

The first place Waugh visited in the Caribbean as head of international was the Turks and Caicos. Relative to the pricey beach resorts of today, the island was still undeveloped. The airport, Waugh recalls, was bare bones. "They needed someone to come out and turn the [runway] lights on," he says, "so we could land." Waugh's wife, Lynne, had accompanied him, and they decided to spend the weekend there. In the morning, they walked out to the beach. Before they departed, they bought a two-bedroom apartment. "That got me a personal connection to the Caribbean." He has since become a significant investor in the country.

People often mention the world's longest undefended border between the United States and Canada—and the US/Mexico border is always controversial. But Waugh described the Caribbean as "the third border." He gained an appreciation of this via the likes of David Rockefeller. It's just a short boat ride from Nassau to Fort Lauderdale or from Cuba to Key West. Many of the islands are close, so flights are short. The Turks, Dominican, and Haiti form a triangle "all within a half hour." Jamaica was the other big connection, but its initial branch was destroyed in an earthquake in 1907.[8] As in Haiti, Waugh says, Scotiabank was known as "the safe bank" in Jamaica, and by far the largest.

Large Jamaican companies banked with Scotia. "We were an integral part of Jamaican society." During times of financial stress, when Jamaica received assistance from the International Monetary Fund, Scotiabank would co-operate locally. The IMF was on standby to assist countries in financial crisis, and Scotia would lend in Jamaican dollars and use Jamaican dollars to pay staff. A key rule operating internationally, Waugh emphasizes, is never to lend US dollars locally. Lend local dollars, he cautions, which can always be repaid by printing the local currency. "Never lend Jamaica USD 'cause you'll get burned," he says, calling the US dollar "the only world currency." It was a way for the bank to do business but mitigate risk. "Jamaica can always print money. Jamaican dollars." He says the bank never lost money there and "Jamaicans never lost their deposits."

As for the Dominican Republic, Scotiabank is the oldest bank there, opening its first branch in 1920. Geographically, the country has a jaw-dropping coastline, fringed by beaches with caramel-coloured sand. The island's verdant interior is broken up by protruding green hills. In towns, motorbikes and scooters weave and buzz around cars and each other like oversized insects. Their riders are mostly helmet-less. In Las Terranas on the northeast coast, a Scotiabank branch sits in a small strip mall, Plaza Rosada.

The Dominican occupies the eastern half of the island of Hispaniola and sits between Puerto Rico and Cuba. A nation of just over eleven million people, the DR is where Columbus landed in 1492. Since then, it's been occupied by the Spanish, French, Haitians, and Americans. The United States occupied the Dominican from 1916 to 1924, and again in 1965 during a civil war. The political history is one of multiple republics. For three decades, the DR was ruled by a murderous right-wing dictator, Rafael Trujillo, who executed sixty-seven thousand Haitians and amassed enormous wealth by controlling more than half of the country's arable land. He was assassinated in 1961. The first peaceful transfer of power occurred in 1978. The DR has also been ravaged by hurricanes and has been highly dependent on the sugar industry, creating a volatile economic structure, and one riddled with corruption. Waugh says it's a democracy, but with a handful of family-owned companies essentially running the economy.

For Scotiabank in the Dominican, the early days were raw. Roy Scott described how customers came into the bank barefoot. Scotia's Frank Irvine happened to mention it at a party and a decree then came down from Trujillo. The dictator ordered the bank's customers to "carry shoes." Customers took it literally, carrying their shoes into branches and putting them on the counter.[9]

There was more. According to the obituary of Edward Dennis Hunter, who spent twenty years at Scotia in the Dominican starting in 1946, a rebellion in 1966 required the closure of the Isabella Catholica branch because it was in a zone held by rebels. Nonetheless, the branch still operated—in a private home, the manager's residence, which was out of the line of fire. This novel solution did not go down well at head office. Hunter, who had risen to the position of manager, was called to Toronto, where Bill Nicks lit into him for not getting head office approval to open a bank branch in a house. Waugh calls Hunter "an icon" who had opened doors for him in New York. Even after Hunter retired, he reportedly still showed up at work.

According to Terry Fryett, who'd worked with both Ed Hunter and Waugh in New York, Hunter apparently had a close call with the dictator, Trujillo. After Hunter died, Cedric Ritchie was flying to the funeral and shared war stories about the late executive. He described Trujillo phoning Hunter.

"Ed, are you married?"

"No, Mr. President."

"Ed, I want you to meet my daughter."

"I'm sorry, sir, I'm not good enough for her," Hunter reportedly replied. After Hunter extricated himself from the call, Fryett said, he phoned Ritchie, who pulled him out of the country. More recently, Wendy Hannam said, "There was a lot of pride in the Scotia bankers there about how long we had been in the DR."

Being a major lender in these countries meant knowing not only the key families but also the heads of government. While Trujillo would phone up Ed Hunter, Waugh, due to the bank's history and significance in the Dominican, would pay his respects to the democratically elected president of the country. Typically, a top executive in the region who reported to Waugh would have an advance visit with the national leader, so each could be briefed before the meeting. "What do I have to do to make the gringo happy?" the Dominican's president would ask Waugh's executive in a light-hearted but respectful manner. Waugh says paying respects to the leaders of so many countries was time-consuming: "It was a real pain in the ass," but necessary given operations in more than fifty nations.

It turns out that in 2003—an extraordinarily trying year for the country and its financial system—much would be expected of the Dominicans if Scotia were to participate in what amounted to a bailout of a failed, fraud-riddled bank, and, in effect, a bailout of the country. Dominicans of a certain age will remember television commercials for a local bank that featured Sammy Sosa, the Dominican-born home-run hitter who sits ninth on the all-time homer list in Major League Baseball. The bank Sosa was advertising was Baninter, the nickname for Banco Intercontinental. Baninter had become the country's third-largest private bank during a comeback in the DR's economy in the late 1990s.[10]

In 2003, Baninter faltered after a multi-year bank fraud was uncovered, forcing the Dominican's central bank to step in to stanch the bleeding. However, it would not be enough. The size of the fraud—essentially, the use of two sets of books to pilfer $2.2 billion—constituted two-thirds of the national budget and 15 percent of annual GDP. The Dominican peso fell by half, public debt shot up, and inflation soared.[11] In addition, two other Dominican banks had to be restructured.[12]

The Baninter fraud had gone undetected since 1989, even by the bank's auditors. It was uncovered after a run on its deposits in 2002. The bank run led to a plan to merge Baninter with another bank in 2003, but the deal fell apart when the acquiring bank looked under the hood. As the *Wall Street Journal* reported, Baninter's "bookkeeping hid a 'vampire bank' inside Baninter—a complex system of secret accounts and corporate entities set up to spirit away assets." The bank had been growing deposits by paying significantly higher interest rates than other banks and heavily marketing those rates. "During hours when the bank was closed, a clandestine computer program streamed up to $100,000 a day out of legitimate accounts and into the hidden coffers," the *WSJ* reported. Baninter was primarily owned by a family that also owned significant media assets in the Dominican, including a prominent newspaper and radio and television stations. The owner, Ramón Buenaventura Báez Figueroa, whose great-grandfather had been the country's president in the 1800s, lived a lavish lifestyle and was close to the country's leaders.[13]

The impact of the Baninter fraud on the country was dire, and a central bank deposit guarantee wasn't sufficient to stabilize matters. The International Monetary Fund was needed, and along with the IMF and the central bank, Scotia was integral in conducting what amounted to a national bailout. Over a period of approximately six months, a deal would be negotiated that would see Scotia acquire Baninter assets (credit card operations and personal and commercial loans), thirty-five branches, and 460 employees. Each party played a role, with each depending on the other. Waugh says Scotia participated, with the guarantee of the central bank, conditional on IMF support, with the IMF's involvement conditional on Scotia's support. Both the IMF and Dominicans needed Scotia. "We orchestrated this," Waugh says, and "we had our choice of assets." That included choice real estate. Scotia executive Tim Hayward, who reckons he spent six to eight months there, picked those assets. By other accounts, Waugh was also directly involved in going through them and choosing. "They were beautiful offices," Waugh recalls.

Given the bank's broad international operations, Waugh says it was one of many situations Scotia faced in countries with corruption, where the bank had to step in with the IMF, but he said the Dominican was "by far the biggest." After departing as governor of the Bank of Canada, David Dodge sat on Scotia's board of directors. "Scotia was the IMF for the Caribbean," he said, "especially for the Jamaicans and for some of the smaller ECCB [Eastern Caribbean Central Bank] islands as well."

Nonetheless, the process started badly. Scotiabank's first meeting in the Dominican about acquiring Baninter was not a good one. It was early 2003 and three bankers from Scotia—Tim Hayward, Jim Meek, who headed up the bank in the DR, and one other—met at the country's central bank. According to Hayward, the meeting lasted about five minutes. "We didn't handle it well," Hayward said.

Hayward joined the bank in 1979, starting in audit, becoming deputy chief accountant and then chief auditor (he said he left that job as soon as he could). After a three-month stint at Harvard, Hayward began working on integrating acquisitions, including Montreal Trust, and oversaw due diligence on the purchase of Inverlat in Mexico, where he spent three and a half years. In 1999, he returned to Toronto and began working in the international division, run by Waugh. With his accumulated experience in finance, operations, systems, and mergers and acquisitions, Hayward was the point person on the 2003 negotiations between Scotiabank and the DR's central bank as well as the subsequent integration (he was executive vice-president and chief administrative officer of international banking).

In that brief initial meeting, Hayward said, one of the Scotia bankers "talked down" to the head of the central bank, who got miffed and kicked them out. "Jim Meek and I were cringing inwardly," he recalled. Of their overly direct and undiplomatic colleague, Hayward said "you can't tell a guy to shut up in the middle of a meeting." Fortunately, Peter Cardinal, Scotia's EVP of Latin America, "was invited back to reopen the door, which he did."

Scotia's reputation and long history in the country was what got the bank in the door. It was also their personnel on the ground. Ed Hunter, Scotia's top person there for years, was known as "the godfather of the DR." Hayward said the Dominicans had nicknamed Hunter "Il Papa," or "the Pope," indicating his and the bank's influential stature there. The country needed a respected foreign bank to solve a dire banking and economic problem. "The bank [Baninter] was completely overloaded, really bad loans," Hayward said. "The central bank had the responsibility to bail out Baninter and rescue it or arrange for it to be rescued. And fund the losses as a result."

The negotiations, which Hayward said began in early 2003, focused on a central issue. If Scotia took over Baninter, not only would there be loans to collect but also loans to write down to get to a sustainable state. The central bank would be responsible for paying for those writedowns.

The essential question was how to establish a value for the loans. Hayward described a push and pull to get the central bank to cover the true cost of the writedowns. In addition to taking over the loans, Scotia took over real estate. To secure what the bank lent, Waugh said, Scotia got local property. "We took over this building and that building." That included Baninter's head office.

Peter Cardinal met Rick Waugh in 1978. Cardinal was a high-school dropout from Ottawa who'd been with the bank since 1964, when he was twenty. He had been kicked out of school for a week for smoking and didn't go back. Luckily, two women came to his rescue, allowing him to build a forty-five-year banking career that saw him become executive vice-president in charge of Latin America. The first was his mother, who, after he got the boot from school, made an appointment for him to see the Scotia branch manager at Carling and Woodroffe in Ottawa. Cardinal pooh-poohed the idea but went. It was a Friday, and the manager said, "Can you start on Monday?" He did, fetching coffee and stamping cheques.

In 1966, Cardinal's wife followed in his mother's footsteps, enrolling him in a nighttime accounting course. When he told her he thought it would be a lot of work, she said, "I paid for it. You're taking it." There's a theme running through this volume's cast of characters, including Waugh: few of them liked accounting, but they held their noses and benefited from it. Despite his initial distaste, Cardinal became a certified general accountant.

After various pit stops across the bank, Cardinal ended up at the main branch in Toronto, where he became assistant manager and began learning about credit—the secret handshake at Scotia. It was there he encountered Waugh for the first time. "He had been parachuted in as another one of these instant bankers," Cardinal cracked. "I tried to train him, but he didn't take to training very well." Waugh irritated Cardinal on one account, in particular. There was a credit application from a textile company, and Cardinal said Waugh took it home and went through it with Lynne, who worked in retail for Simpsons. Cardinal said when Waugh brought it back, it was all marked up. Cardinal told him he wasn't too happy with meddling from home. Waugh laughs about it today.

Meantime, Peter Godsoe wanted Cardinal in Mexico. After the Mexican peso crisis in the 1990s, Scotia wanted to get more involved there. The bank already had a 10 percent interest in the Mexican bank Inverlat. So, Cardinal went and combed through the credit portfolios, but couldn't find any good loans except to government. He reported back to Toronto, saying, basically, "this pig ain't going to fly," which was not what they wanted to hear at King and Bay. Finally, a deal was struck to divide the bank into the good bank and the bad bank. Cardinal was put in charge of credit and Scotia had the option to take control, which it did. Given his credit chops and ability to speak Spanish, Cardinal was by 1999 chair and CEO for Mexico, and in 2003 became EVP for Latin America and the Spanish Caribbean. Not only was he in charge of Mexico but also Peru, Chile, Puerto Rico, Costa Rica, and the Dominican Republic.

This time frame intersected with the banking drama in the DR. While the Dominican was in an economic crisis due to Baninter and needed a solution, Scotiabank wanted more critical mass there. "They [the Dominicans] had a major, major problem with Baninter. And we had a major problem with critical mass in the country," said Cardinal. While Scotia was the oldest bank in the DR, it was nowhere near the largest. There was even talk, Cardinal said, of Scotia getting out of the Dominican—too much effort, too little payback. "We were like a pimple on an elephant." Waugh agreed that "we definitely needed the critical mass," meaning more scale to spread costs and heighten impact. The acquisition of Baninter would not only solve the issue but also be "on-strategy." Cardinal made a bet (a steak dinner) with Jim Meek that he could talk to the head of the central bank and get them onside with a Scotia solution.

"I'm here to help you," Cardinal said he told the central banker, a more diplomatic approach than Hayward's description of the bungled first meeting. Cardinal said it helped that he could describe to the Dominicans that Scotia had assisted the government of Mexico with Inverlat after that country's currency crisis, making it part of a viable Mexican banking system—which "really clicked his interest." Scotia would approach the DR in the same way. It worked.

"We had government reps on the review team," Cardinal said. "We wanted total transparency. We didn't want them to come back and say we screwed them." He said, "I opened the doors," which let Scotia kick the tires. "Jim Meek ran it, and he still owes me a steak dinner."

In the summer of 2003, Scotiabank's jet touched down at La Romana Casa de Campo International Airport in the Dominican Republic. Greeting the plane was Jim Meek, who'd been with the bank since 1966, when he started at a branch in Cornwall, Ontario, after leaving high school. Like Waugh, he'd started at the ground level. After moving to Ottawa for the bank, he'd taken receipt of physical securities as collateral for loans, and with his gold representative hat on, he'd gone down to the Bank of Canada to count gold bars. Over the years, he was moved to Jamaica to clean up the main branch operation, and then to Puerto Rico where he also had responsibilities in the Virgin Islands.

After several years back in Toronto, where he oversaw human resources for the international division, as well as working in the card department and managing Toronto-area branches, Meek was sent back to Latin America, specifically to Peru to be "country head." Scotia had purchased a minority stake in a Peruvian bank (Banco Sudamericano) in 1997, following the deadly years of Shining Path terrorism. That's where Meek met Waugh, then head of international.

Meek describes his family's first couple of months in Peru as "rocky." He and his wife, Tish, were looking to rent a house in a nice neighbourhood, only to be confronted with the sight of a couple of thugs throwing a rat into the car that was stopped in front of them at a traffic light. The passengers jumped out of the vehicle and the attackers then stole it. Separately, their niece was robbed while visiting. And their son Justin, also visiting before going back to college, was on his way home from a club when he was taken hostage at gunpoint by would-be thieves. "We drove around for a while they kept the gun on me, checking my pockets trying to find money," he wrote in an email to his parents, but he didn't have much with him. Fortunately, "after I don't know how long, I finally was let go."[14]

Despite such terrors, Waugh said, "Peru is a treasure," a "goldmine," and one of the better deals he and the bank did ("where there's a crisis there's an opportunity"). He recalled former Deutsche Bank CEO Joe Ackermann phoning him and asking, "How in the hell did you get that?" He said Ackermann said that if Scotia ever wanted to sell the Peruvian bank to call him.

Back in Toronto again, while overseeing the Caribbean region, Meek joked that in his office, he had a picture frame and two photos. One featured Godsoe, the other, Waugh. Whichever executive was visiting, that would be the photo in the frame that day. But on this day in the Dominican, he was out of the office, and it was Waugh disembarking the aircraft. He'd installed Meek to run the bank's Dominican operations that May, just as one of the biggest frauds in banking was coming to light, putting the nation at grave economic risk.

Because of Scotia's long-standing position in the Dominican and the Caribbean at large, Waugh said, "We were the obvious buyer." The government, according to Meek, wanted a well-known foreign bank involved to illustrate credibility and confidence to the IMF. Scotia's involvement also fit Waugh's playbook of uncovering opportunities in crisis. Baninter was a wounded duck; the bank could get it cheap and rehabilitate it. To protect itself, Scotia would participate via the Dominican's central bank. Meek was appointed to run the branches and integrate Baninter with the Scotia ops already there. Meantime, Waugh got intelligence about the DR from Edgar Dao, who owned a bank in Venezuela in which Scotia had purchased an interest. Dao had a home in Casa de Campo, the swanky enclave on the island's south shore where Scotia's jet landed the day Meek met him at the airport. Among others, Waugh got to know a prominent local family that was also a major customer of the bank. They provided Scotia with advice.

Waugh said the country's handful of controlling families each dominated a sector of the economy. One had the coffee company, one had the cement company, and so on. The bank was most certainly known to each of the families. "All of their kids worked for Scotiabank as summer jobs," Waugh said. As a result, the bank was "connected with the country's elite," and they were a helpful source of information on the ground. However, the family that owned Baninter as well as media outlets was not one of those families. Waugh confirmed Baninter was "offering deposits at rates that didn't make any sense to us," multiple points above what other banks were paying,[15] a clue that something had been amiss.

The IMF was declarative. "The failure of a large bank because of fraud has hurt confidence in the banking system," it said as part of the announcement of a two-year "Stand-By Arrangement" for the country that amounted to US$600 million. The quote was attributed to Agustín Carstens, deputy managing director and acting chairman. In 2010, Carstens became governor of the Bank of Mexico, and Waugh would later deal with him there.[‡] In its statement, the IMF did not refer directly to Scotiabank, but to "the resolution of Baninter, a solution for the problems of other weak banks." Waugh said, "We stepped

---

‡ Carstens declined an interview invitation.

up because the IMF wanted us to step up," adding, "we were written into the IMF agreement." The IMF wanted stability. Scotiabank would be the stabilizer.

The "resolution" was the takeover of Baninter in the autumn of 2003, more than doubling Scotia's presence on the island. But initially, it just stanched the bleeding of a deeply wounded economy. In 2002, GDP had grown 4.1 percent, capping a decade of positive economic growth. In 2003, the Dominican was in a deep recession, with GDP at -3 percent. The next year wasn't much better. Inflation in 2003 was 35 percent, after the peso fell by 42 percent.[16] The months of complex negotiations about the value of the loans, who'd cover them, and all the banking and legal minutiae were obviously crucial, but to Waugh, there was a more important issue. He had something he wanted to say to the president of the country.

When Scotia was ready to close the deal, the president's office called Meek's office. Waugh flew in to meet the president in Casa de Campo for a three-hour luncheon and tête-à-tête. While Lyford Cay in the Bahamas is known as an exclusive haunt for the English, Waugh described Casa de Campo as "the Lyford Cay for the Spanish speaking." Casa de Campo—meaning "country house"—sits on seven thousand acres of former sugar mill land, originally conceived and created in the 1970s by an American industrialist. Meek described the president flying in on a government helicopter from the palace and landing on the helipad at the foreign minister's home. "They didn't want it [the meeting] in Santo Domingo," Meek said, because you couldn't keep anything quiet. In Casa de Campo, they could keep it controlled and secure.

While Meek recalled five people being in attendance, the meeting was principally a discussion between the Dominican leader and Waugh. "If I said ten words in three hours, I would be lucky," Meek said. Even at the luncheon "I was asked to stand outside the door" when Waugh and the president spoke privately. Waugh described telling the president

Scotiabank would help and work with the IMF, but that it was important, as a Canadian bank, to be assured of good governance—rule of
law. "I told the president that this guy [who owned Baninter] had to go
to jail," as public proof of law and order. Meek said he was not present
for that part of the conversation. "I'm sure he did say it. I didn't hear it.
But I'm sure he did."

While the bank had leverage, it could not dictate the law, and Waugh
knew it. He said the president replied that if the courts issued a guilty
verdict, those responsible would go to jail. "If he's convicted, he'll go to
jail, which is as much as I could ask." Waugh was satisfied. "They needed
us. They needed a legitimate international bank," he said. "It was like a
stamp of approval from us, which would help with his negotiations
with the IMF." With the hit to the economy, the currency, and the central bank (not to mention inflation), the country needed IMF money.

Once the deal was consummated, "their bank [Baninter] was just
handed over to us," Meek said. The price was not disclosed, meaning it
was not material—an amount that would cause a reasonable investor to
revalue Scotia—and therefore not requiring disclosure. After the deal
was done, Meek said, "everybody [at the bank] was so co-operative."
They wanted to keep their jobs. Meek was made general manager of the
entire bank and took over Báez's luxurious office. On top of the six-
storey building was a helicopter landing pad for chopper rides to and
from luxury yachts and properties.

On October 21, 2007, Ramón Buenaventura Báez Figueroa was found
guilty of concealing information, including hiding records, prior legal
history, accounting books, and other relevant documents with the intent
to obstruct the oversight functions of the Superintendency of Banks.
Additionally, the court found he approved and executed operations
aimed at concealing or covering up the financial state of Banco Intercontinental. He was sentenced to ten years in prison and fined 2.5 million
Dominican pesos. An appeal was unsuccessful, although the appeal court

issued its own guilty ruling and upheld the lower court's sentence of ten years. Compensation to the Superintendency of Banks was set at 50,082,450.10 pesos, plus 18,743,000,000 pesos compensation to Banco Intercontinental, and 44,552,706,192 pesos to the central bank. The case went to the Supreme Court of Justice, which ruled on July 8, 2008, dismissing Báez's final appeal. On May 16, 2013, he signed a thirty-page co-operation agreement with the central bank, acknowledging his conviction was final and irrevocable. The recovery ordered by the state for damages amounts to 44.552 billion pesos (C$1.04 billion or US$734 million). Separately, among assets recovered were boats, helicopters, real estate, and media outlets—the latter recognized as assets of the bank. Báez acknowledged the final and binding nature of the judicial decisions related to the Baninter case. He abandoned a lawsuit against the central bank, the Superintendency of Banks, the Bank of Nova Scotia, and other parties, and permanently gave up any legal remedy, action, or claim. The central bank did not oppose his application for parole, supporting a conditional request without reducing or eliminating imposed penalties. Báez served approximately six years of the sentence. As of April 30, 2023—twenty years after the Baninter crisis—the balance of public funds to be recovered was 58,329,928,298.80 pesos,§ almost a billion US dollars, or C$1.4 billion.

Despite what Meek described as certain difficult moments, the bank became very profitable. Indeed, "It was a lot of risk taking, but we took the risk, and it turned out really well. He [Waugh] was tough, he was

---

§ In a November 5, 2023, interview on CDN (Dominican News Channel), Báez said, "Look, explaining what happened with Baninter, it's sometimes hard to explain. Baninter experienced extraordinary growth and also accumulated significant power through its media outlets, including its radio, television and newspapers. You know, all of that can lead to envy . . . People often think because you own media outlets, you must have ideas of becoming president or some other plan" (Julissa Cepedes, *Reporte Especial: 20 años después: Ramón Báez Figueroa, expresidente de BANINTER, en entrevista exclusiva* [interview with Ramón Figueroa Báez], CDN, November 5, 2023).

strong, he was fair, he was honest and a real delight to work with, a great leader." Waugh came up "through the school of Bell and Ritchie, very much hands-on credit, risk management. Rick inherited that," Cardinal said. "He's smart, he's a good negotiator. I found him a really good boss." While Cardinal said he didn't always agree with Waugh, he added that any disagreement "was more style than substance," adding a friendly barb about how talkative the CEO was.

While the negotiations were difficult and time-consuming because of the situation, Hayward described the Dominican central bankers as "decent" people. However, the closing of the deal was delayed by a mysterious incident. Shortly before the scheduled closing, there was a fire on the seventh floor of the bank's main building, where all the important records were kept. While it was mostly smoke damage, certain loan files burned. In a 2023 television interview, Báez said that computers and archives burned. "It was unreal," Hayward said. "That was the main real estate in the whole transaction." While it didn't come to anything, there was a worry that the fire was an attempt to sabotage the deal and could have a material impact.

Immediately, Scotia wondered whether it had an out, if necessary. While the closing was delayed to assess the damage, it did eventually go ahead. "The bank was so broken in terms of loan value," yet while the purchase price wasn't huge, Hayward said, "We didn't take it off their hands for nothing." A *Financial Times* article, citing a government source, said the price was at least $25 million. Báez stated in his televized interview that Scotia paid US$35 million for Baninter, and that the bank's building and land were worth that alone. He also said that six or seven months prior, Scotia had offered US$700 million for the bank. "Bullshit," Waugh says. "There's no way." He adds, "Why would we pay seven hundred million when we bought Peru for three hundred million?"¶ As for

---

¶ In 2005, Scotiabank paid $390 million to increase its bank holding in Peru after buying a minority interest eight years before. Peru has three times the population of the Dominican, and Scotiabank invested more there in 2008.

taking over Baninter, branch acquisition agreements signed on October 31 and November 7, 2003, between the Bank of Nova Scotia and Dominican authorities including the Central Bank of the Dominican Republic, the Liquidation Commission of Baninter, and the Superintendency of Banks show purchase prices of 6,556,427 Dominican pesos and 34,273,949.25 Dominican pesos respectively. They were signed by Jim Meek. But they only account for a portion of what Scotia purchased. There were at least three other agreements signed, including one for the credit-card portfolio. Tim Hayward recalled the total cost was around $30 million, roughly what was estimated by a Scotia insider in the DR.

The importance of Scotia's bailout was such that Hayward said the president of the country, Hipólito Mejía, was present for the closing. "Baninter could have taken the DR down," Hayward said, adding that the bailout saved the country. The failure of one central financial institution can have a devastating effect on a nation via the negative power of leverage. And while he wasn't party to the discussions, Hayward knew the bank had been assessing whether to exit certain Caribbean countries, possibly the DR. He agreed that the deal gave the bank the critical mass it needed. "Absolutely. It is the deal that bulked us up."

After the loss of the bank in Argentina, many key people there were offered jobs elsewhere in the Scotia system. Miguel Jarsun went to the Dominican Republic. When Waugh visited on one occasion, Jarsun recalled picking him up and driving him around. Waugh's style was to ask questions of those on the ground—the troops—over a beer, coffee in the morning, or in the car. On that ride, Jarsun recalled Waugh asking him what the bank's biggest exposure was. Mortgages, Jarsun told him. How much? Forty percent. That's a lot, Waugh responded. Jarsun said Waugh didn't say anything else, but the comment stuck with him and the operation in the Dominican subsequently diversified its exposures.

Because of the many jobs he'd done over the course of his career at the bank, Waugh said he knew where to go to get the answer to a particular question. "It was the people who knew the combination to the vault," he said. "It's the people who help you on the ground who can get you out of the problem."

On November 11, 2009, as part of the ninetieth-anniversary cele-bration of the bank's presence in the Dominican, Rick Waugh, along with the late Ed Hunter and the late Ariel Perez (both country heads) were awarded the DR's highest civilian honour for the role they and the bank played in the economy in the DR. Jim Meek's wife, Tish, sat between Waugh and the head of the DR's central bank, translating for the two. Waugh spoke, highlighting that Scotia was not only the oldest bank in the Dominican but also "the only foreign bank with retail opera-tions here." Over the bank's almost ninety years in the country, Waugh said, the bank had been "through many ups and downs—including natu-ral disasters—and, of course, more than a few economic downturns," and had continued to work with customers through good and tough times. He added that the bank remained committed "to supporting the long-term growth of the Dominican Republic." Certainly, more than twenty years later, the country is booming. With Argentina and the Dominican, Waugh had experienced two major banking crises. Argentina was about corruption, government mismanagement, and Scotia's questionable decision to invest there in the first place. The Dominican was rooted in fraud, with the perpetrator going to jail. The next—and biggest—crisis would be rooted in widespread greed, reprehensible behaviour, careless credit judgment, appalling risk management protocols, inscrutable financial instruments, lax and fragmented regulation, globalization of financial markets, and that old chestnut, fear of missing out. This time, though, the crisis wouldn't be contained by national borders. It would be worldwide.

CHAPTER EIGHT

Friday Afternoons Were the Worst

On December 3, 2003, with the Dominican crisis comfortably set-tled to Scotia's advantage, Waugh would add the title of chief executive officer to the president's position on his business card, completing an orderly transition following Godsoe's retirement. There were two other contenders for the job—Bob Chisholm and David Wilson—but the board had settled on Waugh. Chisholm and Wilson stayed on as vice-chairs for a time, with Wilson later becoming chair of the Ontario Securities Commission, the country's top markets regulator.

While running a global bank is never easy, in retrospect, the period from 2004 until the summer of 2007 was a relative cakewalk for Waugh. It was a few years after the dot-com crash and 9/11. Financial markets were frothy again. Each deal seemed bigger than the last, as debt piled up. In particular, the housing market in the United States was on fire. It was party time for anyone in finance. As the former chairman and CEO of Citigroup famously said in 2007, "As long as the music is playing, you've got to get up and dance," adding, "We're still dancing."[1] The problem is, you don't know when the music will stop, so you don't know when to sit down.

The music abruptly halted on August 9, 2007, when French bank BNP Paribas froze €1.6 billion of funds invested in US mortgages. The Dow Jones Industrial Average fell 2.8 percent. It was just the beginning. A day later, there was a coordinated response by central banks in Europe, Canada, the United States, Japan, and Australia to inject cash into the global financial system to prevent a credit freeze. But markets the world over had by then become so interconnected—so globalized—that what would follow for the next eighteen months was the equivalent of a financial COVID-19. Major banks—in particular, American and European banks—had let their risk guards down. Lending had been loose, and they'd exposed themselves to the bug of complex financial engineering, which would spread. Worsening in 2008, reaching a fever in autumn of that year, and then extending into 2009, it would be the gravest financial crisis since the Great Depression. While Argentina and to a lesser extent the Dominican were challenges for Waugh and Scotiabank, they would pale in comparison. This was global. Storied financial institutions would fail, central banks would resort to extraordinary measures to keep the banking system functional, and governments would inject previously unthinkable amounts of stimulus to prevent a replay of the 1930s. Canadian banks had generally not been reckless in the preceding years and would survive and ultimately prosper, but the period was not without nerve-wracking days and nights. It was the most trying situation Waugh and his generation of bankers would face.

The situation was such that his office kept a one-page chart handy. It listed all the telephone numbers for each of the big five Canadian bank CEOs. The list included home phones, cellphones, car phones, cottage phones, farm phones, Florida condo phones, office fax numbers, home fax numbers, and the phone numbers of executive assistants. One bank

CEO had eleven phone numbers, not including three for his executive assistant. Waugh could find whoever he needed whenever he needed them—and during the crisis, communication was like breathing. Banks not only lend to customers but also lend to each other, and have an extensive range of funding needs and commitments with varying timelines. A payment needs to go here. Another needs to go there. One of the terrifying realities of what became known as the Great Recession was that many global banks stopped lending to each other. Badly infected securities, filled with curdled pools of bad housing loans, had been sold to financial institutions around the world. Those securities were suddenly viewed as poor collateral for interbank lending. You want to borrow from us and give us collateral like that—bonds stuffed with sick mortgages? Forget it. Trust is the essential currency in banking, and it had evaporated. Liquidity dried up.

The disturbances in the summer and fall of 2007 were the chest pains that would presage a near–financial cardiac arrest in the fall of 2008 with the bankruptcy of Lehman Brothers. A years-long buildup of bad debts was blocking financial arteries. These bad debts were centred in the American housing market, but they had been spread around the world to banks and other financial institutions. Mortgages emanating from the United States—including subprime mortgages whose borrowers had little or no capacity to pay interest—had been bundled up by the hundreds of thousands into securities and sold to institutions globally as investments. The process is known as securitization. Mortgage-backed securities, a type of bond, had been a staple of the American financial system for decades, income-generating investments to be sold so that more credit could be provided. But over time, the asset quality inside those securities—the mortgages themselves—deteriorated. Because banks lend to each other to manage their short-term needs, they need assurance they're lending against sturdy assets. A built-in assumption in mortgage securitization was that housing prices would keep rising. But when that stopped and many people couldn't make their payments, the collateral looked weak. Fear replaced confidence.

"I was seeing definite indications that there were troubles internationally," Waugh says. As the crisis was building, Waugh noticed a shift when he attended international meetings, tension exhibited by several participants. He'd be in a room with twenty people at dinner and "there was obviously concern that the world was not a friendly place." Again, Waugh talked up what he viewed as one of his strengths. "I'm good at reading people." Along with that confidence was a career spent assessing and measuring risk—the downside first—going back to his earliest years at the bank in the investment department, managing the bank's securities portfolio. "And I was good at it."

Waugh recalls a meeting of the Institute of International Finance (IIF), a global industry lobby group with some four hundred members from sixty countries. There were participants from Ireland and Iceland, where there were severe financial stresses. "I could just see through the body language of the CEOs at those banks that something was going on." He says he was not party to what was happening at specific international banks, but during this period, "I remember phoning internally our Treasury [department]. I remember my words. 'I don't know what's going on, but make sure we have lots of liquidity.'"

Calculating the liquidity position of a bank is complicated. It's dependent on the positions the bank is taking and the bank's total assets. Liquidity changes. The world's pre-eminent central bank, the Federal Reserve in the United States, explains the difference between liquidity and capital: "Liquidity is a measure of the cash and other assets banks have available to quickly pay bills and meet short-term business and financial obligations. Capital is a measure of the resources banks have to absorb losses . . . Capital is the difference between all of a firm's assets and its liabilities. Capital acts as a financial cushion to absorb losses. The value of a firm's assets must exceed its liabilities for it to remain solvent."[2]

Certain assets a bank has, though, may not be readily converted into cash. For a bank, loans are assets designed to earn or generate income, but are not necessarily liquid. If a loan is paid back, it's a source of liquidity. If a loan is made, that depletes liquidity, and a bank's loans are dynamic, changing. Government bonds held by banks are also classified as assets and may be sold on the market, although market values fluctuate. Government securities in a financially stable country like Canada are generally considered to be a source of liquidity. However, assets such as real estate can take more time to sell and are therefore less liquid, even though they might be excellent assets. Then there are trading positions involving securities or market instruments, potentially more complex. Are those positions easily or advantageously closed or not? How difficult was it to value certain financial products which were central to the crisis? Algorithms used in trading activities add another layer of complexity to valuing assets and furnishing liquidity. "That's when you have to use judgment and common sense," Waugh said. There is also the issue of time. What are the short-term obligations? Fifteen days is different than thirty days, which is different than three months.

Monitoring liquidity closer than Waugh was Scotiabank's treasurer, the highly respected Bob Brooks, a key behind-the-scenes figure. Born in Saskatchewan to immigrant parents (an Irish Protestant mother and Ukrainian Jewish father), Brooks was set to retire in 2007 when Waugh asked him to postpone. He'd joined Scotia in 1968 as one of the bank's first MBAs. After five years at Scotia, including time in the IT department, which top executive Gordon Bell told him was one of the stupidest moves he could have made, Brooks was made chief accountant of Scotiabank at just twenty-nine years old, reporting to Bob MacIntosh. MacIntosh, who'd also steered a young Rick Waugh, was the closest person Brooks had to a mentor at the bank.

Like Waugh, though, Brooks was yet another banker who didn't like accounting. In fact, he'd been part of the controller group, working cheek by jowl with the accountants. Brooks said he and his fellow controllers looked down on the accountants as bean counters, green-eyeshade types. Controllers had fun—fun to Brooks, at least. Controllers ran the management information systems and profit planning, while accounting was a bore. So, Brooks said he didn't want the job, which resulted in a stern lecture from—once again—Gordon Bell about why he'd better take the job. Being chief accountant was a big deal, a stepping stone. After all, the CEO, Cedric Ritchie, had held the position. So, Brooks took the job. In the late 1980s, he moved to the capital markets side, just as derivatives were beginning to blossom as financial products and evolving into a mind-boggling market of their own. (They would also be central to the spread of the crisis.) Eventually, the group treasurer position Brooks held was created under Godsoe.

The role of treasurer at a bank is critical. Brooks described it as managing the balance sheet to ensure the term structure and interest rate structure of the assets and liabilities are matched as best as can be. "Banks borrow short and lend long in interest rate terms," he said but the extent of that must be managed. You also don't want to use one currency (say US dollars) to make loans in another currency (say the Japanese yen), which would create added risk. Aside from deposits, some portion of the bank is funded via the sale of commercial paper, issued by the institution to fund short-term needs. The terms are in days or months, generally less than a year. The paper is a borrowing instrument that pays interest to the buyer. Ideally, the paper is "rolling over" regularly, with the buyer continuing to purchase it when the term is up, without any disruptions. Liquidity is required to make up for any deficiencies in the event a bank is having trouble borrowing short or rolling over that paper. One way to ensure liquidity is to make sure part of the asset base is easy to sell in a hurry—liquid. In simple terms, it's the rainy-day fund if there's a cash-flow problem or an opportunity arises to lend money fast.

A significant learning from the crisis was that prior regulatory focus was on credit risk or operational risk, not liquidity risk. "When companies fail, it's because they run out of cash," Brooks said. "Banks are no different." On this, he and Waugh were on the same page. Brooks contended that most of the guardrails ultimately mandated by regulators had already been instituted at Scotia, self-imposed rules. To illustrate, he compared the bank's view of Canada versus the United States. Canada, due to a vast branch network, had retail funding through deposits that "isn't going away in a hurry." In Canada, therefore, the bank knew its funding was secure, so the rainy-day fund could be smaller. But in the United States, where it didn't have branches and retail funding, Brooks said the bank would keep significantly more liquidity—20 percent of the size of the balance sheet in the United States.

Brooks, like Waugh, had been through the liquidity crisis and bank run in Argentina, and they'd each also been through the asset-backed commercial paper (ABCP) freeze-up in Canada at the outset of the financial crisis (more on that later). They were battle tested. But this crisis was different. It was global, huge, and a mortal threat to the world financial system. Major players at the bank recall different areas of worry. Brooks said the biggest specific issue for Scotiabank was its very large loan book in the United States. Godsoe and Waugh had built up that business, lending to large American companies. As a result of the subprime mortgage crisis, US-dollar liquidity was drying up as anxious players withdrew from the market. Whatever cash they had, they were hoarding. Meantime, Brooks said, Scotia was sitting with "illiquid corporate loans." The American borrowers were big, such as real estate development companies, but Brooks said the bank did not have "a natural funding source for US dollars," which it needed constantly. In Canada, it had a marvellous funding source, a branch network with depositors. It didn't have that in the States.

Brooks described how, in the United States, Scotia had to fund through commercial paper and certificates of deposit (CDs, the American equivalent of Canadian guaranteed investment certificates, or GICs). He said he had previously overseen those operations and that he'd had confrontations with Waugh because Brooks's team needed access to the American companies that borrowed from Scotia to also raise deposits from them. "Rick was very jealous of his relationships," Brooks said, describing several heated arguments between them. On hearing this, Waugh pushed back. "I had a lot of other things to do than roll over a two-million-dollar CD. And that was his job, and he was very good at it and that's why I asked him to stay. I needed him to do that job. I didn't want to do his job. Those were the arguments."

When it came to the financial crisis, Brooks said, "I started monitoring that book on a daily basis." What he saw was that "the terms kept shrinking." One-hundred-and-eighty-day deposits became ninety-day deposits. Ninety-day deposits became thirty-day deposits. To Brooks, this was a warning sign that the bank might not be able to fund the loan book. Scheduled to retire at the end of 2007, Brooks told Waugh he'd stay on for one more year, "but only one more."

His characterization of the day-to-day management during the financial crisis was chilling. "Funding the bank was an enormous problem," Brooks said. "We didn't know from day-to-day whether we could roll our deposits." The saviour, he said, was the Federal Reserve in the United States, which "treated us like an American bank," allowing Scotia to borrow from the central bank. Brooks stressed that it wasn't just Scotia—other Canadian banks did this as well—and that it was a regular occurrence. "I think we did it non-stop for months."* Indeed, Fed data gathered through extensive research by Bloomberg showed that between August 2007 and April 2010, there were twenty-one thousand loans to banks totalling as much as $1.2 trillion.[3] Given the interconnectedness of global financial institutions and reliance on US dollars, banks around the world borrowed, including a German commercial property lender. The big five Canadian banks borrowed billions, with Scotia topping the list of the number of days borrowing—798 versus 679 for TD, 588 for RBC, 462 for BMO, and 364 for CIBC. TD had the highest daily balance of $2.3 billion—it was a bigger bank in the States—while Scotia averaged $1.9 billion and RBC $1.8 billion. Scotia's peak amount of loans was $9.5 billion, versus $6.9 billion for RBC and $6.6 billion for TD. Both BMO and CIBC's peaks were much lower, approximately $2 billion. Top US banks borrowed in the $90 to $100 billion range.[4]

Stephen Hart, who'd been chief credit officer and later chief risk officer, confirmed Brooks's description. "The treasury area suddenly became the most important area of the bank," he said. "Stuff that used to roll over on a thirty- or ninety-day basis, they were rolling one day at a time." Hart said there was a worry that big depositors might not re-up. He cited the example of an Asian central bank having half a billion dollars on deposit with the bank. "Instead of calling clients [borrowers], you're calling depositors," Hart said. Because Scotia stored a lot of gold for central banks, sovereigns trusted the bank with some of their cash.

---

* BMO's Bill Downe said that with its substantial branch network in the United States, his bank had a natural US dollar funding source. After TD closed its acquisition of Commerce Bancorp on March 31, 2008—just two weeks after US investment bank Bear Stearns faltered—I interviewed TD's CEO Ed Clark and asked for his worst-case scenarios, given the liquidity crisis witnessed at Bear. I incorporated his answer in *Banking on America:* "He indicated that TD had modelled for a total shutdown of the markets, meaning the bank couldn't borrow for the next six months . . . 'We survive it, we do well,' was his calm reply" (159).

While Waugh would not reveal names of customers, he said, "There would have been sovereigns for sure because we were an international bank." The bank's country managers would solicit deposits from the local governments where they operated. Scotiabank was also marketing to the biggest American companies to see whether they had cash to deposit with the bank. "I personally called on Boeing to market to them," Brooks said. Besides sovereigns and large corporations, major private equity firms and hedge funds were depositors as well.

The scale of this crisis was simply not in the bank's playbook. "We tested it once or twice so we knew the mechanics should it ever be necessary. But we never thought it [would be]," Brooks said, adding, "This whole thing was a US dollar thing." He said the European banks that failed did so because of their US exposure. In normal times, there was a foreign exchange market to swap Canadian dollars into American, but that had also dried up. "It was a complete dry-up of US dollar liquidity on a global basis," he said. "So yeah, it was day-to-day." No trust, no transactions, no liquidity. Safety became paramount. Anyone with cash held on to it or parked it in sovereign debt like US treasury bonds, which, next to cash, have been regarded as the least risky financial asset. Sylvia Chrominska, then head of human resources, said Brooks was "on the phone 24/7 trying to figure out what the hell to do."

Meanwhile, at one point during the crisis, certain members of the executive team were talking about the great lending opportunities being served up because of the market dislocation. Brooks recalled screaming that they were in the middle of a liquidity crisis, and they didn't have any money to lend. He said Waugh supported him. "He definitely understood that [liquidity] was the biggest challenge," even though Waugh was a "lending guy" himself. Brooks also said he spent a lot of time on the phone with a deputy governor of the Bank of Canada discussing the idea of a swap arrangement with the Fed, so Scotia could pledge its Canadian balance sheet to them to receive US dollars in return. It had been a daily issue of survival for banks, not unique to Scotia. "This had been so difficult, so stressful. And there was no end in sight." Many a night, Brooks said, he went home wondering "Is it going to roll tomorrow." Would there be enough cash? Then-CEO of BMO Bill Downe said, "A bank that had a very high wholesale deposit ratio, and a lot of it was in US dollars, would have had some sleepless nights." Because the price of US dollars was high and availability low, he said Brooks "probably had a heart attack at least once every twenty-four hours." Despite any arguments, Waugh greatly valued Brooks's battle scars and ability. After all, he'd convinced Brooks, revered by many, to stay on to help steer a safe passage through a financial cyclone.

If treasury was the engine room of the bank, where Brooks had to ensure there was enough liquidity to keep the boiler firing, the ship's bridge, where Waugh stood, afforded another view. While US dollar funding was crucial given the size of Scotiabank's loan commitments south of the border, it was not lost on Waugh that the biggest part of the bank was Canadian, with Canadian customers and Canadian capital, and subject to Canadian regulation. The foundation of the Canadian business was the stability of retail deposits, even though Scotia's share of the market was then the smallest of the big five Canadian banks. Despite that, retail deposits were the bedrock. There were also mortgages, which had been issued via sound lending practices, typically with a 50 percent loan-to-value ratio—powerful assets with "contained" risk. Waugh, in addition to ensuring the bank's overall liquidity via Brooks's assignment, was focused on other specifics: Would the Bank of Canada make liquidity available if needed, and would each of the other major Canadian banks lend to Scotia and each other, given the freeze-up in interbank lending in other parts of the world?

On the first issue, Waugh knew Scotia's mortgage portfolio was sound. Not only was that vital to the bank's stability, but it was also key to securing liquidity from Ottawa, if necessary.

Regarding Brooks's concerns about major deposits rolling over and US dollar funding, Waugh said he didn't doubt at all that those were problems. But it wasn't what kept him up at night. His biggest concern was in retail customer deposits, which is why the bank was allowed to lever approximately twenty times in Canada. If retail deposits are stable, you only have to hold a small percentage and you can lend the rest. Say the bank has $100 in deposits, it can lend $95. "It depends what your view is. I'm at the top. I see the whole picture." It's not only being in the room, he said, but it's also "the room you're in"—frequently with other bank CEOs, the central bank, the Finance Ministry, and regulator giving him a broad perspective.

While Waugh conceded it would have been rough for Brooks, he said he didn't think the US funding issue could have imperilled or unravelled the bank. Waugh was convinced the bank had sufficient diversification in funding and had high-quality assets, like residential mortgages. Others who had granular knowledge of the bank's balance sheet agreed. There wasn't evidence of the imprudent, dumb moves made by US and European banks. Furthermore, he had a different mandate. While the first order of business was survival, as CEO, shareholder returns were also top of mind.

On October 31, 2008, Brooks left the bank. "I was just beat," he said. Waugh, Brooks said, begged him to stay, but he'd spent forty years at Scotia, and he'd had enough. It was a profound loss for the bank, given Brooks's operating abilities and credibility on "the street." Brooks died in November 2024, a little over nine months after being interviewed for this book. His obituary in the *Globe and Mail* said: "As a Junior A hockey goalie, Bob broke his nose three times, earning himself a reputation as 'the guy who'd get the job done.'"[5] By all accounts, he did that at Scotia.

Along with Bob Brooks, another key figure during the crisis, and Waugh's tenure as CEO, was Sabi Marwah. Marwah came to Canada in the late

1970s, carrying a backpack and looking for a job. His brother was already in Canada and sponsored him. Marwah was born in Asansol, 240 kilometres from Kolkata (Calcutta) in the coal mining district of West Bengal. He studied economics in Kolkata and then Delhi, earning a master's and starting a PhD, which he never finished. He did, however, get an MBA in finance from UCLA. While there, he made spending money playing bridge. One of his bridge partners was Omar Sharif, star of *Doctor Zhivago* and nominated for an Oscar for his role in *Lawrence of Arabia.*

With an uncanny knack for numbers and what they mean, Marwah wanted to work as a trader. "But it was a white man's world," he said. "I was the only turban guy on Bay Street, for god's sake. Not just at Scotiabank." There might have been one or two others, but Marwah's point was made. After four months as a programmer at Manulife, he spent thirty-six years immersed in finance at Scotiabank after being hired by Brooks, then chief accountant. Along with audit, Marwah said, finance is a part of the bank where you "get to see everything." In his early forties, he said, he became an executive vice-president of the bank.

He doesn't remember when he met Waugh, but he became chief financial officer in 2001 when Waugh was still running international. The two travelled extensively—to South America and Asia—given the bank's appetite for foreign acquisitions. Eventually, Marwah would become Waugh's trusted number two as chief operating officer. Along with Waugh, he also promoted the bank's frugal, cost-conscious culture. Outright calling the bank "cheap" was a running joke, but they meant it. Fellow executive Dieter Jentsch, who'd started at the bank in the 1980s managing small branches in BC logging country, said Marwah, who made millions of dollars a year, lived humbly and drove a Honda Accord.[†]

---

† On Fridays, loggers cashed their paycheques, but the branch in Pemberton didn't have enough cash, and Jentsch couldn't get enough until the next day. So, paper bag in hand, he went to the town bar, a lender of last resort and source of liquidity, if you will. The bar would be depositing its till at Jentsch's branch anyway, so he asked for it early to cash the loggers' cheques.

Jentsch described the car being in "shabby" shape. Disputing that he was frugal, Marwah says he "lived a normal life" and "felt the bank was managing somebody else's money." Despite his responsible nature, a profile in the *Globe and Mail* highlighted his fondness for office pranks to lighten the mood.

But Marwah observed that following the hell of Argentina, the bank had to pay more attention to macroeconomic risks in countries where it operated. There wasn't just borrower risk or company risk, there was country risk. For most bankers in the first decade of the 2000s, it would have been outlandish to suggest *the United States* could pose the planet's greatest financial risk. Unlike Waugh, who speaks in a ramshackle, congenial gush of consciousness, Marwah is eloquent and precise. He was the key finance person for three CEOs, and readily compared their approaches. "[Ced] Ritchie and [Gordon] Bell ran the bank by fear. Peter [Godsoe] came along, and he ran it by intellect. And Rick came along and ran it by people. Three different styles of management." Waugh, he says, was very good with people. That didn't mean he wasn't tough or stubborn. While Godsoe was known for arguing, "Rick and me used to argue like crazy the first couple of years, especially on financial issues." He said Waugh would debate with him about certain accounting requirements. It's stupid, Waugh would say. It doesn't matter, Marwah would fire back—it's the rule! Although it was confrontational, he said he never felt insecure in his job, even with Godsoe, who was "so smart, so goddammed smart."

While both had witnessed the LDC crisis and Argentina, the greatest test faced by Waugh and Marwah would be the financial crisis. "Most economic downturns are a credit crisis that eventually results in a liquidity crisis," Marwah said. But 2008, he explained, was the reverse—a liquidity crisis that caused a credit crisis. It was the first time he witnessed that in what was by then a thirty-year career. "Liquidity dried up and the dominoes started falling." All the off-balance sheet instruments, he said, assumed that ample liquidity would always be available. "But that assumption turned out to be false." Securities had been created, packed full of mortgages, many of which were subprime or bad loans. The assumption Marwah referenced was that these products could be sold and resold, creating liquidity. When it became clear they were littered with bad mortgages, the market for them died. There were no buyers, and this created a funding problem for banks. Marwah said he'll never forget the day Brooks came into his office saying, "We've got a problem." The funding difficulty had begun. Marwah, who said the treasurer was one of the smartest people he's ever met, recalled Brooks saying to him, "You and me, [we've] got to go talk to Rick."

Of the major Canadian banks, Marwah said, Scotia was the most reliant on wholesale funding—from corporate or government clients—rather than retail deposits.‡ The bank was a large corporate lender, but its retail deposit base wasn't as large as those of the other Canadian banks because of its historically later entry into the country's largest deposit regions. The wholesale reliance was a structural issue, "chronic" in Waugh's words.

"It's probably been a structural problem for the fifty years before I was around," Waugh says. It developed that way, he explains, due to the bank's desire to grow and expand internationally. The push was for the bank to lend. Ritchie was known to direct his staff to put loans on the books, telling them he'd worry about securing funding via the wholesale desk—the markets. Waugh said he and Godsoe were similar. "A good CEO says let me and head office take care of funding. You go out and get the business

---

‡ *Bank of Canada Review* defines wholesale funding as "typically obtained directly from institutional investors in financial markets" through a range of instruments, including short- to long-term maturities and in different currencies. While money can be raised quickly via markets, "cost and availability of wholesale funding depend on conditions in global financial markets, thus making it less stable relative to retail and commercial deposits" (Truno, Matthieu, Andriy Stolyarov, Danny Auger, and Michel Assaf. "Wholesale Funding of the Big Six Canadian Banks." *Bank of Canada Review*, Spring 2017).

and we'll find a way of funding it." He says the bank had dealt with this successfully for a century, even during 2008. Besides, "you have to deal with the deck you've been dealt." Changing the bank's deck, he says, would have been at great cost to shareholders. "We could be the most liquid bank in the world and have no return on equity—do you think our shareholders would like that?"

Nonetheless, he conceded that during the crisis the bank was perhaps more exposed than others, but that it was manageable. There were daily meetings about capital, liquidity, and how the exposures were managed. Terms were extended, unutilized credit lines were pulled back, and the size of the trading book that required wholesale funding was cut back, making the bank less vulnerable. Marwah said this was not unique to Scotia—all the banks were doing similar things. He said Waugh's greatest contribution was that "he was very, very in tune with our risk profile." Marwah said, "He knew it better than me."

While the bank's risk team was looking for potentially uncomfortable exposures and how to manage them, Marwah's concern was on the global macro side, where there was little control. He'd say to Waugh, "What will happen if there's a run on Citibank in Mexico?" Scotiabank had a large exposure to Mexico with its division there, so if there was a bank run on another major institution, would Scotia face the same? His concerns lay outside of the bank, with "the exogenous factors of the environment that we're operating in, especially internationally." One need look no further than what occurred in Argentina—the bank was fine; the macroeconomic environment was not. Scotia was operating in so many countries, and most of them were locally funded, but there were contingency plans if his worst-case scenario became a reality.

When asked whether he shared Marwah's concern, Waugh says such a scenario in Mexico could have been handled. "As CEO, I have access to other resources. I have (the) total toolbox available to a CEO of a major international bank, which is significant." He says he could marshal an entire management team of twenty executive vice-presidents. While discussing this, he projected a steely calm. He was the one who could talk to regulators or the board. "I as CEO can make it a small room or a big room." As well, international problems could be managed, he continues, because the bank was so well respected globally. After all, in the early 1990s the government of Mexico called on Scotiabank to manage one of the country's banks out of a crisis. Later, Scotia bought it and has run it successfully. Also, hadn't BNS been brought in to bail out the Dominican? Waugh may indeed be right, but he may also have been exhibiting the overweening confidence of a successful CEO. He'd been a prudent, motivating leader, and knew how to run his bank. But while Waugh and his team may have been among the world's best risk managers, a roiling sea is bigger than any ship, and any ship can founder in an angry macro ocean.

However, as witnessed by others in Argentina, a calm demeanour was one of Waugh's strengths as CEO. Aside from managing through people and teams, "I view that as one of the most fundamental things of my job," he says—to handle a crisis in a measured way. "If the guy at the top is ranting and raving, you gotta wonder." Also, one of his management maxims is "don't hide from a crisis."

One of Waugh's steelier decisions during the crisis was being the only big five Canadian bank to not issue stock to increase the bank's capital, a buffer against losses. Marwah said "there was enormous pressure" to do so from analysts and the board. Other banks had issued stock at low prices, but by doing so had diluted existing shareholders' holdings. "Everybody had done it, and nobody would have batted an eyelid if we had done the same," Marwah recalls. But Waugh says Scotia didn't need to, and thereby saved shareholders the dilution by not following the pack. "We took a lot of heat from everyone." Marwah said Waugh appeared exceedingly calm throughout the period, a calmness that exceeded his own expectations. Meanwhile, the board was poking. Privately, a board member came to Marwah, saying, "Sabi, what do you really think?" The person was a "very thoughtful" long-serving director, and they met in Marwah's conference room. "It was a very stressful time," Marwah says, "and I told him I agreed with Rick," that he trusted Waugh's judgment on the issue. It was "not the answer he [the director] wanted to hear at the time. The board was very nervous." As the former CFO[§], the instinct would have been to issue equity—i.e., issue more shares in the company to raise money via the stock market—but Marwah lined up with Waugh as a team to say no. While the dilution was avoided, he had to be the front man, defending the decision to analysts, rating agencies, and shareholders who questioned the prudence of not raising more capital.

Meanwhile, there were regular meetings with staff, analysts, and the top ten shareholders to assure them the bank was safe and solvent. Given what was occurring in the United States, there was, understandably, palpable anxiety. Despite the steady public stance, Marwah says his stomach churned for months. "We were telling everybody outside, 'Things are fine, things are fine.' Because that's our job. Inside, your stomach would churn saying, 'Shit, Marwah, why are you out there telling everybody? This could go off the rails.'"

He stresses they were not saying things publicly they didn't believe. He and Waugh knew their balance sheet, their customers, their exposures, their risks—but things were occurring that no one could control. "We were putting on a wonderful front." He gives Waugh "enormous credit" for presenting that calm. For his part, Waugh sharply disagreed with Marwah's characterization that they were putting on a front. "He speaks for himself." Perhaps Marwah was simply expressing what could have been very human anxiety during a distressing time. Other

§ In 2005, Marwah was appointed chief administrative officer, and in 2008, chief operating officer.

executives—Mike Durland, Terry Fryett, Barb Mason, and Wendy
Hannam—all said the bank never felt destabilized during the crisis.
Former board member Indira Samarasekera said the fact that Waugh
was so well-connected internationally was perhaps "where he got his
comfort that maybe Sabi didn't have." That, along with the bank being
conservative in lending and credit risk "contributed to Rick's comfort
level." Waugh was in fact comfortable enough during the crisis to
double his own personal holdings of Scotiabank at thirty-three dollars
per share. "I didn't tell my wife until after the fact," he told the *Globe
and Mail*.[6]

While Waugh strongly believed you should never hide from a crisis,
Marwah did say that he intentionally kept some matters from the
CEO. Marwah cited cyberattacks and privacy issues as examples. "Shit,
you didn't tell me that. You know, you got to tell me," he described
Waugh saying to him. "Rick, I'll tell you everything, but there's some
things you really shouldn't know." It was Marwah's view that if he told
his boss and things went to hell, Waugh would have no one to fire. By
not telling Waugh, the boss could at least fire him. Marwah told Waugh
he had to let him decide what he told him, when and how. Finally,
Marwah said, Waugh agreed with the approach. "Use your judgment,"
Waugh told him.

Marwah said there were many things he didn't tell Waugh, and they
sorted themselves out. Waugh, of course, had a different viewpoint. "I
don't doubt he said that [but] I still want to know." Waugh said that he
might have used the words "I understand," but that didn't mean "okay."
"I don't think I ever backed down on the statement I'd want to know,"
Waugh said firmly. "I want to know. I don't want it hidden on a shelf,"
which he said is one of the biggest mistakes you can make.

A June 18, 2008, bank document described a financial world that had
"spectacularly unraveled."[7] It stated that BNS "did participate in a

relatively small number of structured products (e.g. ABCP, CDOs)⁵ where some losses were incurred." It was prepared by an executive committee chaired by Sabi Marwah. Others involved included future CEO Brian Porter, capital markets head Mike Durland, Anatol von Hahn, and Dieter Jentsch. The document was designed to assess risks, but also opportunities. It said that by May 2008, $380 billion had been written off by global financial institutions. The worst was still to come—the collapse of Lehman Brothers—and the document was not naive in that respect. "Any opportunity identified must be considered in the context of the potential for further shocks from the credit crisis." It pointed out that "the cycle turned with remarkable speed," and noted the fizzy capital markets and record deals of just a year earlier. "The current crisis has undeniably demonstrated the critical importance of liquidity." These words could have come directly from Waugh. "Once investors doubt a firm's ability to meet its obligations as they become due, the institution runs a severe risk of failure, irrespective of the assets on its balance sheet."

The document also mentioned the Institute of International Finance, where Waugh was vice-chair, stating: "The IIF views risk management as a 'business culture' that must pervade an entire organization." Again, this was from the Book of Waugh. Poor incentives—i.e., compensation—across the spectrum of originating and distributing securitized mortgage products was highlighted. Scotia had noticed this trend beginning years earlier in the United States: loose lending practices followed by the sale of loans to other institutions. As a result, the originators worried less about credit quality than selling, "Which we found stunning," one highly placed Scotia executive said. "Risk was not being properly assessed." Everyone collected a fee across the "securitization food chain." Among the most damning words: "the arrangers worked hard to sell the securities to third

---

⁵ ABCP is asset-backed commercial paper, while CDO stands for collateralized debt obligation. Both fall under the category of structured credit products, and both contained subprime mortgages.

parties. As the distance between borrower and ultimate bondholder increased, the quality of the information degraded, and the prospects of predatory behaviour went up."[8] The crisis also exposed credit rating agencies as sorely conflicted, paid by issuers of the debt they judged. Securities containing subprime mortgages had received investment grade ratings. As Waugh would say, follow the money. If people are incentivized improperly, look out. The system had honest players, but there was an oozing swamp of greed threatening to suck everyone down. While many have noted no one went to jail for the causes or excesses of the crisis, there was a recklessness and moral reprehensibility that led to it.

A crucial part of managing the Canadian financial system during the crisis were meetings at the highest levels—and they were frequent. Waugh met with other Canadian bank CEOs regularly, along with the heads of the federal finance department, the Bank of Canada, the Office of the Superintendent of Financial Institutions, and the Canada Deposit Insurance Corporation (CDIC). "The advantage of that was that we could have very specific discussions . . . and not be accused of collusion," he said, because the discussions were taking part in front of political and regulatory masters. This allowed the bankers to speak freely, Waugh says, and not for the advantage of their specific organizations.

Waugh no longer has his office calendars for 2007 and 2008. But the crisis would continue into 2009, with fallout and regulatory discussions well into 2010 and beyond. Calendars do still exist from those years, right up until he left the bank on January 31, 2014. They are handwritten in pencil and in duplicate, one for Waugh and one for his executive assistant, Caroline Stevens. Indicative of what occurred in late 2007 and through 2008, on January 5, 2009, there's an entry about a meeting at CIBC headquarters between the bank CEOs, Finance Minister Jim Flaherty, and Mark Carney, the governor of the Bank of Canada. As with other entries of this ilk, there was also a pre-meeting with the

Early years. *Photo courtesy of Rick Waugh*

Waugh's mentor and former Scotiabank executive, Bob MacIntosh, later president of the Canadian Bankers Association. *Photo by Erin Combs / Toronto Star via Getty Images*

New York years, late 1980s–early 1990s.
Photo courtesy of Rick Waugh

R. E. WAUGH, F.I.C.B., Corporate Research Analyst, Investment Department, General Office.

1971, Corporate Research Analyst, Investment Department at the Bank of Nova Scotia.

Rick and Lynne Waugh with US President George H. W. Bush and First Lady Barbara Bush, date unknown. *Photo courtesy of Rick Waugh*

Former chairman and CEO Bill Nicks, 1964. Nicks launched the Bank of Nova Scotia into the gold business, kicking off a global expansion. *Used with permission of Bloomberg L.P. Copyright © 2025. All rights reserved.*

Scotiabank executive Alan Macdonald portrayed on placard as employees of Scotiabank Quilmes protest in Buenos Aires, demanding their jobs be preserved, June 13, 2002. *Photo by Ali Burafi / AFP via Getty Images*

Employees of Scotiabank Quilmes protest outside the bank, May 21, 2002, in Buenos Aires. Workers of the suspended bank protested in "defence of 1,800 jobs." *Photo by Juan Vargas / NA / AFP via Getty Images*

Argentine ex-president Fernando de la Rúa leaves the Casa Rosada by helicopter after resigning on December 20, 2001 in the throes of an economic crisis. *Photo by Anibal Greco / DYN / AFP via Getty Images*

Waugh, Ed Hunter (third from left), and Ariel Perez (third from right) receive the Dominican Republic's highest civilian honour, 2009. Jim Meek, BNS country head on left, Carlos Morales Troncoso, Minister of Foreign Affairs, second from left, Rosario Arvelo, BNS director of marketing in DR, far right. *Photo courtesy of Jim Meek*

Ex-president of the Intercontinental Bank (BANINTER) Ramón Buenaventura Báez Figueroa waits for the sentence for alleged fraud to be read at the Justice Palace in Santo Domingo, October 21, 2007. *Photo by Ricardo Hernandez/AFP via Getty Images*

Donna Groskorth, a senior Scotia banker in Argentina during the 2001-2002 banking and economic crisis. She was attacked after leaving a grocery store. *Photo courtesy of Donna Groskorth*

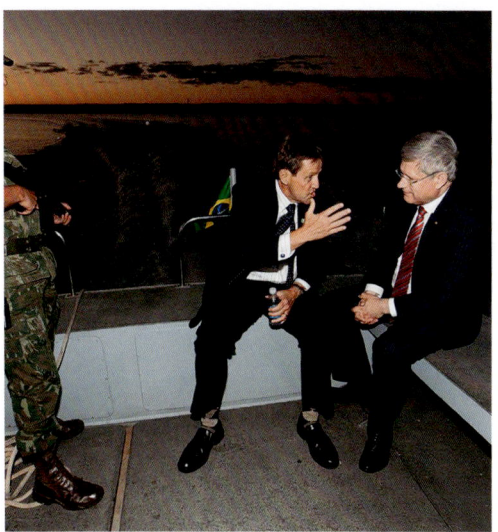

Waugh with the Prime Minister of Canada, Stephen Harper, in Brazil, August 8, 2011. *Photo by Jason Ransom / Library and Archives Canada / Stephen J. Harper fonds / R16093-57117-5. Copyright: Jason Ransom*

Larry Tanenbaum holds the Larry O'Brien Championship Trophy after the Toronto Raptors defeated the Golden State Warriors to win Game Six of the NBA Finals on June 13, 2019 in Oakland, California. *Photo by Lachlan Cunningham / Getty Images*

Waugh's predecessor and mentor, former chairman and CEO Peter Godsoe. *Photo by Dick Loek / Toronto Star via Getty Images*

Waugh with mentor and former BNS chairman and CEO Cedric Ritchie, 2013. *Photo courtesy of Rick Waugh*

Scotiabank COO Sabi Marwah, Rick Waugh, and Chief Human Resources Officer Sylvia Chrominska, October 2010. *Source unknown*

Longtime Scotiabank executive based in Argentina, Roy D. Scott, at former head office of the Bank of Nova Scotia, Havana, Cuba. *Photo courtesy of Maria Cristina Broers*

L to R, Scotiabank executives Stephen Hart, Anatol von Hahn, Sabi Marwah (on scooter), Rob Pitfield, Rick Waugh. *Photo courtesy of Anatol von Hahn*

Former Scotiabank treasurer, Bob Brooks. *Photo courtesy of Rob Wessel, Hamilton ETFs*

Waugh and Mark J. Carney, Governor of
the Bank of Canada (later Governor of the
Bank of England and Prime Minister of
Canada), at the annual meeting of the
Institute of International Finance,
September 24, 2011, in Washington, DC
*Photo by Brendan Smialowski/AFP via
Getty Images*

Waugh as newly elected president of the
International Monetary Conference (IMC), and
Ben S. Bernanke, chairman of the US Federal
Reserve at an IMC event in Atlanta, Georgia,
US, June 7, 2011. *Photo by Chris Rank/Bloomberg
via Getty Images*

Waugh introduces US treasury secretary,
Timothy Geithner, at the International
Monetary Conference (IMC), in Atlanta,
Georgia, US, June 6, 2011. *Photo by
Chris Rank/Bloomberg via Getty Images*

Canadian finance minister Jim Flaherty and
Bank of Canada Governor David Dodge at the
annual International Monetary Fund and World
Bank meetings in Singapore, September 16,
2006. *Photo by Jonathan Drake/Bloomberg via
Getty Images*

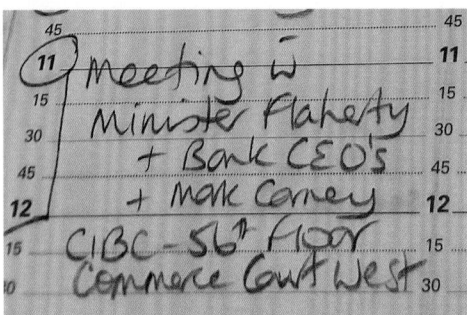

Frequent entries in Waugh's calendar during the financial crisis. *Both photos courtesy of Howard Green*

Waugh's mother didn't believe anything was true unless it was in the *Winnipeg Free Press*. Reprinted with permission, Winnipeg Free Press, October 26, 2013. Article by Martin Cash, photograph by Boris Minkevich

CEOs prior to the wider discussion. Four days later, on January 9, there is an entry about a breakfast of bank CEOs, Tiff Macklem (then a top finance department official, later governor of the Bank of Canada), and Crown corporations.

Of course, at such gatherings there is the issue of who speaks first. Waugh said the order was generally determined according to size. That meant Royal Bank, the largest, went first, followed by TD. Although Scotiabank was not the smallest (it was third-largest), Waugh said he "was quite comfortable being last because I brought in the international perspective." Who said the most during these meetings? "We all did. This was not a competition. It was all in our best interests to work together. That's why those meetings were so successful," ensuring the system continued to function. Canada's banking system was more stable than any other in the world.** Unlike many other countries, "no bank needed a bailout." Waugh maintains that history "has told us [we] never put our country at risk." As far as he could remember, "there was no secretary or anyone taking [official] notes." He says, "These were understandings." Then-CEO of RBC, Gord Nixon, described the sessions as almost daily during the crisis, with Carney as "quarterback." Waugh said the meetings were often held at the finance department's office in the King and Bay neighbourhood, walking distance for five of the big six.

Given fears about interbank lending, Waugh says at one meeting he told his fellow bankers that he (Scotia) would be willing to lend to other Canadian banks if they'd be willing to lend to Scotia. Going around the table, Waugh recalls everyone responding that they'd be willing to do the same. "We sort of all mutually agreed to lend to each other. We just solved the biggest problem in the international [financial] world."9 David Longworth, former deputy governor of the Bank of Canada, says, "I know that Canadian banks did co-operate, including

---

** There was no bailout of Australian banks, but the government guaranteed deposits, and for a fee, the banks' wholesale funding.

in the interbank market. Yeah, that was a great advantage for us over other countries."

So, while the interbank lending market had broken down internationally, it was still operating in Canada. But given the way dominoes were falling, Nixon says it "could have been" a problem. Waugh said "it was under strain." Describing the level of co-operation, Nixon says, "It was the best example of Canada and of the way banks operated. I mean, we compete like hell," he adds, explaining that Canadian banks are more competitive with each other than banks in the United States, but "everybody came together, put quarter-to-quarter earnings aside and said, 'Okay, what's the best thing to do here for the country?'" Nixon said there were things they all did that were not necessarily in the interests of their shareholders but were in the interest of the system, and therefore the nation. He emphasizes that in banking, there is no such thing as last man standing. Big banks were simply too interconnected. BMO's Bill Downe, who was also on the Fed's Advisory Council in the United States, echoes Nixon and Waugh: "If the whole market collapses, there is nothing that one firm can do to protect itself," he says, adding that "it rose above the transactional. It was about the country, right?" Meantime, Canada's banks were profitable and paying dividends; they "were well managed and had the assets," Waugh says. He argues that tackling the issues the same way in the United States would have been impossible, given the large number of banks. "We did it more effectively because we could all get in the same room."

These calls with the Bank of Canada, Finance Canada, OSFI, and the other bank CEOs continued through 2011 as the banks grappled with regulatory reform post-crisis. One was scheduled to last four and a half hours. There were also diary entries for calls with CEOs of American financial institutions, such as Larry Fink of BlackRock, the world's largest asset manager, and Brian Moynihan of Bank of America.

Also clearly noted in Waugh's calendar was a meeting every morning at 8:30 a.m. for the bank's Risk Policy Committee (RPC)—code for assessing credits, or loans. At Scotia, this was the sacrosanct meeting. Loans were the bank's key assets. Waugh said that in addition to reviewing large loans, he used RPC as a "management information system." His executive assistant, Caroline, said Waugh always arrived with his hair wet, after having worked out and showered shortly before arriving. "Rick," she said to him on more than one occasion, "tuck in your shirt." Monday afternoons, there was a standing meeting on bank liabilities, which the CEO chaired, specifically to discuss liquidity. Even when Waugh was travelling to Asia, Europe, or South America, those critical meetings were in his calendar.

Across the top of the calendar, surnames were written in blue ink— top executives who reported to Waugh. If a name was there—e.g., Marwah, Chrominska, Durland, [Rob] Pitfield, McDonald, Porter, [Chris] Hodgson—it meant that executive was travelling. Waugh needed to know. They oversaw significant sections of the bank. Given Scotia's international operations, there were whole weeks or days blocked out for foreign travel: China, India, Turkey, Tokyo, Chile, Puerto Rico, Colombia, Brazil, Thailand, Stockholm, Copenhagen, Basel, Zurich, Austria, the United Kingdom, Washington. Other notable entries: a call with Prime Minister Stephen Harper.

While the banks were doing their bit for the country, the country did much for the banks to keep the financial system operating and oiled. Over the course of the crisis, the Bank of Canada provided extraordinary liquidity based on banks providing an expanded range of eligible collateral. The central bank furnished this via so-called purchase and resale agreements (PRAs), which David Longworth said peaked in December 2008 at $37 billion. He said it was also a signalling measure to let the rest of the financial world know Canada was co-operating internationally, even though Canadian banks were profitable through the crisis.

Nonetheless, extraordinary measures continued and expanded. Among them was an emergency initiative spearheaded, Waugh says, by the federal finance department called the Insured Mortgage Purchase Program (IMPP). Via the Canada Mortgage and Housing Corporation (CMHC), Ottawa would provide liquidity to support the banks if needed and would charge a fee, if the assets were sound. According to the *Bank of Canada Review,* the IMPP "was complementary to the provision of extraordinary liquidity by the Bank of Canada."[10]

To meet Ottawa's requirement, Waugh said, the banks had to make sure their documentation was in order. In the event they had to put up collateral to get liquidity, bank assets had to be packaged up into securities that could be sold. CMHC would be the likely purchaser.[††] The underlying bank assets packaged for the IMPP during the financial crisis were principally mortgages to Canadians, which Waugh says typically had a loan-to-value ratio of 50 percent or better, meaning they weren't high risk. "They made liquidity available to us because they were secured," he said, emphasizing that it was not a handout. "They were secured. That was their role." He added that it was not putting the country at risk. "They were doing what a good regulator [*sic*] does, and they did it safely. And that was [Finance Minister] Flaherty's point. We're not going to take the risk and you're going to pay us a fee."

Waugh assigned a team to work swiftly on this, led by Jeff Heath, who became treasurer after Brooks left. Packaging mortgages into securities was time-consuming. Mortgages were divided by maturity; for example, three-year mortgages would be pooled together, while five-years would be in their own pool. If you were constructing a $200 million bond filled with mortgages that averaged $500,000 each, you needed four hundred mortgages for that one security. The task quickly involved thousands of mortgages. Stephen Hart, who'd been chief credit officer and later

†† It also performed this function in 2020, during the financial stresses caused by the COVID-19 pandemic.

chief risk officer in the last months of Waugh's tenure, said "the government window was very useful," with little or no risk to taxpayers because of the quality of the mortgages and a "standby fee" that would be paid by the banks. In addition to a standby fee, Waugh says there could also be a transaction fee. For his part, Marwah said "that [the IMPP] was our lifeline."

However, during a fireside chat in October 2024 at Schulich School of Business, Waugh indicated that the bank never used it. In subsequent interviews for this book, he responded to Marwah's description. "You always have a lifeline. And hopefully you never have to use it," he said. "We got prepared to use the lifeline, so Sabi is totally correct." Waugh said he "signed off to get the lifeline, to get prepared to pay for the lifeline, but we never had to use it." Dieter Jentsch, one of Waugh's top executives, said "that [the IMPP] saved us. I mean, all the banks." Waugh, immovable on the subject, said, "It helped to save us."

Later, Marwah reflected that perhaps "lifeline" was too strong a word. The IMPP, he says, was not for Scotia alone—liquidity "was drying up for the system" and the IMPP was a relatively easy way to get it and ensure the system functioned. Bank assets—mortgages—were available to be purchased by Ottawa to create liquidity, or, Waugh says, in the form of a loan. Although Marwah says he wasn't directly involved in the program, his recollection differed slightly from Waugh's. "I think we did utilize some of it." When told of this on the phone on December 11, 2024, Waugh says there may have been some, but an immaterial amount—or for such a short term that it wouldn't have been brought to his attention. Another Scotia executive familiar with the IMPP says it was not used but was a case of having securities ready on the shelf in case they were needed "in a hurry" to create liquidity. While borrowing from the Fed in the United States became common among banks—with little stigma attached to it—this executive said borrowing from the Bank of Canada would have been viewed as a bad signal, and that Scotia did not do it.

He said that during the crisis, Scotiabank was one of the few banks globally that could still get funding via the market, even if it was just short-term. Waugh says in the event they had to borrow, all the banks would have had to do so, thereby neutralizing the stigma.

Indeed, Canada was one of the only major economies (Australia was another) that did not require banks to get capital injections or be nationalized. "It's not like the US banks where there's a bailout paid for by the taxpayer," Marwah says. "There was no bailout in Canada. The Bank of Canada provided us liquidity and made enormous profit at it. So, don't say this is a bailout. There was no bailout of the Canadian banks. This is the only system that was not bailed out amongst the G7." Marwah says "a bailout also implies that the taxpayer somehow got screwed. But there was no taxpayer funding, unlike the US."

Some may argue there is room for nuance in the definition of bailout. The provision of liquidity might be loosely described as a form of bridge financing, or even supplemental oxygen standing by if necessary. As BMO's Bill Downe said, without specifying, "some banks needed that [the IMPP] a lot more than others." He added, "It was a signal to the broader system. And for some banks that would have been a very important development." Waugh says because Canadian banks had agreed to lend to each other, "we didn't need the liquidity. They [the Finance Department] still made us pay for it, but we didn't need it. But it was a great fee we paid to have that comfort."[11]

Waugh agrees with Downe and Nixon that the IMPP was a signal to markets. Nonetheless, by the end of October 2008, $66 billion in banking sector mortgages had been purchased by Ottawa through the program.[12] From whom they were purchased is unclear. "Somebody needed it, I guess," Waugh says. By 2010, that number had increased to $69 billion.[13] In the end, it was another measure that protected the financial system—which was at risk—and therefore the country. "If your banking system goes down, all hell breaks loose," Waugh says. He'd seen it in Argentina.

———

Central banks, often referred to as lenders of last resort, are meant to provide liquidity in crisis. Yet while Canada certainly did its bit for Canadian banks, support was modest compared with the United States and other countries. There had been nothing like it since the 1930s. A 2012 paper by the Federal Reserve Bank of New York shows the extent of what the Fed did for major US financial institutions. Under just one program, there were 416 borrowers—including New York branches of foreign banks: German, Japanese, British, and Middle Eastern—*and there were multiple programs*, aside from the Fed's normal market operations. Under just one of the other programs, two American banks had loans of $48 billion each.[14]

Separate from central bank support was taxpayer support—the $700 billion Troubled Asset Relief Program (TARP) via the US Treasury Department, as well as specific support for specific organizations. In August 2022, *ProPublica* published a list of who got what, citing 991 recipients. Scotiabank de Puerto Rico and BMO Harris Bank, NA, are on the list, receiving $2,603,545 and $37,723, respectively, proverbial rounding errors. Insurance company AIG received more than $68 billion; Citigroup and Bank of America received $45 billion each; JPMorgan Chase and Wells Fargo got $25 billion each; and on it goes. The tally shows $635 billion was disbursed, $390 billion returned, and revenues of $353 billion, meaning a net profit to the government of $109 billion. Not to dismiss a profit, but this could be viewed as cold comfort. The American and world financial systems had been through hell, as had people.[‡‡]

---

‡‡ A year later, there was different math from the US Government Accountability Office. The total cost of TARP was $443.5 billion. As of 2023, after repayments, sales, dividends, and interest, the lifetime cost was $31.16 billion. There would be more federal assistance in the United States in 2009—another $787 billion (U.S. Government Accountability Office, "Troubled Asset Relief Program: Lifetime Cost," GAO-24-107033, December 7, 2023).

Janet Yellen, the first woman to serve as both chair of the Federal Reserve and secretary of the Treasury, spoke with David Axelrod, podcast host and former advisor to President Barack Obama, about public anger surrounding the crisis. Yellen estimated nine million people in the United States lost their jobs between 2008 and 2010, and countless lost homes. Axelrod suggested to her that many people paid a terrible price, while those responsible walked away. Yellen responded that such a conclusion was "pretty fair." But then she explained why institutions were bailed out. "It's because if we don't have a functioning financial system in the country that enables people to borrow and lend, no one is going to have a job. And we cannot allow anger about what happened to lead us to destroy a necessary ingredient for our economy to function. We had to have a functioning banking and financial system."[15]

Liquidity in banking is created in a variety of ways. Waugh indicated the bank's major source was the Canadian mortgage portfolio: "I knew we were liquid because we had good assets." The mortgages in its marketable securities, he maintains, were from solid Canadian customers to whom the bank sold other products and services. Interest was being paid on mortgages, meaning cash was coming into the bank. To ensure liquidity, there were other tools. A bank could cut credit lines, call loans, extend terms, sell things. Waugh views these, however, as less palatable measures. He says Scotia was cognizant of who banked with them. Using the example of Sudbury, where occasionally nickel miners would strike, Waugh says the bank would defer their mortgage payments until the strike ended. Banking was about relationships, and strikes end. He says the bank would make every effort to back its customers, "because we need to survive long term with customers. And the best ones we have are the ones we know." Terry Fryett underlines that Waugh didn't panic or close shop. "He [Waugh] knew the storm would pass." Although the bank tightened up, it didn't close its doors. "It was quite bad, but he didn't stop doing business. He did it prudently," Fryett says. "And clients will remember when you just cut them off." He adds that "I thought he [Waugh] was a pretty safe pair of hands during the crisis." Jentsch goes further: "Rick was the right guy for that period."

In Canada, Waugh says, bankers had some preparation for the 2008 calamity. The country had its own financial scare in the lead-up, the so-called non–bank sponsored asset-backed commercial paper crisis. It began in the spring of 2007, and according to then–Bank of Canada governor David Dodge, "in August, everything was falling apart." The market in Canada for $32 billion worth of commercial paper froze on August 13, a few days after the freeze-up at BNP in Europe. Buyers for the paper had vanished.

Investors, reaching for a bit of extra interest versus a bank account or a government treasury bill, had bought these short-term instruments. Commercial paper is issued to investors by companies looking to borrow for terms under one year, and for as little as thirty days. Traditionally, the paper is backed by creditworthy firms. If issued by a bank, the ABCP might be backed by auto loans, residential mortgages, or credit card receivables. A government treasury bill—viewed as risk-free—pays interest, but with the non-bank ABCP, investors would get a few more basis points of return. A basis point is one one-hundredth of one percent. However, a slightly higher yield translated into significantly more risk. Initially, ABCP was a bank-only market, but in the 2000s, other participants began issuing it—financial entities that were unregulated or lightly regulated. Their paper could contain much more exotic, non-traditional assets. With relatively little disclosure required, investors soon discovered that what was contained in the non–bank issued securities was dizzyingly complex—opaque financial products—non-transparent, and difficult to value. And while the paper had short-term maturities, the assets were much longer term. Stephen Hart described it as a classic liquidity squeeze. "Short-term funding, long-term assets." In the summer of 2007, one of the non-bank issuers disclosed that its ABCP had exposure to the subprime mortgage market in the United States.[16] That set off alarms.

While the banks weren't the issuers of the paper in question, some sold it and continued selling it, including a division of Scotiabank, Scotia Capital—the investment dealer side of the bank—despite the revelation of exposure to US subprime. When nervousness hit about the quality of assets like subprime mortgages, investors didn't want to buy the paper or roll over what they had when it matured. The market froze. It took several months of complex negotiations to restructure the market, and years for fines to be levied.

David Dodge described the ABCP situation as "an enormous problem for us. And Scotia was not the worst player, but I would say they were not the best in that regard." He recalled that "by the summer of 2007, it was clear that these vehicles were in very serious trouble." Dodge said, "that was going to mean very serious problems in the Canadian capital market for ABCP, and of course for our banks." The former central banker then explained "the basic rule on securities—they ought to be transparent . . . these were vehicles that had underlying assets. And if you couldn't tell what those underlying assets were and you couldn't value them, [it's] pretty hard to value the security. And that was the issue." As for Waugh's assessment that the ABCP crisis helped Canada prepare for the global financial storm yet to come, Dodge agreed. "I remember very well in September of 2008, sitting with Tim Geithner [president of the Federal Reserve Bank of New York and later Treasury secretary]. Tim was really starting to become aware of the big problems in the US," Dodge said. "All of a sudden, he [Geithner] said, 'Well, you guys just have started to try to deal with this and what's under there?'"

One of Dodge's deputies, David Longworth, focused on system-wide issues and market operations. Longworth was also a deputy under

Dodge's successor, Mark Carney. He said ABCP was not only complicated itself but also backed by other complicated instruments. "And
because the US housing market had deteriorated and people were wondering about the safety of the assets that were backed by mortgages, they
were concerned about all these very complicated instruments that were
based in part on these assets that were backed by mortgages. And so,
there was beginning to be a worry that maybe asset-backed commercial
paper should not be trading at par."

Investors in commercial paper certainly didn't expect it to drop below
par or face value. They were parking their cash to get a bit of interest and
hadn't imagined their principal would be threatened. Buyers of ABCP
could be retail investors with less than a million dollars tied up, or others
with more. "Any significant decline in the asset values would leave them
in a very bad situation," Longworth said. "And so, people didn't want to
buy any. People did not want to roll over the asset-backed commercial
paper." While the non-bank ABCP was the crux of the problem, the
worries were also affecting bank-issued ABCP, a source of funding.[17] "It
was becoming more expensive for banks to raise funds," Longworth said.
Fortunately, both Dodge and Longworth indicated, Canada's banks
were not hugely exposed to this, but it was enough of a fright. The biggest fright was for investors, who couldn't get their funds and faced
losses. It was also a black eye for Canada's financial system.

In September, the late Purdy Crawford, the distinguished dean of
securities lawyers, stepped up to supervise a restructuring of the market
for non-bank ABCP to prevent a default and fire sale that would have
devastated investors. The catchy name of his committee told you all you
needed to know about the swamp of trouble—the Pan-Canadian Investors
Committee for Third-Party Structured Asset-Backed Commercial Paper.
One evening in the fall of 2007, I boarded a flight from New York to
Toronto. I sat down next to a young man with a fat binder spread on his
lap. I couldn't help noticing the byzantine diagrams as he flipped each

page. They looked like something from the Manhattan Project. I soon realized I was looking at the contents of non-bank ABCP. It looked unintelligible, at least to me. The fellow worked at JPMorgan and would be Purdy Crawford's associate on the committee, untangling the web of third-party structured asset-backed commercial paper.

By December 23, 2007, there was a framework for an agreed restructuring under the so-called Montreal Accord (an agreement to keep the market frozen until it was restructured), with completion in 2008 and final approval in early 2009. While the resolution was exceedingly complicated, it boiled down to this: the paper was "eventually converted to floating rate notes with maturities that would match the underlying assets."[18] Essentially, major investors had to agree to hold the paper for years, rather than the short term they expected when they bought. Stephen Hart said, "It took five or six years to unwind that stuff."

Following the restructuring, there were court challenges and enhancements to the plan. But later, seven banks and brokerages faced $139 million in penalties for their involvement in selling the paper. Scotia Capital settled with the Ontario Securities Commission and the Investment Industry Regulatory Organization of Canada for approximately $29 million. At $75 million, National Bank of Canada accounted for more than half of the total fines, while CIBC settled for $22 million.[19]

Since the crisis, the ABCP market has become more regulated and transparent, backed by more traditional assets. Today, 99 percent of the Canadian market is dominated by the big six banks, and typical investors are large and knowledgeable about risk.[20] In the end, retail investors with less than $1 million invested were made whole, while larger investors received restructured, longer-term paper. While it was torture for those investors, Longworth says that, given what was still to come, the ABCP situation "was a bit of a sideshow for the health and safety of the Canadian financial system overall."

———

During the crisis, Waugh was not only being challenged by the bank's board of directors, analysts, and shareholders but he also faced ongoing scrutiny by the key regulator—the Office of the Superintendent of Financial Institutions. The superintendent from 2007 until 2014 was Julie Dickson, a quiet but firm native of Saint John, New Brunswick. Dickson is polite but not given to small talk. She gave off the aura of someone with a job to do, not susceptible to being jollied along by high-powered financial-sector CEOs. Waugh says they spoke "all the time" during the crisis. In addition, he was meeting with American regulators, given his involvement in the IIF.

Dickson would not divulge specifics of her conversations with Waugh or any bank CEO (nor would Waugh), but this is part of an email she sent me on April 27, 2024:

> I would say that I remember him telling me how he turned the lights on at the bank in the morning, and then turned them off at night—meaning he was the first to arrive and the last to leave, and that he knew everything there was to know about the bank . . . he always had a lot to say. He had great pride in the bank so he could be intense if OSFI was suggesting something he didn't agree with. But that was ok . . . He was a plain talker which I really appreciated. I remember seeing him do a presentation at a conference, where he talked about problems that can arise in banking, and at one point said "real estate . . . oh it's often real estate." That stuck with me.

Of course, the 2007–9 crisis was tied directly to real estate.

But if problems were tied to real estate, going deeper into causes meant they were tied to bad decisions. Decisions were made by people, but equally, solutions emanated from people. So Waugh wanted meetings and interactions to be in-person. He strongly believes "we're all social animals," and that working virtually is not the way to hold a major organization together. "There's nothing like a round table to sit around and discuss complexity. And having people in the room." His career was, among other things, about being in the room. "You've got to see the reaction," he said. "Body language for me has always been an important factor." If the person across the table chokes up or there's anguish on someone's face, it's information, he says.

Waugh provided a stark example of giving an order in October 2007, the early part of the crisis, which created anguish amidst the troops, at least certain trading troops. Aside from taking deposits, lending money, and advising people on how to manage their investments and savings, banks also have trading divisions. They are market participants themselves, trading on behalf of the bank's own account. It's an understatement to say that during the crisis there were significant swings in markets. In fact, the ups and downs—mostly downs—could be violent. "There was of course huge volatility in markets, which did affect trading positions that the bank in its normal course of operations had taken," Waugh says. He goes on to describe "a strong tendency to use the bank's balance sheet to make use of market opportunities, and most of the time it's appropriate. It's therefore important to put guardrails around the ability to do that, which ultimately means it gets taken to the top of the bank for final decisions, and you have to tell or enforce—that while the opportunities may look attractive, the risks are too great."

Waugh says most of the risks taken by traders were based on algorithms, mathematical rules about which he has skepticism (Jentsch says Waugh "despised all the modelling"). "I worry about being self-reliant on AI," he says. "Some of the best decisions I have made was [*sic*] understanding the weakness in the algorithm, and AI, from my understanding, just perpetuates the weakness of the algorithm." And in life as in trading, there are so-called black swan events, statistically highly unusual occurrences that can throw mathematical models out of whack. While the odds of a black swan occurring are rare, often infinitesimal, they do still occur. Traders try to factor in those odds.

In one instance, Waugh says, traders reckoned the probability of a black swan at less than one percent. As per risk process, he says, the bank's finance department was then consulted about the impact if such a low probability event did occur. It was determined that while the probability was very low, if it happened, the "hit to the bank was material and we would have to tell the traders to actually eliminate any such positions." In other words, it was a potentially disastrous trade that would hurt the bank, and it had to go. He says he gave the order to "unwind the position and they asked for time, and I said unwind the position in the next few days, which they did." The loss "would have been a headline number," Waugh says. "That's why I say material." By definition, a material amount is an amount that would cause reasonable investors to assign a different value to a stock. Whether it would have moved the stock or not, the loss would have been consequential, perhaps as high as $100 million.

For the traders, it was also material. Their Christmas bonuses were tied to the success of their trading. Eliminating the position meant taking a loss and a hit to bonuses. "It just had to be done." Was it tense, I asked? "Uh-huh. And [there were] a number of very unhappy people." While there were internal limits on trades that were enforced, Waugh says he knew what the bank's positions were. Sometimes he might go to the head of trading himself, or he would have a direct report do so.

While Waugh did what he believed was best for the bank, the crackdown may have underlined what had been an uncomfortable relationship between him and the capital markets group. More broadly, there was something of a cold war between those of the bank's lending culture and those of the deal and markets culture. Waugh vigorously denies the two were like oil and water ("absolutely not"). Regardless, the latter group's roots stemmed from outside the bank, imported with Scotia's purchase of investment bank McLeod Young Weir in late 1987, just days before a massive stock market crash.[§§] To a degree, it was speculated that traditional bankers like Waugh were envious of how much certain markets people made. Again, he douses the assertion. "That's definitely wrong."

After federal and provincial regulatory reform earlier that year (Canada's "Little Bang" followed the "Big Bang" in the UK in 1986) allowed banks to buy securities firms, it was a new world for banks.[21] In fact, Scotiabank had led the charge for the change in regulation, and five of the six big banks soon bought investment dealers, with TD the exception.[22] Buying McLeod Young Weir meant combining two very different cultures, and for many years, the bank and the investment bank ran virtually separately under the same roof, with Cedric Ritchie running the bank, and Austin "Austintatious" Taylor of McLeod Young Weir continuing to oversee the latter. Of course, Waugh was not of the Taylor side; he was of the credit culture, the Scotiabank culture. "The biggest issue was they had to get a chair big enough for Austin," Waugh says facetiously. Taylor was six-foot-four, three hundred pounds.

According to *Princeton Alumni Weekly*, Taylor, who was a graduate, took pride in knowing all twenty-three hundred of his firm's employees by their first names. He retired in 1993 "frustrated by its [Bank of Nova Scotia's] style of management."[¶¶] The two sides weren't technically integrated until 1999 with the establishment of Scotia Capital, the division that had sold the non-bank ABCP. Such lengthy, grinding, years-long integrations are not unusual. Often, you need to wait for people to die or retire before culture melds. For his part, Waugh says traders, branch managers, and investment bankers all come from different cultures. "It's a monumental job to get everyone onto one

---

§§ The crash happened on October 19, 1987, or "Black Monday." The Dow Jones Industrial Average fell 22 percent.

¶¶ According to Walter Isaacson's Elon Musk biography, Musk also left Scotiabank in frustration.

team, one goal," he says, referencing his mantra. Were they hard to manage? "Yep."

There was more to the trade that Waugh shut down. Mike Durland says he was involved in the controversial transaction. Durland grew up in Middleton in the heart of Nova Scotia's Annapolis Valley, a town with not quite two thousand people. "It was one of those towns with two banks," he said, in this case Royal Bank and Scotia, which faced each other. A customer of BNS, Durland did a PhD in finance at Queen's University. He later spent twenty-three years at Scotiabank, working as a top executive, one of Rick Waugh's "direct reports" as group head of Global Banking and Markets. Durland was yet another who cited the bank's family atmosphere as the magnetic pull of working there. Durland said "that really defined how Rick ran the place," personifying what it meant to be a Scotia banker. Waugh was folksy, "just one of them," while at the same time intense, focused, and achievement oriented.

Durland was a slightly peculiar cat when he joined the bank in 1993. He worked on the investment banking and markets side but was viewed by Godsoe and Waugh as a Scotia banker, not an import from McLeod Young Weir. As for that group, "They were not really Scotia bankers in his [Waugh's] mind," Durland said. "He never really embraces that they can become part of the family." Some, but not all of that was related to compensation. Waugh, he said, believed in meritocracy and had a hard time accepting that certain jobs paid more than others if they didn't produce more for the bank. At the same time, Durland said, every major bank in the world was dealing with the same "two class citizen" issue, a by-product of the chipping away at and ultimate repeal of the Glass-Steagall Act in the United States, which broke down the regulatory barrier between deposit banking and investment banking. It was a regulatory shift that had also occurred in Britain and Canada.

So, was Waugh jealous of the investment bankers? "Probably," Durland said. After all, Waugh had proven to be a good dealmaker himself. At the same time, Durland added, it would be unfair to characterize Waugh's views in such a one-dimensional fashion. "It was way more than that. It was his paternal protective instinct," Durland argued, citing all the loyal Scotia soldiers. "In his mind, they were the core of the organization. He was one of them. He was the voice of everybody."

That culture clash came to a head with the trade Waugh snuffed out. The bank's trading side had taken a position in a "synthetic" collateralized debt obligation (CDO). It was deemed synthetic because it was based on a derivative transaction. It was underpinned by contracts that were non-cash assets, rather than a bond, mortgages, or loans. The position's value was based on the movement of credit spreads, the yield difference between certain debt securities. Durland recalled that tens of millions of dollars were at stake, perhaps as much as $100 million. While it was hardly a small amount, he said the trading group generated annual revenue in the billions. But given that the market was moving against them, there was a risk to the bank that it would have to mark the position down: in other words, value it at a depressed level—a hit to the books. Calling it a "shitty" position, Durland said, "It's like having chains around your ankles." While exiting such a position would be difficult, he noted that it would also be a relief, eliminating a risk.

While Waugh says closing the trade angered people whose year-end bonuses would be affected, Durland says he doesn't "remember it as being that traumatic, to be honest." Rather, it was a tough decision that had to be made. "Finance is a world of uncertainty," Durland says, and "this is something that we need to take a hit on or move on . . . We did that." His recollection is that aside from this trade, "the group that did that had a phenomenal year that year," so he didn't believe "that outside of a small number of people that it was that monumental."

What was more monumental, he says, was that not everybody agreed with Waugh's risk assessment. "I think it was more about control." One high-ranking person, Durland said, probably felt micromanaged. "At

senior levels it's a lot about ego," on both sides. A top person in the trading group didn't respect Waugh, Durland says, and "Rick kind of sensed
it." Waugh denies this bothered him, and doesn't agree that it was about
ego. "What I sensed was they weren't on the team." Despite any disagreement, Durland said unwinding the trade was still the right decision and
he respected the process. He believed Waugh was concerned about the
wider, long-term prosperity of the bank, and that both Waugh and
Marwah were highly skilled in making risk-related decisions. "I think the
bank handled itself extremely well during the crisis," making fast, bold,
and thoughtful judgments, including this one.

Marwah also recalls that the trade involved structured credit products
(collateralized loan obligations, or CLOs) that amounted to a sizable
portfolio that was underwater; he estimates its total size at about $2 bil-
lion. Based on the statistical and algorithmic analysis, the probability of
a default was one percent. If the trade worked out, the gain would be
huge, and the Christmas bonuses would reflect that. But if there was a
default, the hit would be substantial.

"All the risk was [being] taken by the shareholders," Waugh says, "and
all the upside was going to [the] bonus of the traders." Get out of it,
Waugh ordered, even if there's a loss. Marwah says he and Brooks agreed
with Waugh—because it wasn't going to get any better. They did get out,
and thank God, Marwah says. Sure, they sold at a 20 to 30 percent loss,
but Marwah estimates that if they hadn't gotten rid of those securities,
they would have been worth 30 percent less by January. "He [Waugh]
took the right decision, sold the damn asset," Marwah says, adding, "All
those investments went down virtually to zero." Waugh couldn't recall
whether that was the case ("probably," he says), but he does remember
checking to satisfy himself that the position had been eliminated.

Of course, not everything was about fighting the crisis. From a human
resources perspective, because the bank's share price was sharply lower
during the crisis, the stock options held by executives were underwater.

Sylvia Chrominska says executives—not Waugh—frequently came into her office "weeping and moaning" (figuratively, not literally crying) about how their options were un-exercisable. The financial world was coming unhinged, and it was all about their pay packets, which Chrominska did allow was "pretty stressful for them." She says board members, though, were startled by how much the bank was paying certain people. The investment bankers would frequently begin by saying, "'Well, Sylvia, this is not about compensation.' And I'd say to myself, 'This is always about compensation with these guys.'"

While compensation may or may not have made Waugh jealous, it's clear that compensation was a management and a risk issue. Waugh says traders were transactional and wanted to know what the cheque would be at the end of the year, whereas bankers like him were paid not just for the short term, but also for the medium and long term. Waugh was certainly a self-confessed "deal guy," but he was also concerned about the long-term prosperity of the bank. And he knew about bonuses and incentives. He had been a recipient over the years and had spear-headed research on the issue of incentives while vice-chair of the IIF, given the role misaligned incentives had played in fuelling the loose lending, securitization, and sale of subprime mortgages that had ignited the financial crisis.

As it turns out, a relatively small percentage of Waugh's compensation was in cash. The bulk came in medium- and long-term compensation—stock and options. Over time, it built. He estimated that at one point, he was the bank's largest individual shareholder. That aside, there was friction between trading and banking. Waugh says David Wilson, who headed Scotia Capital and was a vice-chair of the bank, helped bridge the gap.

The most gut-wrenching moment of the financial crisis—the failure of Lehman Brothers in September 2008—was foreshadowed six months beforehand when Bear Stearns required a rescue. In the same way that a human can die of blood loss, a financial institution can expire from a loss of liquidity. This issue arose in an interview I conducted with the late Alan "Ace" Greenberg, the respected former chairman and CEO of the now-defunct Wall Street investment bank. Bear Stearns was widely known as a scrappy, sharp-elbowed investment bank. Greenberg wrote in his memoir *Memos from the Chairman*—a compilation of his folksy yet pointed memos to staff—that he was looking for employees who were poor, smart, and wanted to be rich. He was, of course, describing himself. Greenberg had long finished his tenure running the company when Bear Stearns became deeply entangled in subprime mortgages. In March 2008 it faced a liquidity crisis that resulted in a Fed–backed forced sale to JPMorgan Chase & Co. over a weekend. Initially, the sale price was two dollars a share, but later raised to ten dollars. Bear's stock had previously traded at well over $100 per share. Some ten thousand Bear Stearns employees lost their jobs, although JPMorgan kept a spot for Greenberg, viewed as a wise owl.

On liquidity, Greenberg expressed disbelief that Bear was buying back its own shares during a period of intense financial stress, when the overnight lending on which it depended had dried up. Beyond that, Greenberg cited upcoming multi-billion-dollar commitments the investment bank had made to major corporations—yet it was using precious cash to buy back its own stock. To Greenberg, it was an incomprehensible use of cash, a depletion of liquidity. He was dumbfounded by the decision made by the company he loved and had helped build. Bear had been valued at many billions of dollars, had survived the 1929 crash and Great Depression, only to fizzle in a matter of days due to liquidity draining away. So, Waugh, during the crisis, watched his bank's liquidity level like a pilot watching the fuel gauge over an icy ocean.

But all gauges would flutter wildly on September 15, 2008, when the global financial system went into code blue. Lehman Brothers collapsed and there was no Fed-organized rescue as there'd been with Bear Stearns.

A sick financial system was now in intensive care. Waugh was in Thailand when it happened. He immediately got on the plane home. Aside from the grave systemic implications, Scotia was also involved in a hair-raising trade with the bankrupt American investment bank,

While American financial authorities helped engineer the takeover of Bear Stearns by JPMorgan, Lehman was a different story. They let it fail, a calamitous moment in financial history that few involved in the system will ever forget. Bankers were staring into the abyss. Lehman was deeply involved in structured credit products at the core of the crisis. It was also highly interconnected and subject to light oversight. As vice-chair of the IIF (and president of the International Monetary Conference, or IMC), Waugh attended meetings with the top banks in the world, the heads of central banks, global finance ministers, and the leader of the International Monetary Fund. "I had a view in the world that not many people did," he said. At one conference, prior to Lehman's collapse, Waugh sat next to Christine Lagarde, then head of the IMF and now president of the European Central Bank. Waugh recalled that Dick Fuld, the CEO of Lehman Brothers, got up and told everyone in the room that Lehman did not have a liquidity problem. "You could just read the body language," Waugh says, adding that the whole room shuddered. "That was the beginning of the end of Lehman Brothers," a storied firm founded in 1850 by German immigrant Henry Lehman, who started with a fabric business in Montgomery, Alabama. As for Fuld, Waugh said derisively, "he [thought he] was the smartest guy in the room." There was the sense "nobody liked the guy.""" A *New York Magazine* profile described Fuld as having an "almost animalistic presence" and "intimidating." By some, he was nicknamed "gorilla" given that he "seemed to grunt rather than speak in full sentences."[23]

*** Gord Nixon said that RBC was "the Canadian institution that was looking at whether we would buy Lehman's."

Was it the right decision to let Lehman go under, given the cascade of trouble it set off? While the critical consideration was that any official action or inaction should not create systemic risk, Waugh says he wouldn't have had access to the information authorities had in September 2008, so he couched his answer carefully. "Over time, if it corrected the crisis and limits the damage," Waugh says, "obviously it was the best that could be done at the time." He adds that the "financial system corrected itself and moved on." However, Waugh concedes systemic disruption was not without enormous costs to taxpayers, employees, and all stakeholders in society. "I would say it was something that I and others would worry about."

After angst-ridden days in Washington, American lawmakers eventually passed the $700 billion Troubled Asset Relief Program, which took bad assets off the hands of financial institutions. As said widely at the time, while profit was privatized, risk was socialized. Although the scenario played out on a global scale, the net result exhibited echoes of the trade Waugh had shut down at his own bank. It was a classic case of misaligned incentives. At the bank, shareholders hold the bag. In life at large, society does.

Nine of the largest American banks had to take capital injections from Washington—a step towards nationalization. General Motors and Chrysler were bailed out, a rescue that included billions from the Canadian and Ontario governments. Short-term interest rates set by central banks were suppressed at emergency (near zero) levels. They effectively stayed that way for fourteen years, arguably creating a society of free-money junkies that distorted valuations in many asset classes. David Longworth of the Bank of Canada says it's an issue he's reflected on many times, but he wondered what the alternative would have been. Letting the entire system collapse?

"Things were happening daily, it wasn't just Lehman," Waugh said. "You just didn't know what you didn't know. [So,] the best place to be is head office with your management team." Waugh's view is that the best information source is to "talk to someone directly," in person—management by walking around. It's important to have your team around you, experts within the bank and their networks. One of the things Waugh has come to realize is that "I always had a great sense of who to contact to get what result I needed within the Bank of Nova Scotia." He cites decades of experience within the bank. When there's a crisis, he argues, get on the ground, or as close to the ground as possible.

Talking face to face was a key part of Waugh's modus operandi. So was the financial media. It still is. By and large, he trusts it, reading—or at least scanning—four major newspapers each morning. They include the *Wall Street Journal, Financial Times,* and the *Globe and Mail's Report on Business.* The fourth may depend on where he is at any given time. Aside from his love of reading newspapers, he might come across a column not directly related to a specific financial world issue but that will nonetheless trigger a connection of some sort.

While you needed to stay abreast of the macro situation, Waugh said, for someone running an international bank "it's the microeconomic that determines your response." The micro, for example, would be if one of your major borrowers couldn't repay a loan, which would affect the bank's liquidity and, in turn, determine how the bank would act.

But with the collapse of Lehman Brothers, the macro and the micro converged. The system was at risk of coming apart—and Scotia had its own specific exposure to the failed firm.

While the unwinding of the trade in late 2007 and the ABCP issue occurred early in the crisis, the "emergency would start around the Lehman default," Mike Durland says, as did everyone who remembered it. David Longworth says the Bank of Canada heard about the Lehman failure in the middle of the night. He'd been awaiting a call from the New York Fed, expecting to hear Lehman's immediate problem had been solved by Barclays in England purchasing the ailing firm. But it didn't happen. Barclays backed away and Lehman went under.

The capital markets group at the bank, which Durland was part of, would have had the most direct relationship with Lehman Brothers and knowledge of Scotia's exposure to it. "It was a very large position, and we were able to work out of it 'cause of a little bit of luck," Durland says. Again, it was a complex transaction that involved the hedging of equity swaps, a derivative contract. Durland boiled it down to this. If the market dropped, Lehman would owe Scotia money; if it went up, Scotia would owe Lehman. When Lehman defaulted, the market dropped, but the bank couldn't claim what it was owed. "That could have been three, four, five hundred million," Durland estimates, much more than the controversial trade in late 2007. "Most executives would have been shitting themselves," he says, recalling that Waugh remained calm.

Then, the unexpected occurred. To prevent panic selling, on September 18, 2008, three days after Lehman failed, market authorities in the United States reinstituted a ban on short selling[†††] (it had been in place for a time in the summer) and the stock market spiked upward. Durland says the bank was then able to trade out of the position with just a slight loss, "a somewhat fairy-tale ending," adding that "Rick and Sabi were unbelievably composed." Durland admitted to having been a bit "flat-footed" himself with respect to the position, saying that "a different boss would have beaten me to a pulp."

Unsolicited, Durland offered up a view of Waugh's "very calm" stance. "Rick was made for the crisis, in many ways." His impression of Waugh's state of mind was that he had survived Argentina. "There wasn't a sense of panic," he says. "He was an adult who had burned his hands before."

[†††] Short selling a stock involves borrowing stock from a shareholder (generally an institution) for a fee, and then selling the shares in the hope of buying them back at a lower price, returning them, and pocketing the difference. The risk is that the stock rises in price, potentially creating infinite losses.

Durland used this metaphor without knowing Waugh's father was a fire-fighter. When I mentioned it and told him that Waugh had dismissed my theory that he'd inherited his father's firefighter gene, calling it "a stretch," Durland says, "that's not a stretch." "There's a wartime CEO and there's the peacetime CEO," he said. "[I'm] not saying he wasn't a good peacetime CEO, but he was a damn good wartime CEO" who would rise to the occasion. If you were part of his family, he trusted you. "We're all in this together and we're going to get out of it," Durland says, adding, "All your energy was on solving the problem." This contrasted with certain unflattering views of Waugh on the markets side. If you were not, in Waugh's mind, a Scotia banker, "you did not like Rick. He was disrespectful. He didn't trust you. He micromanaged you," Durland says. He also said Waugh was privately mocked by people because of his authenticity and his "butchery" of English. "I think he sensed that, and it pissed him off."

Waugh's assertions to Dickson of being the first to arrive and last to leave "and that he knew everything there was to know about the bank" raise the question of CEO oversight and how hard Waugh was on his direct reports. "Oh, I'd hold everybody accountable," he told me. "Whether it's hard or not, it's appropriate." He said "someone on the management team called it tough love." When he retired, a mostly lau-datory article by Tim Kiladze in the *Globe and Mail* described Waugh as a "micro-manager" who put significant pressure on his top-tier execu-tives, with one unnamed source calling it "bad parenting." So, was he a micromanager? "Yeah," Waugh said when I asked. Was that always good? "No." Dieter Jentsch, who held top positions under Waugh (and his suc-cessor Brian Porter) said "he wasn't easy to work for," adding, "I don't think CEOs necessarily should be." Durland says Waugh was more likely to micromanage you if he'd done your job previously. When asked to define "tough love," Waugh said, "Ask tough questions and see how they respond." Was there shouting, I asked? "Not shouting, no," he said.

"However, there was heated discussion and sometimes consequences." While Waugh would talk to his people about anything, he knows he was notorious for losing track of time and leaving a lineup of frustrated people waiting outside his door. He jokes that his wife Lynne complains about how he can turn a short story into a long one.

Waugh seemed unfussed about any criticism of his management style. He laughs at the "bad parenting" rap. "There's always a problem with one of your kids," he says, referring to his direct reports. And after all, he'd had plenty of heated exchanges with Godsoe, to whom he reported through extremely tense situations, including Argentina. Despite his friendly posture, certain things bring him rapidly to a boil. His sentences harden, responses get crisp. A dark cloud seems to form.

Waugh said he would personally express to his team that everyone makes mistakes in judgment, that nobody batted a thousand, and that was okay. Obviously, if a person made too many errors, "that was a different matter." But when his people did make the inevitable mistakes or there were seemingly intractable problems, he said he demanded they not be hidden from him. "I wanted to know as soon as possible."

That brought the discussion to the subject of Friday afternoons, which Waugh says were probably the worst part of the week for him. If something went wrong and couldn't be resolved during the week, the executive responsible knew it had to be brought to the top. "I owned it then," he says. "It hit my desk that afternoon [Friday]." He says his job was to then figure out the available alternatives "hopefully [by] the following Monday." A person who worked alongside Waugh for years confirmed this, saying he was "inundated" on Friday afternoons with "piles" of material. "I used to hate Friday afternoons," the person said. "Everyone would come in with their shit," or there would be tail-between-the-legs calls from people in the bank, saying, "I have to see Rick."

Was it a bit scary that a major financial institution needed an individual as a Friday afternoon backstop, I asked. "I didn't think it was

scary," Waugh says. "I just thought it was part of the job. You're CEO for
a reason, right?" There's truth in that. The president of the United States
decides when to send troops. The football coach decides when to pass,
run, or kick on the last play of the game. "Because I had forty years' experience I could do it," he says, his confidence never wavering. "People are
my strength." There was also that sense of calm described by those in
Argentina and elsewhere. "I thrive on crisis," Waugh said. "My whole
career was a series of crises. That's one thing I'm good at."

After the worst of the crisis passed, the Bank of Canada examined what
occurred between August 2007 and the early part of 2009 and the
extraordinary liquidity actions it took in response to "the financial market turmoil." In a paper published in *Bank of Canada Review* in the
autumn of 2009, the authors said financial institutions worldwide "began
to hoard liquidity for precautionary purposes," leading to significantly
higher borrowing costs and funding difficulty. "At several points during
the period, interbank lending and other short-term funding markets
ceased to exist for terms greater than overnight." This supports Bob
Brooks's heightened level of anxiety about term lengths shrinking, and
whether funding would materialize. While Canada did not have to bail
out its banks during the crisis, inject capital, take ownership positions, or
nationalize them, "The Bank of Canada, along with other central banks,
intervened repeatedly to provide liquidity to financial market participants to mitigate the risks of serious financial disturbances and improve
credit conditions."[24]

Interventions included the overnight buying of Government of
Canada securities from primary dealers, most of whom are the big banks.
On August 5, 2008, amendments were made to the Bank of Canada Act
to allow the central bank more flexibility to buy and sell a wider range of
securities. When a central bank buys securities, it is injecting liquidity
into the financial system. As the crisis wore on, the Bank of Canada

broadened the eligibility of assets it would accept as collateral, including non-mortgage loan portfolios. The latter wasn't phased out until early 2010.[25] National Housing Act mortgage-backed securities, Canada Mortgage Bonds, and provincial bonds were also included.

The facts are sobering. "For a short time in Canada, there was a reluctance to lend in the money market for terms longer than a few days, and for several months activity in some short-term markets (e.g., CP) was reduced for terms greater than one week." Stress in the system had initially spiked during the last months of 2007, intensified again as Bear Stearns was running aground in March 2008, and then peaked when Lehman Brothers collapsed on September 15, 2008. On September 18, "the bank expanded a reciprocal currency swap arrangement with the Federal Reserve in order to be able to provide up to $10 billion of US-dollar funding to domestic financial institutions if necessary (such a need has never materialized in Canada, nor was it expected to)." Nevertheless, during the four weeks after September 19, 2008, the Bank "had injected over $20 billion of term liquidity into the financial system."[26]

Separate from the Bank of Canada liquidity interventions, there were federal government initiatives to provide up to "$200 billion to improve access to financing for Canadian households and businesses." That included the Insured Mortgage Purchase Program, which facilitated government purchases, through CMHC, of "pools of insured residential mortgages from Canadian financial institutions . . . Through the IMPP, these institutions could mobilize assets on their balance sheet and obtain a significant and stable means of long-term financing. Thus, the IMPP enabled financial institutions to continue to provide credit to Canadian households, businesses and the economy." This was in addition to the liquidity provided by the Bank of Canada, which "is legally restricted from acquiring an interest in mortgages."[27] As Professor Louis W. Pauly wrote in an analytical chapter about the crisis: "Notwithstanding their solid domestic foundations, Canadian banks were among the key beneficiaries of both

Canadian and American monetary and fiscal largesse during the darkest days of the crisis."[28] In addition to sound management, it seemed a necessary condition of staying profitable, paying dividends, and not requiring an equity issue. Canadians have always wanted stability in their banks. They got it. But they also had the banks' backs.

Reflecting on the crisis, Waugh points to a difference between American lenders and Canadian ones. At Scotiabank, he said, they would appraise an asset and inspect it themselves. In the United States, however, mortgages that were being securitized had been the by-products of "drive by appraisals." It wasn't just the borrowers and lenders who were the problem; there was a problem with the fundamental valuation of the physical assets—the properties themselves. Waugh explains that in Canada the bank's people were required to get out of the car to inspect the asset. Also, in Canada, mortgages would typically be held to maturity, so the bank would have a vested interest in the quality of the loan. Therefore, it was crucial to know the truth about the asset associated with the mortgage. "The assumption on the American models was, 'it's not going to be on our balance sheet.' Buyer beware," Waugh says. Stephen Hart also emphasizes the fact that Canadian banks kept mortgages on their balance sheets. "We're a buy-and-hold [system]," Hart says. "They're a buy-and-churn." Nobody (or at least few) in the US system knew or cared about the quality because they didn't hold it, he says. But if you buy and hold, you're interested.

Also, a bank that was intertwined with its community meant a lot. While banking has undergone a digital modernization since the days when Waugh was a branch manager, assessing the character of borrowers is critical. A borrower needs the capacity to pay and the collateral to back it up, but "the toughest part is character. We always said you have to meet your customer," he says. When Waugh said "meet your customer," he meant physically meet your customer.

Several times during our discussions, Waugh adamantly expressed that if you ever meet a credit person who tells you they've never made a bad loan—and he said he'd heard that from several senior people in the bank—"that person is not a good banker. It just isn't possible. It's like batting averages. No one hits a thousand." While he wouldn't name or specify a client, he indicated that the bank did get snowed from time to time, saying it was usually a mistake in judgment. "I never held that against any credit officer or bankers 'cause they had bad loans, 'cause that's the nature of banking." If a banker continuously made bad loans, however, that was different. "It's hitting for average not for home runs," he said, and "there's no magic number."

There are a variety of reasons Canada's banks withstood the crisis of 2007–9. Sustained profitability is one. As Waugh would say, that's the first line of defence. During 2008 and 2009, all but one of the big five Canadian banks was profitable. CIBC reported a loss in 2008 but was earning money again a year later. In 2008, the four others combined made more than $13 billion, and in 2009, the five made $16 billion. They also had stable national deposit bases, a legal moat protecting them from foreign acquirers, and were less interconnected and complicated than US banks. In addition, they were better supervised and required to hold more and better-quality capital than banks outside of Canada. And as pointed out by others, they held loans on their balance sheets to maturity, resulting in higher lending standards.[29]

While it's clear there were many disquieting days during the crisis—from Brooks's concerns about funding, to Marwah's macro worries, to trades that went awry, to the alarm Waugh witnessed among global bankers and the extraordinary measures taken by central banks and governments—Scotia, like the other Canadian banks, held up and held up well. During the three years of the crisis, its combined net income was $10.591 billion.[30] Waugh says the bank never came close to saying it had to cut the dividend. During the worst of the crisis, the bank paused the cadence of dividend increases but did not stop paying dividends or reduce payouts. It kept paying, as it had done since its earliest days. But during the crisis, you couldn't expect anything to be a slam dunk.

There was, however, the question of issuing more common stock to the public to shore up capital. During interviews, Waugh mentioned many times that Scotia was the only big five bank that did not raise equity to do so.[‡‡‡] Issuing shares during the crisis meant selling stock at a bargain-basement price. New stock would also dilute existing shareholdings by adding more shares to the public float. Despite widespread worry about the ability of banks to absorb losses, Waugh was convinced Scotia did not need to raise more capital (although it did issue stock for an acquisition—the purchase of SunLife's holding in CI Financial). "Never did I feel exposed." The bank, Waugh says, had liquidity alternatives and, in a pinch, "could have raised capital because the markets were receptive to it." But as CEO, he was accountable. "I made the call that we didn't need to." He did allow that he was challenged by the board on the issue, "appropriately so," he says, adding that good boards do that. Ultimately, the board was satisfied the bank had enough liquidity and capital, "and we were all right." Marwah believes this was one of Waugh's best decisions, and that it saved shareholders a lot of money.

But while Scotia had done well throughout the crisis, there was some international mopping up to do.

[‡‡‡] National Bank, the sixth biggest, also did not issue common stock in 2008 to boost capital.

CHAPTER NINE

In the Room

On Saturday, January 10, 2009, as the financial world struggled to find its footing after the disastrous and unthinkable autumn of 2008, Waugh travelled to Europe and back home in less than forty-eight hours. The bank's jet was scheduled to depart Toronto at 7:30 p.m. His itinerary showed he would be joined onboard by Mark Carney, governor of the Bank of Canada. Carney was to arrive at Toronto's Pearson International Airport on Air Canada flight 461 at 6:09 p.m. He would then be transferred to the private aviation section of the airport. The two were headed to Basel, Switzerland, for Sunday meetings at the Bank for International Settlements (BIS), the central bank for central banks.[*]

Basel is the closest thing to a company town for people who set interest rates and have their names on currencies; this weekend they had global bankers as guests. Among the thirty-five people expected in Room B at

---

[*] Waugh said Carney's predecessor, David Dodge, also flew with him to Basel.

the BIS: Federal Reserve chairman Ben Bernanke; governor of the Bank of England Mervyn King; president of the European Central Bank Jean-Claude Trichet; governor of the People's Bank of China Zhou Xiaochuan; plus the CEOs of the biggest UK, German, Japanese, and French banks, as well as the chairmen and CEOs of Morgan Stanley and debt rating agency Moody's Corporation.[2]

While Waugh attended as president and CEO of Scotiabank, he was there in his capacity at the Institute of International Finance—representing global financial firms from sixty countries—to address concerns arising from the crisis. In addition to running the bank, he had become involved in policy issues facing the entire sector. As well as having sat on the IIF board for ten years, he was vice-chair. Waugh's briefing notes included a list of the top seventy-five global banks by market value or capitalization. The total market value of the big five Canadian banks constituted just 5.5 percent of the global figure. American banks accounted for 20 percent and China 21.5, while Europe and the UK combined for the largest chunk, 29 percent.[3]

A seventeen-page BIS briefing document put bankers on notice. "The immediate measures taken by governments, supervisors, central banks and financial institutions have contained the crisis," but the future was unclear. Conditions had "deteriorated rapidly." The crisis "calls into question key features of financial innovation and bank business models," the document said, and banks were rapidly trying to shrink balance sheets—i.e., unload bad assets (loans)—leading to "severe credit restraint." The BIS went on: "The near total breakdown in credit markets in early October [2008] led governments to announce system-wide rescue measures. Central bank lending policies were widened in unprecedented ways." Still, "the fragility of market conditions has abated only gradually."[4]

As if anyone needed clarification, the BIS said, in underlined text, "<u>High leverage was a key cause of the financial crisis.</u>" Additionally, it added, "insurance and hedging strategies made leverage seem safer than it had been before the early 2000s." From mid-2007 to the end of December 2008, it reported, global writedowns were US$772.6 billion, and the crisis was far from over. Banks had become much more reliant on short-term funding, with non-US banks facing "increasing difficulties in rolling over dollar funding," just as former Scotia treasurer Bob Brooks described. Reflecting the risks of the market, at the end of 2008, the cost of US dollar bank debt had ballooned. By that time, $7.5 trillion had been "committed or actually made available by central banks and governments since mid-2007 to support bank debt funding and capital."[5] Such a number is hard to fathom. Then, it would have amounted to approximately four times the annual value of Canada's economy.

While banks were shrinking their balance sheets—deleveraging— central banks and governments were piling on leverage to save the system. "The only way to deleverage," the BIS said, "is to shed assets." Shedding assets meant cutting lending. Cutting lending might save banks, but it could put a stake through the heart of economies. No lending meant no funding of households, no funding of businesses. If that happened, no economy. Everyone was in a terrible jam because of bad banking practices. The BIS said there had been fifteen banking crises in industrial countries since 1970.[6] Argentina in 2001–2 would have been one of them. But there had been none like this.

For the "Crisis Management" meeting at 2 p.m., a BIS document laid out questions: How advanced was bank deleveraging? How intense was the pressure to do so? How can you prevent a severe contraction of credit to households and non-financial firms while facilitating an orderly reduction of financial system leverage? In other words, damned if you do, damned if you don't. Then, the one that makes banks shudder. "How can banks respond to market demands for higher capital levels?"[7] Years later, the debate continues. Bank CEOs, including Scotiabank's, still maintain that rigorous capital requirements diminish what banks can lend.[8]

As the afternoon progressed, there was no relief. Central bankers wanted to know "How are banks changing their funding strategy? How will banks manage their funding liquidity risks differently in the future?" When discussion turned to "Business models and regulation," the queries were about "the future of the originate-and-distribute" model. In plain English: What would happen to the practice of lending money to unqualified borrowers and then packaging up and selling those loans hither and yon, so you no longer bore responsibility for bad credit decisions? That was, of course, a key, underlying cause of the crisis. Furthermore, what would all the restructuring and consolidation that occurred during the heat of the crisis mean— and how could "the systemic consequences of increased concentration be mitigated?" Was there a need for "simpler indicators" to oversee the buildup of bank leverage?[9] It was the overseers questioning the overseen. And the overseen had some explaining to do. Even though Scotia wasn't a culprit, it was part of the overseen and could be hit with more regulation.

Waugh, of course, had strong views. Capital was an important buffer in the long run, he recognized, and it was dear to regulators' hearts. But liquidity, he believed, was paramount. As well, the asset quality at a bank was more crucial than capital. If the loans were good and the bank was getting paid, it would make money. And a profitable bank was not only good for shareholders, but it also protected depositors and didn't leave taxpayers holding the bag.

As his own notes show, Waugh had his arguments ready. Topping a page of bullet points was a standout line: "the Canadian Model is a bit less in need of 'being fixed.'" Any changes in capital requirements, his notes said, needed to be "fully assessed and globally harmonized before being implemented in Canada to ensure Canada is not at a competitive disadvantage." Any changes to core capital "should recognize our very high starting position." Minimum capital ratios "are higher in Canada than Basel base requirements." As for liquidity, Waugh's notes indicated that individual institutions have differing requirements. This simple sentence—"*Limit hard rules*" (italics added)—stood out. "This is a long-established best practice and has worked well for Canadian Financial Institutions."[10]

Waugh also had notes about the importance of regulatory regimes and good management. He highlighted Canada's Office of the Superintendent of Financial Institutions. The Canadian regulator's key capital requirement was already the highest in the G7—and Canada's banks, Waugh had written, chose to hold even higher levels of capital and the highest quality capital "by choice, not regulation." They had also chosen to not have "large exposures to CDO and structured securities to any large degree—this was management choice, not regulators."

He also noted the regulator buttressed an already conservative Canadian culture—"law, order and good government vs. Liberty, freedom and the pursuit of happiness," the latter being the American way. It may have been a Rick-ism—he got the mottos of both countries slightly wrong—but the contrast he made with the United States was clear. Residential mortgages in Canada, he wanted to tell the Basel group, required 20 percent equity or insurance over that amount, with losses being negligible. Durations were five years or under (much shorter than in the US, so less risky). Keeping mortgages on the banks' balance sheets meant accountability. Each year, the bank started with 20 percent of its "accrued income from our mortgages."[11] The underlying message was: Canada's doing it right. Keep your hands off.

He'd also scribbled there was "no one model" for a global financial institution. Scotia, for instance, had singular characteristics, and "regional differences are important—culture, politics and regulatory." Regarding the "exit strategy of state-owned capital," he scribbled "sooner better . . . State intervening never works in long run." As for compensation, he stressed the "right incentives, structure of compensation, not the amount." Canadian banks were "the best," adding "we received no subsidies, nor equity, nor are we asking for it."

Additionally, over the course of the past year—the height of the crisis—Scotiabank had moved from sixtieth in market value to twenty-ninth (RBC and TD were fourteenth and twenty-third, respectively). "Something must be working," he wrote. In the past few months, he added, Canadian financial institutions had raised billions in private capital. Trumpeting the "Canadian Model," he called Canada "not a bad place to be!" He said the country's model "is not perfect," but "at least it's made it through the crisis in pretty good shape—so far."[12]

The meeting was scheduled to wrap at 5:15 p.m. At 5:30, a bus would take the group to a dinner hosted by Credit Suisse.† At 9 p.m., Waugh would board the company jet alone to fly home, arriving in Toronto at 1:20 a.m. on Monday, January 12. His flight to and from Europe, the luncheon, meetings, and dinner would take just over forty hours, a week's work over a weekend. Indira Samarasekera, a Scotiabank board member from 2008 to 2021, said "the reason that Rick could do what he did, scan the world, be connected externally, was because Sabi [Marwah] ran the bank on a day-to-day basis with Bob Brooks. And it reflected Rick's confidence in Sabi. And their ability to work as a sort of partner-ship." Waugh agrees. "Anybody who thinks their CEO can run the bank solely on themselves," he says, "gets into trouble."

Before the worst of the crisis hit, the IIF had tried to get ahead of what it knew was coming. In October 2007, it established a Committee on Market Best Practices and reported in July 2008. More than sixty finan-cial firms participated "to determine what went wrong and what needed to be done to fix a system with serious deficiencies" and to help facilitate co-operation with regulators.[13]

---

† Fourteen years later, during a banking crisis in March 2023, Credit Suisse would falter and be absorbed by UBS.

While the IIF has a staff of hundreds in Washington, DC, Waugh says without a hint of bashfulness that, "I led the charge on a lot of this stuff."‡ He had initially been reluctant to take on a leadership role at the IIF. But RBC's Gord Nixon, who was on the board, encouraged him to do it. Charles Dallara, who led the Institute and later joined the board of Scotiabank at Waugh's behest, mentions Waugh in his 2024 book *Euroshock*, about the Greek debt crisis. Dallara wrote that Scotiabank had "no exposure whatsoever" to the Greek debt fiasco, but Dallara says he consulted Waugh, describing him as "a very experienced banker" who "had dealt with many sovereign debt problems in Latin America. I often found his independent views quite useful."[14]

In helping lead the IIF's best practices drive (Waugh co-headed the committee with Cees Maas, CFO and COO of ING Group), Waugh interviewed risk managers from global banks and discovered that none reported directly to the CEO. At one conference, Waugh says, he interrupted the then-CEO of Citigroup, who was leading a session on "A Day in the Life of a CEO," to say, "I talked to all your risk managers. Very few report to any of you guys." He adds: "They [the bankers in the room] didn't like it."

As Waugh told *Euromoney* in September 2008, "Those who have got it [risk management] right have been major beneficiaries of this crisis but even more significantly, those who have got it wrong have paid an immense price."

Describing the report of the best practices committee, *Euromoney*'s Peter Lee wrote: "It sounds like a collection of advanced mathematics PhDs having to go back to primary school and learn their multiplication

---

‡ BMO's Bill Downe said Waugh was very well regarded internationally at the IIF, IMC, and IMF, "and would have been much more outward-looking than most of the other Canadian banks." Downe said Waugh encouraged him to join the IIF board to make sure there was a Canadian voice when he left—and ensured when he stepped off as a director of the IMC that Downe was appointed a director. "He was just very generous in sponsoring me."

tables." One bank CEO told the magazine that the underlying loans within the collateralized debt obligations and asset-backed securities his bank bought in the run up to the crisis contained—*wait for it*—exposure to "seven million" individual loans. How could an institution, let alone a regulator, possibly know the vulnerabilities of that many loans—the quality of the assets?

The report addressed a laundry list of issues, essentially an admission the system had run amok: principles of conduct, risk management, compensation policies, liquidity risk, ratings and investor due diligence in securitization markets, transparency, and disclosure. Where to begin? From the report: "some first overestimated the market's capacity to absorb risk. Failures in risk management policies, procedures, and techniques were evident at several firms—in particular, the lack of a comprehensive approach to firm-wide risk management often meant that key risks were not identified or effectively managed."[15]

For his part, Waugh understood risk and knew that managing it had to be a company-wide concern, starting at the top. While the IIF had a significant staff and many would have been involved in the report, his voice echoed through it. "It is critical for governance to embed a firm-wide focus on risk." Consistent "risk culture," the report argued, was the main enabling tool in risk management. "Each firm should: Make clear that senior management, in particular the CEO, is responsible for risk management; Establish the Board's essential oversight role in risk management; and Develop a robust risk culture that is embedded in the way the firm operates."[16]

Furthermore, "Assign responsibility for risk management to an officer at a senior level, in most cases a Chief Risk Officer (CRO) who should have sufficient seniority, voice, and independence from line business management to have a meaningful impact on decisions;" and "Ensure that the CRO has the ability to influence key decision makers in the firm . . . Ensure that risk management does not rely on a single risk methodology, and analyze group-wide risks on an aggregate basis." The report stated that "stress testing was not consistently applied, too rigidly defined, or inadequately developed."[17]

As for the securitization mania during the run-up to the crisis, the report underlined this: "There are a number of parties involved in this process . . . the Committee found that, as the number of structured deals grew, standards weakened at various points in the chain. Pressures to keep costs down resulted in risk assessment becoming an excessively model-driven process."[18] Terry Fryett recalls Waugh on stage at the IIF, telling his fellow global bankers that "Everyone's responsible for risk." Fryett says the bank had always had that in its DNA and referred to the crisis as "the Canadian banks' fifteen minutes of fame." Indeed, following the crisis, the World Economic Forum ranked Canada's banks the world's soundest for several years running.

In September 2011, there was a meeting of the IIF in Washington. It was a closed session with no media in attendance, but what occurred there—a high-temperature squabble resulting in the guest of honour leaving—leaked. The guest was Mark Carney, who that year also became chair of the Financial Stability Board, an international body created by the G20 to help monitor the global financial system and recommend measures to make it more secure. By then, Carney had become a financial star who would later be the first non-Brit to serve as governor of the Bank of England. He was the kind of speaker IIF members wanted to hear.

Also in the room was another financial star, arguably the world's leading banker: Jamie Dimon, chairman and CEO of JPMorgan Chase & Co. Dimon became CEO in 2005 (and remains so in 2025). Growing the bank while navigating financial crises, a global pandemic, and personal issues like cancer and emergency heart surgery, Dimon is a force in business and a thoughtful commentator on economies and global affairs. JPMorgan not only survived the crisis under Dimon but also did well by purchasing Bear Stearns in March 2008 and Washington Mutual six months later, at the height of the crisis. In 2023, it would again be opportunistic, buying First Republic Bank during a mini-banking crisis.

Carney, meanwhile, was born in the Northwest Territories, and attended Harvard (he was the hockey team's backup goalie) and Oxford. He then worked at Goldman Sachs for thirteen years before returning to Canada as a leading finance department official, Bank of Canada official, and then Bank of Canada governor. Until winning the leadership of Canada's Liberal Party in 2025 and replacing Justin Trudeau as prime minister, he was chair of Bloomberg as well as Brookfield Asset Management. Carney is smart and eloquent. So is Dimon, and neither is a shrinking violet.

One participant recalled that the group was meeting in an ornate room at one of Washington's large museums. The bankers were on edge, given that regulators and central banks wanted to strengthen the regulatory net. While the IIF wanted to be open about the industry's weaknesses and mistakes—it recognized that liquidity, capital, and compensation had to be addressed—there was also a view in the room that regulators were moving too fast, and credit could be choked further while economies were still weak due to the crisis. Charles Dallara said the "regulatory pendulum was swinging too far," and regulations were not being developed with a nuanced sense of the economy. The preferred approach, according to Dallara, was for the banks to get their own acts together before regulators did it for them. He added that the history of the Institute was such that while these meetings could be adversarial, concerns were voiced "with a certain degree of politeness" and civility.

Waugh says he was chair of the meeting and that he sat beside Dimon, and that "Jamie and Mark had a back and forth." That was Waugh's polite way of saying there was an altercation. "They were arguing," he says, and "both are opinionated people." A key participant in the room described the interchange in starker terms. "Dimon ripped into him [Carney] in a particularly vicious fashion," they said, describing it as "a cringeworthy moment." Fourteen years later, Dimon challenged descriptions of the exchange. "I wouldn't call it heated," he said, saying he was just being direct. "I was probably less civil than Charles thought I should be. So be it."

Dimon was pushing back against Carney's view on tougher banking regulations—the post-crisis requirement for banks to hold more capital as a buffer against losses—calling the new rules "cockamamie non-sense."[19] He charged they were designed by regulators, academics, and others who didn't know the reality of markets. "And I still think they're cockamamie, and they're still in place," Dimon exclaims. "Obviously," Waugh says, "Jamie was disrespecting the role of the regulator and Carney took it personally because he was, you know, in that capacity." At an international gathering of hundreds of financial firms from doz-ens of countries intent on mopping up after a US-generated financial crisis, Dimon was calling the new rules "anti-American," which he still does. "I was probably the one person who was willing to speak up." It would appear that there was zero introspection over the fact that US banking practices had been central to the problem in the first place.

But many in the room—hardly wallflowers themselves—were shocked. "We watched it. It was a two-way conversation. The rest of us weren't involved in it," Waugh says. If there was a banker certain people looked up to during the crisis, it was Dimon, for his shrewd, articulate, level-headed approach. But on this day, the view was he'd overstepped. Carney, though, didn't need training wheels. A pugnacious, sharp-elbowed character in his own right, with an intellect to match, he was having none of it. In Waugh's retelling, Carney "basically told him [Dimon] to fuck off."

At the highest levels of global finance, emotions were running hot. News accounts reported that Waugh intervened to lower the temperature, to no avail. Waugh downplays the media dispatches, which described him as a referee. It seemed as though Carney felt abused. He "pulled together his papers," another participant said. "I'm not going to sit here and take this," was the sense. Carney "packed up and walked out." For his part, Dimon says, "I remember him getting annoyed and leaving," but adds that he does not recall Carney swearing.

Afterwards, Waugh says he spoke firmly with Dimon. "I said, 'Thanks, Jamie. That's my regulator that you just pissed off or upset.'" Dimon didn't dispute Waugh's recollection. While Carney wasn't technically Canada's banking regulator (OSFI is), he was governor of its central bank, which controls monetary policy and promotes "safe, sound and efficient financial systems."[20] Dimon's comments, in Waugh's view, were simply out of line. "Our guest Mark Carney had left, and he was our guest. And that's no way to treat a guest," Waugh says. He phoned Carney later to smooth things out. Dimon also says that he spoke to Carney afterwards. "I probably even apologized if I felt I was a little harsh, okay? But being harsh and being right are two different things." Dimon characterized the incident as "a little kerfuffle" and maintained he has a good relationship with Carney. "I've spoken to him since he became Prime Minister."[§]

Separately, blithe disregard of Canadian concerns was not unusual in American financial circles, even among some of the best bankers in the world. Sitting in his office at JPMorgan in New York, cameras rolling, I asked Ace Greenberg—the legendary former chairman and CEO of Bear Stearns, long before it ran into mortal trouble—whether he had any sense that a crisis in American banking had created extreme pressures and costs to other countries, like Canada. While Canada was not the epicentre of the financial crisis, the Canadian government did decide to inject $63 billion in stimulus and tax reductions to prop up the economy as a result.[21] Other estimates are higher. Greenberg seemed

_____

§ Carney did not respond to requests for an interview.

mystified by the question, at the idea that anything outside of the United States was relevant. The financial crisis was *an American banking issue, a Bear Stearns issue.* And what was the capital city of Canada anyway, he wondered aloud. "Ossawa?" Here was one of the world's best-known and savviest financiers, someone who'd spent the bulk of his life a mere one-hour flight from Ottawa, and he didn't even know the national capital of the United States' closest ally, let alone the cross-border impact of careless financial practices.

As an attendee of global banking conferences, Waugh came to a similar realization. He knew all the top American and European banking CEOs personally. And yet, "I was stunned," he says. "Not one of them that I recall asked me why Canadian banks did so well and survived [during the crisis]." The truth is, they don't care. But Waugh saw that as a competitive advantage for Canada. It sits next to the world's biggest economy, has historically benefited from that proximity, and was—until Donald Trump's threats to make Canada the fifty-first state via economic force—regarded as a friend. So his attitude was "just suck it up."

Thomas Lewis Dodge was a merchant in Kentville, Nova Scotia, in the 1800s. He became part of the province's legislative council, and his principal assets were shares in the Bank of Nova Scotia. In 2001, his great-grandson, David Dodge, became governor of the Bank of Canada, after stints as deputy minister of finance and deputy minister of health. Once Dodge retired from running Canada's central bank in early 2008, and after an appropriate amount of time had passed, he joined the board of directors of Scotiabank in 2010 for the last few years of Waugh's tenure. He said he liked Waugh and had "sporadic contact over a number of years," first meeting the banker in the 1990s. Dodge said the overriding factor in Canada successfully making it through the crisis was that "our financial system was inherently more risk averse than the American financial system." There weren't the "crappy mortgages" that were originated and then distributed or sold off. "Essentially, our banks were prudent lenders" and, as Waugh has stated, kept mortgages on the banks' balance sheets.

Nonetheless, Dodge talked about how the crisis was in certain respects harder for Scotia than for other banks. Because it had the smallest retail depositor base, it was more dependent on wholesale funding. "And when stress occurs in the system, [to] the extent you are more heavily reliant on wholesale funds, which can run very fast compared to retail deposits, you are more exposed. I mean, that's absolutely true," Dodge said. As a result, he said that the Office of the Superintendent of Financial Institutions had been more vigilant about Scotia's overall risk management than, say, Royal Bank's during that period. Scotia's lending was known to be more judgment-based, particularly in its international subsidiaries.

"That's why OSFI had Scotia in the penalty box for a long time," which Dodge, when he joined the board, felt "was a bit unfair." Credit, after all, was the Scotia culture, the culture Waugh had been trained in and grown up amidst. That judgment allowed for lending to small businesses and immigrants. Restricting it would mean cutting off people who would have been good risks. Also, in subsidiaries like Chile, which Dodge said was the one he knew best, money was lent more on judgment. "He [Rick] fought Nick Le Pan, who was superintendent at the time. He fought Nick on this." Le Pan, Dodge said, had criticized the bank for a weak management information system. In the end, Dodge said, "Scotia had to institute some systems that took away some of that judgment."

This brings up the bank's historic approach to technology. "Scotia also never invested very heavily in technology. That was a long-standing shortfall, and so, you know, we were always criticized," Dodge said. At this point, he was speaking as a former board member. "It was true that we didn't invest enough in technology. I mean all of the banks were slow. But we were probably the slowest, at Scotia, in doing that."

Did the bank misjudge the importance of technology? "Absolutely. Absolutely. That was a fight I had when I was on the board. We were going in the wrong direction on that." Another former board member— Indira Samarasekera—confirmed that Scotia lagged on tech, as did others. "OSFI really held our feet to the fire on the need to have better technology capability," she said. "'You guys might have just dodged a bullet—next time around, you need to have better systems.'" Investments ramped up, she said, after the financial crisis.

Waugh, for his part, calls technology a tool, not a strategy. Not long after he left the CEO position, he told me over lunch that you could buy tech "off the shelf." He wasn't a tech guy. He was a walk-around-and-talk-to-people guy. That worked during his era, but would the string have run out quickly on that approach as digital and cloud technology became more central to all industries? How would the bank have kept up with cybercrime, let alone online banking, or run a bank virtually during a global pandemic—a crisis that restricted social interaction, the mother's milk of the Waugh approach?

When presented with Dodge's view, Waugh says, "I disagree, obviously, 'cause if you're first on technology, he's right. But if you're not first, you can save a lot of money by then investing in technology that's proven itself." He adds, "It's better to be a quick follower of a proven technology that's available." The latest ATM is outdated a year later, he says. "We strategically decided to be a quick adopter rather than a significant investor in new technology." With ATMs, Waugh says, no matter which bank you were, you were behind Canada Trust with its famous Johnny Cash machines. He didn't believe the bank lost customers because it was fourth or fifth on ATMs. On AI becoming more of an enabler, he says, "I'd rather have a pilot in the plane rather than relying on an algorithm."¶

¶ In June 2024, a top bank source said BNS now spends some $4 billion a year on technology. The 2023 annual report said $4.5 billion (Scotiabank 2023 annual report, p. 35). In 2024, it was $4.8 billion (Scotiabank 2024 annual report, p. 34).

Waugh is clear on many things, and one of them is an unwavering belief in the human mind, a bias that he said "absolutely" affected his decisions on tech investments. And as CEO, he had to prioritize. "Was I better off doing [buying a bank in] Peru or was I better off giving it to ATMs?"

As for Waugh's views on regulation, which included his opinion that the quality of assets should be emphasized over increasing capital requirement? "That of course is the banker's argument," Dodge countered, adding that it's not just coming from Waugh but from bankers around the world. "That's fine until you have an SVB [Silicon Valley Bank] that runs into trouble." We were speaking roughly a year after the deposit run at SVB.

"So, the question is always, and always has been, the issue of to what extent do you allow the banks—which are the bedrock of the day-to-day financial transactions and day-to-day funding of business—to what extent do you allow them to get themselves potentially into trouble by making riskier bets?" Dodge asked. "That debate goes on." As for the IIF (and the IMC), where Waugh played a significant role, "they're on the banker's side."

On the debate over the importance of capital, the former chief risk officer of Scotia, Stephen Hart, said: "Capital's shit. I mean it's liquidity that saves you." Hart said Lehman Brothers had lots of capital, but that couldn't save it. Dodge, however, argued that, "you need both." He said, "Underlying capital is fundamental. But if you don't have liquidity," he added, "you can get into a jam in a short period of time that even though you are very solid and fundamentally strong, you can't get out of the jam." Liquidity, of course, is central to the Waugh playbook. "It's correct that in the short run, no matter how solvent you are," Dodge said, "you can be in trouble."

Despite any differences over technology investments and regulation, Dodge has a soft spot for Waugh. "So, I really like Rick," he said. "His style fitted with the history of Scotia . . . It was a family." And the bank's leadership, he observed, was in a sense part of the family, "Rick perhaps more than Peter and more than Ritchie," he added, confirming Waugh managed by walking around. "I liked the culture of Scotia. That's why I joined Scotia," Dodge said; he liked "how they looked at the world."

Indeed, BNS had a culture. Gerry Schwartz had known Waugh since the late 1970s, when the young banker was assessing investments for the bank's pension fund. Schwartz, speaking at his firm's headquarters in June 2024, said he, along with the late Izzy Asper—two fellow Winnipeggers—were trying to raise money for what he called the precursor to Onex. "He [Waugh] turned us down," something Schwartz said each has reminded the other of over the years. But they became friends, and later, Schwartz and his wife, Heather Reisman, went along with Waugh and Lynne on a holiday to Jamaica. On the plane back, Schwartz described a company he was buying personally—Brights, a winery—and mentioned that another bank had turned him down for a loan.

"That's business we'd like to have," Waugh told him, and said he'd have an answer by the end of the week. "And he did." Schwartz said it was a $3 million loan that allowed him to buy Brights. Ultimately, via acquisitions, the business was driven by vintner Donald Triggs. It became Vincor International Inc. and was later sold for more than a billion dollars. Waugh, Schwartz said, was chosen to be Scotia's CEO because he "was the standard-bearer for the culture at BNS," which he said was discernible: "willing to support people that it believed in." Scotia "banked people based on character, not just numbers." Waugh, he believed, was "very, very smart," and very much in the mould of Godsoe, with whom Schwartz was also close.

Isadore Sharp echoed that sentiment. On the morning of April 8, 2024, when I reached out regarding an interview for this book, his wife Rosalie emailed me back within minutes with their home phone number. Although I'd interviewed Issy several times on television, I didn't have his email, but I did happen to have Rosalie's from some ten years earlier. Within nineteen minutes I was on the phone with her. We chatted while Issy finished his cereal. "Scotiabank was his guardian angel," she said. "He used to go on bended knee. He'd nag them to death," she added, laughing. "He had no money."

Issy confirmed her story. His relationship with the bank "goes back to the first money I ever borrowed in business," he said. "The Bank of Nova Scotia . . . never rejected a request of mine and I didn't have the balance sheet." In the late 1950s, he was entering a business about which he knew nothing, but he had an idea and a passion. He was borrowing from a mortgage company and from the trades—and the bank lent him $150,000. In fact, credit chief George Hitchman looked at Four Seasons' short-term commitments and told him, "Your balance sheet shows you're bankrupt." The banker then said, "Let me fix it for you." Sharp recalled Hitchman using a purple pencil** and moving around certain commitments so they would be longer term, giving Sharp's company financial relief. "They looked for ways to help you in your business."

At one point, Sharp said he wanted to take over management of the Ritz-Carlton in Chicago. To take an equity position so he could get the management contract, he needed $3.5 million. The hotel was losing money operationally, but Sharp viewed it as a "magnificent" hotel. He went to Scotiabank to borrow what he needed. During Sharp's meeting with Hitchman, Cedric Ritchie walked in carrying a newspaper with the headline "The Biggest White Elephant in Chicago." Is this what you want us to lend to you for? he asked. Yes, Sharp answered. "Remember," Ritchie warned, "we're lending you the money and we expect you to pay us back." Waugh, Sharp told me, "was groomed on that principle."

** Scotia had a tradition of CEOs using coloured pencils, typically aligning with the first initial of surnames. Ritchie used red. Godsoe used green. Waugh reverted to red again because white wouldn't have worked. He said a checkmark from the CEO's coloured pencil was accepted by the bank's audit department. To this day, Waugh has a huge red pencil in a corner of his office.

Later, when Sharp wanted to build his second hotel, the Inn on the Park in North York, his bank manager on Bloor Street set up a meeting with a more senior banker, Cliff Ash, at head office. Let me explain something, Ash said. I don't have to know your business, but what do you want? "I'm choking at this point," Sharp said. "He said, 'How much do you need?'" Six hundred thousand dollars, Sharp told him. Ash said okay. Sharp then said, "That's it?" Ash said yeah. Sharp reckoned they'd witnessed him successfully building the first hotel, and "whatever I had borrowed from them I had always paid back."

From his later days on Scotia's board, Sharp recalled there was a strategy "to develop a very strong service culture." While Sharp only dealt with Scotiabank, at one point, one of his finance executives suggested Four Seasons should try to secure a second banking relationship. So, he went to see "Gordie" Bell to explain. "Well, that's fine. That's what most companies do," Bell told him. But the banker kept talking: If Four Seasons dealt with three or four banks and something went wrong, he asked, which bank would have Sharp's back? Against everyone's advice, "That taught me that I'm going to stick with one bank" he said. If things went bad, "that one bank is going to have my back."

Sharp and Four Seasons did run into serious problems in 1981, when interest rates were above 20 percent and they owed a large sum to the bank. "You better come down," Bell said. The banker wanted to know how Sharp planned to deal with the extreme rates. He told Bell he thought it was a "temporary blip," and he needed an increase in the amount of the loan to see him through. Bell did not react well. "I brought you down here to find out how you're going to pay back your loan, not increase it," he said. If the latter were the case, Bell told Sharp he would have to pledge all his personal assets. Again, against the advice of lawyers and auditors, "I pledged everything I had personally with the condition that they would continue to support my loans." He said the bank abided by that and rates eventually returned to more normal levels. Sharp said

Ritchie, Godsoe, and Waugh shared the same, old-school principle when running the bank, and that it was "always a company that looked at the character of its clients rather than the balance sheet of their clients."

Nick Le Pan was superintendent of financial institutions from 2001 to 2006, deputy head prior to that, and an assistant deputy minister in the federal department of finance before that. He said he would have met Waugh when Waugh headed the international division at Scotia, as part of building a relationship with the banks. The relatively brief meeting took place in a small meeting room on the bank's boardroom floor. "He looks a little bit boyish," Le Pan recalled. "The arms are flailing." The jocular look, the sideways grin, "that was Rick," Le Pan said. And "he's always leaning in." The next-in-line to be CEO was anything but buttoned down, a trend that Le Pan was beginning to observe at the big banks. While some bank bosses were still formal, "others were starting to be a little bit more, I almost want to say human, in a sense."

As for whether OSFI was more vigilant with Scotia than the other big banks due to its credit culture—as David Dodge suggested—Le Pan said no, even though the regulator was well aware of Scotia's way of doing business. "Every one of the major, the big five, had some element that was different than the others" and that had to be considered when assessing risk. At Scotia, the obvious difference was the international scope of the bank, which could be volatile over a cycle. It was clear, though, that Scotia had a different credit culture than others. "It was very centralized. It was more hands-on," Le Pan said. Godsoe read the credits, he said, as did Waugh, and they prided themselves on that. "They really thought that was something that differentiated them and allowed them to do certain things," he said.

Beyond that, during Waugh's tenure as CEO, Le Pan believed the bank's culture began to change on purpose. While maintaining the primacy of credit, Waugh, Le Pan said, viewed himself as a representative of the bank, not as a personality cult CEO. This fits with my own first impression of Waugh. Among the many Canadian bank CEOs I have interviewed, Waugh is the only one to ever hand me a business card, more Rotary Club than Toronto Club. Whether this shift had anything to do with the chair and CEO roles being split when Waugh arrived as chief executive is difficult to prove. Perhaps it was just the way Waugh was. Le Pan, the former regulator, did not see in Waugh the desire to be an "imperial CEO" like Ritchie or Godsoe. "There would have been a little more space for people [under Waugh]," Le Pan said, a culture shift that, he added, "served the bank well."

That said, "We were definitely aware that Scotia had a particular credit culture," Le Pan said, and as it did with all the banks, OSFI monitored to see whether that culture was working the way it was supposed to work. Le Pan would not reveal confidential conversations; rather, he spoke broadly. If as a bank you were sometimes going with the gut, with centralized involvement from the top, the regulator wanted to know whether you were up to it—who you were extending credit to and how much. Were there signs that decisions were getting overridden in a manner that heightened risk? As to whether Scotia was ever in the OSFI penalty box because of the way it operated, Le Pan said he wouldn't go there. "I don't talk about who's in the penalty box, ever," he said.

He did, however, confirm that Waugh fought with OSFI, as Dodge indicated. "Oh, absolutely," Le Pan said, adding there was nothing wrong with that. While OSFI wasn't running the banks or declaring a culture was flawed, Le Pan said the regulator welcomed lively debate. "We're going to push on stuff and they're going to push back," he said. "I would expect that." He said, "I respected Rick. I think Rick respected the office." While the regulator wanted to push, Le Pan said, it also wanted to hear how things worked in the real world. There were also instances when banks would say, "You know, Nick, it's actually good that you raised that." If, however, a bank was in total denial about an OSFI concern, that's when the red flags would pop up. As for stresses in the wholesale funding market, Le Pan said such situations are always triggered by something. "Often, it's credit. It's a big credit surprise"—meaning bad lending that comes home to roost, such as what occurred in the sub-prime mortgage market in the United States.

Assessing the bank's approach to technology during that period, Le Pan said, "They had adopted a different strategy as to how they want to spend." Given its frugality, Scotia might not have had the prettiest ATMs, but Le Pan said as far as the key issues OSFI cared about—controls and risks or safety and soundness—technology at the bank was not a concern. This of course, was before cyberthreats were what they are now. While Le Pan said he agreed with Waugh's statement that technology is not a strategy, it is, he argued, "a big enabler of strategy."

Given Waugh's involvement in international policy discussions through his participation in the IIF and IMC, Le Pan said they had many discussions over the years, even pre-crisis. He believes "Rick was less effective in his contribution to policy stuff" than he could have been. Quite simply, Le Pan said, "It wasn't a world he came from at all." Waugh, he observed, is a "get it done" kind of guy—a deal guy, a credit guy, a leader guy—and "he's irrepressible." Le Pan, who has made a career out of regulation, policy and legislation, and leading high-ranking global regulatory groups, said Waugh's considerable qualities didn't nec-essarily fit with those of policy-makers, who may be more deliberative. Rather than criticizing regulators that they were putting too much emphasis on capital, Le Pan would have preferred to have heard three specific suggestions on what to do differently. He said he found it easier to have such discussions with Sabi Marwah, who was more deliberative, more inclined to listen. "None of the CEOs were super [on policy]," Le Pan said. "They were leaving it more to the Sabis of the world."

As for Waugh's assertion that policy-makers became too focused on capital levels rather than the quality of assets, Le Pan was clear: "Yes, regulators became overly focused on capital. Why? Because it was easier!" It would be nigh impossible for regulators to assess assets, the soundness of every loan a bank made. "I'm not saying it [the IIF] was all a crock and didn't go anywhere. And he [Waugh] did do a bunch of good stuff," Le Pan said, fired up. However, he added, "The moment you're a banker, you're in an unholy alliance with the government." You are regulated, meaning a level of discomfort. "They [banks] benefit from that," Le Pan said. "The country benefits from that."

For his part, Waugh wouldn't address the specifics of the conversations with OSFI either, saying, "I'm bound by a confidentiality agreement with the regulator." However, he was willing to discuss issues such as the bank's reliance on wholesale funding. "Because of our reliance on wholesale, we had to make sure our assets were well diversified and produced a significant amount of equity and had adequate loan loss reserves, which it did." He was fired up, too, saying, "I felt completely comfortable, and as history has shown, was right. The numbers speak for themselves." The best way to prevent failure, he said, "is to make sure you're a good lender." He added, "If we're making money for the shareholder, the depositor is being well taken care of." The issue, Waugh said, is how much risk does a bank take to protect the shareholder.

On Dodge saying Le Pan had to institute some systems that took away some of the judgment-based credit decisions, Waugh says, "We had to continually show our regulators that our assets were either performing or had been reserved," adding, "I had no problem with the debate with our regulators and they were healthy. I still believe we had one of the strongest risk cultures of any bank," he says, because we devoted so much talent and process to that. "We're totally involved on a daily basis." Waugh describes how every day, he would take home (as did the team) "a suitcase of the largest credits which need to be authorized the next day and go through them—my wife can attest to that." At night, sitting down to grind through the numbers, he'd turn on the jukebox or put on a Blue Jays game to keep him company, adding that he knew what to look for in the documents. The loan requests were then dealt with at the committee meeting by not only credit officers but also the CEO and business heads. "Attendance was required at 8:30 every morning." Over the forty-plus years of Ritchie, Godsoe, and Waugh, he says, they always felt total accountability on the credit decisions that were made. "The CEO was always the chair of the liability committee, which met weekly." Quoting Marwah, Waugh says the goal was for BNS to be known as the Bank of No Surprises. CEO Scott Thomson used the line in front of the Canadian Club in June 2024.

Le Pan's successor as superintendent was Julie Dickson. As with Le Pan, I had interviewed her on what is now BNN Bloomberg. Her tenure also coincided with Waugh's time as CEO and, more significantly, with the financial crisis. After an initial email response to my request for an interview specifically for this book (see chapter 8), she wrote detailed answers to questions about her view of Waugh's international reform work, and whether organizations such as the IIF contributed to greater soundness in the banking system. She also addressed the debate about asset quality versus capital; Scotiabank's frugal culture, culture of credit, and dependence on wholesale funding; and how those impacted supervision as compared with other banks.[22]

Dickson wrote that the IIF's work was helpful because of its straightforward industry explanations and said Waugh did a good job of influencing the organization. But she went on to say it thinks of "shareholder returns," while regulators "have a 100% focus on depositor protection, financial stability and the impact of unlikely but impactful events." She did add that the IIF helped "ensure there are no unintended consequences of regulation which helps promote bank soundness."

As for Waugh's argument that asset quality is more important than capital, Dickson wrote: "I think of this as a statement on how important it is to have high quality assets, versus a statement on capital not being important. History has shown that banks have made lending mistakes (so assets were not as high quality as they thought), and when this happens capital helps deal with the unexpected losses." She also wrote that "capital rules are not always right," given repeated revisions and refinements: "capital rules could be too demanding or not demanding enough (typically not demanding enough). So, you need both assets that are correctly categorized by risk, and capital that appropriately reflects the risk. It is also important to remember that capital covers more than just asset quality/credit risk—it covers operational risk, market risk etc. So even if a bank is generally good at making loans, and may have appropriate capital for that, banks are subject to many more risks for which capital is important."

As for one bank being more frugal than another, "OSFI was more concerned about culture in terms of a bank's appetite for risk taking, whether people felt free to speak up about risk, etc. A frugal culture would not concern OSFI unless it led to a bank deciding not to have proper controls in place," Dickson wrote. She added, "I don't think that a bank's pride in its judgement on credit would affect how OSFI assessed the bank. OSFI would still determine for itself whether credit quality was being well managed and being closely monitored by a bank."

Dickson concluded by writing that each institution is different. Scotia's international exposure "definitely figures" into OSFI's assessment, as did its funding profile of wholesale versus retail.

While respecting the role of regulators, upon hearing Dickson's take Waugh stood by his views. "I believe by far financial institutions, indeed most corporations, go under not because of a lack of capital but because of a lack of liquidity," he told me in his midtown office on May 29, 2024. Waugh pointed to the bank weathering the 2008 storm as proof.

The Grand Hôtel in Stockholm sits like a castle-fortress overlooking the water. In operation since 1874, it drips with European grandeur and overlooks the Old Town and the Royal Palace. From June 3 to 5, 2012, it played host to the top echelon of the world's financial sector, the International Monetary Conference. The IMC comprised sixty-four organizations from thirty-one countries, representing assets of more than $55 trillion, more than twenty-seven times the annual GDP of Canada. The IMC's roots are postwar, the 1950s, and each year it meets in a different country to hear from government leaders, financial authorities, and industry, as well as country experts to promote financial stability and prosperity. It's arguably the gathering of the world's most eminent bankers, a CEOs-only event. While the IIF was work, the IMC was prestige. Waugh called it "the social club of the top CEOs," and Scotia CEOs had participated in the past, a schmoozefest of sorts. Waugh was president of the IMC twice—the second time because the "guy from Brazil got sick." In 2012, he was president of the conference and host, and he and Lynne were housed in an executive suite. Delegates needn't worry about tipping porters at the hotel—IMC had taken care of that. Traditional Swedish candies, as well as fruit, flowers, and chocolates from the hotel, were waiting in the room. Life at the top may be pressured, lonely, and 24/7, but everyone caters to you.

Attendees were met at their planes by an IMC representative and taken to a VIP lounge, where IMC reps were on-hand "to facilitate clearance" through customs and immigration. Discreet, luxury sedans waited to whisk financial royalty to and fro. Scotiabank hosted an evening at Stallmästaregården, Stockholm's oldest inn, dating to the mid-1600s. The food was prepared under the supervision of the royal chef. In attendance: Christine Lagarde, the managing director of the IMF (previously France's finance minister and now president of the European Central Bank); Jean-Claude Trichet, former head of the European Central Bank; the CEOs of major European and UK banks; American bank CEOs, including Jamie Dimon; the CEOs of Visa and IBM; and fellow Canadian bank bosses Gord Nixon of RBC and Ed Clark of TD. On the agenda:

regulation, European banking, shadow banking, the risks and opportunities of evolving technologies, the impact of globalization on emerging markets, and new business models. All discussions were off the record, "not to be repeated outside the conference," adding a coat of elitism to the highest levels of banking. At 5 p.m. on June 4, the King and Queen of Sweden hosted a reception at the Royal Palace. The forty-four spouses in attendance could tour a royal residence. Security was heavy.[23]

As president, Waugh's briefing book was a thick binder, with timing and directions for everything. On page C-16, there is even the correct wording for how to address "their Majesties." He had to speak many times, including to introduce Christine Lagarde. In his notes, he crossed out one line of the introduction that said Lagarde had been ranked the ninth most influential woman in the world by *Forbes* magazine. He'd also scribbled notes in blue ink, not his customary red pencil. At the time, the eurozone was in crisis. Greece was drowning in debt. On pages B-14 and B-15 of his typed script, he made lengthy handwritten notes. "We have a new asset class with substantial risk—sovereign debt and much more significant risk in another, fixed income and bonds. This is an immense challenge to both govts and investors and a critical challenge to all banks, particularly European. The rescheduling/default of Greek debt and impact on each stakeholder has significant implications for the future of both asset classes, investors and issuers alike, particularly govts and banks. . . . new levels of capital . . . are now a given and must be accepted . . . we must accept the capital and funding but push back on the great influx of new rules and regulations. . . . what are the changes to our business models that have to be made and how that affects our growth and profitability, our customers and our shareholders." The list of participants shows no bankers or officials from Greece.[24] Waugh says you had to be a top-fifty bank to attend.

What the crisis and its aftermath played to were Waugh's strengths—credit risk, markets, and psychology. These were his ABCs. But history

is so frequently forgotten or not known. By the time this book is published, it will be approaching twenty years since the great financial crisis.
There are now people running parts of banks or trading floors who were
teenagers then. Memories can be non-existent or fade. And in financial
markets, ignorance of history and fading memories are dangerous.
Despite advances in technology, the basic questions remain relevant.
What are the exposures? Where are they? How much are they? How
liquid are they? How transparent are they? Who's responsible for them?
Are they manageable under a wide and deep range of scenarios? Put
plainly, are the risks understood?

To gauge the impact of its crisis-related work, the IIF hired Ernst & Young
to conduct research. The first report, published in 2009, was based on a
survey of CEOs, CROs, and CFOs at thirty-eight of the largest banks
across twenty countries. Many had not waited for guidance but were
already acting, saying they were looking to reverse "sales-driven" cultures
to make them more risk sensitive. "The area that stood out as having the
greatest impediments was remuneration. Again and again, firms said that
they were revising remuneration structure to make it more risk-based and
were exploring longer horizons in terms of bonus payouts; but they were
not confident that changes would be workable or would last in the face of
pressure from the market." Quite simply, financial types still wanted to
make more money. "Several banks made the point that it would take only
one or two large firms to break ranks internationally and to start poaching
teams by offering higher bonuses or less delayed bonuses for the changes
to start to unravel. Several banks said that without some kind of international regulatory pressure, the changes would not last into the next
boom." Just like economic cycles, greed apparently had not been repealed.
Nonetheless, "Many banks had made substantial changes already in terms
of reducing the percentage of income from bonuses or spreading bonus
payments across several years. This had led to some disquiet. . . ."[25]

However, there appeared to be progress in other areas. Stress testing was more widely accepted, and "in a number of banks, moves have been made to enhance the stature of the CRO, in some cases changing reporting lines so that the CRO reports directly to the CEO," something Waugh advocated. What's more, "CROs in a number of banks are now expected to have a greater role in monitoring and considering liquidity risk," which traditionally had been overseen by treasury departments.[26] Since the financial crisis, regulators had instituted new liquidity standards to encourage deposit-taking institutions to have sufficient liquid assets to withstand a thirty-day stress scenario and to reduce dependence on wholesale funding.[27] On stress testing, the probing had sharpened. "One major bank spoke of now asking the question 'what does it take to bankrupt the bank?'" Banks also recognized flawed techniques for valuing structured products, those bonds stuffed with bad mortgages at the centre of the crisis, conceding they had "relied too heavily on the rating for individual securities" and were focused on improving risk models.[28]

Later, in 2011, there was another IIF-sponsored report from Ernst & Young. It had surveyed sixty-two firms, half of which had been severely impacted by the financial crisis. The top two lessons cited were managing liquidity and the need to strengthen risk culture. Most firms reported increased board oversight, strengthening the CRO role, changing liquidity risk management, and implementation of stress testing. But as time passed, urgency passed. While 78 percent reported revisions of compensation schemes, less than half had completed initial changes. Ninety-two percent reported increased attention to risk culture, but less than a quarter reported a significant shift. And while 96 percent reported an increased focus on risk appetite, only a quarter reported a link to business decisions. Still, in a finding Waugh would appreciate, "respondents consistently expressed the view that companies underestimated the vital importance of the human factor in managing risk. Human judgment, insight and experience . . ."[29]

While stress testing had been embraced, banks struggled with fragmented systems and gathering meaningful data. The report's authors wrote that "One executive told us it takes 150 people across the businesses to analyze the scenarios mandated by both the regulators and the board risk committee." Seventy-three percent of respondents reported increased IT spending "to support more effective risk governance."[30] It was a long way from the days of "big bucks, fast and cheap" in New York.

Discussion of compensation loomed large. While "many firms reported that the CRO and risk teams are increasingly involved in remuneration . . . close to 75% of respondents listed the lack of regulatory consistency together with competitive pressures as their top challenges to changing remuneration policies."[31] Given human behaviour and the lessons of history, people will do potentially harmful things to be paid more. As Waugh frequently says, follow the money.

Since the crisis, the world has only become more complex, and the financial world more complex by extension. New risks have emerged—for example, the spread of information and misinformation via social media and the lightning speed at which deposits can be withdrawn via an app while lying on a couch. There are also financial risks related to climate—extreme weather risks that impact banks, their customers, and their communities, not to mention questions about whether banks are financing businesses that increase climate-related risks. There are new political and trade risks with the rise of populism and authoritarianism in the industrialized, developed world. The basics of banking are still relevant, but the overlay of other issues is substantial.

Waugh stops just short of calling regulation a necessary evil. "Regulation is necessary, time-consuming, and expensive," he says. The purpose is "so that they can make sure it [a crisis] doesn't happen again. The problem with regulation, it just builds. And what they add they can never take away." On top of that, the next crisis will be different than the regulation enacted to solve the last problem. Regulators, he says, are always fighting the last war, adding that regulation is not a predictor of the next crisis. "Regulation builds, builds, becomes more expensive and perhaps less responsive because we don't know what the next crisis will be. But there will be one." While his argument has its strengths and regulation certainly intensified post-crisis, banking has hardly been forced back to the days prior to the "Little Bang" or Glass-Steagall.

At the same time as he argued that regulation builds, Waugh recognized that "the political environment is supposed to reflect Main Street." And why shouldn't it? Main Street typically bears the brunt of crises, either through lost jobs or taxation. As the late Adam Zimmerman, the former chairman and CEO of Noranda, once said to me, corporations operate with public consent. They are incorporated by governments, which are installed via the ballot box. That said, nothing is simple. Banks operate in a byzantine, competitive, global environment. Understanding the various interbank and cross-border financial devices used to keep credit flowing so households and businesses can function is akin to understanding cardiology. It's part of the circulatory system of the economy. Banks and society must operate in a manner that both protects a citizenry of depositors and allows for the meaningful flow of credit so businesses, owners, and households can thrive. That is the tightrope of banking regulation.

Waugh puts much of his faith in central banks. "They're independent usually and they never want to repeat the Volcker years." The Volcker years were the late 1970s and early 1980s, a period of exorbitant inflation that led to Federal Reserve chair Paul Volcker leading a cold-blooded cycle to raise interest rates into double digits, resulting in a brutal recession in 1982—at the time, the worst since the 1930s. But the rate of inflation was tamed, and Volcker became a hero, at least to central bankers, economists, and market players. Waugh cited the power of central banks to print money and operate with strong checks and balances, adding, "and that's why I'm pro-regulation." He said other arms of regulation, like the Office of the Superintendent of Financial Institutions, "are more problematic"—a strong and critical statement by a former bank CEO. Waugh said regulatory auditors spend more time looking at a bank as it is and less time considering where it's going. "But they're the policemen and you have to pay attention," he concedes, because you don't want to get slapped with a ticket or be put in jail.

Waugh pointed to the emphasis on shoring up bank capital, post-crisis. "It was overdone," he said, adding that Canadian banks were well above the requirements (of Basel 2 standards). "There is an underlying assumption that more capital is better than less," Waugh argued, "which I think is far too simplistic." Higher capital requirements mean less money available to lend to the community to help the country (and the financial sector) grow. In the years after Lehman failed—which Waugh said had capital, but bad assets—Waugh spoke out against excessive, prescriptive regulatory rules. It's like "requiring the cars to have more and bigger airbags without taking into account the driver or the passengers. Eventually, you have so many airbags that there is no more room for the passengers and the driver can't see out the window," he told the Empire Club in September 2013.[32] "And you've done nothing really to prevent the collision." Capital, he said, may give comfort and trust, "but it is the quality of the bank's assets that generates profitability and protects it from needing to use capital at all," adding that "prevention is the best medicine." He wasn't like Jamie Dimon going at Mark Carney in front of the world's financial leaders, but in his own way, with just weeks left in his tenure, he was pulling no punches. He'd also been building to it, making the banker's argument. During a 2010 interview with Tara Perkins of the *Globe and Mail*, he said, "You can have a perfectly riskless banking system which will not lend, which will not grow, and that leads to an economy that doesn't grow. So, leaving it just to the regulators is dangerous, leaving it just to the politicians is dangerous."[33]

But leaving it just to bankers in certain countries had also clearly been dangerous. And if it had just been left to bankers, history tells us Canada wouldn't have a central bank. Or, if just left to bankers, big in-country mergers in 1998 could have resulted in an even more concentrated banking system than Canada already has.[††] As former central banker Malcolm Knight pointed out, the latter is a potential weakness in the country's otherwise stable system.[34] In making their cases to merge in the late 1990s, bankers argued they needed to do so in order to compete globally. Clearly, they fared nicely without the mergers. And a decade later, they survived the crisis. The truth is politicians, regulators, and bankers can at times all be right. They can also all be wrong.

Waugh, however, argues that one crisis is different from another. Some, he says, are idiosyncratic, while others are systemic. And if a crisis is idiosyncratic, Waugh advises that regulators shouldn't lard on more rules. Companies need to grow to create jobs, "And you kill the goose." Perhaps that's wise. But he also frequently warns that "history repeats." So, which is it? Julie Dickson recalled him saying crises are often rooted in real estate, implying repeats. Certainly, there are recurring themes: bad lending practices, greed, lack of liquidity, too much complexity, too much interconnectedness, bad management, lack of oversight. And rules don't necessarily stop bad behaviour. Some people break rules. Does that mean rules should be changed?

So, what's the solution? When there's a financial crisis that requires government to step up to backstop the system—backstops that cost taxpayers inordinate sums—the public, represented by government, has an expectation that guardrails will be put in place to prevent it from happening again. Corporations, which provide goods and services, jobs, tax revenue, community support, and returns to investors and pensioners, are creations of the public, which grants them the right to operate. Bankers may complain

---

†† In 2024, RBC closed its purchase of HSBC Canada for $13.5 billion and National Bank announced it was buying Canadian Western Bank for approximately $5 billion.

about more and more regulation, and they may be correct that some is excessive or creates unintended consequences. But it has not stopped them from being extremely profitable. Profitability alone, as Waugh argues, fosters a sound system. So, is the high cost per bank for compliance a reasonable ask to help maintain a safe system? Arguably, yes, and Waugh would agree. "Canadian banks do see a role for proper regulation and it's 'cause we take deposits," even though it costs a lot—hundreds of millions of dollars a year to meet regulations. "Costly, but of value to us."

Waugh's airbag metaphor raises another—the evolution of passenger aviation. Decades ago, there were more frequent major plane crashes. Lots of people died. By the 2000s, major crashes had become very rare and unusual occurrences, in large part because of investigations into past accidents and incidents designed to prevent future crashes. Regulation of the industry is burdensome for good reason. In the early 1990s, I flew to Washington to interview John Lauber, then a member of the National Transportation Safety Board, the agency that investigates air crashes. I've never forgotten something he said. *If you think safety is expensive, try having an accident.*[35]

However, hand in hand with effective regulation goes sound management and tone from the top. "Our job as executives of a large international bank is dealing with one crisis after another, which we certainly have done [at Scotiabank] for almost two hundred years," Waugh says. Certainly, he was considered a very effective manager, as were his contemporaries at the other major banks. But what happens if you have a bad manager atop a bank, an unfavourable macroeconomic environment, or unexpected shock like 9/11 or COVID-19? The owners of the *Titanic* wanted fewer lifeboats so the ship could steam faster. We know the result.

Whatever the work of the IIFs, the IMCs, the BISs, or the Rick Waughs of the world, economic crises are regular occurrences. Like storms and fires, they seem more frequent and worse these days than in days past.

Whether they truly happen more often or with more devastating effects is difficult to say. The Great Depression of the 1930s resulted in unemployment ranging from 19.3 to 27 percent.[36] The financial crisis of 2007–9 was the worst since the Depression, and it certainly put the entire system at risk, but it was not as bad as what occurred in the thirties. Key policy-makers in 2007–9 were students of the Great Depression, so they worked to prevent their crisis from reaching such depths.

However, cyclicality born of human behaviour—the constant tug between fear and greed—now seems supercharged by technology, interconnectedness, and financial "innovation." Things can happen faster. With the rise of generative AI, one can't help wondering what an AI-rooted financial crisis will look like—or whether AI could prevent one. Either way, there are traditionally only two policy levers that can be used to pull economies out of dives: lowering interest rates, and creating fiscal stimulus via spending (usually deficit-funded) or tax cuts. Typically, because central banks of industrialized countries are independent from politics (or strive to be), interest rate cuts are first on the beach. Fiscal stimulus is political, requiring public debate. But each has impacts that can lead to different crises later.

In the case of the financial crisis, the heavy lifting fell to central banks. Rates were suppressed below normal levels for years, helping economies and the financial system survive. But cheap money led to asset bubbles. Increases in housing prices can occur for multiple reasons, but cheap money is an accelerant. So, while we made it through 2008, housing affordability is now a crisis in many places. This intensified during the pandemic, which also showed the power of policy-makers to save economies and financial systems. But their actions were not free. Rates fell again. Home prices rose even more, and inflation exploded across sectors, the latter more due to choked supply chains.

But politicians and central banks have felt the blame, and that has now changed politics. Economies impact politics; politics impact economies. There's no more vivid example than what Waugh dealt with in Argentina. It's a constant feedback loop. We get through one crisis and create another, or are not prepared for the crisis that comes out of the blue, like COVID-19, 9/11, or the rise of authoritarian politics with rash actions such as punitive tariffs. But we muddle through with the system we have. And that includes the unintended consequences of whatever we try to fix.

In a television interview I did with Waugh on BNN on April 16, 2010, he pushed back at the notion that some banks—including the major Canadians banks—are too big to fail. It's the concept that, given their size and crucial roles in the economy, the government will always rescue them, potentially leading banks to take undue risks because, deep down, they know there's a backstop—the taxpayer. Waugh also balked at the criticism that big is bad when it comes to banks, creating greater concentrations of risk to the financial system. Speaking about Scotiabank specifically, he said, "Yes, we've gotten much bigger. We're much bigger than I ever thought we would be, but we're more diversified." As a result, Waugh said, when Lehman Brothers toppled, yes, Scotia took a hit, but nowhere near what others faced. "So, it's too simple to say too big to fail."[37]

The fact is, while Canadian banks are certainly not exempt from major mistakes and big trouble, from a national policy perspective, they are too big to fail. The government needs to stand behind them for the good of the country's financial system and economy. A key figure on the Canadian policy front during the crisis was the late Jim Flaherty, then federal finance minister. A former litigator, Flaherty was short, built like a fullback, hard-nosed, and respected. In June 2010, the G20 met in Toronto. On BNN, I asked him about the issue of "too big to fail."

GREEN: Mark Carney told a conference sponsored by Thomson
Reuters the other day that no bank is too big to fail. Does that
mean the Canadian government would let a major Canadian bank
fail if heaven forbid one were at the brink?

FLAHERTY: Well, our view is that all financial institutions should be
effectively supervised. That's what we do in Canada regardless of the
size of the financial institution. But our top five banks in Canada
are world-sized banks.

GREEN: But . . . my question was would the Canadian government
let a major Canadian bank fail?

FLAHERTY: Well, we're going to regulate them so that they don't.
And we're going to make sure that they have adequate reserves
so that they don't. And we're going to cap their leverage so that
they don't.[38]

The finance minister was never going to answer the question.
Governments the world over were unlikely to say publicly that banks
were too big to fail. That would risk giving banks a "get out of jail free"
card—overtly letting them know they could do anything and the taxpayer would be there as a backstop. A certain ambiguity was required.
But since the crisis, global policy-makers have become more specific.
Several global banks have been identified as global systemically important financial institutions (G-SIFIs). RBC and TD are included in that
list, while BNS, BMO, and CIBC are deemed to be D-SIFIs (domestic
systemically important financial institutions).

But size isn't everything, Waugh suggested. Lehman was not the
largest independent dealer, and the Icelandic banks were not large. But,
he pointed out, each of these was interconnected. Waugh worried that
a raft of new regulation would be created without looking at what

worked—the Canadian system. "The problem is," he said, "we're not an island." Indeed. When he ran Scotiabank, it operated in more than fifty countries. Whatever capital requirements were coming, he said, the bank will manage through it. "The Canadian model again has worked, and we do have to be part of the process but let's be very careful. Don't rush in. Don't rush in. Make sure we get it right because we're going to have to live with the consequences for many, many years." He said, the best way to prevent a crisis in a bank is "ensure they're profitable. You don't have to worry about capital if you're earning 17 percent."[39]

On August 27, 2013, Ann DeRabbie, then part of Scotia's communications team, sent Waugh a memo to prepare him for an interview with Tim Kiladze of the *Globe and Mail*. It would be about the fifth anniversary of the financial crisis, tied to the collapse of Lehman Brothers. The interview would focus on Waugh's recollections of pivotal events and when confidence started to return. Waugh had already been briefed by Diane Flanagan, VP of communications. The memo included a timeline of the crisis, highlighting events from 2007 through 2009.

It's a head-spinning list and a reminder of the chaos of the period. For 2008, the memo cited thirty-one noteworthy events, from the demise of Bear Stearns through TARP. From October 6 to 10, the memo says, "Shit hits the fan. The Dow Jones loses 22.1 percent, its worst week on record, down 40.3 percent since reaching a record high of 14,164.53." Iceland's three largest banks collapse. On October 6, the Fed announces unprecedented emergency assistance of $900 billion in short-term loans to banks; the next day, $1.3 trillion to companies outside the financial sector. On November 7, employment data is released: "240,000 Americans lost their jobs in the last month." On November 12, Paulson decides to give banks cash injections. On December 12 in Canada, "Ontario and Ottawa announce $3.3 billion auto bailout. Actual cost ends up being much higher." On Christmas Eve, the "federal government and three provinces back $4.45 billion ABCP deal."

As Waugh told the Empire Club in early September 2013, five years after Lehman's collapse, "I grew up learning that made in America was a pretty good thing. But you know, I think when it comes to banking, I think made in Canada is probably a better thing."[40]

CHAPTER TEN

Close Calls for a Deal Junkie

While Scotia was still managing through a trying period, by the end of 2007 and the first half of 2008, it was also on the hunt. This was not out of character. Waugh was always scouring for bargains amongst the rubble, even though he had no idea that the worst of the crisis, the unimaginable, was still to come. He would fixate on a big retail bank in the United States that he would miss out on by a whisker. But there were plenty of other deals. Ultimately, during Waugh's tenure as CEO, the bank made some forty acquisitions at a cost of $13 billion.[1]

"Rick liked the deal," Mike Durland said. "He was happiest when he was working on a transaction." Waugh doesn't dispute this, calling himself a "deal junkie." Some of the forty were opportunistic deals, including buying 37 percent of CI Financial from SunLife, which was a motivated seller in the autumn of 2008, as well as E*TRADE Canada and DundeeWealth to build out Scotiabank's wealth management business.* With SunLife, Waugh recalls receiving a phone call from the insurer saying a deal to buy its holding in CI had to be done quickly, so Scotia moved fast. For Dundee, he describes weekends sitting in the cabana at Ned Goodman's cottage near his own north of Toronto, negotiating with the late entrepreneur. Diversification into wealth management was, in Waugh's view, risk management. Wealth management business also came with deposits, cash parked in clients' investment accounts. As well, there were purchases of foreign banks, like in Peru, widely described as a homerun. Buying 51 percent of Colombia's fifth-largest banking group turned out to be less successful.†

There was also the uncharacteristic deal—paying richly for an acquisition that would grow the bank's deposits. On August 29, 2012, Scotia announced it would purchase ING Bank of Canada, known as ING Direct, for $3.126 billion in cash. Its Dutch parent, ING Groep NV, put it up for sale to help pay back a government bailout dating to the financial crisis. It was classic Waugh—buying when a seller was distressed. What was not classic Waugh was agreeing to a non-distressed price. ING Direct was the eighth-largest bank in Canada. It was an online bank; there were no physical branches. But with 1.8 million customers came a mortgage portfolio and $30 billion in deposits. It could operate as a digital stand-alone and boost the retail side of Scotia, broadening its funding. The deal would give BNS the third-largest deposit base among Canadian banks—improving from fifth place during the financial crisis.[2]

---

* Waugh's successor Brian Porter divested Scotiabank's stake in CI in 2014 at a profit. The bank would later buy other wealth management assets, including MD Financial Management and Jarislowsky Fraser Ltd.

† In January 2025, Scotia stepped back from operating in Colombia. It transferred its banking operations there (as well as those in Panama and Costa Rica) to a Colombian bank in exchange for an approximate 20 percent holding in that bank. Waugh "was saddened" by this, given the bank's effort there, but understood the situation had changed. "The country itself didn't progress as planned," he said, "so you deal with the current issues."

The executive running Scotia's Canadian division then was Anatol von Hahn, Waugh's wingman during the Argentina crisis. As head of the bank's biggest division, he knew the bank had a gap, confirming that the deposit issue was "historic" at the bank. In normal times, if there was a shortfall, he said, funds could be raised via the wholesale market. But in times of market stress, von Hahn went so far as to say a shortage of deposits created a funding gap that posed a "near death risk" during the financial crisis. "Was it close? Absolutely." He talked about working "like hell" to collect loans, get deposits, and slow down on credits. "We used the line which was 'we're playing for the house.' That was actually said by us in the Canadian bank" during the crisis. Nonetheless, Scotia reported a profit of $3.1 billion in 2008, raised its dividend that year (but not during the worst of the calamity), earned $3.547 billion in 2009, and was ranked as one of the world's safest banks in 2010 and 2011 by *Global Finance*. It also could have issued equity to a market that had been receptive when other big banks did so, buttressing Waugh's stance that the bank was okay. But 2008 may have been too gut-wrenching. There was certainly a recognition that the bank needed to boost deposits to provide more funding stability.[‡]

Initially, ING's Canadian division, a "well-run, well-oiled machine," was not available. The parent had indicated it wanted to keep it. But in 2012, a window opened. Von Hahn and Scotia executives Robin Hibberd and Vikas Sharma met with two ING executives from Holland. The Dutch bankers came alone, without an investment banker to advise them—unusual. "They were in deep trouble in Europe, and they needed to get liquidity," von Hahn said. When he found out they were putting their Canadian division up for sale, "that was like music to our ears." Von Hahn recalled a small group would be

‡ At Scotia's April 2025 annual meeting, CEO Scott Thomson stressed deposits are a "big part of the strategy," citing a significant increase in Canadian deposits over the previous two years.

invited to bid. "I do think we were the first to be called." Waugh said the opportunity came first to Scotia because of the personal relationships he had with ING, via his international work. "This is where relationships count," he said.

The problem was, Scotia traditionally bought fixer-uppers on the cheap. This was anything but. While it had just 3 percent market share in Canada, ING Direct had unusually wide recognition thanks to an inventive ad campaign. It featured an actor speaking Dutch-accented English, spouting a well-known tagline: "Save your money." As von Hahn said, "it was the anti-bank" and was popular because of it. But that popularity meant it would be expensive. "It was going to be who pays the most," von Hahn said. And pricey "totally went against our ethos." But as Waugh would argue, if you must pay up, make sure you get value. "It had the deposits. It had the technology," Waugh said. It was a fit. ING Direct was deposit rich and asset light, while Scotia was asset heavy but deposit light. "We were asset hogs," von Hahn said. And while Scotia bankers were good lenders whose assets (loans) typically served them well, after the financial crisis they needed to become deposit hogs. One by one, von Hahn said, the bank's top executives were convinced Scotia had to pay a premium—essentially double what it might have paid for the same deposits. "We'll pay the fair price, and we'll do it right away and those reasons resonated with the seller," Waugh said. He took the proposal to the board.

There was, however, a cultural consideration. Colour-wise, Scotia was red. ING Direct was orange. Von Hahn described Hibberd producing a video that showed if you put red and orange together, you'd get brown—shit. So don't wreck everything by forcing Scotia's culture on ING Direct, went the argument. Run them separately. Von Hahn also said then-director Paul Sobey of the Sobeys grocery chain, someone who knew retail, made the same argument. Von Hahn described Sobey dramatically standing up at the board meeting to support the transaction—provided the team didn't combine red and orange and get brown.[§]

It was the largest acquisition in the bank's history,[3] but it wasn't big enough to be transformational. Scotia didn't do transformational. Waugh preferred to plant flags in many places rather than make big bets. He said he was typically unimpressed by the word *big*. "You never bet the bank on any one country," he said. "Other than Canada." An acquisition had to be material and on-strategy: in this case, to bolster deposits. Eventually, Scotia would rebrand ING Direct as Tangerine, an all-digital bank that looked contemporary. All six major Canadian banks had competed to buy it[4]; Scotia held its nose and paid up. Could the willingness to bid aggressively have also been a nod to those who'd criticized Scotia for being a tech laggard? No, von Hahn said, but it was not lost on the Scotia team that the mother ship could take ING's digital technology and test it across the bank, without turning things brown.

Among the most interesting transactions, however, were the ones that got away or went away. The most noteworthy was National City Corp., based in Ohio—potentially a multi-billion-dollar purchase. In that case, Waugh even played the role of mystery shopper, talking to branch managers at the acquisition target, a bank in the American heartland. It brings up the oft-repeated maxim of never letting a crisis go to waste. Waugh and his team were scanning the banking landscape for the wounded, but those with potential for rehab and growth for Scotiabank. "We were keeping our eyes open," he says. While Scotia had a vast international presence, it had yet to enter retail branch banking in the United States, unlike BMO, TD, and RBC. Waugh saw his opportunity in 2008.

Although regulations now force Canadian banks to hold more capital as a buffer for bad times, the reality is that they're such strong businesses that capital builds up anyway. Some goes to dividend increases, share

---

§ Scotia first financed Frank Sobey in the 1920s, starting with a truck of potatoes.

buybacks, and keeping up with technology. But what about the rest? Canada is banked-a-plenty, just like it's over-coffee'd by Tim Hortons. So, in recent decades, the big banks determined they can only grow so much in Canada and must expand elsewhere. Except for Scotia, that has typically been in the United States, an obvious target given the number of American banks, geographic proximity, and size of the economy. TD was fond of saying there are almost as many people in the New York metro area—which includes parts of New Jersey and Connecticut—as there are in Canada (it's not quite that many). But despite appearances, a common language, and cultural crossovers, the United States is still foreign territory, with foreign ways (and under Trump, increasingly hostile ways). RBC initially bought in the southeast and later sold, licking its wounds (it's since returned with a different focus). BMO bought in the Midwest in the 1980s and for years didn't report the return on equity of the US division.[5] TD acquired a significant footprint over multiple years but has never had anywhere near the return it gets in Canada. While there are thousands of banks in the United States, Canada has an oligopoly, albeit a competitive one. The major Canadian banks not only have a protective moat via ownership limits but also their branch networks date to the 1800s, and historically have had lower loan losses. Still, for Canadian banks in the modern era, the objects of desire have been regional banks in the United States, often large organizations that do business in geographical chunks of America—the Midwest, the eastern seaboard, or California.

When TD's former CEO Ed Clark started acquiring banks in the United States, he moved into New England first. In part, he did so

---

[5] Former BMO CEO Bill Downe described the bank's deep history in the United States. It opened its New York Agency in 1819, and in the 1860s, "after the Great Chicago Fire, it was the largest provider of rebuilding capital in the city of Chicago." Downe said one of his predecessors, Bill Mulholland, "acquired a deposit-taking institution [Harris Bank, in 1984] to supplement the large balance sheet of Bank of Montreal in the United States, and it worked out just fine."

because the region is close to head office in Canada and has long, historic ties. You could fly there in an hour. It wasn't like schlepping to South America to inspect branches. But proximity meant paying a premium. Buying elsewhere in the world meant different risk and different pricing. You could buy cheaper if you were willing to shoulder the risk and the jet lag, like Scotia did on other continents.

For Scotiabank, though, the acquisition of branch networks in the United States had not been a priority until the financial crisis. Before that, Waugh said, the price was too high. But with the crisis, Waugh thought Scotia could get in at a discount. "If you buy well, you can sell well." As someone who had spent a decade in New York, he knew the United States and was comfortable there. But while Waugh knew banking in the United States wasn't akin to banking in Canada and was experiencing financial mayhem, he figured that if the price was right, maybe it was time. And the United States had gotten cheap.

This was the flip side of crisis: the scouring for opportunity—otherwise good banks that had been side-swiped by financial turmoil. Such banks presented mouth-watering value for those with the stomach and resources to swallow them, although they could be agonizing to digest. While Waugh would not identify the target, it was reported Scotiabank was interested in acquiring National City Corp., and former Scotia executives from the era confirmed this. Among the tasty morsels a buyer would enjoy—some $50 billion in deposits. That gunny sack of retail funding would help offset Scotiabank's wholesale reliance. So, knowing he had reliable liquidity at home in the largest part of the bank, Waugh was serious. He described how he and a few of his people went to the Cleveland bank's branches and "talked to tellers." To many Americans, Waugh's voice wouldn't sound discernibly Canadian. But when asked by employees where he was from, he'd smile and say, "it's north of here, which was the truth." But it was across one of the Great Lakes, so "you have to know how to swim," he joked years later.

While CEOs get the credit (or blame) for acquisitions, teams are involved. In 2008, Barb Mason, who then ran marketing, sales, and services, "the infrastructure" of the bank (later, she would head up human resources), got a call to be on the bank's jet early the next morning with Waugh and Wendy Hannam, the EVP of retail banking.

The trip was organized so hastily that Scotia had to make some ad hoc immigration arrangements. Mason says she, Waugh, and Hannam, planned to fly into Cleveland and "try to do it without anybody knowing" who they were. "We're sitting on the tarmac, and the pilot comes back and says, does everyone have their passports?" At the same time, Mason said, both she and Hannam said, "Oh, fuck." There they were on the plane with the CEO, on a mission to look at a multi-billion-dollar acquisition, and they were missing basic documentation to cross the border. "Rick said incredulously, '*Both of you?*'" The pilot, Mason said, saved the day. He radioed ahead to make the case that the Scotia trio was only coming in for the day. Could an exception be made at immigration? They were permitted to go, making the short skip across Lake Erie to Ohio.

On the plane ride, the three cooked up a rather weak cover story that they were branch designers or a bank real estate team surveying the layout and parking. Waugh is sensitive about the story. "We had a cover," he admitted, but "we were not lying." The branches were indeed what Waugh, Hannam, and Mason were looking at, he said—and he emphasized that he never expected any of the people working with him to misrepresent themselves or be untruthful. In fact, he said, the Scotia team had the consent of the Ohio bank to go in and talk to staff. Hannam recalled the scene with amusement. Waugh, she said, was wearing a Scotiabank pin on his lapel and carried a Scotiabank folder. "We carried it off fairly well. Barb and I, for sure," Hannam joked. Mason tells a different story: "We were so busted."

When presented with the story, Waugh laughs, saying he wouldn't dispute it but would deny. "I wouldn't have been that dumb. I wouldn't have worn a lapel pin," he huffed, adding that "the people in Ohio would never have recognized it." Nonetheless, Hannam, Mason, and Stephen Hart all said he was wearing the pin. While it sounds like something out of *Inspector Clouseau*, it didn't really matter. The Ohio bank was in serious trouble and was like many American banks, which by then were sitting ducks for takeovers. The staff seemed to indicate to the Waugh squad that they'd seen this movie before. "We've been through this change of ownership many times."

On the plus side, Hannam said, the Ohio-based bank was in sync with Scotia, culturally, brand-wise, and in terms of how customers were treated. "On the ground there was a fit." There were also meetings with the executive team to learn about how the target bank managed deposits, credit processes, and the nuts and bolts of banking. "It would have been a very meaningful operation for us," she said, adding Scotia was acutely aware of the differences between Canada and the United States when it came to banking. Scotiabank was engaged in North American banking associations, so the Toronto bank and the Cleveland bank knew one another. Scotia, she said, had always watched what were considered the top American retail banks, spending time with them. "We were aware the US wasn't just another Canadian location," and the United States was always on Scotia's radar because it had to be. "It was only like 2008 when such drastic things happened in the US market." Conditions were such, Hannam said, "where we couldn't not look at the market."

Waugh said the bull's eye, National City Corp., was well regarded and had a local community culture, "which gave us good comfort." He liked its geographic footprint, and it "was deposit rich." Bingo—the *D* word. It had a respected CEO who mistakenly "did get more involved in the attractiveness of securitized assets than perhaps he should have." This was a polite way of saying the bank got sucked into the vortex of the subprime mortgage crisis. Scotia was serious enough about the possible purchase to have a team of thirty-five people on-site under the supervision of Stephen Hart for four weeks, going through the bank's loans. "They were a good bank in the Midwest," he said. Hart described, however, how this Ohio-based bank, with little expertise, had opened an office in Miami to do real estate loans, and facetiously added: *"real estate never goes down, so you know, give everybody money."*

Aside from the culture of National City Corp. and whether it was a fit for Scotia, a major concern was how big a "black hole" there could be when it came to bad assets, meaning bad loans. Scotia had bought a bad bank before, and Waugh had been the guy who had to clean it up. A top American bank was brought in to help on due diligence "to try to get an estimate on the black hole." Sabi Marwah was particularly concerned about the unknown unknowns. The worst-case scenario was difficult to determine. Hart said Marwah kept asking him, "'How big is the black hole?' I said that's why it's a black hole."

Nonetheless, Waugh describes how Scotiabank got "very close" to buying the bank. Despite the crisis, it was a risk Scotia was initially willing to take. "You can walk and chew gum at the same time," Waugh says. "We were protecting our downside but looking for opportunities on the downside." Did Scotia make an offer? Waugh wouldn't say, but the negotiations were not with the American bank itself but with a key regulator, the Office of the Comptroller of the Currency. "They were serious about it. We had serious discussions with them." The purchase would have given Scotia a major beachhead in American retail banking, which it didn't have. "I was in direct negotiation with regulators."

Hart said Scotia bankers flew in on the company jet so many times that the border guy would say, "Oh, it's you guys again." "We're not really here," Hart cracked. In retrospect, "We should have bought them. We were so close." Waugh was emphatic when presented with that view. "We tried to buy it, and we couldn't," he said, explaining that the American government in the waning days of the George W. Bush administration had provided relief to domestic banks with the Troubled Asset Relief Program, which came into force to stanch the bleeding in the banking system. In essence, Waugh says, TARP was free money for American banks. "We couldn't afford to pay for the American bank because our cost of capital was too big." As was the case with the Argentina experience, a foreign bank like Scotia was a second-class bank. "We wanted it cheap, but we weren't going to risk the bank." He says negotiations took place up until twenty-four hours before TARP was announced.

Marwah indicated that Scotia also assessed other American banks. "We looked at Wachovia," Marwah said, which came up because it imploded. But it was too big. He was "very uncomfortable" because it was large—double or triple Scotia's assets. Wachovia, Waugh says, "just didn't meet the checklist I had." Wells Fargo bought Wachovia at the end of 2008. Meantime, National City Corp. in "Cleveland was very manageable." Marwah described it as a big bank (Waugh described it as the tenth-biggest American bank by deposits), but it started experiencing a run on deposits. "The bank in Cleveland was imploding," he said. "They were desperate for a sale." While Waugh was mystery-shopping the branches, Marwah was talking to the bank's finance people and the CEO, checking the risk profile and balance sheet. "We were deadly serious on this bank in Cleveland." While it was "very tempting to say, 'Fuck it, the US can't be that bad,'" Scotia was "not prepared to risk the parent for the subsidiary," Marwah said. Scotiabank was prepared to take risk, "but not unlimited risk," even though they "were getting it cheap." But with TARP, no deal. "You can't piss into the wind," Waugh says.

Meantime, rather than buying in Ohio during the crisis, Scotia bought in Puerto Rico—branches and loan portfolios, not the bank itself, Stephen Hart stressed. But it didn't work out. Hart said a tax loophole had helped create a pharmaceutical sector on the island, but when it was closed, companies left, and the economy collapsed. Although Scotiabank had been on the island for a century and had "maybe thirty branches," it bought more when Puerto Rican banks were in trouble. Scotia doubled in size, but "within three years we were back to the same size we started in." The problem, he said, was threefold. There was the cost of US regulation, and there was a Spanish-speaking population in a Caribbean lifestyle. And then, he said, to top it all off, there were hurricanes. "It was the wrong mix," Waugh concurred.

There are various takes on what happened in Puerto Rico. By then, David Dodge was a Scotia board member who expressed regrets about the acquisition. "That was a mistake," he said. "I made a mistake. I thought that was a good buy and obviously [it was] a big mistake." He went on: "We had an electricity company [that was] much less strong than we thought, and fundamentally we relied on that company to be providing strength to the economy and it turned out it didn't." Hart said the Puerto Rico Electric Power Authority controlled over 90 percent of the generators and wires on the island. Like all Caribbean islands, Puerto Rico is prone to hurricanes, which kept destroying the infrastructure, "and they never could raise the rates enough to properly fix it. All the local banks including us had to lend to them via government pressure. We spent years quietly writing down our loan bit by bit."[5]

For her part, Wendy Hannam said Puerto Rico required excessive attention. Near the end of the financial crisis, she said, Scotia took over a bunch of loans that the bank got at a deep discount from the Federal Deposit Insurance Corporation in the United States, which manages resolutions for in-peril banks. But Hannam said even with the discount, the loans, which she recalled were broad-based, were worse than anticipated. "I don't recall us feeling that we'd been sold a bill of goods, just regret that even at a deep discount this was a bad purchase."[6]

Mike Durland perhaps framed the Puerto Rico experience the most colourfully. "It was in the category of 'who gives a shit'" (although former executive Dieter Jentsch said that it eventually made money). Were all of Waugh's acquisitions good? No, Durland said. "Thailand was probably one that didn't fit." Still, "I don't think he left the bank with a lot of shitty M&A deals," Jentsch said Thailand was very profitable, but added he'd been through coups there and it was difficult to manage given the distance. The fact was that each country in Scotia's international portfolio was different. Peru and Chile worked, while Argentina didn't. Mexico and Jamaica worked, Colombia less so. As for Puerto Rico, Hart said the bank had to be careful it wasn't imposing a North American governance ethic, but at the end of the day it had to. "That's the difficulty of international. Things run a little looser in certain areas."

It wasn't enough to try to grow in Canada, the Caribbean, Latin America, and the United States: Scotia wanted in on Asian banking, too. Before Thailand, in 2000, BNS was positioning itself to buy an Indonesian bank, and Waugh was running the international division. But why Indonesia? It's hardly an easy commute from Toronto to supervise what's happening in Jakarta. The answer was the size of the market. At the time, Indonesia was home to 214 million people. Now it's 273 million. And no matter the country, no matter the politics, Waugh believed that if you got the right asset for the right price, you could make money. It spoke to Waugh's philosophy of investing, which went back to his earliest days in banking: buy when things are bad and sell when things are good. And either pay as little as you can, or, if you do have to pay up, ensure you get value.

Separately, it's now easily forgotten, but as the year 2000 approached, there was high anxiety about possible techno-Armageddon because no one knew for sure how a now-computerized society would work when the clock struck the start of the next millennium—whether it could handle numbers above 1999. There was a fear that computer engineering hadn't solved for that one yet. So, job one for Scotia was to make sure the Indonesian bank, Bank Arya Panduarta, was "Year 2000 compliant."

Enter *The Year of Living Dangerously*, without Mel Gibson but with Rick Waugh. In the land of Sukarno and Suharto, the government wanted to shut the bank down—but Scotia had just invested time and people. Waugh went to Indonesia to see the minister of finance. He was accompanied by the equivalent of a Green Beret escort to ensure his physical safety. Meantime, the CEO of the local bank said publicly the closure "wasn't BNS' fault," but "it's closed and we're not going to re-open it." Amazingly, Waugh says he was told by the government, "pick whatever other bank you want, and you can have it." This all happened, he says, in the space of twenty-four to forty-eight hours. Meanwhile, he was thinking to himself, I'm "way over my head on this one." With body-guards, he got back to Singapore and "we said forget it." Retelling the story, Waugh repeats the Indonesian government's line in disbelief, "*You can have another bank.*"

At one point, preliminary discussions about buying in Vietnam and China were also intriguing. Waugh, however, says he didn't endear him-self to the governor of China's central bank. While China wanted to be part of the global reserve currency system, Waugh remarked, "How can you be [a] reserve currency if you're not independent?" The reaction he described was understandably chilly, although Scotia did purchase a minority stake in the Bank of Xi'an. India was another story. Scotia tried to buy a minority interest there—he described three brothers will-ing to sell their holding—but, he says, Scotia needed the Reserve Bank of India's agreement. With the help of Sabi Marwah, they finally got word from officialdom in India. "You're not going to be able to buy it. No Indian bank will sell to foreigners. Go buy the Chinese. They're in trouble, we're not." Waugh says it's the same in the United States. "They will not protect foreign banks, only local banks." So, the question becomes, why fool around in any of these countries? "The spreads are good," Waugh explained, and "every country needs a good bank." Scotia also had vast international experience, understood risk, and wanted to expand in Asia. "It was on-strategy." Developing countries, he argued, offered inexpensive entry and fat spreads, due to the higher risk involved. More risk meant a chunkier spread between what it would pay for deposits and get for a loan. "It can work." he said.

Our discussion of the failed merger attempt between BNS and BMO as Waugh was mopping up Argentina raised the question of whether there were other attempts in Canada afterwards. "Yeah," he said at his office on May 29, 2024, while adding that "I had nothing to do with [Canadian] mergers until I became CEO." When he led the bank, Waugh said, he'd had informal discussions with other Canadian bank CEOs. "I was always looking to do something," he says. "There were discussions." Narrowing it down, he said RBC and TD were too big for Scotia, which left CIBC and BMO. Based on accounting and size, "you could get a merger of equals" with the latter two. Such talks, he says, could conveniently occur when all the major bank CEOs met, off to the side, or over coffee. "What mattered was the mathematics and the accounting." The rest, he says, was about the social issues. Given prior government reaction to merger attempts, did he assume he could get past political issues? "I didn't know whether you could or not," he says, but he cites the fact that for a large part of the time he ran the bank, there was a Conservative government in power in Ottawa, and he boasted a constructive relationship with Prime Minister Stephen Harper. He says he advised Harper on the civil service, met with him abroad, and provided intelligence on the eurozone and Greek debt crisis. Whether Harper would have okayed a major bank merger is unknown. Predicting how governments rule on major business deals is like trying to predict how juries arrive at verdicts. After all, the Harper government put up obstacles to BHP buying Potash Corp (now Nutrien) in 2010, depriving Potash shareholders of a significant premium. And after a state-owned enterprise in China bought Nexen in

2013, the Harper government effectively ring-fenced the oil sands. Once politics was involved, nothing was a shoo-in.

One of the defining features and strengths of the Canadian banking system is the country's national network of branches. It has provided extraordinary stability to the system. Ironically, this network is in many ways the product of the mergers and acquisitions in the sector that occurred in the late 1800s and early 1900s, building out each major bank across the country.[7] The establishment of TD with the 1955 merger of Bank of Toronto and the Dominion Bank as well as the 1961 merger that created CIBC capped that trend. While mergers and acquisitions helped build a sound system with a handful of strong banks, at a certain point, further consolidation became viewed as a threat to soundness, not to mention politically unpalatable. Former prime minister Jean Chrétien told Waugh that by quashing proposed in-country bank mergers in the late 1990s and early 2000s, his government saved the country's banking system. He may well be right. If a mega-bank or two had formed because of mergers between the big five or big six, would one of them have become imperilled in 2008 and required a bailout? Would one of those mega-banks have become too aggressive in the United States, buying an asset that was doomed to failure in 2008? "I don't think we'll ever know," Waugh says. And is bigger better when it comes to banking? "Big can be successful or it can be a failure," Waugh explains. "It's worked in Canada. In Europe it hasn't necessarily worked." We spoke of this just as RBC, the country's largest bank, was buying HSBC Canada for $13.5 billion. Did Waugh approve? "The answer is yes," he says. "There is still lots of competition between the banks," he adds, "even though we're an oligopoly."

Despite obstacles to major bank mergers in Canada, Waugh's international work put him in regular conversations with CEOs of the top fifty global banks. He indicated he'd had discussions with many, including "one or two of them about merging." Those would have been non-American banks. While Waugh wouldn't reveal names, given the market value of Scotiabank in 2008, those within range would have been Deutsche Bank, Barclays, National Australia Bank Limited, and Standard Chartered PLC, all worth a few billion less than BNS at the time.

Rick Waugh didn't like sitting on boards. For a lot of CEOs or former CEOs, it's boring. You're not running things and there are hours of reading briefing materials. When Waugh ran Scotia, his board didn't want him distracted by board work at other companies. However, it did want him to sit on one for the experience. The late John Mayberry, an Inco board member who was also chair of Scotiabank, said the miner needed a director. So, Waugh went on the board of Inco, one of the world's largest nickel producers, and it would bring him face to face with one of the biggest merger sweepstakes of the era. At the height of the so-called commodity super cycle in the aughts, two large Canadian miners were up for grabs—Inco and Falconbridge, Sudbury neighbours. The duo were stalwarts of the country's resource sector, not only mining nickel and copper in Canada but prominent in the South Pacific and South America, too. Inco had even entered popular culture, immortalized by country singer Stompin' Tom Connors. As the tune goes, it was the company that no one thought of when the girls were at bingo and the men were getting stinko on a Sudbury Saturday night.

In the corridors of power, though, there was a move afoot to combine the two metal giants, to create what many in Canada's C-suite yearned for—corporate champions. World-beating companies. *Players.* Aside from the banks, which were known globally, during the dot-com craze of 1999–2000, Nortel comprised 35 percent of the market value of the TSX and competed with Cisco and Ericsson. BlackBerry was a pioneer in secure, mobile email, and Bombardier was known everywhere for planes and trains. All three fell on hard times, with Nortel disappearing entirely.

But the view was that the world needed base metals, particularly China, which was trying to move swaths of its population out of poverty and into the middle class. China was building skyscrapers and infrastructure, and it needed nickel for stainless steel, and copper to wire new buildings.

But mining is a global business with global predators. In 2006, the battle for Inco and Falconbridge became an epic takeover drama the likes of which Canada rarely sees. There were multiple actors—Vale of Brazil, Xstrata from Switzerland, Teck from Canada, Phelps Dodge from the United States. Even a proposed combination of Inco, Falco, and Phelps couldn't hold back other foreigners, who outbid everyone. Meanwhile, Inco's board was just twelve people. Therefore, Waugh said, the whole board effectively became the committee dealing with some sort of M&A deal. Then-chairman and CEO Scott Hand recalled Waugh came on the board just before the multi-company takeover saga began. "I promised him a few board meetings," Hand said. But there were at least multiple dozens.[8] Waugh says they even had a CEO picked out for what they hoped would be a combined Canadian company. It was Aaron Regent, the dashing young president of Falconbridge. Coincidentally, Regent joined the BNS board just as Waugh was departing as CEO and would later become chair of the bank's board.

But according to Waugh, the Canadian government did not encourage a made-in-Canada solution. In fact, the saga was so prolonged that *two* Canadian governments did not encourage it. Aside from business considerations, an in-country deal hinged on politics. One of Inco's board members was David O'Brien, the former CEO of Canadian Pacific Limited, which spun off its individual divisions into stand-alone companies—rail, ships, coal, hotels, and oil and gas. The latter was PanCanadian Energy Corp., which later combined with Alberta Energy Company to form Encana, for years one of the biggest independent energy companies. Hand said O'Brien advised him to speak with the prime minister to ask for public support to help seal an Inco-Falco deal. O'Brien had done so, Hand said, to prevent Exxon from buying PanCanadian.

Hand heeded the advice and went to Ottawa to see then-Prime Minister Paul Martin. Martin, Hand said, turned him down, saying that if the government came out in favour of combining Inco and Falconbridge, it would affect foreign investment in Canada. Soon, though, Martin lost an election to Stephen Harper. But Harper's Conservative government was also not supportive. Hand described being at the Four Seasons Hotel in New York meeting with investors when the Prime Minister's Office called. It was awkward. Although he had a conference room, he was amidst hedge fund types and had to scramble to find a private place to take the call. He rushed into the bathroom. "But I had to sit on the 'can' —no chair!" From there, he spoke with Prime Minister Harper and Industry Minister Maxime Bernier, who, like Martin, told him no.

Waugh went so far as to say the cabinet minister in charge, Bernier, hindered the mining deal ("Bernier screwed us"). Waugh says, "He basically made the decision overnight allowing a foreign hostile takeover." Hand confirmed Waugh's take.

So, Vale bought Inco while Xstrata bought Falconbridge. The consolation was that the two were sold at peak prices. "All of us unanimously put up our hands to sell because of the price," Waugh says, which was not a bad outcome for shareholders. But Canada became a much-diminished player in the mining industry. "We lost it all," he says, despite the high price. While the government most certainly wouldn't allow a foreign bank to buy a major Canadian bank—harkening back to the "widely held" rule put in place in the 1960s—in-country control of two significant mining companies was gone.

The fact that an in-country merger couldn't get done, no matter the government, makes one wonder whether the Harper government would have approved a bank merger. The truth is, Ottawa's decisions about mergers are a hodgepodge. Major in-country bank mergers and foreign purchases of Canada's banks aren't permitted, yet RBC was allowed to buy HSBC's sizeable Canadian operations, increasing its dominance. Within another Canadian oligopoly—telecom—Rogers Communications was allowed to buy Shaw Communications, widening Rogers's moat. And while Inco and Falconbridge were not protected and were snapped up, when foreign-owned miner BHP tried to buy PotashCorp, it was blocked. A couple of years later, *a state-owned Chinese company*, CNOOC, was permitted to buy oil sands company Nexen. There's no knowing. Almost always, politics plays a role, as it did in Thailand, India, Argentina and the US when TARP got in the way of purchasing the bank in Cleveland.

Deals and winning were important to Waugh, particularly if they were designed to build the institution into an enduring force. But at many companies and in many cases, they're just trades—one thing bought, one thing sold, then maybe rebought and resold, taken private, taken public, moved in and out of hands as new leaders take over and strategies shift. What's more likely to endure, change lives, and leave legacies is far beyond mergers and acquisitions.

CHAPTER ELEVEN

Does She Mind Going Down One Floor?

I n 1901, the manager of a Bank of Nova Scotia branch had a question for head office. Should he install a high screen "around his first female employee, to shut her off from the observation of the public"?[1] Today, that manager would no doubt be overwhelmed trying to conceal more than half of the bank's staff, given that women now constitute almost 55 percent of employees in Canadian financial services.

The fact is that much of the twentieth century was still the Dark Ages for women in banking. Until 1964, women couldn't have their own bank account without their husband's signature.[2] And for women who had them during the first couple of decades of the 1900s, there were limits on how much they could deposit.[3] Even though Scotia's staff had become predominantly female after the Second World War, women were not deemed eligible for the company pension fund until 1967, four years after Royal Bank included them in its plan. Although Rick Waugh began working for the bank three years after the fund was established, he remembers when, except for secretaries, women were not permitted on the executive floor of the bank's headquarters. To underline the point, there was no women's washroom on that floor. It was typical, Waugh says, of a lot of companies. *"Does she mind going down one floor?"*

Gender inequality was, and has been, the norm in society at large. After all, Canada's Parliament didn't remove the gender barrier in voting until 1918.[4] And in banking, the obstacles for women were not confined to Scotia. CIBC was twenty years old before it even had a female employee. A 1931 staff newsletter at the bank proclaimed that women didn't have the capacity for management. Routine tasks, it said, were more appropriate for females.[5] A history of TD Bank published in 1958 refers to "girls" on the staff of the Bank of Toronto and the Dominion Bank, TD's predecessors.[6] In 1966, Bank of Montreal opened a women-only branch in Montreal called "Le Salon." A female could be a customer if she kept $2,000 in her account.[7] In 1976, Royal Bank's CEO, Earle McLaughlin, put a big wingtip in his mouth when he pronounced there wasn't a qualified woman to sit on the bank's board, which then consisted of about forty directors. Rod McQueen wrote in the *Toronto Star* that after a national clamour, two women were soon appointed.

As for Scotiabank, it was historically a laggard in promoting women. Volume five of the history of CIBC quotes a 1988 survey in the *Globe and Mail* that ranked Scotia last among the big five with women who reached the rank of vice-president or higher. BNS had just 13 percent versus 24 percent for CIBC, Royal, and BMO. In a glaring example of archaic, controlling attitudes in the 1960s, the head of personnel (later human resources) "would tell employees, during staff meetings, that two children were enough for any banker."[8]

Not surprisingly, gender inequality wasn't just an issue in Canada. Peter Cardinal, who headed Scotia in Mexico, recalled the bankers club in Mexico City also had no women's washroom. "Mexico is very macho," he said, describing the club as a big dinner, big cigar, tequila kind of place. In the 2000s, when Scotiabank in Mexico appointed a female CEO, Nicole Reich de Polignac, Cardinal said the club had to install a women's washroom. (One can imagine many more hastily constructed women's washrooms in 2024, when Mexico elected its first female president.)

At the highest levels of Scotiabank, until a concerted effort began in the 1990s under Peter Godsoe and was later expanded by Rick Waugh, there were virtually no top female executives or female board members. As Robert MacIntosh wrote in his 1991 history of Canadian banking, this was not Scotia-specific. "Fifty years ago, it would not have occurred to banks to have women on the board of directors any more than it would have occurred to the prime minister to have a woman in the cabinet."[9] Indeed, Canada did not have its first female cabinet minister until 1957, Ellen Fairclough.

Waugh's tenure as CEO ended in late 2013, before DEI (diversity, equity, and inclusion) became a go-to acronym in the corporate world. Within a few years of his departure, Indigenous people, LBGTQ2SIA+ people, and people of colour all became focal points for inclusion, inside major organizations and in their outward-facing material. During Waugh's time as chief executive, there was, however, a determined focus to advance women at Scotia and other Canadian banks, culminating in a global award for Scotiabank from Catalyst, a non-profit supported by leading CEOs and companies "to help build workplaces that work for women."[10]

This initiative wasn't Waugh's typical operating zone. It wasn't multi-billion-dollar deals, international acquisitions and firefighting, or navigating the global financial crisis. *It wasn't even banking.* But improving the career prospects of women may be one of the most meaningful things Waugh did while running the bank. "I'm proud of it," he said while sitting at his kitchen table in June 2024, dressed in a T-shirt and jeans. It was also an extension of his philosophy of managing via people—all people. It was good for women, the bank, and society.

Waugh says his involvement in Catalyst and supporting the progress of women in business are rooted in his days at the University of Manitoba. In the late 1960s, the commerce faculty where he studied was typical—predominantly male. However, he says, he recognized there was a small female cohort that was both smart and strong. It included Bonnie Lovelace, who is still one of his closest friends. Lovelace had a successful career as a top civil servant, reaching the rank of assistant deputy minister.

Waugh describes Freshie Week tradition among male commerce students ("maybe two hundred guys") to have a stag at a hotel, which included the usual accoutrements. Waugh says Bonnie and other women in the class insisted they be invited. They were right, he thought. Why shouldn't they be included, even if the situation might be uncomfortable? Waugh goes on to describe that when he ran for student president in high school, he made sure he had a female running mate, who also happened to be Jewish. To him, a diverse approach was common sense. The slate would have wider appeal. "I won by a landslide."

In banking, women are a vast part of the workforce, so joining with Catalyst was obvious to Waugh—the bank simply "had to be at the table." The table included CEOs from other banks—notably Bill Downe and Gord Nixon—who were equally committed. Not only was participating appropriate in a societal context but also it was "the right thing to do as the head of a Canadian bank," Waugh says. Catalyst, he adds, was also a fount of data. As with assessing a loan application, Waugh knew you couldn't argue with facts, and as a research organization, Catalyst had the facts about women being stifled as they tried to move up the ranks. "They [Catalyst] weren't basing this stuff on hearsay."

The key research finding Waugh says he focused on was what looked like a ceiling when it came to women in senior roles. According to the data, women couldn't get above 30 percent representation on boards or in executive positions (the CEO job was, and continues to be, another matter entirely). Waugh says Catalyst's researchers even adjusted the results for the fact that women took parental leave, but a barrier persisted. "We couldn't get past 30 percent." At the end of the second quarter of 2006, six of twenty EVPs—30 percent—were women. A slightly higher number were VPs, while there were fewer senior vice-presidents (SVPs).[11]

Unsurprisingly, another finding that jumped out at Waugh was that tokenism doesn't work. The research showed that if there was just one woman on a board, she would undeniably feel alone. If you were the only woman, everyone would be watching you. While gender parity is obviously the goal, and competency is crucial, Waugh says the data at the time revealed the magic number was at least three. "At least if there's three women in the room, you can diffuse it." Deborah Gillis, who headed Catalyst Canada and later the global organization, said when there were more women represented, "You were no longer expected to speak for your gender. You were clearly there for your skills and experience." That said, Waugh emphasizes "the goal was not 30 percent, the goal was 50 percent."

Waugh couldn't help but think about his wife and what she'd sacrificed for his career. "She gave up some pretty good jobs." Lynne Waugh was an A-plus student who wanted to be a teacher. Upon moving from England to Canada for graduate work, her funding evaporated. So, she found a job. Despite finding success, she later gave up the position so her husband could accept a major promotion—the executive position in New York. "It was her choice in our personal lives," Waugh says. While Lynne had an instinct that her husband was headed to the top of the bank, she found herself mostly on her own when they were living in New Jersey. Waugh was gone before sunrise and not home until late. "It was hard," she reflected. A self-described introvert, she volunteered and, in later years, upon returning to Toronto, started an etiquette training business. But her career had not been what she'd hoped for while he moved up the ladder.

According to Scotia's history of women in the organization, it was "the first Canadian bank to appoint women branch managers." Gladys Marcellus of Ottawa and Shirley Giles of Toronto were appointed in 1961, by which time 56 percent of the bank's staff were women. Newspaper photo captions regarding the two were reflective of the era, referring to them as "Miss Marcellus" and "Mrs. Giles." A page on BNS's website, titled "Women in Banking: A Case Study of Scotiabank," says the two were "acutely aware of their roles as pioneers." Giles was quoted as saying, "I really feel that I have to make good. I have to work at it because it seems like all eyes are on me"—the precise point Waugh made about the challenge of being the lone woman on a board.

Strides began to be made in the 1940s with the appointment of women economists. By 1958, Dr. Lucy Morgan headed Scotiabank's economics department and became the bank's first female supervisor. Much later, Helen Sinclair, a Scotia banker, became executive director of the Canadian Bankers Association. In 1993, Peter Godsoe, then president, appointed an independent task force "to find out why so few women held upper management positions (77 percent of bank staff were women, but only 6.97 percent had reached positions of upper management) and to determine how to improve this situation." Barbara Mason, who would later lead the human resources department, headed the task force. Ten thousand employees were surveyed, "asking for their perceptions, attitudes, and suggestions on the issue of women in banking."[12]

That same year, Wendy Hannam became one of the first female line vice-presidents at the bank and the first VP at the bank to have a baby. But there were still dinosaurs roaming Scotia's halls. Hannam recalled a going-away party for someone in the 1980s, and her boss getting up to speak. "Oh, I just love women employees. They work twice as hard for half the pay." Clearly pregnant, at meetings she said male colleagues were "terrified that I was going to have the baby at work." Hannam rose to executive vice-president of retail banking in Canada, then EVP retail international and EVP Latin America, which meant mostly Mexico.

In 2004, when Waugh became CEO, Godsoe's initiative was relaunched, "with the goal in mind of improving the representation of women in senior leadership positions at Scotiabank, to ensure that a culture that values and builds a diverse pool of employees with the broadest range of skills, knowledge and talent was created."[13] The steering committee was called AoW, Advancement of Women, and Waugh championed it. Aside from doing the right thing, the initiative was in line with Waugh's strategic interest in people and how they could drive the bank's performance. As for Hannam, Waugh called her a role model for other women at the bank.

Sylvia Chrominska first met Rick Waugh when he was on crutches. He'd slipped the day beforehand and injured his leg. "He had on the worst tie I've ever seen," she recalled, wide and covered with fish. "Christ, this guy's going to head up corporate banking?" Clearly, Waugh was bright and brimming with leadership qualities, but he was "unpolished, if you will, which is part of his charm."

Prior to that first meeting, which took place while Waugh was running the main branch, Chrominska had started as a credit analyst, "the lowest form of life," she said wryly, describing it as "penance." She wrote profiles of prospective customers, big companies, so "the marketing guys" could go and pitch the bank. When Scotia set up a corporate credit division, she said she was the only female in the department. That led to her droll observation that "it was easy to distinguish myself one way or another." Peter Godsoe and Bruce Birmingham were her sponsors and mentors.

"One of the great things about the bank then made it a great place to work and a bad place to work," she said. No one stood on ceremony, and as a junior person, she could find herself answering a future CEO's questions. She recalled smoking a cigarette with her feet in her desk drawer when Godsoe came along to grill her. "We kind of went to who we thought had the answer," an un-bureaucratic, "action-oriented," personal structure, one which Waugh embraced.

Like Gladys Marcellus and Shirley Giles, Chrominska was a pioneer. She spent thirty-three years at the bank, becoming SVP of credit, the first female executive vice-president (1995) and then head of human resources, a thankless but immensely powerful post. While Godsoe had promoted her, Waugh knew Chrominska well. She'd been one of the key credit judges scrutinizing his lending requests during his New York days, an intense but rewarding time for the Waugh gang. Although Chrominska was in Toronto, Waugh made her feel part of the team. And Waugh, she added, "had a great relationship with his team."

In contrast, Chrominska said she always felt like her own team in the risk department were "second-class citizens" within the bank, as popular as the guys in audit, she cracked. Waugh, however, included her, inviting her to conferences. This was motivating for Chrominska and her associates—to be seen as facilitators as opposed to obstructionists. She recalled one closing dinner on a tight deal where the bank had thought it would take a bath but didn't. Waugh took them to the 21 Club in New York City. "Talk about starry-eyed," she said. "Here I am, a girl from Stratford. And here I am at the 21 Club." Once Waugh was running the bank, she, along with Sabi Marwah, rounded out a triumvirate. "They were the three amigos at the top of the chain," according to Stephen Hart, who worked for Chrominska.

However, "Not in my wildest dreams did I aspire to be an HR person," she said. Godsoe, Chrominska believed, put her in the job to transfer the unbureaucratic behaviour in the corporate credit department to the rest of the bank, which was "hugely bureaucratic." Despite this historic promotion to group head—one rung below CEO—the move didn't make her happy. "I felt like my male colleagues were waiting for me to self-destruct." As the lone woman at the prime table, she said men were stealing her ideas as their own, interrupting her, all the classic behaviour women experience in the corporate sphere. "It was horrible," she said, until she eventually found her sea legs.

Chrominska was careful to say she never got such treatment from Waugh. "Rick and I made huge strides on the advancement of women in the bank." Chrominska knew she was blunt, but thought Waugh welcomed her directness. "It was my job to tell him things he didn't want to hear." Besides, she had proven herself in credit, which Waugh respected. With her hard-won expertise, inner toughness, and perhaps air cover from Waugh, Chrominska was one of the top women in banking.

She said Waugh set up the strategic investment committee and the human investment committee, an acknowledgement that he needed a team. Chrominska recalled Godsoe, in his day, saying, "I could do that with one arm tied behind my back" or "I could do that on the back of an envelope." She said she loved Godsoe, whom others have called an "iconic" CEO, but added, "Peter was a bit of an intellectual bully." Certainly, Chrominska indicated, Godsoe was a high-wattage intellect, in command of the details. While she didn't want to take anything away from Waugh, she said that "Rick was not Peter" from an intellectual standpoint. Chrominska said Waugh had a differentiating strength. He realized that he needed input by harnessing capabilities across the spectrum of people, embracing diversity. She implied that this energized her, empowering her and other executives to do their jobs.

Inevitably, though, scar tissue remains. Chrominska remembers what she calls "either the worst or the best thing that happened" to her as a top female executive at Scotiabank. At the time, she was senior vice-president of risk. One afternoon, she noticed all of her male colleagues getting dressed up in tuxedos for a splashy dinner event. "All the boys were going to this black-tie dinner" and she hadn't been invited. "I was just mortified," she said. She went home and told her partner. He said to her, "Why do you give a shit, anyway? You don't want to go." But that wasn't the point. It was a terrible hurt. A few years later, she was invited to the same event and realized it was a totally tedious evening, which took the sting out of the insult and now makes her laugh. But clearly, she hasn't forgotten the unfairness.

And of course, there was the washroom issue Waugh had described. When Chrominska moved to the seventh floor, then the executive floor of the bank and where the board met, she told Bruce Birmingham, "There's only one washroom down here." Laughing as she described his terse comeback, she said fondly that you had to know Birmingham. "*So, use it!*" he told her. She did. "They ended up putting some women's toiletries in that washroom."

While Godsoe was still CEO, Chrominska attended the Catalyst honours dinner in New York on behalf of the bank. The bank, she said, had purchased two seats and she occupied one of them. As a believer in Scotia's culture, she remembered sitting there yearning for the bank to receive the kind of recognition she witnessed other companies received that evening. Right then and there began a few years' work to assemble a submission from the bank. Later, when Scotia did make its submission, Waugh was running the bank, and Chrominska said, "he bought in."

The effort was part of a larger strategic priority. Waugh, Chrominska said, would speak to the financial analyst community about the importance of leadership as an engine of the bank's success. And by that, he didn't just mean at the CEO level but throughout the organization. The bank's people, he argued, would drive its success and profitability. He was extrapolating from his own experience. As an employee himself, he had moved the profit needle for the bank. Therefore, so could others, and "others" meant anyone at the bank. For Chrominska, as the executive in charge of human resources, there couldn't have been a better message from a CEO. "I still am a believer that analysts should pay a helluva lot of attention to how we develop our people." She felt it herself. In 2012, she was asked to speak at the bank's annual general meeting, a vote of confidence. "It was the first time a woman [executive] spoke at the Scotiabank annual meeting," the first time a head of HR had done so, and the first time the bank spoke about people development.*

But prior to that, it was all about the business case. "That's what we harped on—the business case," Chrominska said. Internal employee surveys showed female employees were less satisfied, and less satisfied employees were likely to be less engaged. Customers would feel that, hitting the bank where it hurts: profitability. *But why were female employees less satisfied?* Put plainly, they didn't see a path to career advancement. "There was a glass ceiling at the VP level. Women couldn't seem to break that glass ceiling."

The bank started looking at the so-called pipeline of talent at the assistant general manager level, the level just below VP. The research did not show a good reason why women were not advancing. Clearly, it was prejudice. Committees were struck: HIC ("only Rick could come up with this," Chrominska joked), for Human Investment Committee, and STIC, for Strategic Investment Committee. They met regularly and talked about high-potential people and filling vacancies. Chrominska said these initiatives worked. "I give Rick a ton of credit. That was entirely his baby." She said Godsoe used to make a lot of decisions himself but was less likely to have those sorts of meetings with group heads. However, Waugh wanted input. "I think it gave him insight into how his key people were coming at things," and "we had been taking a number of steps to force out biases." You couldn't just fill a vacancy with your favourite person. Chrominska said each business within the bank had to demonstrate it had looked at a diverse slate of candidates. "At the time,

---

* In a September 8, 2024, email, Chrominska added: "I am fairly confident that I was the first woman period to address the meeting."

we were principally concerned with women," not the broader DEI initiatives of ensuing years (according to RBC's Gord Nixon, gender equality was the focus during that period at Royal as well). In addition to work inside the bank, Chrominska said Waugh supported women's issues externally via philanthropy.

The bank also began encouraging women to make lateral moves—to think about how their skills were transferable to other positions so they could broaden their experience and enrich their resumés. Typically, she indicated, women were hesitant. Quite simply, Chrominska said many women felt differently than men. "Well, they shouldn't feel that way," Waugh told Chrominska, trying to send the message that women should feel like they could advance at Scotia. "Well sorry, Rick, they do," was her reply.

As the work evolved, Chrominska recalled getting questions from vice-chairs at the bank. "Could we have a bit more information about the pipeline" and whether it's reasonable to assume people (read: women) will be ready for top jobs? Chrominska viewed that as an unfair question. When you set mortgage targets for your guys, she shot back, how confident are you that you can meet those targets? "That kind of pushed them over the edge."

"People metrics" were also showing up on the so-called balanced scorecard, a tool used by major companies to monitor key components of the business: profitability, earnings per share, return on investment, and operations. The financials always had the heaviest weighting, and were therefore the most influential. But gender diversity, Chrominska said, would have been part of the people metric. The result was that "it was certainly far better than it had ever been before."

Part of it, she implied, was pushing outward herself. Chrominska had certainly, as a woman, known the difficulty of getting a word in edgewise at the executive table, experiencing what she called "shitty meeting etiquette." As the first and only female executive vice-president when she

was appointed, she felt "mortified," apprehensive when presenting to
the board. The directors consisted of titans like New Brunswick frozen
food billionaire Harrison McCain ("they were all Ritchie's cronies,
okay") and Sir Graham Day, a Nova Scotia lawyer who'd been in British
prime minister Margaret Thatcher's cabinet, her "Mr. Fixit." There were,
however, two female board members: former Mulroney cabinet minister Barbara McDougall and the former president of the University of
New Brunswick, Elizabeth Parr-Johnston. "Well, silly girl," Chrominska
described them telling her, "we were looking for you to succeed."
Chrominska, though, said she got support from some of the men.
Graham Day had worked for arguably the most powerful woman in the
world. "These were tough-ass guys," Chrominska said. But Day, she
said, went to bat for her. "Peter, are you sure you're paying her enough?"
she quoted Day saying to Godsoe.

One situation could have been extremely awkward for her and, in
today's climate, unthinkable. While in Saskatchewan, the chair of the
human resources committee told Chrominska he wanted to have a private meeting with her given that she was head of HR. "So where to have
a private meeting?" she wondered. As it turned out, they had breakfast in
his hotel room. "It didn't cross my mind it was inappropriate at the
time." Chrominska stressed that there was nothing untoward. She said
he had simply wanted to know in confidence what was going on at the
bank, and the two remained close confidants.

Deborah Gillis, the former head of Catalyst, offered a view on why
Sylvia Chrominska would be hesitant to speak up about poor treatment
from colleagues. "Not wanting to rock the boat. Not wanting to be seen
as the woman. All of those things." When your CEO is chair of Catalyst,
cares about it, and talks about it publicly, and the team involved gets
recognition, Gillis said, there's a lot of profile and it's celebrated. People
get jealous and feel threatened. Janet Yellen, the first person in American

history to have held the top three economic posts in the country—Chair of the White House Council of Economic Advisors, US Treasury Secretary, and chair of the Federal Reserve—put it this way in an interview with former presidential advisor David Axelrod: "I think that trying to get ahead in a world that has barriers, and some hostility, certainly leads me to think twice before I say something."[14]

Reflecting on the issue, Waugh said that when Chrominska worked in credit, she was a colleague with male peers. "But once you're head of HR, that is one of the most influential positions in any organization," with control over colleagues. For men reporting to a woman, "not every guy can take that," Waugh says. For her part, Chrominska said the problem with CEOs is "they think when they say something, that it happens," implying that whatever a boss says or the tone the boss sets, it still needs to filter through an organization.

An official encounter with a Canadian bank CEO was understandably intimidating for Deborah Gillis, who had grown up in a Cape Breton fishing village in a home with no central heating along a gravel road. But Rick Waugh wasn't what she expected of a bank boss. He was approachable and "treated everyone he met the same," she said, which put her at ease. The first person in her family to get a university education, Gillis had worked on constitutional issues for the Ontario government, in the province's cabinet office, and later in the private sector at PWC and Grant Thornton. As a high-school student, she recalled being struck by women lobbying for gender equality in the Charter of Rights and Freedoms. After a bout with breast cancer, in 2006 she was hired to run Catalyst Canada.

"It changed my life," she said when we spoke at her office, coincidentally on International Women's Day. Catalyst formed in 1962 and, initially, Bank of Montreal's CEO Tony Comper brought Catalyst to Canada. In 2007, Waugh became chair of the Canadian arm and sat on the global board, and Gillis worked with him. In that role, Waugh would convene quarterly meetings at Scotiabank's boardroom. "Gord [Nixon of RBC] came all the time," he said. "Bill Downe [Comper's successor at BMO] came a lot." Linda Hasenfratz, the long-time CEO of auto parts maker Linamar, also participated. For Gillis, having bank CEOs like Waugh and Downe and Nixon stand up and say this was the "right thing to do and the smart thing to do had an impact."[†] And while in those days the focus was on demonstrating the business case for gender equality, "The conversation shifted from give me the data," Gillis said, to "what do I need to do?"

"Someone in Rick's position as CEO of Scotiabank saying to the business community, this is a priority, here's what it's done for my institution," Gillis said, "that has a ripple effect more broadly." She also personally appreciated Waugh reviewing the agenda and topics beforehand and sharing advice as a business leader if she needed help navigating an issue. "He was enormously generous with his time."

Meantime, three bank bosses who were clearly fierce competitors—Waugh, Nixon, and Downe—were all prepared to sit around the table together on a crucial societal issue. "There was always this friendly competitive joking and poking each other a little bit," she said. Gillis recalled Waugh relished chairing the meetings at Scotia, where the other CEOs had to *come to his turf*, and, as chair, he could even cut them off. Given the size and influence of the Canadian banks, Gillis believes they have a responsibility to lead on such issues "and they have done so." They supported Catalyst, she said, because the data existed to support business decisions, impacting the culture and bottom lines of their own organizations. "This matters to me and my institution," it said to them, and "it's

---

† Both Gord Nixon and Bill Downe were honoured by Catalyst Canada, in 2012 and 2014, respectively, and Downe was chair of the Catalyst Canada Advisory Board. After Scotiabank was honoured in 2007, both RBC and BMO also won the Catalyst Award, bestowed at a gala in New York, under Nixon (2010) and Downe (2017). BMO also won in 1994, TD in 1999, and RBC in 2021.

hugely impactful." Gillis said in the almost two decades since, there's been more progress. "It's the journey from compliance to commitment," she said. It's "one thing to check a box . . . as a regulated industry," while it's another to "getting to a stage of commitment."

As Nixon described it, "what they [Catalyst] really encouraged were building these long-term programs [to help women succeed in the workplace], not just appointing people to hit targets." Looking back, when Waugh, Nixon, and Downe started their careers, parental leave to care for newborns was a fraction of what it is now. Downe said "Rick created energy in Canada," was successful at recruiting people for the board, and convinced him to chair it when he stepped down.

Gillis, meanwhile, has experienced her own moments of gender-related discomfort. At a Catalyst event, no less, she said a top Canadian business leader looked her "up and down" and suggestively said, "you look great," clearly inappropriate. What do you say, she wondered as she described the uncomfortable, sexist situation? You ignore it, she said, and move on. But at the same time, when you overlook it and don't say something, "it's death by a thousand cuts."

Nixon said, "the percentage [of women] who have had negative experiences with men—the stats are staggering." During his days as an investment banker at Dominion Securities, he said the trading room was a bit like a locker room. "That was tolerated at the time. That is not tolerated today."

Barb Mason joined Scotiabank in 1982 to begin what would be a forty-two-year career. Armed with a degree in urban geography, she started as a branch location analyst. She also became one of the bank's top executives, running wealth management, and was Chrominska's successor as chief human resources officer (CHRO). We spoke not long after she retired. "When you're CHRO, you have few friends." While Mason previously had deep relationships with her teams and peers, as CHRO, she had to distance herself in order to be impartial. "You're the CEO's confidante," contributing to big decisions around compensation and who gets what position. "It's a lonely job." Nonetheless, like Chrominska, dating to the early 1990s Mason was deeply involved in figuring out how to move more women into leadership roles at the bank.

Her own trajectory can be traced to the bank's unenthusiastic roll-out of bank machines. In the early 1980s, Scotia's tradition of being a tech follower was again writ large. In the 1970s, the bank initially said no to using Visa (then Chargex) and then had to play catch-up with credit cards.[15] Then, as other banks like Royal were installing hundreds of ATMs across the country, Scotia had just fourteen. "Mr. Ritchie and Mr. Bell thought it was a fad," Mason said. The grizzled bankers raised on inkwells thought customers weren't going to use such new-fangled gizmos. Grudgingly, Mason said they put together a group in early 1983 and declared they wanted a national network by October of that year. Previously, she had worked for two years in marketing at Colgate-Palmolive, so they said, "you figure out where to put the machines." As it had for Chrominska, the lack of bureaucracy worked to Mason's advantage.

But Scotia's laggard approach, Mason said, led to declining deposits. While Scotia dawdled on ATMs, Canada Trust was wallpapering the country with Johnny Cash Machines. Canada Trust (purchased by TD in 1999) had grown into a populist, retail banking juggernaut and was maxing out the marketing coup of an endorsement from Johnny Cash, the famous country singer. Armed with a perfect surname for the job, the Johnny Cash machines became a cultural and marketing phenomenon. That led to Mason and her boss, Rick Robida, travelling to the United States to see what the Americans were doing.

In Philadelphia, they looked at a shared service among community banks. Judging it to be brilliant, she said, Scotia approached National Bank, which wanted ATMs outside of Quebec, and voila, the IDEAL network was born in Canada. Hockey superstar Guy Lafleur was National Bank's spokesperson, while Olympic diver Sylvie Bernier was Scotia's. Mason described Lafleur visiting Scotia's lobby at 44 King Street West to demonstrate the card. She said he needed eight attempts to get it to work. But Mason said RBC noticed and wanted in on the network. So did other banks, and Interac was born.

The launch, Mason recalled, was held at the York Club, a stuffy Toronto haunt in the old Gooderham family mansion at the edge of the University of Toronto. The club would not vote in favour of women joining until 1992. So, when Mason went, she described being asked to enter via a less-visible passageway than the main entrance. Inside, she watched as club staff handed out cigars to the men while they walked past her. She said she whistled to call one of them over, helped herself to a cigar, and smoked it.

By 1993, she was central to the bank's Advancement of Women initiative. More than thirty years later, the bank now has more women executives and board members than ever, but she said fundamental issues remain. She believes "that we [women] own part of this," that it's not just a "white [male] senior executive problem."

Part of her view is rooted in the bank's internal research, performance appraisals, and what had been a paper-based system for assessing who'd be assigned what jobs. Scotia asked employees where in the bank and in the world would they be willing to work. Men, she said, would answer "anywhere," while women would say operations or support jobs, not the divisions of the bank where financial results were measured. "Women were risk averse, more conservative," whereas men would say "show me the opportunity and I'll figure it out." Separately and unfairly, in the days of a paper-based jobs system, women were ignored for jobs they didn't even know existed. As a result, Mason said, the system was changed and jobs were posted electronically for everyone to see.

That said, she maintained that as the bank began tackling the advancement of women, it promoted some too quickly. "We were so desperate" to move women from SVP to EVP, she said. "What we didn't do was proper assessments of skills to do the job technically and behaviourally," and therefore "promoted too fast or into the wrong job." Certain high-level jobs in the bank, she said, require the ability to perform at rapid-fire pace immediately. Only years of experience could prepare someone. What's left unsaid is that this had happened with men since time immemorial, so there were bound to be promotion misfires with women.

The first time Mason met Rick Waugh was when she presented the findings of the 1993 task force study to all the bank's executives, EVP and above. This took place at an off-site, held at a downtown hotel, "And it was all men." Mason then corrected herself, saying there was at least one female executive in attendance—Sylvia Chrominska. But her point was made: the top tier was grossly lopsided. After the presentation, when Mason said she was leaving with another female colleague involved in the report, Peter Godsoe and Rick Waugh asked them, "Hey, wanna go for drinks?" Here was an invitation from the CEO and one of his key executives. So, Mason said, they went, emphasizing it was not uncomfortable. Instead, she viewed it as a networking opportunity.

She said she also entered golf tournaments with the guys, adding there may have been chatter that she was doing this to get ahead or assumptions that were worse. But why not, she thought? Men networked socially, why shouldn't women? "I'm not going to be a victim to anybody," Mason said. If a situation became untoward, she would simply remove herself from that situation. And if she was at a bank or industry event where she was the only woman, "I walked into the room as a professional, not as a woman," adding, "What's said behind my back, I don't know."

Mason may have had helpful internal wiring to prepare her for her roles. Due to her father's job at General Electric, the family moved frequently when she was a child. She went to thirteen schools, constantly adapting as the new kid, developing a thick shell. Nonetheless, she conceded there's been an emotional cost, what she described as something akin to PTSD, implying it had not been formally diagnosed. Despite all her success, she said, the thought of entering a room full of strangers makes her recoil. "It's like a burn." Yet, while she said things don't roll off her easily, she added, "I'm very resilient."

The fact remains, reality simply intrudes for so many women. A huge societal obstacle to more women moving into top jobs is the attitude towards stay-at-home dads. Society, Mason said, is still unaccepting. She experienced this first-hand, witnessing how difficult it was for her husband, who retired early, to assume this role. "Now I'm Mr. Barbara Mason?" he'd say.

So, was a successful career as a bank executive worth it? I asked. There was a very, very long, almost excruciating pause. She then said she's had to have very honest conversations with her children. "They went through 'where's Mom?'" She also said, "There's no work-life balance here. Not for a minute," adding that, "One day you're a great mom, you're an A mom, a C at work, a B wife, a D daughter. And the next day it's different again." She said, "Just try to be an A-plus at everything, you'll kill yourself." Mason said we need more role models—and acceptance of stay-at-home fathers—so society produces the best people to run the country and its companies. "If that changes, women would be freed, and then watch out. And then the numbers would skyrocket."

On the difference between Godsoe and Waugh, Mason said she had significantly more interaction with Waugh as CEO. "Peter did think he was the smartest guy in the room. And often he was," she said, adding that he was good at modulating it. "But once in a while it would let loose." On one occasion, she said, he was very rough on her team, and afterwards she confronted him on it. "He called me the next day [saying] 'I'm very sorry.'" Waugh, on the other hand, respected you for what you could do, was very social and good-natured. But that didn't mean he didn't grill you or that he wasn't very demanding. "He would go through line by line," she said. "He really made sure that you knew what you were talking about." It was like a test to see if you really knew your business. If it was Waugh and Marwah, "the two of them together—dynamite."

When she did get the position on the executive floor, the seventh floor, she ensured there was a women's washroom for assistants. And now the pipeline, she said, is "very, very good. Best I've ever seen it"— and includes women who she thinks will be CEO candidates, if not in the next round, then the following, depending on how long the current CEO stays.‡

On March 21, 2007, Sylvia Chrominska's wish became reality. At the Waldorf Astoria on Park Avenue in New York City, Chrominska, Rick Waugh, Deborah Gillis, and the elite of North American business gathered for the annual Catalyst Awards dinner. Waugh and Scotia would share the stage that evening with PepsiCo, Goldman Sachs Group, and PricewaterhouseCoopers LLP, the other winners that year. Waugh credited Chrominska with doing the hard work—a thirty-one-page submission—and the ideas to push for the "Advancement of Women" initiative, which had been "conceived and launched by women, and continues to be monitored by women at the bank" and "supported and championed" by Waugh. Chrominska's co-chair had been another female EVP at Scotia, Alberta Cefis.[16]

"Scotiabank was not maximizing every employee's contribution," and "not benefitting from diversity in decision-making," leading Waugh to commit to funding the initiative for five years. As a result, "Everyone at the VP level and above has accountability for women's advancement."[17]

The results were real. "Scotiabank has significantly improved the representation of women at the senior-management level from 18.9 percent in

---

‡ In 2023, Barb Mason was honoured with the Catalyst Community Spotlight Award.

2003 to 31 percent in 2006. Representation of women at the most-senior EVP/corporate officer level has increased from 26.7 percent to 36.8 percent from 2003 to 2006. Employee satisfaction scores rose nine points and Return on Equity in the same period went from 17.6 percent to 22.1 percent."[18] When Scotia won, Chrominska added, "Rick was able to sit on the stage with the who's who of North American business." Displaying a mischievous sense of humour, she said that at the celebration afterwards, "he was buying a lot of champagne, unbeknownst to him."

Research about the so-called glass ceiling points to what seems like an obvious feedback loop. In a paper for *American Economic Review*, Northwestern and Stanford professors David A. Matsa and Amalia R. Miller, write that "increasing the share of women on corporate boards can lead to subsequent increases in the share of women in top management." And "the presence of more female managers increases the qualified pool of potential female board members." Each bolsters the other.[19]

"It's a tree and it broadens out to a base," Waugh said, reflecting years later about the evolution of women's advancement at the bank. And indeed, it had. In a speech on March 27, 2013, Chrominska talked about how the AoW had been "designed to attract, retain and advance women," and she updated the data. In 1995, she had become the first female EVP at the bank. "In 2003, 27 percent of EVPs were women, by 2010, 36 percent were."

Boards of directors have also changed. In 1960, Scotiabank's board had thirty-two members. All were men, with more than half having business connections to the bank. In 1982, the bank's 150th anniversary, the board had thirty-five directors, two of whom were women, and there were no people of colour on the board.[20] By 2001, there were twenty-two directors, four of whom were women. In 2002, two years before Waugh became CEO, the board had twenty directors, and three were women. When Waugh departed the job on November 1, 2013, there were fifteen on the board, four of whom were women, 26.66 percent. It wasn't 50 percent gender equality, or even past 30 percent. But it was an improvement over the 15 percent representation when he'd arrived in the top job. By 2025, five of the twelve board members were women, or 42 percent.

The landscape was better in senior management. In Waugh's last year running the bank, of the sixteen executive vice-presidents, half were women—hugely significant. Clearly, more women were progressing into top jobs. They were in the pipeline. However, as his tenure wrapped up, the five executives leading the bank's major businesses and reporting directly to Waugh were all men.[21] By 2025, four of the bank's top twelve executives featured on its website were women, while the ratio of executive vice-presidents had fallen slightly below half.[22]§ Overall, eleven of thirty-two executives were women, or 34 percent.[23]

On January 22, 2024, the *Globe and Mail* published an editorial about how boardroom doors in Canada were slowly starting to open. Citing a 2023 diversity report by law firm Osler, the editorial highlighted that it took until 2022 for all S&P/TSX index companies to have at least one woman on their boards. Clearly, gender equality wasn't just a Scotia issue or a banking issue. Among the largest firms on the index, which included banks, 36 percent of board members were women. As for corporate executives, among the companies that disclose such data, 20.8 percent were women. As for CEOs, only 5 percent of companies in the index had a female chief executive. The figures for visible minority and Indigenous representation were even lower.[24]

---

§ A DBRS Morningstar report in December 2023 sampled Canadian financial institutions, including credit unions. At the end of 2022, 45 percent of boards were women. At banks, only 33 percent of executives were female. In C-level roles, a higher proportion of women populated the chief legal officer and chief human resource officer roles (Maria-Gabriella Khoury, Ahmed Al-shaibani, and Michael Driscoll, "Women at Canadian Banks: Thick Glass Ceiling," DBRS Morningstar, March 8, 2023).

Setting aside executive positions and board representation, other sectors have posed steep challenges for women. Air Canada didn't hire Judy Cameron, its first female pilot, until 1978. In 2024, the Canadian Press reported not quite 8 percent of Air Canada's pilots were women, almost twice that of American carriers. The mining, oil and gas, and railroad sectors have historically been dominated by men.[25]

Certainly, Scotiabank was far from alone in its historical treatment of women. As previously cited, progress was glacial across industry and banking. Former BMO chairman and CEO Tony Comper devoted a chapter to the issue in his memoir, *Personal Account*. He described the treatment of women as "unconscious systemic discrimination." Like Scotiabank, prior to the Second World War, "most of our employees had been men. They all went off to war, so the Bank hired women to fill the vacant spots. Even after the war, the women stayed on in those positions, quickly transforming our workforce." Nonetheless, while the ratio of women to men had permanently changed, women were not to be found in management. Before he got the top job, Comper was chief operating officer at BMO and told his boss, CEO Matthew Barrett, that 74 percent of the bank's employees were women, but in the executive ranks, they represented only 6 percent. Before that, as a computer programmer at the bank, Comper had been immersed in data, and that data clearly showed female employees were as educated as the men at the bank. Moreover, performance "levels were equal to or better than men." On more than one occasion, Comper indicated that in his view, discrimination against women was not "deliberate, conscious . . . intentionally malicious."[26]

With all due respect to Comper's thoughtful analysis, as well as his bringing Catalyst to Canada and serving as its first chair—and despite all the ink spilled over this issue, all the speeches, dinners, and conferences—the number of female CEOs of major Canadian companies sits at just 5 percent. It is difficult to not see at least part of that as deliberate, conscious, or worse. Aside from more women in the leadership pipeline, how much has really changed since Comper spoke to Barrett? As of this writing, there has yet to be a woman running one of the big six banks.

While women have progressed up the ranks, and undoubtedly did so during Waugh's tenure at Scotia, on March 18, 2024, Stefanie Marotta of the *Globe and Mail* reported on the next round of CEO succession for Canada's major banks. On the same day as the *Globe* story was published, the *Wall Street Journal* reported that another top female executive had departed Goldman Sachs in the United States, citing "an exodus of top female talent" from the firm. More than a decade after Waugh left the job, it appeared none of the major Canadian banks were any closer to having a female CEO.

During Waugh's era, women had been stuck at the VP level, and he'd consciously helped them move up to EVP and group head positions. Yet not every woman progressed as far as she had hoped at Scotiabank. Colleen Johnston, who'd held senior financial positions at Scotia, left in 2004 to join TD Bank, recruited by its CEO Ed Clark. Not only did she get a good financial offer but also she'd been expressly told she would be on a track to become the bank's chief financial officer. She did, was highly regarded, and was one of the most senior women in Canadian banking. Waugh admitted that Johnston's departure from Scotia "was a big loss" but believed that by the time he heard about the situation, "it was a fait accompli." Johnston, he said, simply got a better opportunity at TD. "Happens all the time," he said. "I assume she got a dream job." Despite losing her to a competitor, when pressed, Waugh responded sharply: "Eighty-five thousand people [employees], you're going to piss some people off and somebody's going to leave. Sometimes that's a woman."

Where gender-related progress has occurred in banking is at the board chair level. Among the major banks, there have now been female board chairs at two of the big five (Kathleen Taylor and Jacynthe Côté at RBC and Kate Stevenson at CIBC), yet "there's been no [female] CEO and it's been unfortunate," Waugh said. Among other factors, he said, that's a function of the number of women in the pipeline. If women are blocked by a 30 percent ceiling, men have an immediate advantage, just on sheer numbers. But, he said, "I think it's going to happen, and you just sense it." That may be true eventually, but it's also true the same was predicted in 2010 by Gord Nixon during an interview on BNN. "I'd say there's a very good chance that sometime in the next round of succession there will be a female [bank] CEO."[27] By 2024, it hadn't happened. Reflecting on that fourteen years later, Nixon said he felt some surprise but put it down to circumstance. At the time, he said, across five banks, there may have been fifteen candidates to be CEO, with probably five of them being women. He indicated that the probability lies in the numbers: if 40 percent of your executives are now women, "there's a 40 percent chance the CEO is going to be a woman."¶

The harsh truth, however, is that discomfort among genders remains. In 2017 in New York City, I attended a private event of business leaders. The meeting, held at an elegant midtown hotel, took place shortly after blaring headlines of sexual harassment and assault by male executives, the MeToo scandals. Among the many discussions and speakers about various subjects at the event, there was also a panel discussion about the MeToo issue and the C-suite. There were four panellists—three females and one male. The male was the CEO of a major financial institution. While he courageously took part as the lone man in a candid, sensitive conversation, I glanced around the room at what had been primarily a male audience. At least half of the participants had excused themselves for much of that hour. The room looked mostly empty. One couldn't help wondering why each of the men who had been in attendance for other sessions that day had chosen to leave for this one. Who can truthfully say? But it certainly wasn't a good look for the corporate upper crust, and none of the other sessions at the event had such a low turnout. It was

¶ In 2021, Jane Fraser became CEO of Citigroup in the United States.

glaring, and one couldn't help but conclude that there was deep-seated queasiness with the issue.

Reflecting on Scotiabank receiving the Catalyst award, Deborah Gillis said, "I remember obviously a sense of pride as a Canadian to have a Canadian organization win and be on stage" with the top companies and business leaders in North America. "I enjoyed working with Rick . . . he was an easy guy to be around. It meant a lot to me that he put people at ease. I was pretty intimidated," she said. "I was very grateful for [the] support and leadership that he demonstrated around the boardroom table and in the business community in Canada."

When we spoke, Gillis was CEO of CAMH (the Centre for Addiction and Mental Health) Foundation, but her office featured mementos from her Catalyst days.** Citing her own personal story, she said there was "no straight path from where I started" to standing on stage at the Waldorf Astoria in New York with leaders like Waugh. "You don't know where potential lies in people." Rick Waugh might say the same of himself— the teller who became the CEO.

** In late 2024, Gillis announced she would step down from her role at CAMH in 2025.

EPILOGUE

In December 2023, Peter Godsoe passed away. Rick Waugh had known him for decades. Back in the day, he said, they debated issues fiercely, "code words for we'd have fights." Godsoe was known as argumentative, while Waugh can be unyielding. Nonetheless, they were from an era when people had heated arguments in the workplace without being accused of microaggressions, or even macro ones, apparently. Waugh had immense respect for the CEO who'd helped guide him to the corner office. The final time he saw his old boss was on a golf course in the spring of that year, near where both had summer homes. Sadly, for someone recognized as one of the most brilliant financial minds anywhere, Godsoe's memory had faltered significantly. Waugh says when he said hello to him, Godsoe didn't appear to know him.

Waugh and I were meeting for interviews the week his predecessor died, so he was on Waugh's mind. "Peter Godsoe had a great quote. He knew he was retired when he got into the back of the car and it didn't go anywhere." It was a line Waugh appeared to use to comfort himself when he had to accept that he was no longer CEO, an uneasy transition.

It was also funny. And humour was key to Waugh's own success. In a world of friction, laughs are a lubricant. While Waugh frequently mentioned how he likes people and has an aptitude for reading them, Anatol von Hahn said it's more than that. Waugh could get people to follow him. He could quickly assess issues, connect humanly, and make rapid decisions. He got things done through people, just like back in his university days when a parade float had to be built in short order. Curiously, though, if you transcribed what Waugh said in conversation and read it, you might be totally confused. His jumbled syntax would baffle any AI-generated transcription service, and it may well have baffled some of his employees and peers. But when you listened to him at a round table, his preferred venue, you got the drift. The noise-to-signal ratio could be high, but the signal was strong.

Waugh frequently says history repeats, while Mark Twain said it rhymes. It most certainly echoes. In December 2023—the week Godsoe died—Argentina devalued its currency by 54 percent to deal with rampant inflation, reported to be anywhere between 140 and 200 percent. This time, though, it was not a left-leaning Peronist in power. Instead, a far-right libertarian was president.[††] While Scotia's debacle in Argentina two decades earlier had been searing, financially it was only a one-quarter blip. But that crisis had revealed Waugh's inner fibre, his ability to handle chaos.

The same week Godsoe died, the almost two-hundred-year arc of Scotiabank's history added one more turn. Scott Thomson had become CEO earlier that year, and in December 2023, he announced a strategy to pull Scotia's stock out of the doldrums, where it had largely resided for several years. Thomson announced a focus shift. Capital would be redirected to Canada, the United States, and Mexico—the USMCA (formerly NAFTA) trade zone. While Nicks, Ritchie, Godsoe, and Waugh had continued to build and broaden Scotiabank's international footprint—and Waugh's successor Brian Porter more tightly concentrated it from fifty-some countries to thirty, with special emphasis on

---

[††] In April 2025, the IMF announced it would send funds to Argentina for the 23rd time.

just a handful—Thomson was now sharpening the focus even more.

On August 12, 2024, Thomson took Scotiabank where Waugh had wanted to go in 2008: Ohio, spending $2.8 billion to purchase 14.9 percent of KeyCorp of Cleveland. It operated some one thousand branches under the name KeyBank. Finally, Scotia had dipped into American retail banking, albeit via a passive investment. Waugh still liked the geographic footprint and thought it could work. So much so that when the stock dropped after the announcement, he bought Scotia shares. But later, given TD Bank's enormous legal issues in the United States, Waugh said in an email that it "makes one wonder with now all the five major banks singing from the gospel of the US market" whether you're better off staying home or expanding in other parts of the world where you have a competitive advantage. So, in retrospect, was Waugh relieved Scotia didn't get the other Ohio bank in 2008? "Not on the terms we had negotiated," he wrote, adding Scotiabank had measured the downside, and the acquisition of retail deposits would have lessened its reliance on wholesale. Price and risk still mattered. Besides, he wasn't the CEO anymore; the world had evolved, and Waugh respected Thomson's right to pursue a new strategic direction. Thomson's era would be unavoidably fluid. Just weeks into his second term as president, Donald Trump ignited a belligerent trade war with Canada and repeatedly stated his desire to make Canada the fifty-first state.

Waugh's tenure as CEO predated trade wars with the United States, the COVID-19 pandemic, and the AI age. On the latter two, he would have hated managing virtually, and the intensification of algorithm usage concerns him. He was and is a people guy, a credit guy, and a crisis guy. That compound made him a leader in Canadian and global banking.

But since Waugh left the top job, the proliferation of technology and social media, while providing powerful distribution platforms for receiving and transmitting information, can drastically shrink the time available to think and react. This became starkly apparent in 2023 when there was a deposit run at Silicon Valley Bank after issues arose that had been unforeseen by management. Customers and depositors of the bank shot first and asked questions later. They were communicating in real time on social media, and with digital banking having arrived in full force, money was being withdrawn in seconds. It's a different epoch.

Otherwise, on the people front, the former superintendent of financial institutions Nick Le Pan said the ascendancy of Waugh to chief executive represented the end of what he viewed as the era of the imperial bank CEO. Put plainly, Waugh was anything but a pinstriped banker. Indeed, Waugh and others in his peer group, like Gord Nixon, Bill Downe, Ed Clark, former CIBC CEO Gerry McCaughey, and National Bank's Louis Vachon were a break from stuffy tradition. They also didn't chair their boards, a nod to good governance. JPMorgan's Jamie Dimon and others would ask Waugh about it at international gatherings. "Rick, how can you Canadians not be chairman?" Dimon would say. Waugh says, "I think it was a step forward with a non-executive chair and I never had any problem being the first non-chairman of BNS. And I think it's one of the reasons why we're a safer banking system." Having a separate chair creates one more layer of accountability. A chair who is also CEO, Waugh says, is never going to fire him- or herself.

While bankers are frequently reviled, the world clearly needs responsible, risk-conscious bankers like Waugh and his contemporaries. Bank failures and financial crises are deadly serious, with repercussions that stretch on for years, even decades, and well beyond the economy. Most certainly, the 2008 crisis helped fuel populist politics and deep societal divisions that persist to this day. Those who pay the price are typically not the bankers. Their compensation, of course, is part of the corporate governance bucket. And it's also fair to say that executive compensation levels don't fall or even stay static. They rise, and often at a higher rate than everyone else's. When I put compensation-related questions to business leaders and economic seers, it's not been uncommon for them to flippantly respond that sports stars and entertainers make huge amounts, so why shouldn't CEOs? But they're hardly comparable. The careers of sports and entertainment stars can be very short. Also, basketball players and movie actors don't pose a risk to the global financial system. Bankers do.

As it happens, Waugh's compensation was always something we talked about—*twenty years* of spirited debate. But the facts are laid out on dozens of pages in a document public companies file with regulators, the annual management proxy circular. Scotiabank's 2013 circular captures Waugh's last year on the job. It was a year of record profits and performance. The bank beat targets on key measures: return on equity, diluted earnings per share, and productivity ("the strongest of all the Canadian banks").[1] Scotia's net income that year was the same as TD Bank's, an organization that booked $6 billion more in revenue for the year but earned the same amount. That meant every dollar of revenue at Scotia generated more profit than at TD.[2] Total shareholder return during Waugh's last year was 21.7 percent, with a five-year compound return of 14.2 percent. Over ten years it was 10.9 percent. The latter period included the financial crisis, and the circular boasted the bank had "outperformed peers from a shareholder perspective for the past several years."

For his last year as CEO, Waugh was awarded a compensation package of $11,120,000, up slightly from the previous year. In a "Say on Pay" vote, 94.4 percent of shareholders approved the bank's compensation disclosure, and separately the bank received plaudits for governance. The stated compensation philosophy was that CEO pay should align with "the bank's business performance and strong returns to shareholders." In Waugh's case, it did. He worked at the bank for forty-three years, and the "board believes the compensation awarded to Mr. Waugh reflects his exemplary contribution and leadership in 2013."[3]

Forgive the pun, but the deeper one travels into the circular, the richer it gets. It shows the CEO would be awarded just 14 percent of compensation in base salary of $1.5 million. The rest would be "at risk," in annual incentives (bonus), mid-term incentives (three-year performance period), and long-term incentives (up to ten years). Outside of these categories, there were also benefits, pension, and $85,612 in perquisites. The biggest chunk—44 percent—would be in mid-term incentives, while 29 percent would be long-term.[4]

To prove his commitment, as chief executive officer Waugh was required to own shares in the bank valued at seven times his base salary and hold those shares two years into retirement. By the end of his tenure, his ownership far outstripped the requirement. Waugh owned forty-five times his base salary, or $67,004,981 in total ownership. Of that, $16,933,064 was in direct share ownership, $34,305,561 in deferred stock units, and $15,766,355 in performance stock units. On December 31, 2013, Scotiabank common shares closed at $66.43, indicating Waugh had a stake of approximately a million shares in one form or another.[5]

Separate to the ownership outlined above, page forty-five of the report specified the number of stock options granted to Waugh from 2004 to 2013—3,057,232—as well as the option exercise price for each of those annual grants. The exercise prices—the price at which he had the option to buy shares—ranged from $39 to $63.98. If the stock was trading higher than the exercise price, he could then sell them for more, making a profit. Each option grant expired in ten years, but when he retired, the "value of unexercised in-the-money options" was $50,400,451. The value that had not yet vested was $15,766,355, and the last three years were part of the PSU (performance share unit) category under his total ownership. In addition to his base salary, annual, mid-term, and long-term incentives, Waugh was eligible for an annual pension from the bank of $2 million (total accrued value was $29,449,000).[6] By all measures, Waugh had done extraordinarily well financially, in step with how the bank performed. The board and shareholders agreed to pay Waugh these amounts.

Without question, he'd put every ounce of his being into Scotiabank, taking the organization to new heights. The bigger question is whether, in the main, CEO and executive compensation is excessive from a societal point of view. After Scotia's 178th annual meeting, held in April 2010 in Newfoundland, Waugh faced reporters' questions about compensation and being the so-called ten-million-dollar man, a quip about his pay packet that year (his total compensation in 2010 was $9.7 million, $700,000 less than his counterparts at RBC and TD). He countered by saying he'd started at BNS at $7,400 a year and never dreamed he'd make the money he had. Furthermore, if he could do it, other Scotia bankers could do it too. Indeed, in front of an audience at York University's Schulich School of Business in October 2024, Waugh said he hadn't had a grand plan to become CEO; he simply strove to do the best job he could as he progressed up the ladder.

Waugh told me that at the peak, he held between three and four million share units in the bank. With the stock closing 2013 at more than $66 a share, this could have amounted to hundreds of millions of dollars. In an exit interview with Gordon Pitts of the *Globe and Mail*, published January 30, 2014, the day before he left the bank, Waugh said, "I'm still going to be one of the bank's most significant shareholders."[7] In interviews for this book, he said that at one point he believed he was the bank's largest individual shareholder and that he had monetized the last of his holdings at approximately $90 per share (in March of 2022, BNS stock traded above $92). In September 2024, it was back in the mid-sixties, roughly where it was when he'd departed. On his last day as CEO, Scotia's market value was more than C$76 billion, a solid third, following RBC at C$100 billion and TD at C$87 billion. After he left, the gap between Scotia and the top two widened sharply, which irks him.

But Waugh was buying the stock again in mid-2024 and again in August 2024, after Thomson announced the minority position in KeyCorp. Not only did the news resonate with his own history but also Waugh's rallying cry of "One Team, One Goal," which had disappeared under his successor, was now coming back into vogue. Thomson, he believed, was trying to nurse the bank back towards the Scotia culture Waugh was proud of and thought worked. But Waugh also recognized that while the bank's culture had worked for employees and shareholders during his era, cultures also evolve. He allowed that maybe it needed more discipline than he provided. But he was who he was, and had been enormously successful at being himself, and fitting into the groove that was Scotia.

While I had frequently irritated Waugh with compensation-related questions, he often raised it himself. Perhaps that was in anticipation of me doing so, or due to his sensitivity about it, or simply because he wanted to be understood. When I mentioned Cedric Ritchie was paid $400,000 in 1982 (according to the Bank of Canada's inflation calculator, that would be just under $1,200,000 in 2024), he said: "Ritchie got to be CEO for twenty years. I got ten. You're comparing a twenty-year term with a ten-year term."‡‡ To be sure, Ritchie's pay over twenty years was still nowhere near what Waugh made, given the emergence of stock options and celebrity culture. GE's CEO Jack Welch set the pace. He was paid orders of magnitude more than his predecessor, Reginald Jones, who lived modestly in a house like that of a GE engineer.[8] This is to say nothing of the proposed and legally contested packages such as Elon Musk's ($56 *billion*), which makes a ten-figure package look paltry in comparison.

Waugh's compensation was of course public information, so I felt free to ask him about it. Apparently, the subject was also fair game for a family member, and it led to an amusing story, which Waugh laughingly shared with me. On one occasion, Waugh's brother Ron, who had been a banker for CIBC and Barclays, was watching me ask him on TV about his compensation. The brothers are close, and Ron couldn't help making some mischief. After watching Rick defend his pay packet, Ron showed

---

‡‡ Mather B. Almon, the second president of the bank, held the top title for thirty-three years.

their mother the bank's proxy filing that laid out how much Rick earned. Meantime, from when Waugh was a young man through seven years of his CEO tenure, Mrs. Waugh sent him twenty-five dollars every Christmas. When she saw in black and white how much he was earning as chief executive officer, she stopped sending him the money, her version of "say on pay."

Over lunch at Biff's Bistro on April 28, 2015—after I'd left BNN and he'd left the bank—Waugh mentioned what Ted Turner had once told him about television hosts (Turner employed a lot of them at CNN). The media mogul said TV anchors were like streetcars. You miss one and another one comes along. The late Bill Dimma, a corporate governance commentator and regular guest on BNN, said the same thing about CEOs during a panel discussion on executive compensation: *another one always comes along.* Jim Gray, the energy industry legend in Calgary, was also on that panel and said this of CEO compensation levels: they all want superstar packages, and only some of them, like Steve Jobs, were in fact superstars. Steve Jobs was certainly in a league of his own, but in global banking, Rick Waugh was undeniably a standout.

And he firmly believes in incentives, not just compensation-related but as management tools. He describes a period when the bank's operation in Mexico was susceptible to frequent robberies. Waugh says the crimes occurred when security guards were present. So, the bank got rid of the guards, who were on the take, and told its bank managers that if there's one robbery, you get a second chance. If there's a second, you're out. The robberies stopped, he says. Incentives worked.

While Sabi Marwah told me Waugh led through people, former EVP Wendy Hannam said she would add "heart" to that description as well. "He cared for us and the bank," she said. "Rick was just so well liked throughout the bank. From the teller through the executive team. That's really his legacy." Hannam recalled that when Waugh became CEO, her boss, John Young, had been her advocate and set up a lunch for her with Waugh. "Here he was, a new CEO, and he was so generous with his time." She said Waugh must have paid multiple visits to branches, to meet people and be seen on the ground. "It meant so much to the branch staff."

Waugh, of course, had once been the underling himself. Long retired, Ed (E.D.) MacNevin had been VP and general manager of the Toronto Central region. And for a time, he was Rick Waugh's boss. When Waugh began running the main branch at just thirty-one, he'd taken over from MacNevin, who couldn't resist telling a story about giving Waugh hell one night. The young banker, MacNevin said, made a computer-related mistake that could have been quite serious. He described phoning Waugh at home in the evening to chew him out. "Well, I may as well quit," Waugh said. "*I may as well quit*," he repeated, obviously distraught. But MacNevin said he knew Waugh was on an upward trajectory at the bank, so he didn't accept his threat to resign. Waugh said he didn't remember the incident, but did recall MacNevin at one point telling him, "One day I'm going to be reporting to you."

One of the most telling moments I've had with Waugh occurred as he was handing off the CEO job to Brian Porter at the end of October 2013. I had professional relationships with both executives and was asked by the bank's communications department to emcee the passing-of-the-baton event at the Metro Toronto Convention Centre. It would be my job to help make it a bit of a show for the some eight hundred Scotia bankers in attendance. The event was a hit. There were lots of laughs interspersing serious discussion. Afterwards, as we took off our micro-phones in the wings, Waugh blurted out at high volume: "Howard, we must be paying you a lot for you to have done this!" He was giving me the gears, ironically compensation-related given our long-running dis-cussion about the subject. I smiled at Waugh's good-natured jab and didn't say anything. But one of his handlers quickly whispered in his ear and his expression changed. Waugh immediately came over to me, his face pained as he looked me square in the eye.

"Howard, I owe you an apology. You did this for nothing because of your sister."

To be clear, Waugh did not owe me an apology. He could not have known my sister Susan had passed away shortly beforehand due to cancer. And because I was still on the air at BNN and would be interviewing Waugh, Porter, and others from Scotia, I would not accept money for hosting the event. But the bank's communications people had wondered whether, in lieu, the bank could donate to a cause. I said sure—to breast cancer research, please, which they did. While I had always viewed Waugh as a decent, stand-up person, the way he rushed over to me to address a concern that he'd said something inappropriate simply confirmed my impression. He wanted to do the right thing. It was all you needed to know about Rick Waugh's leadership abilities, values, character, and, for that matter, good governance.

Aside from Waugh's facility with people and expertise with credit, and despite MacNevin's recollection of the computer-related flub, there was one other ingredient that made him the leader he was: his ability in a crisis. While it's peculiar to cite a tennis star's autobiography in a book about banking, Billie Jean King and Rick Waugh have something in common. They're both children of firefighters. Waugh idolized his father, who could literally handle the heat. As King wrote about her dad, "He was known as one of the coolest heads in the fire department under duress . . . As a rule, the bigger the problem, the better he was."[9] The same might be said of Rick Waugh.

ACKNOWLEDGEMENTS

This book would not have been written without the trust Rick Waugh placed in me. Our relationship dates to when he first became Scotiabank's CEO. Over more than two decades, I have been fortunate to hear his stories, views, and, yes, his frustrations with me. The latter, which have been the exception, have been manifested in his index finger poking me in the chest, complaints about taking up too much of his time, and questions about why I needed so much material. Cheerfully, I reminded him that I never told him how to run a bank, so he shouldn't tell me how to write a book. Despite a few ornery moments, Waugh was exceedingly generous with his time, providing access to personal papers, notes, calendars, documents, and photographs. Of course, leavening all the serious talk, there was also a lot of laughter, a trademark of his character. Because we often met for three-hour sessions between 11 a.m. and 2 p.m.—and we both get grumpy if we don't eat around noon—sandwich lunches were part of the meetings. Subjecting oneself to an author's questions for hours at a time can be mentally exhausting. I am grateful he put up with me, particularly during the weary and irritating times. It was a privilege to write this book.

I also would like to acknowledge the trust and support of Lynne Waugh, Rick's spouse for half a century. She was unfailingly helpful, candid, and hospitable. Also, my profound appreciation to the Waugh Family Foundation for its commitment to the recording and writing of business history and for its support of York University's Schulich School of Business, which contracted me to write an independent book.

While the school received a grant from the Waugh Family Foundation, neither it nor the foundation had any control over the content, which rested with me. Although I had independence and carte blanche to write the book as I saw fit, Waugh requested two conditions, which I understood and accepted. He would not reveal confidential information. Long after his retirement, he respected confidences. Any references in the book to such things initially came to me via other sources, not through Waugh. He also requested that I not quote anonymous sources about him. He was certainly receptive to hearing alternative views, criticism, and debate about his decisions, character, and memory of events, but he felt people should attach their names to such statements. Since this is a history book, I agreed to and respected that request. That said, in certain instances, I have written about selected matters on a not-for-attribution basis because I judged them as worthy, providing context or detail. However, respecting our agreement, those passages are not about Waugh himself but rather about specific situations, events, stories, people, or decisions that I felt would bolster a reader's understanding.

A crucial part of the Waugh world is Caroline Stevens, Rick's long-time executive assistant. Caroline cheerfully assisted with my list of asks, always game to help—connecting me with people, helping root out a file, or sharing a chuckle. Bonnie Lovelace, one of Rick and Lynne's long-time friends, runs the foundation and assisted behind the scenes. Both have my gratitude.

The dean of Schulich at York, Detlev Zwick, was an enthusiastic supporter from the get-go. While I'm not a historian by training, I tried to write a book with a dash of academic rigour, while still crafting an absorbing, meaningful story people would want to read, a nod to my journalistic roots. Professor Andrew Thomson, with his expertise in business history, was an immense help as a sounding board. He not only was the first reader of embryonic chapters and rough drafts, but also assisted with research queries—a friendly, intellectually curious presence with whom to discuss the project from its earliest stages. Christina Niederwanger helped sort out the nuts and bolts of my association with the university. Heartfelt thanks to all three.

I am also indebted to both Joe Martin and Dimitry Anastakis of the Canadian Business History Association and the University of Toronto's Rotman School of Management for their unwavering encouragement from the outset, to say nothing of their deep commitment to the importance of the subject matter. In addition to being something of a project matchmaker, Joe was also co-author, with the late Christopher Kobrak, of a superb volume about the history and comparative differences between Canadian and American banking. It was an essential source, as was Robert MacIntosh's *Different Drummers*, a thoughtful history of Canadian banking. The 150-year history of Scotiabank by Joseph Schull and J. Douglas Gibson helped me understand how the bank started and evolved until the early 1980s, a reminder that corporate histories are valuable societal contributions. To become versed in the bank's involvement in the southern hemisphere, Roy D. Scott's privately published *My Days with Scotiabank in Latin America* was a godsend. Bursting with background, flavour, and detail, it's written by an eyewitness and born raconteur.

Regarding Scotiabank's 2002 loss of Scotiabank Quilmes in Argentina, I owe thanks to a research paper authored by four individuals who were on the ground and up-close—Anatol von Hahn, Donna Groskorth, Gerry Moylan, and Roy Scott. Their written observations (plus my interviews with Anatol, Donna, and Roy) provided crucial details that added to Waugh's own gripping account of events. I also leaned heavily on Paul Blustein's book *And the Money Kept Rolling In (and Out): Wall*

Street, the IMF, and the Bankrupting of Argentina—a blow-by-blow account of Argentina's financial crisis in 2001–2. A superb chronicle of events, it assisted with understanding timelines and the macro picture, helping me frame what happened to SBQ. For a spirited recounting of the birth of Toronto's NBA franchise, I am grateful for Alex Wong's *Prehistoric: The Audacious and Improbable Origin Story of the Toronto Raptors.* Meanwhile, chapter one, on Rick Waugh's early years, and portions of chapter four draw significantly on a private history of the family.

Foundational to this book have been the people who worked with Waugh in various positions at Scotiabank, in Canada and abroad, or somehow intersected with his story. I have been struck by their generosity in giving their time and sharing recollections and thoughts. It was also not unusual after interviews for them to email me additional information or links to articles and documents that have been extraordinarily helpful. I am thankful to all of them and list a number below.

Aside from those mentioned above, for the chapter on Argentina, Miguel Jarsun, Claudio Hernandez, and Eduardo Oteiza were pivotal. Former BNS vice-chair Bob Chisholm and Tom MacDonald, the former Canadian ambassador to Argentina, also contributed meaningfully. Posthumous thanks to Peter Godsoe for speaking to me back in my broadcasting days—on TV and over lunch. Nick Le Pan and Julie Dickson, both former superintendents of financial institutions during Waugh's tenure as CEO, each responded with helpful insights. I equally appreciate the contributions of former Bank of Canada governor David Dodge; former deputy governor of the Bank of Canada David Longworth; Rosalie and Isadore Sharp; Gerry Schwartz; and the former CEOs of BMO and RBC, Bill Downe and Gord Nixon, as well as Jamie Dimon, chairman and CEO of JPMorgan Chase.

Among those who worked closely with Waugh, all have my sincere thanks: Sabi Marwah, Rick's loyal number two, is a savant with numbers and finance—few anywhere are more knowledgeable about banking. The late Bob Brooks's raw descriptions of being in the trenches as treasurer during 2008 and the Argentina crisis were central to the book. When we spoke on Zoom, I had no idea he was a legend. I regret he didn't live long enough to see the book. Sylvia Chrominska not only possessed sharp recollections and documents but also shared fantastic french fries over lunch. Jim Meek kindly shared recollections of the Dominican Republic and contributed research assistance (along with his wife, Tish, plus assists from Clifton Ramirez). Peter Cardinal was equally generous, as were Wendy Hannam, Terry Fryett, Stephen Hart, Dieter Jentsch, Seth Mersky, Barb Mason, Jim Tryforos, Stephen Lockhart, Tim Hayward, Charles Dallara, Mike Durland, Indira Samarasekera, and Deborah Gillis. For the history of the Raptors, my gratitude goes out to former Ontario premier David Peterson, Larry Tanenbaum, Gary Slaight, John Bitove Jr., David Coriat, Borden Osmak, and Russ Granik.

James D. Frost's seminal research on the Bank of Nova Scotia from 1880 to 1910 provided valuable insights into the bank's culture of credit and its expansion outside of the Maritimes. Thanks to an old Halifax friend from the neighbourhood, John March, for connecting me with him. Given my virtually non-existent Spanish, Elizabeth Meneses Del Castillo assisted with research about the Dominican Republic. Related thanks on that to Oakland Ross.

Others who helped: Arni Thorsteinson, Gary Doer, Scott Hand, Tony Wilson-Smith, Kristine Owram, Colleen Johnston, Jocelyn Dunbar, Alison Woodbury, the ever-helpful Ferawan Susanto at Staples Studio, and Doreen and Stuart for the idyllic writer's cabin on Lake Huron. I'd also like to thank current Scotiabank CEO Scott Thomson, chair of the bank Aaron Regent, Meigan Terry, Clancy Zeifman, Heather Armstrong, Katie Raskina, Jay Fitzgerald, and Nicola Ray Smith. Regarding certain events, situations, or background, others spoke to me on a not-for-attribution basis. I thank them as well.

My agent Rick Broadhead is tireless. Despite his impish sense of humour, this project would not have blossomed without his unwavering support and sage counsel. Profound thanks to editor Nick Garrison at Penguin for his wise suggestions and for believing in this book almost instantaneously. Others at Penguin who were instrumental: Zainab Mirza ably shepherded the book through the brisk production process, Linda Pruessen, the precision copyeditor who kept me on all ten toes, Eleanor Gasparik, Rhiannon Thomas, Aruna Dahanayake, Matthew Flute, Sarah Fallarino, Nathaniel McKenzie, Susan Roman, and Catherine Knowles. An appreciative shout out as well to readers Stephen Poloz, Geoff Smith, Rob Wessel, Diane Flanagan, Amber Kanwar, and Bob Kelly.

Endless thanks to my mother Roselle Green—a historian at heart— for her love and for listening. The book's publication date is her ninety-seventh birthday. And, of course, an ocean of gratitude to Lynne Heller for her love and counsel, and for putting up with me for forty years.

A note on sources: Unless otherwise indicated, quotes from Rick Waugh and others are from original interviews for this book. In other instances, articles, books, broadcasts, calendars, emails, personal notes, regulatory filings, reports, speeches, or other documents have been cited. Any errors or misapprehensions of which I am unaware are mine to bear.

BIBLIOGRAPHY

BOOKS AND THESES

Bank of Nova Scotia. *The Bank of Nova Scotia: One Hundredth Anniversary, 1832–1932.*

Blustein, Paul. *And the Money Kept Rolling In (and Out): Wall Street, the IMF, and the Bankrupting of Argentina.* Public Affairs, 2006.

Bothwell, Drummond, and John English. *Canada, 1900-1945.* University of Toronto Press, 1987. Pg 248.

Buera, Francisco J., and Juan Pablo Nicolini. *The Case of Argentina.* PhD diss., Washington University in St. Louis and Federal Reserve Bank of Minneapolis and Universidad Di Tella, n.d.

Comper, Tony, with Bruce Dowbiggin. *Personal Account: 25 Tales About Leadership, Learning, and Legacy from a Lifetime at Bank of Montreal.* ECW, 2020.

Dallara, Charles H. *Euroshock: How the Largest Debt Restructuring in History Helped Save Greece and Preserve the Eurozone.* Rodin Books, 2024.

Dundas, Deborah. *On Class.* Biblioasis, 2023.

Gower, Dave. *Perspectives on Labour and Income: Autumn 1992* Vol. 4, No. 3 Article No. 3, A note on Canadian unemployment since 1921.

Green, Howard. *Banking on America: How TD Bank Rose to the Top and Took on the U.S.A.* HarperCollins, 2013.

Greenberg, Alan C. *Memos from the Chairman.* Workman, 1996.

Greenberg, Alan C., with Mark Singer. *The Rise and Fall of Bear Stearns.* Simon & Schuster, 2010.

Hernandez, Christian. *Neoliberal Globalization and the Argentine Great Depression: Desconstructing Discourse of the IMF and Private Finance.* PhD diss., University of Birmingham, 2017.

Iger, Robert. *The Ride of a Lifetime: Lessons Learned from 15 Years as CEO of the Walt Disney Company.* Random House, 2019.

Isaacson, Walter. *Elon Musk.* Simon & Schuster, 2023.

Isaacson, Walter. *Steve Jobs.* Simon & Schuster, 2011.

King, Billie Jean, with Johnette Howard and Maryanne Vollers. *All In: An Autobiography.* Vintage, 2021.

Kobrak, Christopher, and Joe Martin. *From Wall Street to Bay Street: The Origins and Evolution of American and Canadian Finance.* University of Toronto Press, 2018.

MacIntosh, Robert. *Different Drummers: Banking and Politics in Canada.* MacMillan Canada, 1991.

McQueen, Rod. *A History of Canadian Imperial Bank of Commerce* Vol. 5, *1973–1999.* ECW Press, 2021.

McQueen, Rod. *The Money Spinners: An Intimate Portrait of the Men Who Run Canada's Banks.* Totem Books, 1984.

Mussio, Laurence B. *Whom Fortune Favours: The Bank of Montreal and the Rise of North American Finance* Vol. 2, *Territories of Transformation, 1946–2017.* McGill-Queen's University Press, 2020.

Pauly, Louis W. "Canadian Autonomy and Systemic Financial Risk After the Crisis of 2008." In *Crisis and Reform: Canada and the International Financial System* Vol. 20, *Canada Among Nations,* edited by Rohinton Medhora and Dane Rowlands. Canadian Institute for Governance Innovation, 2014.

Schull, Joseph. *100 Years of Banking in Canada: The Toronto-Dominion Bank.* Copp Clark, 1958.

Schull, Joseph, and J. Douglas Gibson. *The Scotiabank Story: A History of the Bank of Nova Scotia, 1832–1982.* Macmillan of Canada, 1982.

Scott, Roy D. *My Days with Scotiabank in Latin America.* Privately published by Impreso Por Artes Graficas Integradas (Argentina), 2019.

Sorkin, Andrew Ross. *Too Big to Fail. The Inside Story of How Wall Street and Washington Fought to Save the Financial System—and Themselves.* Penguin, 2010.

von Hahn, Anatol, Gerry Moylan, Donna Groskorth, and Roy Scott (contributors). *Lessons Learned—Argentina 2001–2002* (unpublished). n.d.

Wong, Alex. *Prehistoric: The Audacious and Improbable Origin Story of the Toronto Raptors.* Triumph Books, 2023.

Wright, Robert E. "Banking System Stability/Fragility: The Roles of Governance and Supervision in Canada and America." In *Becoming 150: 150 Years of Canadian Business History*, edited by Mark S. Bonham. Canadian Business History Association, 2017.

PERIODICALS

Andriotis, Anna Maria. "Stephanie Cohen Is Latest Senior Goldman Executive to Depart." *Wall Street Journal*, March 18, 2024.

Asian Wall Street Journal. "Charges Dog Banker, Nation: As Dominican Republic Thrived, So Did Mr. Báez; Now Both Reel." July 3, 2003.

Associated Press. "Newmont Acts to Foil Pickens' Hostile Bid: Makes Deal with Top Holder to Pay $2.2 Billion in Special Dividends." *Los Angeles Times*, September 22, 1987.

Bank of Canada. "As Part of the G7 Action Plan, Bank of Canada Introduces New Measures to Provide Liquidity to the Canadian Financial System," October 14, 2008. https://www.bankofcanada.ca/2008/10/part-g7-action-plan-bank-canada-introduces-new-measures-provide-liquidity/.

Bank of Canada. "Primer on ABCP." *Canadian Fixed-Income Forum*, June 2024. https://www.bankofcanada.ca/wp-content/uploads/2024/06/primer-canadian-abcp.pdf.

Bennett, Robert A. "Big Credits Stir Debate Because Money Is Tight." *New York Times*, August 10, 1981.

Bhutani, Angela. "Women and Philanthropy: A Conversation with Deborah Gillis." Burgundy Asset Management, *Minerva* 4, 2020. www.burgundyasset.com/minerva.

Bloomberg. "Bloomberg Uncovers the Fed's Secret Liquidity Lifelines." August 22, 2011.

BNAmericas. "Mejia: Scotiabank to Finalize Baninter Purchase." July 7, 2003.

Braithwaite, Tom. "Dimon in Attack on Canada's Bank Chief." *Financial Times*, September 26, 2011.

Buettner, Russ, and Charles V. Bagli. "How Donald Trump Bankrupted His Atlantic City Casinos, but Still Earned Millions." *New York Times*, June 11, 2016.

Byers, Jim, and Chris Young. "It's a Deal Queen's Park, NBA Accord on Lottery Clears Way for Toronto Franchise." *Toronto Star*, February 10, 1994.

Campbell, Neil A., with files from Robert MacLeod, Harvey Enchin, and Dave Shoalts. "Slaight, Bitove Battle for Raptors' Ownership: Debate over New Arena May Be Root of Breakup." *Globe and Mail*, October 19, 1996.

Canadian Press. "Court Okays $60 Million ACBP Plan." March 14, 2012.

Canadian Press. "Scotiabank to Purchase ING Bank of Canada for $3.1 Billion."
    August 29, 2012.

Carhart, Jeffrey, and Jay Hoffman. "Canada's Asset Backed Commercial Paper
    Restructuring, 2007–2009." *Banking and Finance Law Review* 25, no. 1 (2009): 35–58.

Carmichael, Kevin. "Carney v. Dimon: A Clash of World Views." *Globe and Mail*,
    September 27, 2011.

Carmichael, Kevin. "Carney, Waugh Spar over New Banking Rules." *Globe and Mail*,
    September 25, 2011.

Catan, Thomas. "Argentine Strikes Raise Fears of Renewed Rioting." *Financial Times*,
    April 22, 2002.

CBC News. "BMO-Scotiabank Merger Talks Quashed by PMO: Report." October 29,
    2002.

CBC News. "Scotiabank Files $600 Million Claim Against Argentina." April 7, 2005.

Christie, James. "Bitove Group Gets NBA Franchise: Underdog Bid Proves Success."
    Globe and Mail, October 1, 1993.

Christie, James. "Bitove Succeeds by Laying Cards on Table: An Exciting and Detailed
    Plan Made the Difference for the NBA in Awarding New Franchise." *Globe and Mail*,
    October 1, 1993.

Christie, James. "Canada's in for NBA Expansion Team: League Will Take Its Time
    Deciding Among Three Strong Toronto Bids and One from Vancouver." *Globe
    and Mail*, April 28, 1993.

Christie, James. "Clock Still Running on Toronto's NBA Bid." *Globe and Mail*,
    January 27, 1994.

Christie, James. "The Group Behind the Bid that Got NBA for Toronto." *Globe
    and Mail*, October 1, 1993.

Christie, James. "Two Toronto Groups Await Word from the NBA." *Globe and Mail*,
    February 17, 1993.

Christie, James, and Robert MacLeod. "Silence on Raptors' Homefront." *Globe and
    Mail*, July 13, 1994.

Christie, James, with files from Neil A. Campbell. "Slaight Wins Raptor Bidding:
    Sources Say Bitove Unable to Secure $88 Million Needed to Block Bid from Fellow
    Club Owner." *Globe and Mail*, November 15, 1996.

Class of Fifty-Two. "Austin Edward George Taylor '52." *Princeton Alumni Weekly*, December 4, 2013. https://paw.princeton.edu/memorial/austin-edward-george-taylor -%E2%80%9952.

CNBC. "Jeff Immelt, Who Got Over $200 Million When He Left GE, on CEO High Salaries: 'The Good Ones Are Probably Worth More.'" March 2, 2021 (updated May 21, 2021).

Cordoba, Jose de. "With a Banker Facing Charges, a Nation Questions Its Success." *Wall Street Journal*, June 30, 2003.

Craig, Susanne. "Scotiabank's Latin Obsession." *Globe and Mail*, April 10, 1999.

Cummins, Carolyn. "Disgraced Developer George Herscu Dies." *Sydney Morning Herald*, September 20, 2013.

Dean, Kelly A. "Crisis in Canadian Banking." *Lehigh Preserve Institutional Repository*, 1988.

Diario Libre. "Central Bank to Reveal Deal with Ramón Báez Figueroa." September 2, 2013.

Dow Jones Newswires. "Scotiabank Can Leave Argentina." August 21, 2002.

The Economist. "New World for Canadian Banking." In "International Banking 1968: A Survey." November 16, 1968.

The Economist. "Why the IMF Should Bail Out a Serial Deadbeat." April 3, 2025.

Eicher, Leah. "The Serendipitous Side of Networking." *Globe and Mail*, January 7, 2012.

Erman, Boyd. "Banks and Watchdogs near ABCP Deal." *Globe and Mail*, December 8, 2009.

Erman, Boyd. "Investors Burned by ACBP Set for Settlement." *Globe and Mail*, February 16, 2012.

Erman, Boyd. "Plan to Unfreeze ABCP Gets Final Nod." *Globe and Mail*, January 13, 2009.

Erman, Boyd. "Scotiabank Feels the Cost of ING Acquisition." *Globe and Mail*, March 6, 2013.

Erman, Boyd, and Tara Perkins. "With ABCP Fines Out of the Way, Spotlight Is on Watchdogs." *Globe and Mail*, December 18, 2009.

Erman, Boyd, Jacquie McNish, and Tara Perkins. "ABCP Deal: Panel Asks Ottawa for Billions to Backup Seized-up Investments." *Globe and Mail*, December 11, 2008.

Erman, Boyd, Tara Perkins, and Jacquie McNish. "Asset-Backed Commercial Paper: Banks Brace for Battle over Fine." *Globe and Mail*, July 31, 2009.

Farrell, Maureen, and Anupreeta Das. "Pay for Lawyers Is So High, People Are Comparing to the N.B.A." *New York Times*, July 1, 2024.

Financial Post. "Miss Marcellus, Mrs. Giles: They Made History." September 23, 1961.

Financial Times. "Banking in Argentina." May 21, 2002.

Finkle, Derek. "The Trader's Revenge." *Toronto Life*, June 1, 2008.

Fishman, Steve. "Burning Down His House." *New York Magazine*, November 27, 2008.

Flannery, Nathaniel Parish. "Top Ten Severance Packages of the Last Decade." *Forbes*, January 19, 2012.

Francis, Theo. "The Highest Paid CEOs of 2023." *Wall Street Journal*, May 21, 2024.

French, Cameron, and Euan Rocha. "Scotiabank Buys ING Direct Canada for $3.1 Billion." Reuters, August 29, 2012.

Frost, James D. "Fyshe, Thomas." *Dictionary of Canadian Biography*, vol. 14 (1911–1920), 1998–2016. https://www.biographi.ca/en/bio/fyshe_thomas_14E.html.

Frost, James D. "The 'Nationalization' of the Bank of Nova Scotia, 1880–1910." *Acadiensis* 12, no. 1 (Autumn 1982).

Galea, Irene. "A Glimpse into a Moneyed Past." *Globe and Mail*, December 26, 2023.

Galea, Irene, and David Milstead. "Shopify Gave CEO Tobi Luke $200 Million in Options, Shares, in February." *Globe and Mail*, March 18, 2024.

Galt, Virginia. "Deregulation Caused Sale of Brokerage." *Globe and Mail*, October 2, 1987.

Galt, Virginia. "Scotiabank Cuts McLeod Bid by $64 Million." *Globe and Mail*, December 12, 1987.

Galt, Virginia. "Scotiabank Sees New Brokerage as Separate Line." *Globe and Mail*, January 20, 1988.

Gladwell, Malcolm. "Was Jack Welch the Greatest CEO of His Day—or the Worst?" *New Yorker*, November 7, 2022.

Globe and Mail. "Depth, Scope, Key to Ownership." December 9, 1994.

Globe and Mail. "The Doors to Canada's Boardrooms Are (Slowly) Starting to Open" (editorial). January 22, 2024.

Globe and Mail. "Pay CEOs for Performance, Not Failure" (editorial). April 10, 2024.

Globe and Mail. "Scotiabank Buying Peruvian Bank." December 5, 2005.

Globe and Mail. "Scotiabank to Pay on Quilmes Debt." March 13, 2003.

Globe and Mail. "Some ABCP Answers from the Man Who Knows." August 20, 2008.

Goñi, Uli. "100 Days of Javier Milei." *New York Times*, March 24, 2024.

Government of Canada. "Government of Canada Announces Additional Support for Canadian Credit Markets," November 12, 2008. https://www.canada.ca/en/news /archive/2008/11/government-canada-announces-additional-support-canadian-credit -markets.html.

Granger, Alix, "Estey Commission." *Canadian Encyclopedia*, February 7, 2006 (updated, December 15, 2013). https://www.thecanadianencyclopedia.ca/en /article/estey-commission.

Green, Howard. "Disney Heiress Abigail E. Disney on the Treatment of Theme Park Workers and the Reckoning Around Inequality." *Toronto Star*, June 2, 2022.

Greenwood, John. "National Bank Shines, But is Anyone Looking?" *Financial Post*, November 4, 2013.

Gryta, Thomas, Joann S. Lublin, and Mark Maremont. "GE's Board Was Kept in the Dark About CEO's Extra Plane." *Wall Street Journal*, October 29, 2017.

Guthrie, Amy. "A Kinder, Gentler Foreign Bank." *LatinFinance*, August 2006.

Hanke, Steve H. "The Dominican Republic: Resolving the Banking Crisis and Restoring Growth." Foreign Policy Briefing No. 83, Cato Institute, July 20, 2004.

Houston, William. "Raptors' Owners Set for Run at Stavro: Labatt Also Could Pursue MLG." *Globe and Mail*, August 6, 1994.

Howlett, Karen, and Peter Kennedy. "Scotiabank's Profit Plunges 90% on Charge: Takes Major Hit from Operations in Embattled Argentina." *Globe and Mail*, March 6, 2002.

Institute of International Finance. "Culture Has Move to Center Stage as Financial Services Firms Continue to Revamp Risk Management Functions." July 30, 2013.

International Monetary Fund. "IMF Approves Two-Year US$600 Million Stand-By Arrangement for the Dominican Republic." Release No. 3/147, August 29, 2003. https://www.imf.org/en/News/Articles/2015/09/14/01/49/pr03147.

International Monetary Fund. "Public Information Notice: IMF Concludes 2003 Article IV Consultation with the Dominican Republic." October 14, 2003. https://www.imf.org/en/News/Articles/2015/09/28/04/53/pn03123.

James, Canute. "Dominican Republic Relies on IMF to Avert Bank Crisis." *Financial Times*, July 23, 2003.

James, Royson. "Disappointed Bidder Still Plans Arena at the CNE." *Toronto Star*, October 2, 1993.

James, Royson. "For 'Mr. Basketball' It's Fantasy Come True." *Toronto Star*, October 2, 1993.

Jarvie, Richard, and Camila Russo. "Argentina Says Bank of Nova Scotia Drops $600 Million Claim." Bloomberg, July 26, 2011.

Kalawsky, Keith. "Argentine Shuts Down Scotiabank Subsidiary: Paul Martin to Intervene: 'The Crisis Is Unprecedented in Our Bank's History." *National Post*, April 20, 2002.

Kiladze, Tim. "Scotiabank's Rick Waugh: Perfect Timing and a Tough Act to Follow." *Globe and Mail*, October 31, 2013.

Kiladze, Tim, Tara Perkins, Grant Robertson, Jacqueline Nelson, Boyd Erman, Joanna Slater, Jeffrey Jones, Paul Waldie, and Greg Keenan. "The 2008 Financial Crisis: Through the Eyes of Some of the Major Players." *Globe and Mail*, September 14, 2013.

Knight, Malcolm D. "Surmounting the Financial Crisis: Contrasts Between Canadian and American Banks," First Thomas O. Enders Memorial Lecture. *American Review of Canadian Studies* 42 (2012): 311–20.

Lamarche, Rubén. "Exclusive Interview with Rick Waugh." *Mercado Magazine*, October 2009.

Langan, F.F. "Bruce Birmingham Helped Oversee Major Expansion of the Bank of Nova Scotia." *Globe and Mail*, July 19, 2010.

Langton, James. "Banks Compensation Practices Still Need Improvement." *Investment Executive*, September 3, 2010.

Lee, Peter. "Banks Struggle to Put Their House in Order Before Outsiders Do It for Them." *Euromoney*, September 2008.

Lexpert. "Scotiabank Purchases Baninter Assets." 2003.

Ljunggren, David. "Canada Raises Scotiabank Claim Case with Argentina." Reuters, November 13, 2010.

Lukpat, Alyssa, Theo Francis, and Denny Jacob. "Tesla Wants Shareholders to Approve Elon Musk's Pay Package. Again." *Wall Street Journal*, April 17, 2024.

Maclean's. "An Off-Court Struggle." November 4, 1996.

Marotta, Stefanie. "Bank CEO Succession Is the Talk of Bay Street, but Women Are Not Likely Candidates." *Globe and Mail*, March 18, 2024.

Marotta, Stefanie. "Scotiabank Shifts Capital to North American Operations from Latin America." *Globe and Mail*, December 13, 2023.

Marotta, Stefanie. "TD Bank CEO Took Pay Cut in 2023 amid U.S. Regulatory Probe." *Globe and Mail*, March 12, 2024.

Matsa, David A., and Amalia R. Miller. "Chipping Away at the Glass Ceiling: Gender Spillovers in Corporate Leadership." *American Economic Review* 101, no. 3 (2011): 635–39.

McCarthy, Shawn, Jacquie McNish, and John Partridge. "How the Scotiabank-BMO Merger Fell Apart." *Globe and Mail*, November 2, 2002.

McFarland, Janet. "ABCP Reporting Under Scrutiny." *Globe and Mail*, December 7, 2007.

McGlaughlin, Grant, Richard Steinberg, and Paul Blyschak. "'Greed, for Lack of a Better Word, Is Good': The Case for Superstar CEO Pay." *Globe and Mail*, March 6, 2024.

McNish, Jacquie. "The Mother of All Blanket Immunity Deals." *Globe and Mail*, March 26, 2008.

McQueen, Rod. "From Sweeping the Vault Floor to the Top Job at Royal, He Was the Last Great Canadian Banker." *Toronto Star*, June 29, 2024.

Milner, Brian. "Scotiabank Should Play Its Latin Hand Carefully." *Globe and Mail*, March 6, 2002.

Milstead, David. "Proxy Advisors Recommend Investors Vote 'No' on Shopify Executive Pay." *Globe and Mail*, May 15, 2024.

Milstead, David. "Shopify CEO Tobi Lütke Plans Stock Sale of More than $200 Million." *Globe and Mail*, September 6, 2024.

Milstead, David. "Shopify Executive Earned US$76 Million in 2023, Far Outpacing CEOs Compensation." *Globe and Mail*, May 12, 2024.

Mohamed, Susan, and Duncan Hood. "Cashing In: Canada's CEO Salary Surge." *Maclean's*, May 1, 2009.

Monegro, Jose P., "Dominican Officials Say Bank Deal Reached." *Midland Daily News*, July 7, 2003.

Murphy Jr., Bill. "99 Brilliant Charlie Munger Quotes that Explain Why Warren Buffett Liked Him So Much." *Inc.*, December 23, 2023.

Murray, Matt. "GEs Welch, in Year of Decisions, Got $16.7 Million in Salary, Bonus." *Wall Street Journal*, March 12, 2001.

Nelson, Jacqueline, Grant Robertson, and Boyd Erman. "Scotiabank Snares ING for $3.1 Billion." *Globe and Mail*, August 30, 2012.

New York Times. "Dominican Bankers Linked to Embezzlement." May 16, 2003.

New York Times. "Newmont's Gold Loan." February 12, 1988.

The New Yorker. November 17, 1951, 31.

Obituary, Edward Dennis Hunter. *Globe and Mail*, October 15, 2011.

Otaola, Jorge, and Walter Bianchi. "Argentina to Devalue Peso, Cut Energy Subsidies to Fix Economic Crisis." Reuters, December 12, 2023.

Ovsey, Dan. "Scotiabank's Outgoing CEO Rick Waugh: Customers May Not Like Us but They Feel Comfortable and Safe." *Financial Post*, October 31, 2013.

Partridge, John. "Rumour of BMO-Scotiabank Merger Helps Lift Bank Stocks." *Globe and Mail*, August 27, 2002.

Partridge, John. "Scotiabank Buys Additional 70% of Banco Quilmes." *Globe and Mail*, July 3, 1997.

Partridge, John. "Taylor Quits ScotiaMcLeod: 'Austintatious' Giant Led Firm from Glory to Glory." *Globe and Mail*, September 18, 1993.

Partridge, John, and Jacquie McNish. "Big Changes Seen at Two Banks: Death of BMO-Scotiabank Merger Talks Means Hard Decisions Have to Be Made." *Globe and Mail*, October 30, 2002.

Pérez, Nino Germán. "Ramón Báez Figueroa Initiates Legal Action Against Baninter Liquidation; Asks to Investigate Former Central Bank Officials." *Proceso*, October 26, 2023.

Perkins, Tara. "ABCP Road Show Hits Brick Wall." *Globe and Mail*, April 3, 2008.

Perkins, Tara. "Canadian Bankers Tell G20: Don't Suffocate Our Growth." *Globe and Mail*, April 8, 2010.

Perkins, Tara. "Who'll Be the First Female Bank CEO?" *Globe and Mail*, August 26, 2010.

Perkins, Tara, and Jacquie McNish. "Scotia Capital Named in ABCP Lawsuits." *Globe and Mail*, December 6, 2007.

Pitts, Gordon. "Rick Waugh's Candid Take on Leadership." *Globe and Mail*, January 30, 2014.

Postmedia News. "Did Canadian Banks Receive a Secret Bailout?" *Financial Post*, April 30, 2012.

Potts, Mark. "Pickens Bids $5.7 Billion for Newmont." *Washington Post*, August 31, 1987.

Quash, Harold. "Hurricane Ivan Devastates Grenada." *Independent*, September 9, 2004.

Reuters. "Loss-Making Warner Bros Discovery's CEO Pay Rises to $50 Mln in 2023." April 19, 2024.

Reuters. "Tesla Shareholders Advised to Reject Musk's $56 Billion Pay Package." May 25, 2024.

Reynolds, Christopher. "Air Canada's First Female Pilot Recalls Sector's Sexist Hurdles on Route to Success." Canadian Press, February 4, 2024.

Robertson, Susan Krashinsky, and David Milstead. "Loblaw Paid New CEO Per Bank $22 Million in 2023." *Globe and Mail*, April 1, 2024.

Sanati, Cyrus. "Prince Finally Explains His Dancing Comment." *New York Times*, April 8, 2010.

Schecter, Barbara. "Behind the Blowup Between Dimon and Carney." *Financial Post*, September 26, 2011.

Schwartz, Carl, and Nicolas Tan. "The Australian Government Guarantee Scheme, 2008-15." *Bulletin* (Reserve Bank of Australia), March Quarter 2016.

Scoffield, Heather. "Argentine Judge Grills Scotiabank Executive." *Globe and Mail*, March 13, 2002.

Scoffield, Heather. "Canadian Bank's Argentine Subsidiary Raided." *Globe and Mail*, March 6, 2002.

Scoffield, Heather. "How One Complaint Set Off Argentine Probe." *Globe and Mail*, March 2, 2002.

Scoffield, Heather. "No Cash for Argentina: Scotiabank." *Globe and Mail*, May 2, 2002.

Scoffield, Heather. "PMO Misinformed on Argentine Probe." *Globe and Mail*, March 26, 2002.

Scoffield, Heather. "Quilmes Workers Said Worried They Won't Get Paid." *Globe and Mail*, May 16, 2002.

Scoffield, Heather. "Scotiabank Executives Face Legal Quagmire in Argentina." *Globe and Mail*, March 7, 2002.

Scoffield, Heather. "Scotiabank Quilmes CEO Stays Calm: Macdonald Would Stay in Argentina, Travel Ban or Not." *Globe and Mail*, March 2, 2002.

Sloane, Leonard. "Jones Made $1 Million in His Last Year at G.E." *New York Times*, March 18, 1981.

Srikantiah, Ashwini. "The Toronto-Dominion Bank and Canada's 'Little Bang' of 1987." Case study prepared under the supervision of Prof. Joe Martin, Rotman School of Management, University of Toronto, 2012.

Stewart, Sinclair. "Scotiabank Pressing Argentina for Redress: Demands $600 Million over Quilmes Loss." *Globe and Mail*, April 8, 2005.

Stewart, Sinclair. "Scotia's Sage Works His Playful Side." *Globe and Mail*, December 8, 2006.

Stinson, Marian. "Scotiabank in Argentine Deal: Paying $57 Million for 25% of Private Commercial Bank." *Globe and Mail*, September 15, 1994.

Toronto Star. "Bruce R. Birmingham Obituary." July 2010.

Toronto Star. "Rosedale Mansion of F. William Nicks, President of the Bank of Nova Scotia, Was Damaged by an Explosion this Morning." January 31, 1968.

Trichur, Rita. "When Will a Big Six Canadian Bank Have a Female CEO? At this Rate, Never." *Globe and Mail*, December 31, 2021.

Truno, Matthieu, Andriy Stolyarov, Danny Auger, and Michel Assaf. "Wholesale Funding of the Big Six Canadian Banks." *Bank of Canada Review*, Spring 2017.

Venkat, P.R. "HSBC to Sell Argentina Business in Latest Market Exit." *Wall Street Journal*, April 9, 2024.

Wahlquist, Calla. "Allan Bond: The Rise, Spectacular Fall and Rise Again of the America's Cup Hero." *Guardian* (international edition), June 5, 2015.

Waitzer, Ed. "We Must Do Away with 'Zombie Governance' in the Corporate World." *Globe and Mail*, February 27, 2024.

Waldie, Paul. "Argentine Bank Says Scotiabank Raising Stake." *Globe and Mail*, July 1, 1997.

Waldie, Paul. "Scotiabank May Sell Unit in Argentina." *Globe and Mail*, May 8, 2002.

Waugh, Richard. "The Bond Market in Canada." *Canadian Banker & ICB Review* 84, no. 1 (January–February, 1977): 41–45.

Waugh, Richard. "The Canadian Money Market." *Canadian Banker & ICB Review* 83, no. 6 (November–December 1976): 46–51.

Waugh, Richard. "Equity Investment and the Canadian Stock Market." *Canadian Banker & ICB Review* 84, no. 2 (March–April, 1977): 40–45.

Weber, Terry. "Scotiabank Grabs Dominican Branches, Assets." *Globe and Mail*, July 8, 2003.

Weber, Terry. "Scotiabank Hit by Argentina Charges." *Globe and Mail*, March 5, 2002.

Weber, Terry. "Scotiabank's Argentina Unit Suspended." *Globe and Mail*, April 19, 2002.

Whittington, Les. "Canada's Banks Facing Crisis in Confidence." *The Washington Post*, October 24, 1985.

Willis, Andrew. "Are Big Banks' Cash Hoards Too Much of a Good Thing?" *Globe and Mail*, December 18, 2008.

Willis, Andrew, and James Bradshaw. "Former Scotiabank CEO Peter Godsoe Went from Bank Teller to CEO." *Globe and Mail*, December 14, 2023.

Wong, Tony, and David Grossman. "Young Cagers Ecstatic over Deal to Bring New Team to Toronto." *Toronto Star*, October 2, 1993.

Younglai, Rachel, and Philipp Halstrick. "JPMorgan's Dimon's Aggressive Style May Hurt Banks' Cause." Reuters, September 29, 2011.

Zarum, Dave. "James Naismith." *Canadian Encyclopedia*, June 8, 2010, updated July 26, 2019.

Zochodne, Geoff. "Scotiabank Is Buying 51% of Peru-based Lender, Boosting Its Latin American Footprint." *Financial Post*, May 10, 2018.

Zorn, Lorie, Carolyn Wilkins, and Walter Engert, "Bank of Canada Liquidity Actions in Response to the Financial Market Turmoil." *Bank of Canada Review*, Autumn 2009.

REPORTS

Ackerman, Josef, Klaus-Peter Müller, Rick Waugh, and Charles Dallara. "Compensation Reform in Wholesale Banking 2010: Progress in Implementing Global Standards." Institute of International Finance in Collaboration with Oliver Wyman. September 2, 2010.

Blejer, Mario I. "Some Lessons from the Recent Financial Crisis in Argentina (2001/2)." Seminar on Crisis Prevention in Emerging Markets. Singapore, July 11, 2006.

Blejer, Mario I., Alejandro Henke, and Eduardo Levy-Yeyati. "The Argentine Crisis: Issues for Discussion." National Bureau of Economic Research, November 2002.

Bordo, Michael D., Angela Reddish, and Hugh Rockoff. "Why Didn't Canada Have a Banking Crisis in 2008 (Or in 1930, Or 1907, Or . . .)?" National Bureau of Economic Research, Working Paper 17312. August 2011.

Ernst & Young. "Making Strides in Financial Services Risk Management." 2011.

Ernst & Young. "Risk Governance—Agenda for Change: Survey of the Implementation of the IIF's Best Practices Recommendations." 2009.

Fleming, Michael J. "Federal Reserve Liquidity Provision During the Financial Crisis of 2007–2009" (Staff Report No. 563). Federal Reserve Bank of New York. July 2012.

Government of Canada (House of Commons). "Chapter 1, Canada's Economic Action Plan, of the Fall 2011 Report of the Auditor General of Canada." In *Report of the Standing Committee on Public Accounts*. December 2012.

Institute of International Finance. *Final Report of the Committee on Market Best Practices*. July 2008.

Khoury, Maria-Gabriella, Ahmed Al-shaibani, and Michael Driscoll. "Women at Canadian Banks: Thick Glass Ceiling." DBRS Morningstar, March 8, 2023.

Macdonald, David. "The Big Banks' Big Secret." Canadian Centre for Policy Alternatives. April 2012.

McDougall, Andrew, John M. Valley, Jessie Armour, and Aliza Zigler. 2023 Diversity Disclosure Practices: Diversity and Leadership at Canadian Public Companies. Osler, October 11, 2013. https://www.osler.com/en/resources/governance/2023/report-2023 -diversity-disclosure-practices-diversity-and-leadership-at-canadian-public-companies.

Privy Council Office. "Report of the Inquiry into the Collapse of the CCB and Northland Bank / by the Honourable Willard Z. Estey, commissioner." August 1986.

Scotiabank. *2001 Annual Report*. https://www.scotiabank.com/ca/common/pdf /about_scotia/archived_report5915.pdf.

Scotiabank. *2002 Annual Report*. https://www.annualreports.com/HostedData /AnnualReportArchive/B/TSX_BNS_2002.pdf.

Scotiabank. *2007 Fourth Quarter and Full Year Results*.

Scotiabank. *2008 Annual Report*.

Scotiabank. *2008 Fourth Quarter and Full Year results*.

Scotiabank. *2009 Annual Report*.

Scotiabank. *2009 Fourth Quarter and Full Year Results*.

Scotiabank. *2012 Annual Meeting of Shareholders and Management Proxy Circular*. https://www.scotiabank.com/ca/common/pdf/about_scotia/MPC_(Eng)_-_2012 _-_FINAL.pdf.

Scotiabank. 2013 Annual Meeting of Shareholders and Management Proxy Circular. https://www.scotiabank.com/ca/en/files/14/03/BNS_PROXY_CIRCULAR _ENGLISH.pdf.

Scotiabank. *2013 Annual Report*. https://www.scotiabank.com/ca/en/files/13/12 /BNS_2013_Annual_Report.pdf.

Scotiabank. 2023 Annual Report. https://www.scotiabank.com/content/dam
/scotiabank/corporate/quarterly-reports/2023/q4/Annual_Report_2023_EN.pdf.

Scotiabank. *Implications of the Credit Crisis.* June 18, 2008.

Scotiabank. "Update on Advancement of Women," in *Scotiabank Third Quarter
Report 2005.* https://www.scotiabank.com/content/dam/scotiabank/canada/common
/documents/pdf/about_scotia/quarterlyReports11594.pdf.

U.S. Government Accountability Office. "Troubled Asset Relief Program: Lifetime
Cost," GAO-24-107033. December 7, 2023.

Zelmer, Mark. "Better Safe Than Sorry: Options for Managing Bank Runs in the
Future" (Commentary No. 677). C.D. Howe Institute, October 1, 2024.

WEBSITES, PODCASTS, VIDEOS, AND SOCIAL MEDIA

Websites

Board of Governors of the Federal Reserve System. "What Is the Difference Between
a Bank's Liquidity and Its Capital?" December 2019.

Department of Justice. "Attorney General Merrick B. Garland Delivers Remarks
Announcing TD Bank's Guilty Plea for Bank Secrecy Act and Money Laundering
Conspiracy Violations in $1.8B Resolution," October 10, 2024. https://www.justice.
gov/opa/speech/attorney-general-merrick-b-garland-delivers-remarks-announcing
-td-banks-guilty-plea-bank.

Elections Canada. https://www.elections.ca/content.aspx?section=res&dir=his
/chap2&document=index&lang=e.

ProPublica. "Bailout Tracker." August 18, 2022.

Royal Bank. "Milestones at a Glance: Woman at Royal Bank." n.d. https://www.rbc
.com/en/about-us/history/milestones-at-a-glance/women-at-royal-bank/.

Scotiabank. "Scotiabank in the Caribbean and Central America." n.d. https://tc
.scotiabank.com/about-scotiabank/inside-scotiabank/scotiabank-in-the-caribbean
-and-central-america.html.

Scotiabank. "Women in Banking: A Case Study of Scotiabank." 2019. https://www.
scotiabank.com/ca/en/about/our-company/archives/our-exhibits/breaking-barriers.html.

Securities Industry and Financial Markets Association. "Financial Crisis Timeline."
December 2, 2008.

Statistics Canada. "Women's History Month: The Remarkable Life of Sylvia Ostry."
   October 11, 2022. https://www.statcan.gc.ca/01/en/plus/1980-womens-history-month
   -remarkable-life-sylvia-ostry.

Podcasts and Videos

Axelrod, David. *The Axe Files with David Axelrod*, episode 596, "Secretary Janet Yellen."
   October 3, 2024.

CBC. *The Nature of Things*. Season 32, episode 3, "Air Crash." Aired October 16, 1991.

Green, Howard. *Connexion with Howard Green* (*Toronto Star*), episode 12, "Abigail
   Disney." June 2, 2022.

New York Times. The Daily. "Can an 'Anarcho-Capitalist' President Save Argentina's
   Economy?" December 11, 2023.

NPR. *Planet Money.* "How the Dominican Republic Became Latin America's Economic
   Superstar." May 16, 2024.

Weinbach, Jon, dir. *The Redeem Team*. Netflix, 2022.

Social Media

Charlie182x. "TV Commercial Dominicano: Sammy Sosa — Baninter." 2011.
   Television ad, 1:08. https://www.youtube.com/watch?v=Vkcm9T_lIpE.

Jose Dorin Cabrera Mercadelogia. "Commercial Baninter: Sammy Sosa. 2020.
   Television ad, 1:00. https://www.youtube.com/watch?v=fH0Xg7VGvHM.

OceanMiramar. "Baninter: Sammy Sosa." 2013. Television ad, 0:29. https://www
   .youtube.com/watch?v=UYxknwI3Yqo.

REMARKS AND WORKING PAPERS

"Banking Sector Challenges After the Crisis of Confidence: Issues for discussion for the
   meeting at the BIS at 14:00 on Sunday 11 January 2009, Centralbahnplatz 2, CH-4002
   Basel. Bank for International Settlements." January 6, 2009.

"Banking Sector Challenges After the Crisis of Confidence: Note
   for a meeting at 14:00 on Sunday 11 January 2009 at the BIS." January 8, 2009.

"Banks, Buyouts and Brain Drain." Remarks by Richard E. Waugh, Senior Vice-
   President, Corporate Banking, Scotiabank. November 21, 1989. Commerce Students'
   Association Business Banquet, University of Manitoba, Winnipeg, Manitoba.

Bernanke, Ben. "Liquidity Provision by the Federal Reserve." Federal Reserve Bank of Atlanta Financial Markets Conference. Sea Island, GA, May 13, 2008.

"BIS Meeting re: IIF Steering Committee, Global Financial Institutions & Operating Model, Canadian Model" (printed and handwritten notes). January 11, 2009.

Chrominska, Sylvia. "The Business Case for Diversity: Scotiabank's Advancement of Women Initiative," March 27, 2013. Speaking notes for the "Where Have All the Women Gone" panel, IBA Employment and Discrimination Law Conference, April 2013.

"Discussion Points on Regulatory Initiatives." Notes for January 11, 2009, meeting at Bank for International Settlements, Basel, CH.

Freedman, Charles. "The Canadian Banking System." Revised version (March 1998) of a paper delivered at the Conference on Developments in the Financial System: The Jerome Levy Economics Institute of Bard College, Annandale-on-Hudson, NY, April 1997.

Scotiabank Group. "Top 75 Global Banks by Market Capitalization, Valuation as at December 31, 2008 (in U.S. Dollars)" (prepared by finance department for Rick Waugh in advance of January 2009 meetings at Bank for International Settlements, Basel, CH).

Scotiabank Group. "Unlocking Potential, Delivering Results: The 7 Keys to the Advancement of Women at Scotiabank." Catalyst 2007 Award submission. June 2, 2006.

Waugh, Rick. Address to the Empire Club of Canada. Toronto, ON, September 5, 2013.

Waugh, Rick. "Regulatory Regime & Good Management Also Important." Notes for January 2009 meetings at Bank for International Settlements, Basel, CH.

Waugh, Rick. "Remarks, Dominican Republic cocktail reception." November 11, 2009.

Waugh, Rick. "Tribute Response Remarks, Rick Waugh." Exit speech, Institute of International Finance. n.d.

Waugh. Rick. PowerPoint slides: Environment—Credit Crisis, Swiss Big Banks; Environment—Does Scale Matter?; Does Size and Scale Matter—International Banks; Does Size and Scale Matter?—Canadian Peers; Does Size and Scale Matter?—Shareholder Return International; Does Size and Scale Matter?—Shareholder Return Canadian Peers; Agenda.

RICK WAUGH, PERSONAL PAPERS

International Monetary Conference detailed program, agenda, speaking notes, and
itinerary, for Rick and Lynne Waugh. SE, 2012.

International Monetary Conference president's itinerary, briefing book, and speaking
notes. Stockholm, SE. 2012.

International Monetary Conference program, speaker biographies, excursions, and
participants. Stockholm IMC-2012. Grand Hotel, SE. June 3–5, 2012.

Meeting of CEOs and Governors, Bank for International Settlements, Room B.
List of Participants. January 11, 2009, Basel, CH.

Waugh, Rick. Handwritten notes in red pencil. Fall 2007, 2008.

Waugh, Rick. Personal calendars. 2009–17.

Waugh, Rick. Travel itineraries.

LEGAL

Banco Central de la Republica Dominicana. "Agreement between Ramón Buenaventura
Báez Figueroa and Dominican Central Bank." September 3, 2013.

Bank of Nova Scotia, Liquidation Commission of Baninter, Central Bank of the
Dominican Republic, and Superintendence of Banks of the Dominican Republic.
Branch Acquisition Agreement. November 7, 2003. https://cdn.bancentral.gov.do
/documents/transparencia/oficina-de-acceso-a-la-informacion/documents/Contrato
-sucursales-BANINTER.pdf?v=1730910201442.

Ramón Buenaventura Báez Figueroa appeal. Court of Appeals (DR), No. 0052-TS
-2008, April 17, 2008. https://www.sb.gob.do/media/nhac5gsw/enj-sb-compendio
-regulaciones.pdf.

Ramón Buenaventura Báez Figueroa appeal to the Supreme Court of Justice (DR).
Final order No. 2085-2008, July 8, 2008. https://www.oas.org/juridico/pdfs/mesicic4
_repdom_casos1.pdf.

Ramón Buenaventura Báez Figueroa decision. First Tribunal of the Criminal Chamber
of the National District's Court of First Instance (DR). Decision No. 350-2007,
October 21, 2007.

INTERVIEWS AND PERSONAL COMMUNICATIONS

Quotations from Rick Waugh and others are taken from interviews with the author, unless otherwise cited. The following are the dates and locations of book-related interviews/conversations with Rick (and Lynne) Waugh.

July 26, 2023 (cottage)

August 1, 2023 (cottage)

September 7, 2023 (office)

September 11, 2023 (telephone)

October 16, 2023 (condo/also with Lynne separately)

November 10, 2023 (telephone)

November 13, 2023 (condo)

December 1, 2023 (telephone)

December 14, 2023 (office)

December 19, 2023 (office)

December 21, 2023 (office)

December 22, 2023 (condo/with Lynne as well, briefly)

February 6, 2024 (office)

February 15, 2024 (office)

March 6, 2024 (telephone, from Turks & Caicos)

April 27, 2024 (Zoom, from Turks & Caicos/with Lynne)

May 13, 2024 (condo/including Lynne)

May 29, 2024 (office)

June 5, 2024 (condo)

June 12, 2024 (telephone)

September 3, 2024 (telephone)

September 9, 2024 (Zoom with Schulich School of Business)

October 2, 2024 (Schulich School of Business private dinner, fireside chat with dean and students, car ride home)

November 13, 2024 (condo and office)

November 20, 2024 (condo and office)

November 28, 2024 (telephone)

December 11, 2024 (telephone)

January 29, 2025 (telephone from Turks and Caicos)

February 10, 2025 (Turks and Caicos)

February 11, 2025 (Turks and Caicos)

February 12, 2025 (Turks and Caicos)

April 2, 2025 (telephone, from Turks and Caicos)

April 6, 2025 (telephone, from Turks and Caicos)

April 10, 2025 (telephone, from Turks and Caicos)

May 7, 2025 (downtown Toronto)

May 29, 2025 (telephone)

Published or Broadcast Interviews

BNN. "Interview with Ace Greenberg." *Headline with Howard Green,* August 30, 2010.

BNN. "Interview with Dan O'Neill." *Business News with Howard Green.* n.d.

BNN. "Interview with Jim Flaherty." *Headline with Howard Green.* June 27, 2010.

BNN. "Interview with Peter Godsoe." *Business News with Howard Green.* n.d.

BNN. "Interview with Rick Waugh." *Headline with Howard Green.* April 1, 2009.

BNN. "Interview with Rick Waugh." *Headline with Howard Green.* January 22, 2010.

BNN. "Interview with Rick Waugh." *Headline with Howard Green.* April 16, 2010.

BNN. "Interview with Rick Waugh." *Headline with Howard Green.* August 16, 2010.

BNN. "Interview with Rick Waugh." *Headline with Howard Green.* November 22, 2010.

BNN. "Interview with Rick Waugh." *Headline with Howard Green.* September 22, 2011.

BNN. "Interview with Rick Waugh." *Headline with Howard Green.* September 14, 2012.

BNN. "Interview with Rick Waugh." *Headline with Howard Green.* October 21, 2013.

Cepedes, Julissa. *Reporte Especial: 20 años después: Ramón Báez Figueroa, expresidente de BANINTER, en entrevista exclusiva* (interview with Ramón Figueroa Báez). CDN (Dominican News Channel). November 5, 2023. https://www.youtube.com /watch?v=72JRT3g8egw

Green, Howard, and Brian Porter. Fireside chat. Scotiabank/UJA event, February 8, 2018.

Green, Howard, and Rick Waugh. Fireside chat. SIBOS Conference, Metro Toronto Convention Centre, September 21, 2011.

Green, Howard, Rick Waugh, and Brian Porter. Fireside chat. CEO handover event. Metro Toronto Convention Centre, October 31, 2013.

Kipping, Matthias, and Andrew Thomson. Interviews with Rick Waugh. Schulich School of Business, York University, Toronto, ON, January 22, 2020, and October 25, 2021.

Report on Business Television. "Interview with Rick Waugh." *Business News,* July 21, 2004.

Waugh, Rick, and Detlev Zwick. Fireside chat. Schulich School of Business, York University, Toronto, ON, October 1, 2024.

MISCELLANEOUS

Berkshire Hathaway Annual Meeting, 2005. Omaha, Nebraska.

https://cba.ca/fast-facts-the-canadian-banking-system.

https://www.pnc.com/en/about-pnc/company-profile/legacy-project/artifacts/national -city-bank.html#:~:text=In%202008%2C%20PNC%20acquired%20 National,documents%20that%20tell%20its%20story.

NOTES

INTRODUCTION

1 "Banking Sector Challenges After the Crisis of Confidence: Note for a meeting at 14:00 on Sunday 11 January 2009 at the BIS," January 8, 2009, 16.

CHAPTER ONE: *Great Timing*

1 Robert MacIntosh, *Different Drummers: Banking and Politics in Canada* (MacMillan Canada, 1991), 114.
2 "Banks, Buyouts and Brain Drain." Remarks by Richard E. Waugh, Senior Vice-President, Corporate Banking, Scotiabank. November 21, 1989. Commerce Students' Association Business Banquet, University of Manitoba, Winnipeg, Manitoba.

CHAPTER TWO: *As Canadian as Hockey and Tim Hortons*

1 Christopher Kobrak and Joe Martin, *From Wall Street to Bay Street: The Origins and Evolution of American and Canadian Finance* (University of Toronto Press, 2018), 11 and 77.
2 Kobrak and Martin, *From Wall Street to Bay Street*, 66.
3 Kobrak and Martin, *From Wall Street to Bay Street*, 63.
4 MacIntosh, *Different Drummers*, 15.
5 In Collaboration, "William McMaster," *Dictionary of Canadian Biography*, Vol. 11 (1881–1890) (University of Toronto, 1982–2024).
6 MacIntosh, *Different Drummers*, 16.
7 Kobrak and Martin, *From Wall Street to Bay Street*, 77, 98–101.
8 MacIntosh, *Different Drummers*, 11.
9 Kobrak and Martin, *From Wall Street to Bay Street*, 28 and 33.
10 Kobrak and Martin, *From Wall Street to Bay Street*, 11.

11 Malcolm D. Knight, "Surmounting the Financial Crisis: Contrasts Between Canadian and American Banks," First Thomas O. Enders Memorial Lecture, *American Review of Canadian Studies* 42 (2012): 311–20.

12 Michael D. Bordo, Angela Reddish, and Hugh Rockoff. "Why Didn't Canada Have a Banking Crisis in 2008 (Or in 1930, Or 1907, Or . . .)?" National Bureau of Economic Research, Working Paper 17312, August 2011, 3.

13 Joseph Schull and J. Douglas Gibson, *The Scotiabank Story: A History of the Bank of Nova Scotia, 1832–1982* (Macmillan of Canada, 1982), 19.

14 Tony Comper with Bruce Dowbiggin, *Personal Account: 25 Tales About Leadership, Learning, and Legacy from a Lifetime at Bank of Montreal* (ECW, 2020), 186.

15 Privy Council Office, "Report of the Inquiry into the Collapse of the CCB and Northland Bank / by the Honourable Willard Z. Estey, commissioner," August 1986, 1–21.

16 Alix Granger, "Estey Commission," *Canadian Encyclopedia,* February 7, 2006 (updated, December 15, 2013).

17 Kelly A. Dean, "Crisis in Canadian Banking," *Lehigh Preserve Institutional Repository,* 1988.

18 Kobrak and Martin, *From Wall Street to Bay Street,* 4.

19 MacIntosh, *Different Drummers,* 76, 70, 72, and 78.

20 MacIntosh, *Different Drummers,* 114.

21 MacIntosh, *Different Drummers,* 114–23.

22 Charles Freedman, "The Canadian Banking System," revised version (March 1998) of a paper delivered at the Conference on Developments in the Financial System: The Jerome Levy Economics Institute of Bard College, Annandale-on-Hudson, NY, April 1997, 7 and 22.

23 MacIntosh, *Different Drummers,* 118.

24 MacIntosh, *Different Drummers,* 105, 112, and 127.

25 MacIntosh, *Different Drummers,* 137.

26 Knight, "Surmounting the Financial Crisis," 313.

27 Kobrak and Martin, *From Wall Street to Bay Street,* 202.

28 MacIntosh, *Different Drummers,* 158–61.

29 Howard Green, *Banking on America: How TD Bank Rose to the Top and Took on the U.S.A.* (HarperCollins, 2013), 118–20.

30 MacIntosh, *Different Drummers,* 163–64.

31 MacIntosh, *Different Drummers,* 168.

32 Joe Martin, "The Toronto-Dominion Bank and Canada's 'Little Bang' of 1987" (case study prepared by Ashwini Srikantiah, Rotman School of Management, University of Toronto), 2012, 9.

33 Green, *Banking on America,* 100–1.

34 Kobrak and Martin, *From Wall Street to Bay Street,* 162.

35 MacIntosh, *Different Drummers,* 157.

36 Kobrak and Martin, *From Wall Street to Bay Street,* 215.

37 Green, *Banking on America,* 102.

38 Green, *Banking on America,* 147.

CHAPTER THREE: *From Halifax to the World*

1 Schull and Gibson, *The Scotiabank Story*, 1–35.
2 Schull and Gibson, *The Scotiabank Story*, 20.
3 Schull and Gibson, *The Scotiabank Story*, 53 and 67.
4 Schull and Gibson, *The Scotiabank Story*, 62–68.
5 Schull and Gibson, *The Scotiabank Story*, 68.
6 Schull and Gibson, *The Scotiabank Story*, 70–71 and 77.
7 Schull and Gibson, *The Scotiabank Story*, 103–34.
8 Schull and Gibson, *The Scotiabank Story*, 137–39.
9 Schull and Gibson, *The Scotiabank Story*, 154.
10 Kobrak and Martin, *From Wall Street to Bay Street*, 4.
11 *The New Yorker*, November 17, 1951.
12 Schull and Gibson, *The Scotiabank Story*, 190.
13 Schull and Gibson, *The Scotiabank Story*, 204, 209, and 240.
14 "Rosedale Mansion of F. William Nicks, President of the Bank of Nova Scotia, Was Damaged by an Explosion this Morning," *Toronto Star*, January 31, 1968.
15 Schull and Gibson, *The Scotiabank* Story, 264.
16 Rod McQueen, *The Money Spinners: An Intimate Portrait of the Men Who Run Canada's Banks* (Totem Books, 1984), 158.
17 McQueen, *The Money Spinners*, 168.
18 James D. Frost. "The 'Nationalization' of the Bank of Nova Scotia, 1880–1910," *Acadiensis* 12, no. 1 (Autumn 1982): 3–38.
19 Frost, "The 'Nationalization' of the Bank of Nova Scotia," 3–38.

CHAPTER FOUR: *No, Mr. Trump: Lending to Americans*

1 McQueen, *The Money Spinners*, 260.
2 Russ Buettner and Charles V. Bagli, "How Donald Trump Bankrupted His Atlantic City Casinos, but Still Earned Millions," *New York Times*, June 11, 2016.
3 Green, *Banking on America*, 38.

CHAPTER FIVE: *How to Snag a Raptor*

1 David Coriat, email message to author, February 4, 2025.
2 Alex Wong, *Prehistoric: The Audacious and Improbable Origin Story of the Toronto Raptors* (Triumph Books, 2023), 6, ebook.
3 *The Redeem Team*, directed by Jon Weinbach (Netflix, 2022).
4 Russ Granik, email message to author, April 10, 2024.
5 Wong, *Prehistoric*, 24, ebook.

CHAPTER SIX: *Good Wine, Rotten Barrels*

1   MacIntosh, *Different Drummers*, 124.
2   Roy D. Scott, *My Days with Scotiabank in Latin America* (privately published in Argentina Impreso Por Artes Graficas Integradas, 2019), 13–14, 37.
3   Scott, *My Days with Scotiabank in Latin America*, 95–96.
4   Scott, *My Days with Scotiabank in Latin America*, 25, 6, and 159.
5   Scott, *My Days with Scotiabank in Latin America*, 55–56.
6   Scott, *My Days with Scotiabank in Latin America*, 97–105.
7   Scott, *My Days with Scotiabank in Latin America*, 135–36.
8   Paul Blustein, *And the Money Kept Rolling In (and Out): Wall Street, the IMF, and the Bankrupting of Argentina*. Public Affairs, 2006, 16–17, 23–24, 28, 33–34, 52, 66, and 162–67.
9   Scotiabank, *2002 Annual Report*.
10 Blustein, *And the Money Kept Rolling In (and Out)*, 166–67.
11 Blustein, *And the Money Kept Rolling In (and Out)*, 134 and 167.
12 Blustein, *And the Money Kept Rolling In (and Out)*, 49.
13 Scott, *My Days with Scotiabank in Latin America*, 149.
14 Scott, *My Days with Scotiabank in Latin America*, 149–50.
15 Scott, *My Days with Scotiabank in Latin America*, 136.
16 Marian Stinson, "Scotiabank in Argentine Deal: Paying $57 Million for 25% of Private Commercial Bank," *Globe and Mail*, September 15, 1994.
17 Anatol von Hahn, Gerry Moylan, Donna Groskorth, and Roy Scott (contributors), *Lessons Learned—Argentina 2001–2002* (unpublished), 8, 9, 13.
18 von Hahn et al., *Lessons Learned*, 10.
19 von Hahn et al., *Lessons Learned*, 23.
20 Rick Waugh, email message to author, November 25, 2023.
21 Tom MacDonald, email message to author, January 26, 2024.
22 Mario I. Blejer, "Some Lessons from the Recent Financial Crisis in Argentina (2001/2)," Seminar on Crisis Prevention in Emerging Markets. Singapore, July 11, 2006.
23 Partridge, John. "Scotiabank Buys Additional 70% of Banco Quilmes," *Globe and Mail*, July 3, 1997.
24 Susanne Craig. "Scotiabank's Latin Obsession," *Globe and Mail*, April 10, 1999.
25 von Hahn et al., *Lessons Learned*, 11.
26 *Globe and Mail*, May 1, 2002.
27 Scotiabank, *2002 Annual Report*.
28 von Hahn et al., *Lessons Learned*, 14.
29 Heather Scoffield, "How One Complaint Set Off Argentine Probe" and "Scotiabank Quilmes CEO Stays Calm: Macdonald Would Stay in Argentina, Travel Ban or Not," *Globe and Mail*, March 2, 2002; "Canadian Bank's Argentine Subsidiary Raided," *Globe and Mail*, March 6, 2002; "Scotiabank Executives Face Legal Quagmire in Argentina," *Globe and Mail*, March 7, 2002; "Argentine Judge Grills Scotiabank Executive," *Globe and Mail*, March 13, 2002; "PMO Misinformed on Argentine Probe," *Globe and Mail*, March 26, 2002.

30 Keith Kalawsky, "Argentine Shuts Down Scotiabank Subsidiary: Paul Martin to Intervene: 'The Crisis Is Unprecedented in Our Bank's History,'" *National Post*, April 20, 2002.

31 Scoffield, "PMO Misinformed on Argentine Probe," *Globe and Mail*, March 26, 2002.

32 Shawn McCarthy, Jacquie McNish, and John Partridge, "How the Scotiabank-BMO Merger Fell Apart," *Globe and Mail*, November 2, 2002.

33 von Hahn et al., *Lessons Learned*, 23.

34 Sinclair Stewart. "Scotiabank Pressing Argentina for Redress: Demands $600 Million over Quilmes Loss," *Globe and Mail*, April 8, 2005.

CHAPTER SEVEN: *Every Country Needs a Good Bank*

1 Schull and Gibson, *The Scotiabank Story*, 243.

2 Scott, *My Days with Scotiabank in Latin America*, 90.

3 Schull and Gibson, *The Scotiabank Story*, 210 and 212.

4 Scott, *My Days with Scotiabank in Latin America*, 43.

5 Scott, *My Days with Scotiabank in Latin America*, 43–44.

6 Schull and Gibson, *The Scotiabank Story*, 212–13.

7 Scott, *My Days with Scotiabank in Latin America*, 44.

8 Schull and Gibson, *The Scotiabank Story*, 92.

9 Scott, *My Days with Scotiabank in Latin America*, 42.

10 International Monetary Fund (IMF), "IMF Approves Two-Year US$600 Million Stand-By Arrangement for the Dominican Republic," Release No. 3/147, August 29, 2003.

11 Jose de Cordoba, "With a Banker Facing Charges, a Nation Questions Its Success," *Wall Street Journal*, June 30, 2003.

12 IMF, "IMF Approves Two-Year US$600 Million Stand-By Arrangement for the Dominican Republic."

13 Jose de Cordoba. "With a Banker Facing Charges, a Nation Questions Its Success."

14 Justin Meek email to parents, January 27, 2025.

15 Cordoba, "With a Banker Facing Charges, a Nation Questions Its Success."

16 IMF, "IMF Approves Two-Year US$600 Million Stand-By Arrangement for the Dominican Republic."

CHAPTER EIGHT: *Friday Afternoons Were the Worst*

1 Cyrus Sanati, "Prince Finally Explains His Dancing Comment," *New York Times*, April 8, 2010.

2 https://www.federalreserve.gov/faqs/cat_21427.htm.

3 Bloomberg, "Bloomberg Uncovers the Fed's Secret Liquidity Lifelines," August 22, 2011.

4 Louis W. Pauly, "Canadian Autonomy and Systemic Financial Risk After the Crisis of 2008," in *Crisis and Reform: Canada and the International Financial System;*

Canada Among Nations, vol. 20, ed. Rohinton Medhora and Dane Rowlands
(Canadian Institute for Governance Innovation, 2014), 165.

5   https://www.legacy.com/ca/obituaries/theglobeandmail/name/robert-brooks
-obituary?id=56826209.

6   Tim Kiladze et al., "The 2008 Financial Crisis: Through the Eyes of Some Major
Players," *Globe and Mail,* September 14, 2013.

7   Scotiabank, *Implications of the Credit Crisis,* June 18, 2008, 8, 5, 7, 9, and 14.

8   Scotiabank, *Implications of the Credit Crisis,* 15 and 28.

9   Rick Waugh and Detlev Zwick, Fireside chat. Schulich School of Business,
York University, Toronto, ON, October 1, 2024.

10 Lorie Zorn, Carolyn Wilkins, and Walter Engert, "Bank of Canada Liquidity
Actions in Response to the Financial Market Turmoil," *Bank of Canada Review,*
Autumn 2009.

11 Waugh and Zwick, Fireside chat.

12 Zorn et al., "Bank of Canada Liquidity Actions in Response to the Financial Market
Turmoil," 21.

13 Pauly, "Canadian Autonomy and Systemic Financial Risk After the Crisis of 2008," 167.

14 Michael J. Fleming, "Federal Reserve Liquidity Provision During the Financial
Crisis of 2007-2009" (Staff Report No. 563), Federal Reserve Bank of New York,
July 2012.

15 David Axelrod, *The Axe Files with David Axelrod,* episode 596, "Secretary Janet
Yellen," October 3, 2024.

16 Bank of Canada, "Primer on ABCP," *Canadian Fixed-Income Forum,* June 2024,
3 and 4.

17 Bank of Canada, "Primer on ABCP," 4.

18 Jeffrey Carhart and Jay Hoffman, "Canada's Asset Backed Commercial Paper
Restructuring, 2007–2009," *Banking and Finance Law Review* 25, no. 1 (2009): 42.

19 *Reuters,* "Canada Banks to Pay C$139 Million in ABCP Settlement," December 21,
2009.

20 Bank of Canada, "Primer on ABCP," 5–7.

21 Ashwini Srikantiah, "The Toronto-Dominion Bank and Canada's 'Little Bang'
of 1987" (case study prepared by Ashwini Srikantiah, under the direction of Prof,
Joe Martin), Rotman School of Management, University of Toronto, 2012.

22 Virginia Galt, "Scotiabank Sees New Brokerage as Separate Line," *Globe and Mail,*
January 20, 1988.

23 Steve Fishman. "Burning Down His House," *New York Magazine,* November 27, 2008.

24 Zorn et al., "Bank of Canada Liquidity Actions in Response to the Financial Market
Turmoil," 3–4.

25 Zorn et al., "Bank of Canada Liquidity Actions in Response to the Financial Market
Turmoil," 5–6, 8, and 9.

26 Zorn et al., "Bank of Canada Liquidity Actions in Response to the Financial Market
Turmoil," 5, 7–8, and 15.

27 Zorn et al., "Bank of Canada Liquidity Actions in Response to the Financial Market
Turmoil," 21.

28 Pauly, "Canadian Autonomy and Systemic Financial Risk After the Crisis of 2008,"
    164.

29 Green, *Banking on America*, 147; and Knight, "Surmounting the Financial Crisis,"
    311–20.

30 Scotiabank, *Annual Reports*, 2007–9.

CHAPTER NINE: *In the Room*

1   Waugh, travel itinerary, Bank for International Settlements (BIS), Basel, CH,
    January 10–12, 2009.

2   Meeting of CEOs and Governors, BIS, Room B, List of Participants. Basel, CH,
    January 11, 2009.

3   Scotiabank Group: "Top 75 Global Banks by Market Capitalization, Valuation as
    at December 31, 2008 (in U.S. Dollars)," (prepared by Finance Department for
    Rick Waugh in advance of January 2009 meetings at Bank for International
    Settlements, Basel, CH).

4   Bank for International Settlements (BIS), "Banking Sector Challenges After the
    Crisis of Confidence: Issues for discussion for the meeting at the BIS at 14:00 on
    Sunday 11 January 2009, Centralbahnplatz 2, CH-4002 Basel. Bank for
    International Settlements," January 6, 2009, 1.

5   BIS, "Banking Sector Challenges After the Crisis of Confidence," 1–2, 4, 5, and 8.

6   BIS, "Banking Sector Challenges After the Crisis of Confidence," 8, 15, and 16.

7   BIS, "Banking Sector Challenges After the Crisis of Confidence," 1–2.

8   Scott Thomson, remarks to Canadian Club, Toronto, ON, June 2024.

9   Waugh, "Banking Sector Challenges After the Crisis of Confidence," 1–2.

10 Waugh briefing note for BIS meeting prepared by Scotiabank.

11 Waugh briefing note for BIS meeting prepared by Scotiabank.

12 Waugh briefing note for BIS meeting prepared by Scotiabank.

13 Institute of International Finance (IIF), *Final Report of the Committee on Market
    Best Practices*, July 2008, 7.

14 Charles H. Dallara, *Euroshock: How the Largest Debt Restructuring in History Helped
    Save Greece and Preserve the Eurozone* (Rodin Books, 2024), 173.

15 IIF, *Final Report of the Committee on Market Best Practices*, 9.

16 IIF, *Final Report of the Committee on Market Best Practices*, 9.

17 IIF, *Final Report of the Committee on Market Best Practices*, 9–10.

18 IIF, *Final Report of the Committee on Market Best Practices*, 14.

19 Rachel Younglai and Philipp Halstrick, "JPMorgan's Dimon's Aggressive Style
    May Hurt Banks' Cause," Reuters, September 29, 2011.

20 https://www.bankofcanada.ca/publications/annual-reports-quarterly-financial
    -reports/annual-report-2020/mandate-and-planning/.

21 Government of Canada (House of Commons), "Chapter 1, Canada's Economic
    Action Plan, of the Fall 2011 Report of the Auditor General of Canada," in *Report
    of the Standing Committee on Public Accounts*, December 2012.

22 Julie Dickson, email message to author, May 27, 2024.

23 IMC president's briefing book, 2012 International Monetary Conference, Stockholm, SE. Includes detailed program, agenda, speaking notes, and Rick Waugh's handwritten notes.

24 International Monetary Conference, Stockholm IMC-2012. Program/speaker biographies/excursions/participants, June 3–5, Grand Hotel, SE.

25 Ernst & Young, "Risk Governance—Agenda for Change: Survey of the Implementation of the IIF's Best Practices Recommendations," 2009, 8–11 and 22.

26 Ernst & Young, "Risk Governance," 11, 14, and 18–19.

27 Mark Zelmer, "Better Safe Than Sorry: Options for Managing Bank Runs in the Future" (Commentary No. 667), C.D. Howe Institute, October 2024, 9.

28 Ernst & Young, "Risk Governance," 25, 29, 34, and 36.

29 Ernst & Young, "Making Strides in Financial Services Risk Management," 2011, 1–4 and 4–6.

30 Ernst & Young, "Making Strides in Financial Services Risk Management," 30 and 34.

31 Ernst & Young, "Making Strides in Financial Services Risk Management," 16.

32 Rick Waugh, Address to the Empire Club of Canada, Toronto, ON, September 5, 2013.

33 Tara Perkins, "Canadian Bankers Tell G20: Don't Suffocate Our Growth," *Globe and Mail*, April 8, 2010.

34 Knight, "Surmounting the Financial Crisis," 318–19.

35 *The Nature of Things*, season 32, episode 3, "Air Crash," October 16, 1991.

36 Canada, 1900–1945 by Robert Bothwell, Ian Drummond, and John English, University of Toronto Press, 1987. Pg 248. And: *Perspectives on Labour and Income: Autumn 1992* (Vol. 4, No. 3) Article No. 3, A note on Canadian unemployment since 1921, Dave Gower.

37 Interview with Rick Waugh," *Headline with Howard Green*, April 16, 2010.

38 Interview with Jim Flaherty," *Headline with Howard Green*, June 26-27, 2010.

39 Interview with Rick Waugh," *Headline with Howard Green*, April 16, 2010.

40 Waugh, Address to the Empire Club.

CHAPTER TEN: *Close Calls for a Deal Junkie*

1 Waugh Empire Club speech, September 5, 2013.

2 Jacqueline Nelson, Grant Robertson, and Boyd Erman, "Scotiabank Snares ING for $3.1 Billion," *Globe and Mail*, August 30, 2012.

3 Scotiabank, *2012 Annual Report*.

4 Cameron French and Euan Rocha, "Scotiabank Buys ING Direct Canada for $3.1 Billion," Reuters, August 29, 2012.

5 Stephen Hart, email message to author, February 6, 2025.

6 Wendy Hannam, email message to author, February 6, 2025.

7   Freedman, "The Canadian Banking System," 6.
8   Scott Hand, email message to author, October 11, 2024.

CHAPTER ELEVEN: *Does She Mind Going Down One Floor?*

1   MacIntosh, *Different Drummers*, 142.
2   Statistics Canada, "Women's History Month: The Remarkable Life of Sylvia Ostry,"
    October 11, 2022.
3   MacIntosh, *Different Drummers*, 144.
4   Elections Canada. https://www.elections.ca/content.aspx?section=res&dir=his
    /chap2&document=index&lang=e.
5   McQueen, *The Money Spinners*, 205–7.
6   Joseph Schull, *100 Years of Banking in Canada: The Toronto-Dominion Bank*
    (Copp Clark Publishing, 1958), 169.
7   Laurence B. Mussio, *Whom Fortune Favours: The Bank of Montreal and the Rise*
    of North American Finance Vol. 2, *Territories of Transformation, 1946–2017*
    (McGill-Queen's University Press, 2020), 37.
8   McQueen, *The Money Spinners*, 164 and 220.
9   MacIntosh, *Different Drummers*, 154.
10 www.internationalwomensday.com/Giving/Catalyst.
11 Scotiabank Group, "Unlocking Potential, Delivering Results: The 7 Keys to
    the Advancement of Women at Scotiabank," 2007 Catalyst Award Submission,
    June 2, 2006, 23.
12 Scotiabank, "Women in Banking: A Case Study of Scotiabank," 2019.
13 Scotiabank, "Women in Banking."
14 Axelrod, *The Axe Files*, October 3, 2024.
15 Schull and Gibson, *The Scotiabank Story*, 280-1.
16 Scotiabank Group, "Unlocking Potential, Delivering Results," 2.
17 Scotiabank Group, "Unlocking Potential, Delivering Results," 4.
18 Scotiabank Group, "Unlocking Potential, Delivering Results," 7.
19 David A. Matsa, and Amalia R. Miller, "Chipping Away at the Glass Ceiling:
    Gender Spillovers in Corporate Leadership," *American Economic Review* 101,
    no. 3 (2011): 639.
20 Schull and Gibson, *The Scotiabank Story*, 404–9.
21 Scotiabank, *2013 Annual Report*.
22 https://www.scotiabank.com/ca/en/about/our-company/executive-management.html.
23 Scotiabank, Management Proxy Circular, Annual Meeting of Shareholders, April 8,
    2025.
24 *Globe and Mail*. "The Doors to Canada's Boardrooms are (Slowly) Starting to Open"
    (editorial). January 22, 2024.
25 Christopher Reynolds, "Air Canada's First Female Pilot Recalls Sector's Sexist
    Hurdles on Route to Success," Canadian Press, February 4, 2024.
26 Tony Comper with Bruce Dowbiggin, *Personal Account,* 108.

27 Tara Perkins, "Who'll Be the First Female Bank CEO?" *Globe and Mail*, August 26, 2010.

EPILOGUE

1 Scotiabank, *2012 Annual Meeting of Shareholders and Management Proxy Circular*, 36.
2 Scotiabank, *2012 Annual Meeting of Shareholders and Management Proxy Circular*, 28.
3 Scotiabank, *2012 Annual Meeting of Shareholders and Management Proxy Circular*, 21–22.
4 Scotiabank, *2012 Annual Meeting of Shareholders and Management Proxy Circular*, 29.
5 Scotiabank, *2012 Annual Meeting of Shareholders and Management Proxy Circular*, 32 and 33.
6 Scotiabank, *2012 Annual Meeting of Shareholders and Management Proxy Circular*, 48.
7 Gordon Pitts, "Rick Waugh's Candid Take on Leadership," *Globe and Mail*, January 30, 2014.
8 Malcolm Gladwell, "Was Jack Welch the Greatest CEO of His Day—or the Worst?" *New Yorker*, November 7, 2022.
9 Billie Jean King with Johnette Howard and Maryanne Vollers, *All In: An Autobiography* (Vintage, 2021), 18.

INDEX

Note: n appended to a page number
   indicates a footnote.

Abbott, Sir John, 26
Ackermann, Joe, 154
AI (artificial intelligence), 67, 75, 196,
   229, 249
AIG, 189
Air Canada Centre, 90, 95
Argentina, 266
   corruption in, 137–138
   crisis events, 110–117
   economic history of, 101–103
   employee impact, 112–113, 115,
      121–124
   Scotiabank entry into, 97–101,
      103–105
   Scotiabank exit from, 127–136
   Waugh's handling of crisis, 115,
      117–120, 128–137, 138–139, 250
   See also Quilmes
Arrell, Tony, 17
Ash, Cliff, 233
Asper, Izzy, 231
asset-backed commercial paper (ABCP)
   freeze-up, 168, 191–194
ATMs, 229, 290
   See also Johnny Cash machines
Axelrod, David, 190, 287

Báez Figueroa, Ramón Buenaventura,
   148, 157–158, 158n, 159

Banco Bansud SA, 131
Banco Comafi SA, 131
Banco Intercontinental. see Baninter
Banco Nacional de Cuba, 144
Banco Quilmes, 105
   See also Quilmes
Banco Sud Americano (Chile), 101, 134
Banco Sudamericano (Peru), 153
Baninter, 148–149, 150–151, 152–153, 154–160
Bank Act, 26, 27, 31, 32
Bank Arya Panduarta, 266–267
Bank for International Settlements (BIS),
   215–220
Bank of America, 184, 189
Bank of Canada, 28, 30, 41, 182, 184,
   185–186, 187–188, 206, 210–211
Bank of Canada Act, 210
Bank of Montreal, 28, 34, 35, 124–127,
   170, 251, 259, 259n, 268, 275
Bank of Toronto, 35, 269, 275
Bank of Xi'an, 267
banking
   branch banking network model,
      26–27, 36, 269
   history of, 25–37
   regulation, 29, 218, 230, 244–248
   technology, 249, 304
   treasurer role, 167–168
   women in, 274–300
Banking on America (Green), 32, 34
Barbarians at the Gate, 60
Barclays (UK), 207, 270

Barclays Bank of Canada, 35
basketball. *see* Raptors
Batista, Fulgencio, 143
Bear Stearns, 202–203
Bell, Gordon (Gordie), 58, 82, 105, 166, 167, 175, 233
Benson, Edgar, 14
Bernanke, Ben, 216
Bernier, Maxime, 272
Bernier, Sophie, 291
BHP, 268, 273
"Big Bang," (UK) 34, 198
Birmingham, Bruce, 48–49, 49n, 51, 54, 62, 70, 80, 118, 127, 128, 140, 280, 283
Bitove, John Jr., 73, 76, 77, 78–80, 81–82, 84–85, 86–92, 95–96
Bitove, John Sr., 76
Black, Conrad, 75
black swan event, 196–197
BlackBerry, 270
BlackRock, 184
Blue Jays. *see* Toronto Blue Jays
Blustein, Paul, 102
BMO. *see* Bank of Montreal
BMO Harris Bank, NA, 189, 189n
BNP Paribas, 163, 191
BNS. *see* Scotiabank
Bombardier, 270
Bond, Alan, 65
Boyles, Thomas, 42
Brights, 231
Brooks, Bob, 79–80, 106, 166–173, 176, 201, 217, 220
Bryce, Robert, 30
Buffet, Warren, 20

Cameron, Judy, 297
Canada Deposit Insurance Corporation (CDIC), 182
Canada Mortgage and Housing Corporation (CMHC), 186, 211
Canada Savings Bonds, 23
Canadian Bank of Commerce, 26, 28
Canadian Bankers Association, 41
Canadian banking. *see* banking
Canadian Commercial Bank (CCB), 28, 29, 32n

Canadian Imperial Bank of Commerce. *see* CIBC
Cardinal, Peter, 138, 150, 151–153, 159, 183, 275–276
Carney, Mark, 182, 215, 223, 224–226, 251
Carstens, Agustín, 155
Cartier, George-Étienne, 25
Castro, Fidel, 143
Catalyst, 276–278, 283, 286, 287–289, 297
Catalyst Awards, 288n, 294–295, 294n, 300
Cavallo, Domingo, 104, 105, 111
Cefis, Alberta, 294
Chase Manhattan Bank, 32–33, 49, 61n
Chávez, Hugo, 71
Chemical Bank, 49, 61, 61n
Chile, 99, 101, 107–108, 134, 266
China, 267, 271
Chisholm, Bob, 112, 125, 126, 127, 162
Chrétien, Jean, 34, 35, 124, 125, 269
Christie, James, 78
Chrominska, Sylvia, 51, 52, 53–54, 111, 124, 202, 280–287, 294, 295
CI Financial, 214, 255, 255n
CIBC, 26, 34–35, 79, 84–85, 170, 194, 213, 251, 268, 269, 275
Citibank, 32
Citigroup, 162, 189
Clark, Ed, 170n, 240, 259–260, 298
Clark, Scott, 36
CNOOC, 273
Cohl, Michael, 77
Colombia, 255, 255n, 266
Comper, Tony, 126, 287, 297–298
Confederation Life, 35
Connolly, Cyril, 105
Connors, Stompin' Tom, 270
Coriat, David, 75, 78, 87
corralito, 102, 105, 110, 115
Côté, Jacynthe, 298
Cox, Victor, 143
Craig, Susan, 119
Crawford, Purdy, 193–194
Cuba, 142–144

Dallara, Charles, 221, 224
Dao, Edgar, 155
Davos, 104, 105
Day, Sir Graham, 286

DeRabbie, Ann, 252
Deutsche Bank, 270
Dickson, Julie, 195, 238–239
Different Drummers (MacIntosh), 30
Dimon, Jamie, 223–226, 240, 304
diversity, equity, and inclusion (DEI),
  276–278
Dodge, David, 135, 149, 191–193, 215n,
  227–231, 265
Dodge, Thomas Lewis, 227
Doer, Gary, 14, 16
domestic systemically important financial
  institutions (D-SIFIs), 251
Dominican Republic (DR), 141, 145–149,
  152–153, 154–161, 158n
Dominion Bank, 35, 269, 275
Dominion Securities, 289
Dow Chemical, 15
Downe, Bill, 170n, 172, 183, 184, 188,
  221n, 259n, 277, 288, 288n, 289
Doyle, Kevin, 34
Duhalde, Eduardo, 124
DundeeWealth, 254, 255
Durland, Mike, 181, 199–201, 206–208,
  265–266

E*TRADE Canada, 254
Ecuador, 99
Encana, 271
Ernst & Young, 242–244
Estey, Willard, 29
Euroshock (Dallara), 221
Evita (film), 103
executive compensation, 199, 202,
  219–220, 244
Exxon, 33, 272

Fairclough, Ellen, 276
Falconbridge, 270–273
Falkland Islands, 100
Federal Reserve, 41, 165, 169, 187, 189,
  211, 245
Finance Canada, 184
Fink, Larry, 184
Flaherty, Jim, 182, 250–251
Flanagan, Diane, 252
Fonda, Jane, 60
Four Seasons, 232–233

Frost, James D., 43
Fryett, Terry, 51, 53–54, 55–57, 66–67, 79,
  147, 190–191, 223
Fuld, Dick, 204
Fyshe, Thomas, 43–44

Galt, Alexander Tilloch, 26
Geithner, Tim, 192
Giles, Shirley, 279
Gillis, Deborah, 278, 286, 287–289,
  294, 300
Glass-Steagall Act, 199
global financial crisis (2007-9). *see*
  Great Recession
global systemically important financial
  institutions (G-SIFIs), 251
Gluskin, Ira, 17
Godsoe, Peter
  and Canadian credit market, 62
  and Caribbean market, 141, 152, 154
  and Latin American market, 101,
    104–106, 109, 112, 118, 120–121,
    131, 134, 135
  and potential BMO merger, 125–126,
    127
  and Raptors, 74, 75, 77, 79, 80, 91, 93
  as Scotiabank CEO, 42, 104, 140,
    162, 175, 176–177, 234, 293
  and US business diversification, 54
  and US credit market, 45, 48–49, 51,
    52, 58, 168
  and women in banking, 276,
    279–283, 286, 292
Goodman, Ned, 255
Gordon, Walter, 33
Granik, Russ, 81, 85, 90
Granovsky, Phil, 77, 80–81, 86
Great Depression, 29–30, 249
Great Financial Crisis. *see* Great
  Recession
Great Recession
  asset-backed commercial paper crisis,
    191–194
  Bank of Canada assessment of,
    210–212
  BIS meeting regarding, 215–220
  Canadian banks during, 182–184,
    218–220, 223, 227

executive compensation during,
    201–202
government support during, 185–189
liquidity in, 165–168, 171–172,
    203–206, 218–219
overview of, 163–165, 252–253
Scotiabank assessment of, 180–181
Scotiabank proprietary trading during,
    196–201
Scotiabank structural issues revealed
    by, 175–178
Scotiabank's day-to-day management
    during, 169–171
Scotiabank's Lehman exposure,
    206–207
Scotiabank's position during, 228
Waugh's assessment of, 212–214
Waugh's management during,
    172–173, 178–180, 184–185,
    190–191, 195–198, 207–210
Greenberg, Alan "Ace," 203, 226–227
Grenada, 144
Griffiths, G.A. ("Bonzo"), 143
Groskorth, Donna, 110–111, 112, 114, 115,
    120, 131, 134
Guevera, Ernesto "Che," 143

Haiti, 141–142
Hamilton, Alexander, 26, 27
Hand, Scott, 271–272
Hannam, Wendy, 144, 147, 261–262, 265,
    279–280
Harper, Stephen, 135, 185, 268–269, 272
Harper, Susan, 132
Hart, Stephen, 52, 58, 170, 186–187, 212,
    230, 263
Hasenfratz, Linda, 288
Hayward, Tim, 149–151, 159, 160
Heath, Jeff, 186
Hernandez, Claudio, 113, 120, 129, 131
Herscu, George, 64–65
Hibberd, Robin, 256, 257
Hincks, Sir Francis, 26
Hitchman, George, 20–21, 24, 29, 49,
    82, 232
HSBC Canada, 247n, 269, 273
Hudson, Dave, 13

Hunter, Edward Dennis, 146–147, 150,
    161
Hurricane Ivan, 144

IDEAL network, 290–291
IIF September 2011 meeting, 223–226
IIF Committee on Market Best Practices
    report, 220–223
Imperial Bank of Canada, 35
Inco, 270–273
India, 267
Indonesia, 266–267
ING Bank of Canada. see ING Direct
ING Direct, 255, 256–258
ING Groep NV, 255
Institute of International Finance (IIF),
    165, 181, 204, 216, 220–226, 221n,
    230, 238, 242–244
Insured Mortgage Purchase Program
    (IMPP), 186, 187, 211
Interac, 291
International Monetary Conference
    (IMC), 204, 239–241
International Monetary Fund (IMF),
    102, 145, 149, 154, 155–156, 157,
    204, 220
Inverlat, 152
Investment Regulatory Organization
    of Canada, 194
Irvine, Frank, 146

Jamaica, 40, 43, 141, 145, 266
Jarsun, Miguel, 115, 129–130, 131, 139, 160
Jefferson, Thomas, 27
Jentsch, Dieter, 136, 174–175, 174n, 181,
    187, 191, 196, 208, 266
Johnny Cash machines, 229, 290
Johnson, F. Ross, 60
Johnson, Magic, 77
Johnston, Colleen, 298
JPMorgan Chase and Co., 33, 61n, 189,
    203, 223–226

Kiladze, Tim, 208, 252
King, Mervyn, 216
Knight, Malcolm, 27, 32, 247
Kobrak, Christopher, 26, 32

Kohlberg Kravis Roberts and Co. (KKR), 60–61
Korthals, Robin, 58

Labatt Brewing Company, 84
Lafleur, Guy, 291
Lagarde, Christine, 204, 240, 241
Lambert, Allen, 32, 33
Lauber, John, 248
LDC (least developed countries) crisis, 29, 107
Le Pan, Nick, 228, 234–238
Lee, Peter, 221
Lehman, Henry, 204
Lehman Brothers, 164, 181, 202, 203–207, 230, 246, 250, 252
"Lessons Learned," 112, 120
leveraged buyouts (LBOs), 60–61
liquidity, 23, 165–166, 167–168, 203, 210–211, 218–219, 230, 239, 243
"Little Bang," (Canada) 34, 198, 245
Lockhart, Stephen, 50–51, 65, 66, 68, 69–70
Longworth, David, 183, 185, 192–193, 205, 206–207
Lovelace, Bonnie, 13–14, 14–15, 277

Maas, Cees, 221
Macdonald, Alan, 109, 112, 121–122, 123–124, 128–129
Macdonald, Sir John A., 25
MacDonald, Tom, 110, 116, 120, 121–122, 137–138, 139
MacIntosh, Robert (Bob), 18, 19, 24, 30, 33, 49, 166, 276
Macklem, Tiff, 182
Macmillan, Hugh, 30
Macmillan Commission, 30
Manulife, 25
Maple Leaf Gardens, 83
Maple Leaf Gardens Ltd., 93
Maple Leaf Sports & Entertainment, 92–94
Maple Leafs, 83, 89, 91–92
Marcellus, Gladys, 279
Marchi, Sergio, 138
Marotta, Stefanie, 298

Martin, Joe, 26, 32
Martin, Paul, 34, 35, 124, 272
Marwah, Sarabjit (Sabi), 125–127, 173–180, 187–188, 201, 214, 220, 236, 238, 263, 264, 267, 281, 294
Mason, Barbara (Barb), 261–262, 279, 289–294, 294n
Mathew, Himal, 85
Matsa, David A., 295
Mayberry, John, 270
McCain, Harrison, 286
McDougall, Barbara, 286
McKinnon, Neil, 31
McLaughlin, Earle, 275
McLeod, J.A., 41
McLeod Young Weir, 197–198
McMaster, William, 26, 28
McQueen, Rod, 45, 275
Meek, Jim, 149, 150, 152–158, 160
Meek, Justin, 154
Meek, Tish, 154, 161
Mejía, Hipólito, 159
Memos from the Chairman (Greenberg), 203
Mercantile Bank, 32, 32n
Merchants Bank of Halifax, 40
mergers and acquisitions, 34–36, 40, 124–127, 268–273
Mersky, Seth, 61–62, 63–65, 66, 67–68
MeToo, 299
Mexico, 100, 101, 101n, 137, 150, 152, 153, 177–178, 266, 275–276
Miller, Amalia R., 295
Ministry of Finance, 28
Molson Bank, 106
Montreal Accord, 194
Montreal Canadiens, 80, 85
Montreal Expos, 73, 73n
Moody's Corporation, 216
Morgan, John Pierpont (J.P.), 41
Morgan, Lucy, 279
Morgan Stanley, 216
Morton, David, 79–80
Moscow Narodny Bank, 143
Moynihan, Brian, 184
Munger, Charlie, 20

National Australia Bank Limited, 270
National Bank of Canada, 32n, 34, 194
National City Corp., 258, 260–264
NBA. *see* Raptors
Newmont Mining Corp., 63–64
Nexen, 268, 273
Nicks, Bill, 19, 42, 64, 98, 107, 136, 147
Nixon, Gord, 183, 184, 204n, 221, 240,
    277, 285, 288–289, 288n, 299
Nokes, Jane, 17
non–bank sponsored asset-backed
    commercial paper (non-bank
    ABCP) crisis, 191–194
Nortel, 270
Northland Bank, 28, 29, 32n

O'Brien, David, 271–272
Office of the Superintendent of Financial
    Institutions (OSFI), 29, 182, 184,
    195, 219, 228, 229, 234–237, 239
Onex, 17, 67, 231
Ontario Securities Commission, 162, 194
Organization of the Petroleum Exporting
    Countries (OPEC), 100
Osmak, Borden, 79, 80–81, 84, 85, 87,
    90–91
Oteiza, Eduardo, 122–124, 129

PanCanadian Energy Corp., 271, 272
Pan-Canadian Investors Committee for
    Third-Party Structured Asset-
    Backed Commercial Paper, 193
Parr-Johnston, Elizabeth, 286
Pauly, Louis W., 211
Pearson, Lester, 33
Perez, Ariel, 161
Perkins, Tara, 246
Perón, Evita, 103
Perón, Juan, 103
Personal Account (Comper), 297
Peru, 99, 137, 153–154, 159n, 266
Peterson, David, 73, 76–77, 78–79,
    80–81, 84, 85–86
Peterson, Jim, 34
Phelps Dodge, 271
Pickens, T. Boone, 63–64
Porter, Brian, 136, 137, 181, 255n
Porter Commission, 32

Porter Report, 32
Potash Corp, 268, 273
Prentiss, Charlie, 68
Puerto Rico, 264–266

Quilmes
    and Argentina banking crisis,
        105–106, 110–120
    early problems of, 108–109
    employee impact, 128–130, 131
    establishment of, 105–106
    suspension and disposal of, 101,
        120–121, 130–131, 134–136

Raptors, 72–92, 96
RBC. *see* Royal Bank of Canada
Regent, Aaron, 271
Reich de Polignac, Nicole, 276
Reid, Angus "Gus," 16
Reinsdorf, Jerry, 89
Reisman, Heather, 231
Reynal, Alejandro, 129
Richardson, Frances Mary, 12
Ritchie, Cedric, 19–20, 24, 42–43,
    47, 50, 51, 52, 58, 69, 82, 107–108,
    136, 139, 147, 175, 176, 198, 232,
    234, 290
Robida, Rick, 290
Rockefeller, David, 32–33, 145
Rockefeller, John D., 33
Rogers Centre, 90
Rogers Communications, 273
Roosevelt, Franklin, 29–30
Ross, F.W., 143
Royal Bank of Canada, 34–35, 40, 143,
    170, 183, 204n, 220, 247n, 251, 258,
    259, 268, 269, 273, 274, 288n, 291
Royal Commission on Banking and
    Currency, 41
Royal Trust, 35
Rúa, Fernando de la, 111
Russia, 103

Samarasekera, Indira, 180, 220, 229
San Antonio Spurs, 83
Schwartz, Gerald (Gerry), 67, 79, 231
Scoffield, Heather, 123–124
Scotia Capital, 192, 194, 198, 202

Scotiabank
  Asian expansion of, 266–268. *see also*
    individual country entries
  Canadian expansion of, 39, 40, 43
  Canadian merger & acquisition
    considerations, 40, 124–127,
    254–273, 268–269, 269–270
  Caribbean expansion of, 40, 43,
    141–161. *see also individual country*
    entries
  corporate aircraft of, 80, 133, 134,
    142
  credit rating of, 51
  culture of, 231–239
  dividends, 29, 41
  as D-SIFI, 251
  gold business of, 98–99
  history of, 28, 36, 38–39, 41–42
  lending policy of, 43–44
  mortgage portfolio of, 190
  Raptors involvement, 77, 79–80,
    84–85, 88–89, 90
  risk appetite of, 65–67, 136, 177
  South American business of, 99–101,
    152. *see also individual country*
    mentions
  and technology, 228–230, 229n, 236,
    290
  US business diversification of, 48, 49,
    51–67, 168–169
  US expansion of, 39, 43, 260–266
  wholesale reliance of, 176–177
  women in, 279–300
Scotiabank de Puerto Rico, 189
Scotiabank Quilmes (SBQ). *see* Quilmes
Scott, Roy, 98, 99, 104–105, 108–109, 111,
    121, 122, 123, 143–144, 146
Sharma, Vikas, 256
Sharp, Isadore (Issy), 135, 140, 231–234
Sharp, Rosalie, 231–232
Shaw Communications, 273
Shields, Jim, 128, 128n, 129, 132–133
Silicon Valley Bank (SVB), 67, 230
Simpsons, 21, 22, 152
Sinclair, Helen, 279
Slaight, Allan, 73, 74–75, 77, 79, 80, 82,
    86–87, 88, 89, 90–93, 95, 96
Sobey, Paul, 257–258, 258n

Sosa, Sammy, 148
Sprott, Eric, 17
St. Maarten, 144
Standard Chartered PLC, 270
Stavro, Steve, 87, 89
Stern, David, 73, 81–82, 83, 84, 85, 88
Stevens, Caroline, 182
Stevenson, Kate, 298
stress testing, 223, 243–244
SunLife, 254–255
Sutton, Bill, 122

Tanenbaum, Larry, 73, 76–77, 78, 82–84,
    87–89, 91, 92–95, 96
Tanenbaum, Max, 76–77, 82
Tangerine, 258
Taylor, Austin "Austintatious," 198
Taylor, Kathleen, 298
TD Bank, 32–33, 34–35, 58, 60, 94, 136,
    136n, 170, 170n, 198, 220, 251,
    259–260, 268, 269, 275, 288n, 290
Teck, 271
Texaco, 57
Thailand, 266
Thatcher, Margaret, 100
The Bank of Nova Scotia. *see* Scotiabank
The Money Spinners (McQueen), 45
Thomson, Dick, 32–33
Thomson, Scott, 62, 101n, 137, 238, 256n
Thorsteinson, Arni, 17, 18, 19
too big to fail, 35, 36, 120, 250–251
Toronto Blue Jays, 73, 83, 84, 85
Toronto-Dominion Bank. *see* TD Bank
Trichet, Jean-Claude, 216, 240
Triggs, Donald, 231
Troubled Asset Relief Program (TARP),
    189, 189n, 205, 252, 264, 273
Trujillo, Rafael, 146, 147
Trump, Donald, 33n, 46–48, 48n, 227, 259
Trump, Robert, 46
Tryforos, Jim, 49–50, 57–58, 60, 61, 70
Turks and Caicos, 144–145
Turner, John, 35
Turner, Ted, 59–60

Union Bank of Prince Edward Island, 39
University of Manitoba, 13, 18, 277
Uruguay, 98–99, 129, 132

Vale, 271, 272
Venezuela, 71, 155
Vincor International Inc., 231
von Hahn, Anatol, 107–109, 112, 122–123, 128–131, 132–133, 135, 137, 181, 256–257

Wachovia, 264
Washington, George, 26
Waugh, Earl Francis, 11–13
Waugh, Lynne, 21, 70, 278–279
Waugh, Richard Earl. *see* Waugh, Rick
Waugh, Rick
    on Argentina, 103, 106
    and Argentinian banking crisis, 111, 113, 115–116, 117–124
    Canadian business connections of, 78–79
    as deal junkie, 254–255
    and DEI, 276–279
    and Donald Trump, 46–48
    early banking career of, 16–21, 42
    early signs of banking acumen, 22–24
    escape from Argentina, 132–134
    as Inco board member, 270, 271–272
    lending approach of, 48–49, 51–60, 53–54
    management style of, 67–68, 70, 138–139, 159, 175, 178, 230
    marriage of, 21–22
    as president of 2012 International Monetary Conference, 239–241
    Rick-isms, 68
    risk approach of, 62–63, 65, 65–67, 177–178
    and US business diversification, 58–59
    views on regulation, 37, 219, 230, 244–248
    youth of, 11–16
Waugh, Ron, 12
Webster, Ben, 77
Wells Fargo, 189, 264
West Indies, 40, 141, 144
Wilson, David, 162, 202
women in banking
    generally, 274–275, 296–300
    at Scotiabank, 275–296
    See also Catalyst; Catalyst Awards; Chrominska, Sylvia; Gillis, Deborah; Mason, Barbara (Barb)
World Economic Forum, 104, 233

Xiaochuan, Zhou, 216
Xstrata, 271, 272

Yellen, Janet, 190, 286–287

Zimmerman, Adam, 245

01 14